CLINICAL APPROACH
TO
ALLEVIATION OF POVERTY

CLINICAL APPROACH TO ALLEVIATION OF POVERTY

E.D. SETTY, Ph.D.

AKANSHA PUBLISHING HOUSE
NEW DELHI-110002 (INDIA)

AKANSHA PUBLISHING HOUSE
4649-B/21, Ansari Road
Darya Ganj, New Delhi - 110 002
Email: ektabooks@yahoo.com
Ph. : 23263193 / 9811582579

Clinical Approach to Alleviation of Poverty

First Published 2007
ISBN 978-81-8370-106-8

[The responsibility for the facts stated, conclusions reached etc. is entirely that of the Author. The publisher is not responsible for them, whatsoever.]

PRINTED IN INDIA

Published by M.P. Misra for Akansha Publishing House, New Delhi and Printed at Aryan Enterprises, Delhi.

DEDICATED
TO
SRI BHAIRON SINGH SHEKHAWAT
Vice-President of India

Shri D.K. Adikesavulu
Member of Parliament
has sponsored and patronized
publication of this book

CHARANJIT SINGH ATWAL
DEPUTY SPEAKER, LOK SABHA
PARLIAMENT HOUSE, NEW DELHI

Foreword

The most apparent and deplorable human problem is poverty. Poverty may be termed true in case of human beings and not in respect of other species. Although it is a very complex problem and is not related to food only but an intake of less than 2400 calories of nutrients consumed by an individual in a day is how we define poverty. In fact, the moment someone desires or needs something more than what he has, that moment he becomes poorer by it but as far as minimum basic needs of an individual are concerned someone who does not have basic access to food, shelter, clothing, health, sanitation, literacy are termed below poverty. We all know that rich world has become richer only because it exploited the resources of the poor world. The phenomenon is deep rooted in lesser developed countries. In fact the poor are the result of exploitation by the rich.

Time and again poverty has been discussed with great authority and will and a number of measures have been adopted for eradication of poverty. But poverty has been assuming gigantic proportions day by day and has become a problem out of hands of government and people. Mankind's desire to create wealth is a noble idea but mankind's desire to accumulate and possess wealth is what creates the bane. Impropriety in distributing wealth among all as well as impropriety in distributing the profits adds to the problem a great deal. Various schools of thought like Marxism, communism, socialism and capitalism have dealt with poverty in their own way but poverty has always slipped out of their purview. It needs an integral school of thought. In our culture more emphasis is laid on becoming richer by wealth than to have a happy, peaceful and healthy life, the problem of poverty goes on assuming new proportions. It is just not the government alone which needs to address this problem but together society as a whole and government have to address this issue in a holistic manner. Government alone cannot eradicate poverty by simply changing its course. Communism tried to create commune with equal distributable wealth divided among individuals but it failed because there was no motivation. Capitalism tried this by creating wealth and by creating competition and motivation but failed because unless there is an equal level playing field you cannot expect that it will eliminate poverty.

Eradication of poverty is a very complex task. It needs sustainable development, equal distribution of resources, equal level playing field, motivation, healthier competition and above all a holistic society. Poverty is not only an economic issue but it is aiso related to our personal selves. Dr. E.D. Setty has authored this book encompassing critical issues causing poverty and multiple ways for mitigating poverty. Dr. Setty with his wide national and international experience especially in rural development has put forth his inspiring ideas and strategies and has aptly called it 'Clinical Approach to Alleviation of Poverty.' I congratulate him for his efforts for bringing about this volume.

CHARANJIT SINGH ATWAL

कुमारी सैलजा
KUMARI SELJA

राज्य मंत्री (स्वतंत्र प्रभार)
आवास और शहरी गरीबी उपशमन
भारत सरकार
निर्माण भवन, नई दिल्ली–110011
MINISTER OF STATE (INDEPENDENT CHARGE)
HOUSING AND URBAN POVERTY ALLEVIATION
GOVERNMENT OF INDIA
NIRMAN BHAWAN, NEW DELHI-110011

MESSAGE

I am happy to know that Dr. E.D. Setty is bringing out his new book titled ***'Clinical Approach to Alleviation of Poverty'***.

Poverty is a complex problem which includes not only the basic necessities of food, clothing and shelter but also takes into account the problems of sanitation, health, literacy and a clean environment. Eradication of poverty has been one of the major goals of the Country since independence. A large number of schemes and programmes have been launched by Government of India for poverty alleviation in both the rural and urban areas. However, Central, State and local Governments and the stakeholders have to work in tandem to implement the schemes and programmes in the most effective ways in order to eradicate poverty.

This book by the Author analyses the critical issues causing poverty and suggests ways to eradicate it. I congratulate the Author for sharing his ideas and experience in the book, and wish the publication all success.

(Kumari Selja)

JUSTICE N.Y. HANUMANTHAPPA
Former Chief Justice of
Orissa High Court
Member of Parliament
(Lok Sabha)

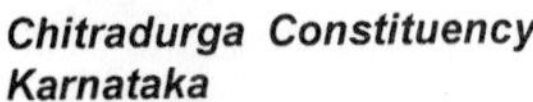
Chitradurga Constituency
Karnataka

No.361, 14th Cross, 4th Main,
Sadashivanagar,
Bangalore-560080
Phone: 23613707

No. 18, Ferozeshah Road,
New Delhi-110001
Phone: 23315775

MESSAGE

Dr. E.D. Setty's treatise on "Clinical Approach to Alleviation of Poverty" is a wonderful book in the field of "Micro and Macro" Economics. He has rightly dealt mostly on the maladies existing in our Rural economy and prescribed the remedies. It is diagnosis is rightly and impartially understood then it will be one o the epoch making attempts suggesting in many ways how there shall be rural development which is one of the important goals of our Indian economy.

While appreciating Dr. Setty's sincere and timely efforts to throw light on the sphere of our Rural Development, I feel that this book deserves to be read understood and acted upon by all those who are interested in nation building activities.

I also appreciate Shri D.K. Adhikeshavalu, MP who is a great philanthropist for his patronage and encouragement to bring out this work to be used by all.

(Justice N.Y. Hanumanthappa)

Preface

Before we move into the Preface, I would like to briefly mention an anecdote which lead to taking up the present study. I have proposed to Sri Chandrababu Naidu, Ex-Chief Minister of Andhra Pradesh, the following 4 book projects:

1. A practical Guide on working with people.
2. Clinical Approach to Alleviation of Poverty
3. Dynamics of Dalits Development
4. A Total Systems Approach to Village as a Unit of Development.

Sri Chandrababu Naidu has given me an appointment in February 2005. I went to his residence in Hyderabad on the date of appointment. I met him. Before we could discuss the above mentioned book projects there was a family waiting to meet him and he asked me to sit in a small room where usually he meets individuals on appointment. While he was with this family interacting in another larger room, I moved into as he asked me to a small room where he would meet me. In the small room when I entered I saw two people sitting on a bench. One I could recognise as a Minister in Sri. Chandrababu Naidu's cabinet, but I was not able to recall his name. Next to me on my right side was another gentleman. I was sitting with these two people nearly for 10 minutes until the arrival of Sri Chandrababu Naidu. While I was sitting with these two people in the interview room, I kept silent and didn't have any interaction with my two neighbours. When Chandrababu Naidu came and occupied his seat in front of us, I just tried to tell him that though the suffix in my name is Setty (E. Designu Setty) for some clarity that I belong to Setty Balija community and that I am not a Vysya. On my sharing this real identity with Sri N. Chandrababu Naidu he immediately pointed out that the gentleman sitting on my right side on the bench is also Setty – Naidu a Balija. This man was Sri D.K. Adikesavulu – Member of Parliament. Though I have known his name for a couple of years, I have not seen him. Immediately I felt very happy that I was meeting Sri Adikesavulu and greeted him.

Then I briefly explained to Chandrababu Naidu and Sri Adikesavulu the purport and objectives that would be met with and their usefulness once the book projects are completed. In an unprecedented way Sri Adikesavulu with all the enthusiasm said that he would support two book projects mentioned below:

1. Clinical Approach to Alleviation of Poverty
2. Dynamics of Dalits Development.

In brief I would like to mention that Sri Adikesavulu is a patron of these two studies. The entire credit goes to him in bringing out these two books. Now we move on to the preface to this book.

The introductory part (chapter-1) spells out the concept of poverty and below poverty line detailing the reasons for that kind of destitute state for nearly 30% of the population in general. The second chapter highlights the clinical approach as an analogy taken from medical treatment in respect of human individuals. This chapter emphasizes all development efforts should follow the principle of clinical approach. Chapter 3 highlights the landlessness as a major factor causing poverty especially in rural areas as well as to some extent in urban centres also. Chapter 4 focuses on Gender issue especially referring to women folk and the kind of sufferings and deprivation they go through. In a word, it is women who suffer a great deal amongst the poor. Chapter 5 is a very brief field based study covering 100 households, 50 from Districts of Kanya Kumari and Chittoor. It may be mentioned here the field study though, it brings out the profile of the poor it cannot be taken as representative highlighting the deplorable conditions of the poor in India and elsewhere.

If one goes around the villages in India he could witness the stages and the conditions in which several segments of the population live today. Owing to historical reasons more especially of the foreign colonial administration and diverse princely states ruling for some centuries, to a greater extent the villages have been neglected entities in terms of minimal humane standards of living. The problems are multifarious and the needs are enormous. With all commitment, sincerity and attention, the state has been attempting to improve the conditions of living in rural communities for the past fifty years in terms of planned and organized development. Since the problem is so vast and the machinery of development is not properly tuned across the entire chain and in spite of good intensions, owing to laxity in terms of realistic assessment of the problems, needs and resources, we have not been able to achieve development as we visualized. One may point out several lapses. In a way, the development efforts have been something like broadcasting of seed without paying detailed attention to certain segments of population and sectors of development. Though there have been ethnic-wise, class-wise programmes, either owing to lack of resources on the part of the government and initiative and response from the people, we are still moving rather slowly with halting paces in the march towards development. Examining the way in which we have been working all these years, one realizes what is needed today is what we may call a clinical approach to rural development. The present volume based on the extensive field experience of the author discusses the clinical approach to rural development. It may be mentioned that some of the aspects discussed in this volume are not new but unfortunately, attention has not been paid to some of the strategies and methods of development. These are some of the missing links in what has gone on so far. As a kind of a remedial measure, the chapters that are contained in this volume focus on and highlight the importance of these missing links and the way to go about making rural development a successful endeavour with tangible results.

We may briefly mention the aspects discussed in different chapters. In the introductory part, as mentioned above, the significance of clinical approach to rural development is emphasized. Chapter 6 focuses on the lessons from rural development spelling out the kind of shortcomings and failures in several areas in the field of rural development.

We may consider chapter 7 on programme planning as a basic and systematic process in formulating plans in meeting people's needs. It could definitely serve as a guide giving directions to the planners the way they have to go about in formulating plans to meet people's needs.

Chapter 8 speaks of the need to take each village as a unit of rural development. This operationally links to what is emphasized in this volume: a clinical approach. Chapter 9 speaks of the role of the local institutions as primary agents of social change.

In the entire gamut of rural development, local leaders are expected to play a contributory role. Chapter 10 & 11 speak of the role of local leaders and youth in improving the conditions of living in rural communities. Chapter 12 highlights the part played by innovative Janmabhhomi programme initiated in Andhra Pradesh in 1997. The Government of Andhra Pradesh having analyzed the earlier experiments in rural development arrived at a conclusion that there cannot be a global approach to development but it is to be periodic, sectoral development focusing on one or two sectors in a particular period. With this philosophy, the Government of Andhra Pradesh has initiated what is called Janmabhoomi as a clinical approach to multi-sectoral and segmental development. Chapter 13 focuses on caste dynamics influencing both positively and negatively in alleviating poverty.

Development cannot be mechanical. Social forces influence and operate on any development activity. Caste which is unique in the Indian context for several centuries, though, it is on the decline still plays a significant role both positive and negative in the field of rural development. The life of the Scheduled Castes who are now called Dalits has been a sad story for centuries. They constitute fifteen per cent of the population in India. Though there are several provisions in helping and improving the life of the Dalits, there is a need for special attention to be paid to them. Chapter 14 provides ethnic-wise, region-wise statistics pertaining to the Dalit population in India.

Compared to several countries, the sanitary conditions in rural areas in India can be described as deplorable. It needs special attention and it is a perennial problem. Chapter 15 recommends a need for perspective plan on rural sanitation.

Related to rural sanitation, conservation and judicious use of water for all needs is a crucial issue. Chapter 16 recommends an integrated approach in management of water supply and sanitation.

Chapter 17 discusses the indispensable need for securing people's participation in all endeavours of development since people's participation is an integral part of development in order to create the sense of accomplishing of projects on the part of the people.

Chapter 18: The case study in respect of the Valayar of South India is representative in all details the way the poor live. Chapter 19 deals with the model schemes for individuals, families and small groups. These are rural based cottage enterprises based on natural and organic resources. These mini enterprises are based on the following resources. Cereals and Pulses, Ghani Oil, village leather, manufacture of cane, gur and khandsari, palm gur, non-edible oils, beekeeping, village pottery, fibre, carpentry and blacksmithy, lime manufacturing, fruit processing and fruit preservation and bamboo and cane work.

Chapter 20 spells out some measures which would help alleviating poverty. As one could visualize and imagine alleviating poverty cannot be an instantaneous work, it takes time, but efforts should be combined and coordinated with effective delivery system. It is hoped that this volume emphasizing a clinical approach in alleviating poverty could be of some use right from the top level of administration and down to the village panchayat and several other development agencies.

Rural development is a generic concept, subsuming several fields of development that fall under economic development, democratic growth and social justice. There have been several scores of books on this subject. The present volume emphasizing clinical approach spells out the significant factors that the planner, the organizer, the administrator and the field worker has to take care of and be sensitive in understanding people, their needs and problems and working with them for their advancement and welfare. There is no straight highway to development. Depending upon the ethnicity and subculture within the fold of Indian ethos, one may have to charter in multiple ways, but may remember and apply the clinical approach irrespective of the programmes focused upon. The planners, administrators, organizers and field workers, the teaching and the training community concerned with and working in the field of development would find this volume interesting and useful.

E.D. SETTY

Acknowledgements

I would like to express my profoundest thanks to Sri Charanjit Singh Atwal, Deputy Speaker, Lok Sabha, Parliament House, New Delhi for his highly valuable, significant and encouraging Foreword to this book.

I owe a great deal of thanks and indebtedness and heart-felt thanks to Sri D.K. Adikesavulu, Member of Parliament who has supported this book project. He is the patron of the study. Throughout the work of this book he has been the constant encouraging factor. I cannot simply say these things in words, but I owe him a great deal of indebtedness.

I am especially thankful to Sri P. Krishna Moorthy for his continued assistance and encouragement throughout the work of this book.

My sincere thanks to Sri S. Rama Krishna, Stenographer who has prepared the manuscript.

My sincere appreciation to my wife Smt. E. Vishalakshi, for her support and encouragement extended to me during the time I worked on this book.

E.D. SETTY

Contents

Contents

CHAPTER 1

Introduction

Poverty is a complex phenomenon. It relates to particular segments of the population in India and abroad. The study of the causes of poverty is the study of the causes of the degradation of a large part of mankind. The emphasis in alleviation of poverty is improving the material well-being of the poor. In developed countries, the dependency of families in rural communities on government is far less, the opposite is the situation in developing countries. In the primitive stage of mankind say in Paleolithic and Neolithic stages when hunting and gathering were the only means of survival there was no question of rich or poor. The question of poverty did not arise then. With migration of people and with futuristic vision, hard work and with adopting ever growing technology and with forceful occupation of land and with increased effort and industry, some of the families and the communities were able to advance in terms of their acquisition of property, increased production with an enhanced image of the family or a segment of the community. One could just scan through history and see that some of the families and communities, may be they were satisfied what they were and where they were *vis-à-vis* economic wealth and influence. In a sense, a section of the families or population all over the world were contented and continued with the minimal needs of day-to-day existence and there was no tomorrow for them. On the other hand, some of the families and the communities were all the time exploring and acquiring land and technologies to advance their production and reach higher level of earnings and attain the status of influencing other communities and at the same time increased their wealth and extent of property enjoyed by them.

It is quiet evident to see that poverty and dalit ethnicity go together. Unfortunately, it is a long history of deprivation. Now, the question is how to remedy the damage and gradually help the poor and the people below the poverty line pull up themselves. In view of long suffering in poverty and deprivation and poor image of themselves and very little of expectations and scope for redemption, a large number of people who have been suffering with a large number of limitations with just physical existence have come down to limited aspirations and expectations. Here, we may just mention the Valayar of South India as a Case Study illustrating the dynamics of poverty and the way in which they cope up with the limited resources and the income derived from such limited resources.

Essentially, poverty is a relative concept. People are poor if they cannot afford those things in life that the society in which they live regards as a normal part of their standard of living. In many rich countries families which cannot afford a car are often considered 'poor'. But, in the developing world, the prevalence of destitution, hunger and disease requires an additional absolute concept of poverty to be used. The concept of poverty line is an attempt to set a minimum standard of living in terms of diet, clothing, sanitation – one that permits a family to lead a relatively healthy and active life, even if they are deprived in other areas such as work and schooling. The poverty line is not an accepted standard of living, but it is usually based upon incomes calculated to be necessary to keep an average family at the 'minimum' standard of living.

CONCEPTS OF POVERTY

According to Seebohm Rowntree, "Poverty has always had several not entirely separable meanings and is always defined according to the conventions of society in which it occurs[1]". It can also be viewed from various angles for the purpose of analysis. One may draw distinction between 'primary' and 'secondary' poverty as enunciated by Rowntree in his pioneering studies and which were later adopted with variations in the works of Bowley[2] and Beveridge[3]. Rowntree defined families whose total earnings are insufficient to obtain the minimum necessities for the maintenance of mere physical efficiency as being in primary poverty.

Another way of examining the concept is to distinguish between absolute and relative poverty. Absolute standards for poverty emphasize subsistence and economic insufficiency as the frame of reference for poverty. Relative standards, however, stress economic inequality as the primary indicator of poverty. While the concept of absolute poverty approximates the primary category of Rowntree, his 'secondary' poverty could be viewed as a component of the 'relative' type.

A further way of examining poverty is to conceptualize it in terms of 'relative deprivation'. "Poverty", declares Townsend, "can be defined objectively and applied consistently in terms of the concept of 'relative deprivation[4]'. "This way of looking at the issues makes the concept too amorphous and brings in dynamic elements of change. It involves an inter-related network of deprivation and can be stretched to incorporate political deprivation as well. The relevance of this conceptualization has greater meaning from the point of view of advanced industrial countries where change is fast in all its manifestations. This is not only because as society gets wealthier the absolute level of old standards becomes outmoded, but also because economic growth alters the availability of different types of commodities and radically changes life styles, thus leading to the composition of old standards becoming irrelevant. In such societies there rises a dual problem. Not only the objective conditions change but the perception of felt-needs also changes. In such situations, the social scientist can be the unwitting servant of contemporary social values, and in the study of poverty this can have disastrous practical consequences. If, by the contrast, he feels obliged or is encouraged from the start to make a formal distinction between scientific and conventional perspectives, he is more likely to enlarge knowledge by bringing to light information which has been neglected and so create more elbow room for alternative forms of action, even if, in the end, some colouring of scientific procedure by social attitudes and opinions or individual variation is inescapable.

In practice while the standards of poverty adopted represent a combination of the absolute and relative concepts, the nature of the combination is governed by its appropriateness to the society under study. The use of absolute standards will be more prominent in nations, where much of the population suffers from severe physical deprivation.

Standard of living may be low that even if one reached it, he could still be the victim of serious deprivation of basic needs. As the average standard of living becomes higher, we find relative standards coming more into play either implicitly as they affect the setting of the absolute standards to be used, or explicitly in designating the bottom segment of the population 'poor'. Even, the latter represents a mix in which selection of the cutting point is guided by an implicit absolute standard.

A great variety of studies on poverty have selected one standard or another in estimating the proportion of population suffering form economic insufficiency. For instance, the *United Nations Committee of Experts* (1954) emphasized the desirability of pluralistic approach in defining levels of living and combined both relative standards and a variety of measures. By standardizing rates of health, education, clothing, housing etc., it is possible to make national and international comparisons of poverty.

TOOLS OF MEASUREMENT

Though the resolution of conceptual issues is unavoidable in understanding poverty from an objective and scientific angle, its quantification is not less basic from an operational point of view. The problem can only be comprehended in terms of concrete figures before any strategy is designed for its mitigation and eventual elimination. Further, they form the basis in evaluating the success or otherwise of policy measures pursued in the alleviation of poverty. In general, the poor, defined by some criteria are counted either in numbers or as a proportion of the total population. The head count method, is usually the adopted approach. The other measure, a more sophisticated one, revealing the intensity of deprivation, is the poverty index put forth by Amartya Sen using an axiomatic framework based on ordinal welfare concept. There are also other measures like the poverty-gap and its related variables. Though these measures describe the same objective phenomenon, they have a distinct value in the context of policy formulation in the eradication of poverty.

Poverty and below poverty is defined in terms of the extent of calories of food intake in a day. It is indicated that if the calories of food intake in a day is below 2400 calories per day is considered to be people below poverty line.

The poor and very distressing condition of the generality of the poor and people below the poverty line was attributed to the karma of the people in their previous life. The Karmik theory and the way in which it is interpreted and advocated and justified was thrown as a cause and reason in respect to their housing conditions, the families therein, the richness of the quality food they take and the kind of miserable life they lead in a comparative sense.

The concept of poverty, the recognition of poverty as a socio-economic problem and the attention bestowed on alleviating poverty has been in operation may be for the last few centuries. No country at this moment developed, developing and under developed could claim that they have eradicated poverty in toto. Even in the USA one in eight is a poor person. When it comes to developing and under developed countries you have a considerable number of people poor or below poverty line. In terms of ideals, objectives of human development you cannot simply be a witness and a silent spectator of distressing and pitiable situation of the poor people. The question of poverty as mentioned earlier is a complex phenomenon.

Eradication of poverty is assumed to rest on the Government, rarely rich people in the local communities who could extend some help to the poor below poverty line rarely thought of helping them. A few philanthropic non-governmental organisations have been educating the poor and rendering some services and guiding them to go in for some mini enterprises.

POVERTY CONDITIONS IN BANGLADESH AND NEPAL

We may briefly mention the situation in respect to the poor in Bangladesh and Nepal.

A. Bangladesh

Introduction and Backdrop

Poverty in Bangladesh is so widespread that more than 51 per cent of the rural populations live below the poverty line and have insufficient income to meet the minimum nutrition standard (defined as 2, 122 calories/day/person). Poverty as measured by low income, malnutrition, lack of education (net primary enrolment rate), low life expectancy (infant mortality rate, under-five mortality rate, nutrition-natal mortality, chronic disease) and substandard housing (or lack of housing) etc., result in lower ability to work and lower productivity and income. Thus the rural poor in Bangladesh are caught in a vicious circle of poverty.

Action Research Programmes

Recently, there has been a growing realization that attempts to create employment for the rural poor by outside agencies should be replaced by schemes for self-employment of the rural poor for sustainable solution of the problem. It is necessary to mobilize the rural poor, improve their technical skills and management capabilities through training and assist them with production inputs and credit. The rural poor should be encouraged to select small and medium scale activities and manage them by themselves with management and financial support from a catalytic agency like the Bangladesh Rural Development Board (BRDB).

1. Programme Objectives

The specific objectives of the Action Research Programme were to:

- Mobilize and organize selected rural poor in groups to enable them to have access to various supports and services and to pursue productive income earning activities with a view to improve their present socio-economic status and standard of living.
- Oversee the progress and determine the programme impact for future action.

2. Training Activities

All the members received training in agriculture, homestead production, animal husbandry, free plantation and horticulture, vegetable production, family Planning and population control, accumulation of savings, proper utilization of credit and health and sanitation care. Five female members received training on sewing and dress making under the guidance of Japanese experts Women's Training Institute, Tangail. Training was provided to all group members on management and account keeping skills.

B. Nepal

Introduction

Nepal's economy is primarily based on agriculture which provides employment to 90% of the population. The average land holding size is small. The growth of population (2.1%), has nullified the growth of food production (1.5%) which is mainly due to marginal lands being brought under agriculture.

The estimated calorie intake of the poor is only 75 to 80 percent of the daily requirements. The other indicators of the physical quality of life have compounded poverty in Nepal; the literacy rate is 39.6% with 75% of women illiterate, the infant mortality rate is 107:1,000 and life expectancy at birth is 54. The under-five mortality rate is 165 per thousand live births and 50 percent of under-five children suffer from severe to moderate malnutrition. The maternal mortality rate, at 850 per 100.000 is one of the highest in the world. The GNP per capita is estimated at US$ 180.

Most of the poor do not have resources and are under-employed. An increase in the per capita GNP and the institutional credit programme may not be sufficient to bring about effective change in the conditions affecting the poor and the reduction of poverty. The poor must have access and opportunity to use the services and goods through employment and increase in income, resulting in an increase in purchasing power and economic empowerment. The steady economic growth, income transfer or education, health, nutrition, household food securities are essential for the reduction of poverty. Hence the country needs development policies and programmes that would raise incomes in general and would reduce poverty in particular. The convergence of programmes that would lead to economic development, alleviate poverty and provide social services would significantly contribute to improving the situation of poor communities.

The ending of the second millennium in modern man's march through history has often been bannered as the decade when the Cold War and its concomitant hot wars may finally end, when ideological rigidities crumble before a new pragmatism, when the world's talents and resources can finally marshalled to eradicate mankind's ancient yet, no other continent presents such a marked contrast between rich and poor nations, between advanced and low-income economies, as the Asian-Pacific region today.

Deprivation of basic needs is one definition of poverty. However, the subsequent effects of this lack of essentials on a person's well-being acquisition of skills and access to employment opportunities create a vicious cycle that starts and ends with low income for the poor.

C. ANALYSIS AND CONCLUSIONS AT THE NATIONAL WORKSHOP

After the participants have studied critically the 17 surveyed villages, the following reflections on rural problems were found out. The variety of causes which created rural poverty are noted below:

1.1 The Have Not

This stems from the fact that the rural poor do not have any right of ownership in the land they till. Production capital for feeds, fertilizers, pesticides, etc. is not available hence, they resort to borrowing from usurers who charged 60 to 120 percent per annum on loans.

1.2 Lack of management skill

The poor management of available natural resources makes living worse for the rural poor. Their resources are not being used wisely.

1.3 The exploitative nature

The exploitative nature of the middlemen and business companies also cause rural poverty. They promote economic crops like Stevia, tobacco, tapioca and corn for cash, but they buy it at a price which cannot even augment for their production expenses.

1.4 The promotion of incomplete circuit for agriculture

The promotion of incomplete circuit for agricultureis a worse method to assist the rural poor in agricultural production. Agricultural production is being promoted and encouraged only to a certain extent. But after the harvest, their produce cannot be sold at the appropriate price because they were not oriented with marketing scheme.

1. Educational Poverty is one of the symptoms of rural poverty. And what is even worse, their education did not help them creatively.
2. Rural Health Poverty. Poor sanitation, poor service of health care, ignorance of nutrition and preventive medicine are the causes of poor, rural health conditions.

In the following chapters we look into the ways and means in a clinical sense to eradicate poverty.

It is not simple, but it is a question of providing the poor and people below the poverty line, a combination of supplies and services which over a period of time will help the poor educate themselves get enlightened, motivated and strive to wriggle out of the trap of poverty.

REFERENCES

1. B.S. 'Rowntree, *Poverty and Progress*, London, Longmans, 1941, p. 460.
2. A.L. Bowley and M.H. Hogg, "Has Poverty Diminished?" *New Survey of London Life and Labour (1930-35)*, London, 1935.
3. Social Insurance and Allied Services (The Beveridge Report) 6406, London, 1942.
4. Peter Townsend, "Poverty as Relative Deprivation – Resources and Style of Living", In: Dorthy Weddereburn (ed.), *Poverty Inequality and Class Structure*. Cambridge University Press, pp. 15-41.

CHAPTER 2

A Framework for Clinical Approach

In the Clinical Approach to alleviation of poverty, we bring in the analogy of medical treatment, the way the physician tries to know from the patient what his problem is and he on his own tries to diagnose the nature of the ailment or the disease and the cause for it and starts prescribing treatment and follows it up. Here physicians pay individual attention to the patient, sometimes it may be a preventive measure or a cruative thing. Similarly in view of the complex and varied development needs of the poor what is desirable and pragmatic is clinic approach in understanding the need and the problem of every segment in the population. Then depending on the resources available at the disposal of the administration and the technology that could be used in development programmes and the resources at the disposal of the people, the areas in which they can mobilize and their readiness for the programmes development action may be initiated. In the case of a patient and physician neither the physician tells patient the formulae of his treatment nor seldom the patients asks the physician the chemical content of the medicine he has prescribed. Here the patient is a mute receiver of treatment and largely dependent on the physician but whereas in the case of any kind of improvement or development among the poor, the people have a right to know and need to know the details and advantages and the limitations of any development programme introduced by the development agency. Very often we assume the needs and the problems of the people and without taking into account the views and suggestions from the people who move into action. Sometimes, the assumed needs or problems of the people may be right but in the psychological sense there is a need to give an opportunity to the people to share their ideas, views, suggestions so that they will have a feeling that they are partners in development.

We find three methods used in development programmes— (1) suggestive, (2) Prescriptive and (3) Directive'. In the suggestive method of development, the changee has the opportunity to reflect upon the measures suggested, weighs each one and opts or chooses some or all for action. Here you give an opportunity to the changee to reflect over the possible course of action he would choose depending on his interest, his resources and the kind of improvement that he anticipates in him, in his family and the community.

In the Prescriptive Method, the individual or the community may have some alternatives and options for improvement in the case of the individual, family or community. Though prescriptive sounds rather fixed yet one may have some options within the ambit of prescriptive things. But difficulty arises when the development agency gives directives for a particular activity to the people which we may call as Directed Development.

Development cannot be mechanical, it needs human touch. May be the development agency has everything, it could meet all the requirements of the largest population but there is a need to create a sense of achievement on the part of the beneficiary that they have accomplished things. It is not that easy and it depends on the change agents and development administration.

Whether it is a rural poor or urban poor, each is a unit of target for improvement / development. The emphasis here is on creating in a realistic way an atmosphere or an environment wherein the individuals in the community feel that they have been consulted with, and they had an opportunity of sharing their ideas for the way in which the segments in the community or the whole community are to be developed. Over a period of time, the development agency has to draw people closure and move closure to the people and create a sense among the people that they are the ones who came forward with assistance to the development agency. Development here is not mere physical or material development but it is to be a simultaneous development of the human individuals and the material / physical development. One may lay roads, one may bring in power, one may extend financial assistance, introduce new technology, but in all these endeavours the human individual is not to be neglected and forgotten. The human individual is to be No. 1 rest of the things may be either numerals or zeros.

One could observe during the past half a century the multiple development agencies have with all eagerness and intention and commitment initiated a score of rural development programmes embracing a large number of needs and problems assuring the people that they would meet all these needs and solve the problems faced by the people. This kind of continued and periodic assurances by the administration at higher and lower levels has created what is called a 'Cargo Cult'. Usually most of the communities have been managing their problems and meeting their needs at their level. With the advent of programmes of rural development, sometimes with over enthusiasm we have increased the expectations on the part of the people. And today, they look toward the government to fulfill the needs or solve the problems which they could solve by themselves. Here we try to emphasise the psychology of expectations on the part of the people. Though, we have initiated and announced several development programmes, we have not been able to fulfill a large number of them. But there is a need to educate the people at every level that the communities simply cannot totally depend on the government machinery to meet their needs and solve their problems. The administration through the change agents operating at every level may have to remedy this expectation psychology on the part of the people. In this context, close and personalized contact with the people and the leaders appraising them the limitations in meeting most of the expectations of the people which they themselves could have met with and solve. Here it is to be emphasized that the dependency syndrome is to be gradually reduced, of course, over a period of time. This could happen when the general community needs are met with like water, transport, communication, power, finance. Then the dependency will get reduced over a period of time. The government may have to work towards self-reliance on the part of the community. This self-reliance encompasses local leadership, advanced technology and every element that contributes to the advancement of the poor and the rural communities in general. In this context, clinical approach is quite relevant. We will have to get down to the people establishing rapport with them, appraise them the possibilities and the limitations to development.

Keeping this in view that there is a psychological and pragmatic need to adopt clinical approach to development, irrespective of unit of development whether it is the individual, the family, the community or the larger society. The present work details the factors and the approach that matter in the clinical Approach to alleviation of poverty. Though the primary focus of the present study is alleviating poverty among the poor, the work in a larger sense covers various approaches and measures to bring about growth and development of the entire community. In a generic sense rural development or integrated rural development is a comprehensive attempt to alleviate the varying poor living conditions of the total population in rural areas.

Some of the measures suggested in book in general relate to rural development with a focus on improving living conditions related to physical, environmental, cultural and socio-psychological realms. The main focus in clinical approach is on generating employment maximally utilizing the natural resources physical as well as human as mentioned earlier taking each family as a unit of development. Further even in respect of the family one may think of three generational approach: Programmes for the old, youth and children. The major emphasis in the approach is paying sincere and genuine attention to each unit of development creating conducive environment extending needed help and sustaining the development activity until the poor and the people below the poverty line reach a socially acceptable way of life.

CHAPTER 3

Landlessness and Poverty

Millions of inhabitants of rural Asia are tied by a primeval bond to land. They depend upon it as their primary means of survival. Their living standards, their life's activities, social position, power and prestige, their dreams and aspirations are all closely linked with ownership and access to land. However, there is substantial evidence to indicate that ownership and access to land is decreasing at an alarming rate among a major portion of the rural population in the countries of South and South-East Asia. In fact, a substantial number of studies indicate that increasing levels of poverty and inequality are due largely to increasing landlessness among the inhabitants of rural Asia.

The World Conference on Agrarian Reform and Rural Development (WCARRD, 1979) called for devising appropriate policies and strategies aimed at increased self-reliance, improved nutrition and amelioration of the lot of the poor and the landless. The alarming rate of increase in the numbers of landless people has triggered concern among governments and policy makers worldwide, more so in the Asian countries where the burgeoning population growth is exerting serious pressure on fixed resources—mainly land. CIRDAP initiated a comprehensive study to analyse the problems of landlessness in the Asia-Pacific region with a view to providing policy recommendations for the governments of the countries in the region towards reducing its incidence. The specific objectives of the study was to define rural landlessness, to arrive at a sample objectives of the number of landless households in the participating CMCs, to identify and analyse the causes of landlessness, to identify currently-executed policies and programmes to deal with this problem and examine their efficiency, and finally, to suggest measures to overcome the problems of landlessness, or at least, to contain its magnitude.

The study was carried out in the following countries: Bangladesh, Indonesia, Nepal, Philippines and Thailand. The study findings of these countries were presented at the "Expert Consultation on Landless in Rural Asia" (February 7-9), 1987 Hanoi, Vietnam). Identification of landless groups and the measurement of landlessness have tended to vary from country to country depending on major socio-economic variables. A steady deterioration in the economic condition for a particular group of the rural poor may be traced to the decline of the control over land by this group. Bangladesh ranks high in the figure for landlessness. The land-man ratio in 1961 was 0.14 hectares which declined to 0.10 hectares in 1980. This was due largely to poverty, rapid increase in population and family size and the insignificant rate of increase of arable land. The figure for the landless and the near-landless in Bangladesh is currently 62%. In Indonesia, out of over 25.1 million farm households, 27% were landless while 38% cultivated on land averaging less than 0.5% hectares. There was, however, considerable variation within Indonesia regarding these figures. The Gini coefficient for irrigated operational holding of land for villages (the micro study) was 0.68%, not significantly lower than that of *land ownership, implying also that the inequality of distribution of cultivated areas is also quite high*. In Nepal, of the 4037 sampled rural households only 10.4% could be classified as landless. Households operating small farms comprised 31% of the sample followed by marginal farms comprising 25.8%. In the Philippines a person on average owns 0.34 hectares of cropland. About 30% of the rural households were classified as landless. This figure was found to vary significantly among the different islands of the Philippines. For Thailand, considerable regional variations were recorded. In Thailand, landless people having no land whatsoever would be around 10%. However, roughly 33% of rural households in Thailand fall within the category of landless, near-landless and marginal farmer.

To tackle the problem most governments have adopted land reform and land redistribution measures and have enacted laws to regulate tenancy and share cropping arrangements. Some countries have attempted to open up new employment avenues in the non-farm sector while others have declared minimum wages for farm labour. Most of these policies have been formulated as components of a larger rural and agrarian reform programme. Land reform in Vietnam has brought immense benefits by way of securing NGO involvement, specially in launching small-scale projects and pilot programmes that directly enlist the participation of grassroots communities.

The consultation reached the following conclusions: (1) landless rural households needed separate attention since they have so far received very little benefit from development programmes; (2) the dynamics of the process of becoming landless needs further study; (4) rural development efforts should pay special stress on the welfare of poor families; (5) land reforms have to be brought about and group farming be encouraged to obviate the problem of uneconomic size of fragmented holdings; (6) more opportunities of non-farm and lean season employment for the rural people must be made available; (7) improvements in rural and agrarian have to be ensured by the market mechanism for the growers; (8) a participatory approach to rural development and community level involvement must be adopted in all uplift programmes; and (9) women should be involved in various income generating and resources mobilizing activities. It was resolved that CIRDAP, in collaboration with relevant governments and international agencies, should undertake further studies and actions to promote, devise and implement policies on the basis of broad issues identified during the expert consultation.

In the recent years intensive efforts aimed at speedy rural development have been launched in the countries of the Asia-Pacific region. In these countries the rural people constitute the bulk of the total population and a major portion of the gross domestic product (GDP) comes from the agricultural sector, providing also the majority of employment to the rural people. In most of these countries, land is considered as the most important source of livelihood, and also the base of the rural power structure. The lack of access of the rural people to land constitutes the leading cause of poverty, insecurity and powerlessness.

CONCEPTUAL AND MEASUREMENT ISSUES

The concept and the measures of landlessness may vary from country to country, depending largely on the way it is defined and on the variations in socio-economic settings of each nation. In spite of such conspicuous variations it is desirable to work with a comparable concept and a quantitative measure of landlessness in relation to rural poverty. Linked with this aspect is the need to demarcate clearly the landless groups from other groups of assetless people.

BANGLADESH

Bangladesh ranks high among the countries experiencing acute poverty in the Asia-Pacific region. It has an area of 1,43,999 Sq. km. with a population of about 100 million. The density of population is one of the highest in the world, currently standing at 694 persons per sq. km. The growth rate of population is about 2.4% per annum. It is the eighth most populous country of the world. The pattern of landownership in Bangladesh is highly skewed. The land-man ratio which was 0.14 hectares in 1961 fell to 0.10 hectares in 1980.

Concept of Landless

Many published reports are currently available relating to the concept of landlessness in Bangladesh. The landlessness people are categorized as follows:

Group I: Absolute landless households; that is, households having no land whatsoever;

Group II: Households which own some land, apart from its homestead (if any), not exceeding 0.20 hectare;

Group III: Households owning land exceeding 0.30 hectares but not exceeding 0.40 ha.

Those assigned to group II may be termed as 'functionally landless' while Group III is comprised of the 'land poor stratum'. The micro study of the villages made a thorough analysis of the situation with respect to these three groups. For the whole country, the census of agricultural and livestock of 1983-84 reveals that the percentage of households which cover groups I and II is about 49.8%, while about 12.2% of households fall within group III. The number of landless households in Bangladesh could be as high as 62% of the total number of households.

However, it should be remembered that landless is not the only cause of poverty or the landless groups are not the only disadvantaged people. Poverty, in fact, is more pervasive in Bangladesh. It is estimated (on the basis of calorie requirements) that nearly 87% of the rural population could be placed below the poverty line and about 54% of the total population were placed below the extreme poverty line in 1980.

INDONESIA

Rural Java

The salient findings from the Indonesian study are as follows:

The micro study points to overall estimates on the landless and the near-landless households. More than 36% of all households in rural Java are landless, while another 49% belong to a class of very small farmers owning below 0.5 hectares, on average, close to 0.2 hectares. These groups accounted for 85% of the total households in rural Java;

Those landless households with access to tenancy markets constituted only 31% of the total and with an average area of cultivated land of 0.35 ha; 68% were under share-cropping arrangement, 22% on rental system and another 10% on mortgage system or a combination of them;

The major features of landless households are shown below:

a) Few household members of working age;

b) Higher proportion of female household heads;

c) Household heads are younger compared with those of other groups;

d) Ownership of few consumer durables (of little economic value) and a fewfarm animals.

During 1974-83, the income growth pattern of the landless, small, and large farmer groups was 46%, 56% and 24% respectively. The major contributing factor for the pattern of the first two groups was the notable increase in productivity, while for the third it was the increase in hours worked.

The non-agricultural sector provided the major stimulus to income growth, contributing 64% to the increment of income of the landless group. The same is true for the small and large farmer groups which recorded incremental changes of 46% and 60%, respectively. The contribution of the agricultural sector to income growth was as high as 50%, 56% and 21% for the landless, small and large farmer groups, respectively.

Policy Issues to Improve the Conditions of the Landless Poor

Non-Agricultural Sector

From 1973-1983, the massive programme of construction and infrastructure development of Indonesia had absorbed many unskilled labourers from the rural areas either directly or through a propellant/multiplier effect through the activities of the informal sector: construction, manufacturing, "beca" (pedicab) driving, petty trades (peddling of clothing, foodstuffs, kitchen utensils and the like). The concern now is the continuity of operation of these propellant industries.

Agricultural Sector

Macro/Micro Policies Needed

Micro Level

The following observations are worthy of note:

Land as an asset, connotes two major elements: the land as a productive factor, and man as the manipulating factor for its use and development for generating incomes.

The problem arises when there is limited land as a productive factor when more and more people depend on it as a source of livelihood. This holds valid under the assumption that there is not much employment opportunity outside the agricultural sector and no improved technologies to absorb the increasing number of people as work force in both the sectors. This refers to what are commonly labeled as "closing land frontiers" and "decreasing land/man ratio".

Regarding the two aspects related to landlessness, i.e., land and man, very little can be done to augment land expansion, though more can be done with the skewed structure of land ownership and use. Technology application that increases the productive use of land per unit area can also solve the problem. Man, the component that manipulates the land as a productive factor, can be trained through various policies on human resource development.

A long-run, integrated solution is needed to resolve the issue of landlessness. Land policy alone cannot resolve the multifaceted (socio-economic and political, etc.) issues relating to landlessness. A more broadbased employment-oriented strategy on agricultural, agro-industrial sectors, linked to increasing agricultural output is needed.

NEPAL

Nepal is characterized by a predominantly agrarian economy with over 90 percent of the labour force being engaged in agriculture.

The extent of landlessness in Nepal, considering both the landless and near landless, is quite high. The National Planning Commission Sample Survey (1977) shows that of the total number of rural households in Nepal 10.4% belong to the landless category i.e., they do not operate any land at all. Another 25.8% were classified as marginal farmers with landholdings of 1.02-2.38 ha. in the Tarai and 0.20-0.51 ha in the Hill.

In Nepal, the landholding pattern is highly skewed. The 1981 sample census of agriculture shows that two thirds of the total farm households operate landholdings of sizes of less than 1 ha. Which in total makes up less than one-fifth of the total arable land area? The majority of the farm households in the rural areas consist of marginal and small farmers. The small size of landholding is largely responsible for the poverty of the rural masses as the produce from land is insufficient to meet their basic needs. Moreover, the widespread prevalence of the tenancy system deprives farmers of the opportunity to benefit from the new technology of production using modern inputs such as improved seeds, chemical fertilizers and pesticides.

It has been suggested that the following groups of rural households be also included in the category of landless households, viz.,

1) Farm households without any operational land and mainly depending on wage earning in agricultural occupations.

2) Owner operators, tenants and sharecroppers operating land holdings of unto 0.5 ha. in the Hill and Tarai and 1 ha. in the mountains.

The basis for the above 'cut off' point is the minimum nutritional requirement and the level of income required to meet the basic needs of a farm household. According to this classification, the target group consists of about 52% of the total rural farm households in Nepal.

The problems faced by the landless households are serious and deserve immediate attention of policy makers and planners. Poverty, malnutrition among children and illiteracy are the major problems arising out of landlessness. The heavy dependence of landless households (including marginal farmers) on wage labour in agriculture makes this group vulnerable to fluctuations in farm employment opportunities and wage rates. The lack of access to arable land leaves rural farm households in the grip of poverty given the existing employment situation in non-farm sectors and seasonal nature of farm employment

Historically, the age-old land tenure system, unbalanced economic development and poor resource endowment of landless households could be identified as the principal causes of landlessness and rural poverty in Nepal. The migration of people from the Hills to the Tarai in search of arable land has further aggravated the problem.

In the past, various programmes have been launched to improve the economic status of the landless households. Planned resettlement in the Tarai was carried out by converting forest land to arable land through deforestation. The government has so far resettled 80.000 landless families in about 70.000 ha. of land. Since the 1960s, i.e., after malaria was totally eradicated in the tarai, the magnitude of spontaneous migration from Hills to Tarai outpaced Government resettlement efforts while a larger number of people encroached in the Tarai forest than could be legally settled.

As far as agrarian reform measures are concerned, the most important step was the land reform programme following the enactment of the Lands Act, 1964. The land reform programme could not achieve significant results in so far as appropriation of land in excess of the legally-fixed land holding ceiling and redistribution among landless tillers and tenants was concerned. Even the provision of security of tenancy could not safeguard the interests of the sitting tenants many of whom were evicted by the landlords through clever manipulation of the legal loopholes.

Share tenancy still exists. The tenants are most often debarred from avoiding institutional sources of credit as they are unable to provide tangible assets as collateral. Hence, in order to improve the economic condition of the landless households it was deemed necessary to introduce programmes that would directly help in raising the income of the landless households and make them self-reliant. The Small Farmers Development Programme (SFDP) has tumed out to be a viable institutional framework to improve agricultural practices. Raise farm and non-farm incomes and improve the social condition of the landless, marginal and small farmers.

Planned resettlement, based on non-farm activities, should be emphasised as an alternative to a land-based resettlement programme. Increasing employment opportunities for the landless could be achieved through the adoption of new production technologies. The rural works programmes should aim at providing employment during the slack agricultural season.

THE PHILIPPINES

Landlessness in the Philippines may be categorized into three groups, namely:

(a) Those agricultural labourers who are neither owners of land nor leaseholders/tenants and who do not own any land for productive and profitable cultivation except perhaps that for a small homestead with a small garden, the produce of which is just enough for home consumption. In return for their services, these people are remunerated in cash or in kind.

(b) Those rural workers who exhibit the following characteristics:

   i) Landless—they neither own nor have tenants' rights to land;

   ii) Rural based—that is they live in the country side and are dependent mostly on rural forms of employment, particularly farm work; and

(iii) Workers—they sell their labour, together with the labour of their family.

(c) The small and marginal farmers, owners and/or tenants (including share-croppers) with operational land holdings of inadequate size or of inferior soil quality which do not provide reasonable livelihood throughout the year.

Landless people are most often engaged in agriculture and other farm related economic activities in the rural areas. They are either farm wage earners or self-employed and unpaid family workers. In particular, they are the agricultural labourers, tenants and leasers, without ownership right over the land they are tilling, and small owner-operators with 50% or more of their income derived from cash wages, and in kind. They are distinguished from the other categories of rural poor since the latter are dependent primarily on non-farm related activities/occupations, such as fishing, trading, cottage/small industries, crafts, services, carpentry, etc.

Based on the trends seen in micro level studies, the total labour force consisting of farm labourers and marginal farmers, and the agrarian reform beneficiaries, rough estimates indicate that there are about 5 million landless households, including those of tenants and leases in the country, following the current conceptual definitions and measurement of landlessness.

Almost all of the landless people live at standards that lie below the poverty line. Studies have shown that the major causes of poverty are the following: 1) landlessness; 20 inadequate size of land holding to support a family; 3) poor productivity, such as pòor soil, steep slopes of land, 4) adverse climatic conditions; 5) lack of peace and order, 6) lack of access to markets; 7) insufficient delivery of government services; 8) high growth rate of population; 9) lack of skills and education; and 10) cost-price squeeze in agriculture.

Landless agricultural labourers are hired as wage earners for such jobs as land preparation, planting and/or transplanting, weeding, harvesting, etc. These means of livelihood are not, enough to occupy their time for the entire day or the whole season. They have to additionally engage themselves in non-farm occupations like carpentry, trading, driving, working in rural development programmes etc. A number of landless agricultural labourers are underemployed. The extent being 22.4% of the total landless.

To help the government visualize its future course of action, the following pragmatic policy approaches are hereby suggested, based on the critical assessment of the causes of landlessness and its relationship with poverty in the Philippines:

1. Instituting a more comprehensive agrarian reform programme:
2. Creating a conducive environment of free enterprise to encourage higher agricultural production;
3. Introducing institutional adjustments in order to strengthen
4. Adopting group farming schemes.
5. Developing appropriate technology for optimal utilization of rain fed areas;
6. Providing post-harvest facilities;
7. Increasing and expanding rural welfare programmes;
8. Creating non-farm job opportunities for the landless and other types of rural poor; and

9. Assisting the participation of NGOs and the landless in government programme formulation and execution.

THAILAND

In Thailand, farm households are classified into following four groups:

Group 1: Landless, with no land whatsoever.

Group 2: Near-landless, with no more than 0.8 hectares of land;

Group 3: Marginal, with 0.8 – 1.6 hectares of land;

Landless rural households are those whose members are farmers who have no land and are usually employed in agricultural activities, as hired farm labourers.

1. In a series of surveys which cover about three-fourths of the country's total rural population, the absolute landless have been found comprising of 10% of the total farm households surveyed.
2. The near-landless and the marginal farmers have been estimated at 11% and 12% respectively. Rural landlessness is increasing but at a very slow rate.
3. More than half of the landless could be regarded as being poor.
4. The principal causes of landlessness are indebtedness, population pressure, land fragmentation, limited land availability and poverty itself.

Lao PDR

The Lao People's Democratic Republic (Lao PDR) is a land-locked country in South-East Asia, with a total land area of 236,800 sq.km. It is administratively divided into 17 provinces, 111 districts, 945 sub-districts, and 10,994 villages. It has a population of 3.6 millions of whom 90% are subsistence farmers.

At present the population growth rate stands at 2.9% per annum. It is estimated that by the year 2000, the population density will increase from the present 15 per sq.km. to 23 per sq.km. When compared with other countries in the Asia-Pacific region, Laos has rather low population density.

Land-use

Out of the total landholding of 23.7 million hectares, only four million hectares are potential agricultural land, of which two million hectares are arable and two million hectares are suitable for pastures. It is estimated that the ratio of potential agricultural land to agricultural population is 1.28 ha. per capita.

The land area presently under agricultural production is about 900.000 ha. or 3.8 percent of the total land or 24.3 percent of the total agricultural land. There is roughly 0.29 hectares of cultivated land per capita in rural areas. The ratio of cultivated land to agricultural labour force is estimated at about 0.7 ha. per capita.

Lao PDR is a country with enough land compared to the needs of her little population. The development of its agricultural and forestry resources is important, as these, forms the basis of industrial development. Since the land-man ratio is still very encouraging, landlessness is not a serious problem for Lao PDR. Therefore, it is believed that suitable policies aiming at the development of agriculture and forestry resources will go a long way in reducing poverty and improving the living standards of the people.

PAKISTAN

Pakistan with a population of about 100 million is predominantly an agricultural country with 72% of its population living in rural areas and depending directly or indirectly on land. It has been estimated that about one-half of the population is directly engaged in agriculture, while for the rest too, agriculture provides some kind of support. Thus, the economic and social well-being of the rural population directly depends on their access to land. The estimated 25% of the population who live below the poverty line belong mostly to the category of landless rural people.

Causes of Landlessness

The causes of landlessness in Pakistan are many and these vary with the historical, economic, and socio-political conditions as outlined below:

1. the historical process of privatization of land and formalization of transferable land rights by the colonial rulers;
2. the rapid increase in population;
3. the laws of inheritance;
4. indebtedness of marginal farmers;
5. the acquisition of land by Government for development purposes;
6. natural calamities like changes of river course, floods and repeated earthquakes;
7. political problems like refugee movements and ethnic strife;
8. the increasing dependence of the farm sector on expensive machinery, water, fertilizer and insecticides;
9. the successive land reform programmes induced self-cultivation by the landlords and the eviction of tenants converting them into landless labourers.

Living Conditions of the Landless

1. According to the 1980 Agriculture Census, 34% of private agricultural farms are of size less than two hectares, but their cultivated area is only 6 percent of the total farm area.
2. Out of ten million households representing about 60 million population, 6.5 million households are classified as agricultural, 3.5 million as non-agricultural of whom two million are engaged in agriculture-related crafts and trade.
3. Due to the decline in the number of tenant operated farms, the figure for the absolutely landless agriculturists has increased from 0.7 million in 1977 to 1.3 million in 1984.
4. Estimates based on dietary food intake indicate that about 20-25% of the rural population cannot afford the minimum 2200 calories per head per day despite the fact that the national average calorie intake exceeds this figure.

5. While opportunities of employment, except during the peak season have declined due to mechanization and self-cultivation, real wages have considerably increased during the period 1978-83, according to a sample field survey done in the Punjab. Rural unemployment has risen from 1.3% in 1963-64 to 2.7% in 1982-83.
6. Figures for income distribution for the lowest 20% of households as a percentage of national income show a decline from 8.2% in 1978 to 7.6% in 1984. This shows that the growth-oriented development during this period had no trickle-down effect on the rural poor or on the landless and that the inequality of incomes has gradually increased.
7. The landless are making their living through pressing the maximum number of their family members into work. Migrations to urban areas and to countries of the Middle East and incoming remittances from abroad are allaying the poverty crisis

Policies and Programmes for the Landless

The following policies and programmes are in operation in Pakistan to improve the conditions of the landless people:

1. Land Reforms;
2. Reclamation and Settlement;
3. Widening Employment Avenues;
4. Organisation of the Landless;
5. Export of Labour;
6. Industrialisation.

SRI LANKA

Until the middle of the 19th century, Sri Lankan peasants had sufficient land to pursue whatever form of cultivation they cared to engage in. The introduction of European-owned plantations brought to a close their unrestricted access to land, which the peasantry had enjoyed as birth right for centuries under their traditional government.

The peasantry in Sri Lanka can be generally classified as 1) paddy farm operators; 2) home gardeners; and 3) Chena cultivators. The extent of land which home gardeners own varies between a quarter of an acre to five acres, where they grow minor crops such as cloves, cinnamon, betel, and some vegetables. Chena cultivation is a vague mixture of paddy home garden and other operations. According to relevant socio-economic indicators of Sri Lanka, in 1983,30% of the rural population belonged to the landless labourer category. Their number is certainly on the increase; their incomes are the lowest and most irregular and their living conditions are characterised by poverty-related factors. The vast majority (43% of the agricultural operators) in Sri Lanka are small holders or micro-operators working on less than one acre. Their number has increased by almost 50% in the last few years. About 25% to 30% of the paddy land is operated by share croppers who pay more than 50% of crop share to the land owners.

VIETNAM

In Vietnam, agriculture plays a prominent role in the economy. More than 80% of the population in the rural areas depend upon farming for their living, land being their most important economic asset. Quite understandably therefore, following the success of the August Revolution in 1945, the Vietnames Government paid attention to the problem of land and the peasantry.

In the process of rural transformation and the development of agricultural production, a series of policies and measures have been introduced through a two-phase programme:

1. Land reform, and
2. Mobilization for the collectivization of agriculture.

Before the August Revolution in 1945, Vietnam was a colonial and semi-feudal country with a basically agricultural economy. The arable land acreage per head of population was only 1,200 square meters; the production technique was primitive. The distribution of land was unequitable. The peasants who directly produced food accounted for 97% of the rural households but this category owned only 36% of the farming land, while 59% of them had no land at all. Landlords who accounted for only 3% of the households in rural areas owned more than 60% of the arable land.

Land tenants were subjected to very heavy rent often constituting up to 50% to 80% of the output. In addition to this was the exorbitant interest rate of their debts to the landowners which accrued annually, finally turning them into slave labourers.

CONCLUSION

Rural Asia is almost the same all over. The same poverty conditions prevail in most Asian countries. Landlessness is common to most of the countries of the region.

The disadvantaged position of landless rural workers can be attributed to the lack of participation in economic and political decision-making and the general dearth of systematic and coordinated government machinery working for the alleviation of their problems. While it is true that governments have undertaken various-projects to improve the working and living conditions of the rural poor, it is not known how much of these have really benefited or directly affected the landless rural workers.

In seeking a solution to this common problem, it may be fruitful to examine the role of existing NGOs. These organisations have a crucial role to play in the group organisation and education at grassroot levels involving the basics sectors which include farmers, landless rural workers, fishermen, forest dwellers, women and rural youth. Through local organisations they can optimize on development and mobilize various sectors for productive and income generating projects based on the needs of the people.

NGOs can play a pivotal role in developing a grassroots or village-based information network and development planning capability in the villages. These initiatives can assist in structuring a village level planning service which can help villagers to voice their needs and aspirations at the micro level to be fed into the local governments system of local consultation, ultimately reaching the regional development bodies.

A third broad area of NGO involvement is in the articulation or advocacy of specific programmes of keen interest of the grassroots communities that they serve.

A fourth broad area of NGO involvement is in the development and management of pilot programmes in collaboration with a specific government agency.

A prerequisite for tangible government and NGO cooperation is the need to institutionalize communication linkage to facilitate the NGO-Government partnership.

Assuming that a strong flow of communication can be established, a good flow of ideas can be developed. In such an environment, both the government agencies and the NGOs can take initiatives in developing project ideas and programme proposals for pilot-testing.

Taken from a total perspective the NGOs can also be involved in monitoring and evaluation of existing or new projects as they can more easily assess the impact of programmes on the people without being biased.

[Source: *Landlessness in Rural Asia*, Centre on Integrated Rural Development for Asia and the Pacific, 1987].

CHAPTER 4

Gender Issues in Poverty Alleviation

South Asia contains 46.4% of the poor in the developing world while its population is 31% of the total population in the developing world. The total number of poor in South Asia was estimated at 520 million in 1985 accounting for 51% of the population, whereas the number of the extreme poor is about 300 million, accounting for 29% of the population. No more than 3% of the total consumption is needed to lift the people in extreme poverty above the poverty line whereas 10% of the aggregate consumption is needed to lift all the people living in poverty (as against extreme poverty) above the poverty line.

In terms of relevant social indicators characterizing poverty in South Asia, the performance of South Asia is below the average for the developing world as a whole. For example, while the infant mortality is 172 per thousand, the average life expectancy is 61 years and net primary school enrollment is 74%.

The large majority of the poor in South Asia live in the rural areas and most of them are employed in agriculture or in related occupations. The poor tend to have large families and have a high dependency ratio. The poverty amongst children is of particular concern. It is difficult to find clear evidence that women are universally poorer than men but in terms of access to social services, i.e., health and education and in terms of participation in the labour force women are more disadvantaged than men.

The rural poor in South Asia are predominantly small farmers and landless labourers. For example, in Bangladesh 84-93% of the rural population owning less than one acre of land are below the poverty line whereas 68% of the rural population owning between 1.5 and 2.5 acres are below the poverty line.

The extreme poor amongst them are those who often do not have access to food which provides minimum nutritional requirements. Also, since they do not have access to productive assets, they cannot benefit from development projects which require:

a) resource base to expand production or income; b) substantial physical energy requirements for performing additional work; and c) personal savings for investment, which might divert initial income gains away from being used for acquiring food. The extreme poor not only include landless labourers and tenants who are unable to offer collateral for loans, procure inputs and take risks; but also they include women who are heads of households and not allowed to own land. The assetless rural poor are heavily dependent on non-farm income. They face a wide range of conceptual arrangements in the labour market characterized by gender segmentation, low geographical mobility and patron client relationships. Those without any assets or stocks to fall back upon suffer most when agricultural output declines due to natural disasters like floods, droughts or policy induced failures in production. They are unable to provide for unexpected costs of sickness, death and other social obligations.

In South Asia, lack of land and rural malnutrition is highly correlated. In Sri Lanka, whereas one-third of the farm households are calorie deficient, amongst the landless calorie deficient households constitute 56%. In Pakistan, energy deficient households are larger in size and more dependent on off-farm earnings. In Bangladesh, in farming households with less than once acre, four times as many households are found to be malnourished than in the group with more than one acre. Frequently, in South Asia, high rates of malnutrition are observed in the groups with particularly low shares of off-farm income as well as in those who have a high share of off-farm income. Among households with a less specialized, more mixed income source, the prevalence of malnutrition is lower.

The magnitude of poverty in selected Asian countries is seen below.

Table I

Percentage of Population below the Poverty Line

India (1953)	43
Pakistan (1984)	23
Sri Lanka (1982)	27
Bangladesh (1985-86)	35.9

POVERTY ALLEVIATION: ISSUES AND POLICIES

What is the appropriate development strategy for alleviating poverty in these countries? The perception amongst economic policy makers and analysts regarding the appropriate policies for alleviating poverty has undergone significant changes over the years; in fact, it has wavered between economic growth and redistribution as the potent weapon for assault on poverty. During the 1960s it was widely believed that the benefits of economic growth would "trickle down" to the poor and would reduce poverty. Therefore, concentration on accelerated economic growth was the most effective way of reducing poverty. By the early 1970s, the perception changed significantly and redistributive measures such as redistribution of assets or direct income transfers to the poor gained popularity. As the 1980s dawned, the debt crisis, on the one hand, and the adverse external trade environment, on the poor, led to the pressure for structural adjustments in many countries, causing slow down in economic growth and in the government expenditures on social sectors in many developing countries. In many cases, poverty worsened.

Economic growth is frequently associated with increasing inequality, unless income redistribution, specially the redistribution of assets, is undertaken at the inception of the growth process. As economic growth accelerates, inequality worsens first and improves only late. However, if inequality worsens very considerably, it may more than offset the positive effect of income growth, on poverty and as a consequence, the latter may worsen. Income inequality increases in the initial stages of growth because the better endowed regions in a country as well as households with higher education skills, organizational and entrepreneurial ability respond to and take advantage of the growth opportunities much faster than others. The demand for human capital increases fastest and hence those endowed with human capital gain high increase in income.

DIRECTING GROWTH PROCESS IN FAVOUR OF THE POOR

As stated earlier, economic growth is a necessary condition for reducing poverty but the pattern and nature of growth needs to be broad based with a bias towards increasing the productivity and income of the poor.

There are two ways in which a pro-poor bias in the growth process can be introduced – one is to promote a broad based development, which is highly labour intensive and makes efficient use of assets which the poor have. For example, in agriculture it will imply an increased productivity of the small farmer on the one hand, and on the other hand, an expanded employment opportunity for the landless labourers in farm or in non-farm activities. In South Asian countries even though the share of agriculture in GDP is on the decline (in Pakistan, India, Sri Lanka, it is around 30-35% of GDP), it is still a predominant source of employment and income in the rural sector. Furthermore, a predominant proportion of the population of these countries live in the rural areas i.e. 70–80% of the population. Also the major share of employment in the rural areas is provided by agriculture.

The first step in the direction of promoting a broad based development, therefore, was accelerated agricultural development. A second set of measures was needed so that the growth process was to have significant impact on poverty. These measures included a greater access for the rural poor to land and other assets and inputs.

The access to technology, infrastructure, credit, training and extension etc., as well as the degree of competition which local industries, both household and small scale, face vis-à-vis the products of the urban industries, determine the degree and magnitude of the response of the rural non-farm activities to the demand stimulus originating in the agricultural sector. The availability of transportation and communication facilities determines not only the extent of market dispersion but also the degree of interlinkages between villages and towns or semi-urban areas.

The lesson of the spread of Green Revolution in South Asia is the recent past are as follows: Because of an increasing pressure of population on land, growth in agriculture was mainly due to yield-increasing technological change. In the regions and for crops which benefited from new technology, higher farm profits accrued to all producers including small farmers. Increased production led to an increase in demand for agricultural labour as well as for purchased inputs, marketing and transport services which in turn expanded employment. At the same time, increased consumer spending out of the higher profits fueled the demand for rural trades, services and consumer goods. Real rural wages tended to rise or at least did not fall in spite of the increasing population. Workers migrated from the poorer areas to take advantage of the expanding income and employment opportunities in the growing areas.

In this connection mention might be made of the largest scheme of this type in South Asia which was the Integrated Rural Development Programme in India. This programme made grants and loans at below market rates of interest to about 30 million rural households over the last ten years or so. The loans were disbursed by local officials on the basis of eligibility criteria related to average household income. Given the poor state of data and given the possibility that the local officials could manipulate the eligibility of borrowers, the scheme kept the door open for corruption or misdirection of resources to the unintended beneficiaries. An identification of the poor by means of such clear indicators as the size of holdings or location in disadvantaged regions might have worked better.

Grameena Bank in Bangladesh and similar credit institutions elsewhere in South Asia, demonstrated that the poor farmers when organized into groups, had achieved under "peer pressure" not only a much higher rate of repayment than the big farmers, but also they not only were willing and able to pay high interest rates and made at the same time an efficient use of credit facilities. The cost of supervision and management, including the organization of groups amongst the borrowers and the training of often illiterate rural poor in the operation of the credit mechanism was very high; a certain amount of subsidy to the cost of administration of small loans could not be avoided. What was needed was not only a close supervision but also a strict enforcement of contractual liabilities and obligations involved in loan transactions.

The delivery of inputs and services to the poor through appropriate targeting was not only difficult to accomplish because the benefits tended to be deflected to the non-poor in view of the latter's political power; but also frequently there were very high transaction coasts in dealing with a widely dispersed large number of individuals, each requiring a very small amount of services or inputs. If the poor got together in order to provide economics of scale as well as to gain bargaining power, the transaction costs and leakages in the delivery system could partly be scaled down. Similarly, at the initial stages of introduction of new technology such as fertilizer or pesticide, when the high cost new technology was not yet mastered by the farmers and the risks were high in terms of low or uncertain returns, a subsidy for a temporary period might be needed. The argument that a subsidy once introduced could not be reduced or eliminated was not valid as the recent experience of South Asian countries indicated. In this context what was most important was to ensure an abundant supply of inputs and credit at the market price or at the opportunity cost of inputs; once scarcity developed, the rationing was inevitable and the poor were likely to lose. It was not easy to prevent the rich and the powerful from preempting resources for themselves through their dominance or influence over the delivery system and the administrative or implementation machinery.

Also, a broad based rural and agricultural development strategy required a decentralization of decision making functions or authority, including the mobilization and use of resources, at the level of local governments. However, in order for decentralization involving people's participation to succeed, it was necessary to ensure an overall democratic environment in which multiple parties with free press, free and fair elections and freedom of association are allowed to function. In other words, a system of representative, democratically functioning local governments cannot effectively survive in an environment in which the national government was not based on democratic practices and institutions. In some South Asian countries where authoritarian national governments introduced local governments based on local level elections, it was easily subverted and made to become a part of the overall, national authoritarian process.

THE CRUCIAL ROLE OF SOCIAL EXPENDITURES: ACCESS TO HEALTH, NUTRITION AND EDUCATION

Poverty has many dimensions. A lack of access to income and food are very important but not the only aspect of poverty. A lack of access to health, nutrition and education facilities/services which are both important components of welfare and of human capital formation constitute the other dimensions of poverty. These different dimensions of poverty synergistically interact with each other.

An increase in income for the poor causes an increase in demand not only for food, clothing, shelter, transport and trade-related services but also for health and education services. At the same time, an increased access to health, sanitation and education facilities not only improves welfare but also enable individuals to make an efficient use of the income earning and the productivity enhancing opportunities opened up by the growth in income.

However, the health and education services in response to increase in individual demand, if they are to be provided through the market mechanism, will have to wait a long time until the income of the poor reaches a very high level. The divergence between the private and social costs or benefits, especially in the provision of primary education and health care, justifies a very prominent role for public or state action.

Education, as evidenced in South Asian countries as well as elsewhere in the developing world, contributes to increased productivity of labour by the growth of skills, and entrepreneurial ability at all levels. The small farmers, when educated and endowed with skills of numeracy and literacy, have productivity; they can use and manage inputs more productively and respond to the opportunities – the market and technological opportunities – more effectively. This is also true of small non-farm enterprises such as rural and urban trading and services, including those in the urban informal sector.

Even though it is true that primary education for the landless labour in South Asia does not lead to their increased productivity on the farm, on which production decisions are taken by farmers and not by the workers, it still nonetheless improves their prospects of higher income by enabling them to seek alternative opportunities or employment, both rural and/or urban. They can make effective use of resources placed at their disposal, for example, credit for financing self employment in various non-farm activities in the rural areas.

Similarly, the improvement of health has an impact on productivity, mostly for the very poor. The greater physical capacity for hard work is often constrained by lack of adequate food and nutrition. During peak agricultural season, requiring hard work for harvesting, for example, adequate food intake has a significant impact on productivity and wages. Also in year-round agricultural operations, it has been found that for casual agricultural workers, there is a close relationship between energy intake, nutritional and real wages.

Secondly, there is the question of priorities for the allocation of resources between public expenditures on human capital formation, on the one hand and physical capital development, on the other. Even if it is accepted that human capital formation promotes in the long term and often indirectly, increase in productivity and growth, in the short term a larger allocation of resources to social services may dampen growth. A heavy burden of social expenditures in a stagnant economy cannot be sustained for long. On the other hand, the higher is the level of income in the later years, the greater is the amount of resources which can be made available for expenditure on social services. At higher levels of income and investment the short term dampening effect of social expenditures on growth of increased social expenditures is less severe.

First, each country must decide on an appropriate balance between social and investment expenditures keeping in mind that at the extreme there is an important trade off between growth and poverty reduction. In most countries of South Asia the balance so far has been titled against social expenditures.

Second, there is the need for increased efficiency in the use of resources within each of the social sectors, i.e., education and health, etc., with a view to enhancing their impact on the poor. In the health sector there is the need for a shift in emphasis away from curative health services, mostly concentrated in the urban areas, towards preventive health and primary and secondary health care services, particularly in the rural areas, which have been neglected in the past. In the education sector, the required shift is from expenditures on higher educational institutions in the urban areas to rural primary and secondary education as well as technical education, in both rural and urban area. South Asia, as compared with East Asia, spent relatively larger amounts in higher education vis-à-vis primary education; consequently East Asia had literacy rates as well as levels of enrollment in primary and secondary education higher than in South Asia. Also, the pressure of unemployment amongst those with higher education was much greater in South Asia. The need for a redirection of the social expenditures towards the poor does bring into clear relief the possibility of conflict of interests between the poor and the non-poor.

Third, the appropriate method of financing education, health and nutrition services needs careful consideration. This in turn is linked up with three interrelated issues i.e., (a) degree of decentralization to the local government for financing and implementation; (b) relative role of public and private enterprise; and (c) extent to which these services, particularly the specialized health services and higher educational institutions catering to the needs of the rich or the non-poor, are to be paid for by the beneficiaries. For example, in several South Asian countries in the past, private enterprise with assurance from the government played an important role in the provision of both primary and secondary education. In some countries, such as Bangladesh, the government recently embarked on a large scale" nationalization" of primary and secondary schools, which resulted in a greatly increased burden on the government budget. However, this is not to deny that in the provision of education and health services, particularly primary education and health services the public action should play the most predominant role. In fact, the role of local governments in the provision of such services is crucial in terms of both mobilization of resources as well as effective participation of the beneficiaries in the design and implementation of such services.

DIRECT POVERTY ALLEVIATING MEASURES FOR THE POOR

The two sets of policies enunciated before, i.e. (a) a broad based employment oriented development strategy which involves the poor in the growth process, and (b) increased social expenditures directed towards the poor, are not enough to improve the conditions of those who are very poor. In this latter category are included those whose wages and income adjust very slowly or those who are unable to take advantage of the growth opportunities in the short or medium run or those who are located in distant, unproductive and low potential areas. Except the aged, sick and disabled, most of the poor are expected in the long run to participate in the growth process through participating in income and employment generating activities, but in the short and medium run they may be left behind; in the interim, therefore, other measures are needed to alleviate their poverty.

A question has often been raised as to how far the poverty alleviating measures can be narrowly targeted towards the real poor. How costly, both administratively and financially, the targeting schemes are as compared to the non-targeted schemes? Moreover, even when targeting may be more cost effective it may be less sustainable politically. It has been argued that the poverty alleviation schemes which bring benefits to the non-poor, ranging from the direct participation in an imperfectly targeted scheme to external benefits associated with or guaranteed by such a scheme, is often politically more feasible. This is because schemes with wider coverage often permit the formation of political coalitions which mobilize support for roads or irrigation canals can be far more widely distributed than the wages of the participants. Again the participation in public works projects is potentially open to anyone willing to accept the required conditions of employment. Today's well-off farmers or landless labourers could be tomorrow's target groups because of a decline in income or employment. The potential participants in public works programme are therefore larger than the actual participants at any one time. Many do not participate in such schemes may still value the insurance benefits of such a scheme.

Among a few successful well targeted poverty alleviating measures, is the Maharashtra Employment Guarantee Scheme in India. It provides employment to the unskilled manual labourer on small scale rural public works projects such as roads, irrigation facilities and reforestation, etc., at wage rates which are at par with the prevailing agricultural wages. It was introduced in the mid-1970s and it expanded to reach an average annual employment of about 750,000 persons during the period 1977-1983. By 1984-1983 growth of employment amounted to 180 million person days representing 3% of total rural employment. It was variously estimated that the scheme alleviated three-quarters to one-third of the extent of unemployment among landless or near landless households in 1977-1978. During 1978-1979, a survey indicated that 90% of the workers participating in the scheme were living below the poverty line, whereas in the state as a whole, only 49% of rural households were below the poverty line. The mean income of the participating households was found to be 20% below the poverty line, while 53% higher than that of the same classes of rural poor who did not participate in the scheme. The wage bill for the employment scheme has typically represented 70% to 80% of the governments' total expenditures. Excluding the foregone earnings of the workers, their net gain was 50% to 60% of the wages they received.

The guarantee of employment helped to mobilize the rural poor as a political force. The scheme was funded by taxes on the urban rich who did not resist the increased tax burden because they felt that the scheme kept the rural from migrating to the city, thus overburdening its physical and social infrastructure and the overcrowded slums. Several questions were, however, raised about the scheme; one related to the claim that a disproportionate share of the extra benefit emanating from the projects (i.e. roads, buildings, soil conservation, reforestation, irrigation, drainage, etc), for the scheme. Second, the recent requirement that wages paid should be equal to the statutory minimum wage, while in private employment legal minimum wages were often avoided, was expected to increase excessively the financial burden of the scheme by diverting the unemployed away from private employment to the more attractive employment opportunities under the scheme. Third, the productivity of the assets created by the scheme was likely to be kept low, to the extent that labour inputs tended to be maximized and inadequate provisions were made for non-labour inputs. Roads without adequate provision of culverts and bridges etc., did not last long.

Another well known employment scheme for the poor in South Asia was the Food-for-Works Program in Bangladesh. This was introduced in the mid-1970s and had grown considerably over time. The scheme organized employment for wages paid in kind, on such projects as construction and maintenance of roads, irrigation, drainage and embankment projects, etc., and was successfully targeted towards the poor. While 25% of the rural households had per capita income of Taka 1500 during 1980 – 1982, 60% of the households who participated in the scheme came from this income group. Seventy-five percent of the participating households were landless or had land less than half an acre whereas for the rural population as a whole the proportion of landless labourer was only 45%. Seventy percent of the food aid used to finance Bangladesh's food for work project was disbursed to the participating workers. Of the wages received 50% to 60% were net gains accruing to the participants after deductions were made for foregone earnings.

The employment schemes for the poor, as analyzed above, provided for a self selection of participants who were very poor and were in search of employment. This minimized the possibility of leakages, of direct benefits going to the non-poor. Also the chances of missing the target group were very small. If the targeting was to be based on such poverty indicators as the size of land holdings the implementing agency would have been provided with considerable discretion in the selection of beneficiaries; this could have opened the possibility of corruption and leakages.

The full development potential of long-term employment and income generating programme as described is often constrained by the need to provide a maximum of amount of employment for unskilled labour out of a given budgetary provision for such schemes. The constraints which were thus imposed upon the quantity of non-labour inputs detracted from the quality of assets which were created.

As mentioned earlier, the Maharashtra scheme was financed largely by special taxes i.e., income taxes on urban professionals, sale taxes and a surcharge on irrigated land and partly by general revenues. The immediate incidence of the cost of financing was probably the heaviest on the urban non-poor. Bangladesh's Food for Work programme was financed by food aid. As the South Asian countries achieved increased self-sufficiency in domestic food production, they would be able to use domestic food surplus for rural public work programme. However, this would pose the problem of finding resources for financing the procurement and storage of surplus food by the public sector agencies.

CONCLUSION

In most of these countries growth in the per capita income needs to be accelerated as a part of the poverty alleviating development strategy. In view of the fact that the large majority of the poor are in the rural areas, an accelerated increase in rural income is a necessary condition. The key to an increase in rural income in South Asia is held by agriculture and non-farm rural activities linked to the development of agriculture. Infrastructure, technology, credit and appropriate macro and sectoral policies, including output and input price policies are essential ingredients of an employment oriented, broad based agricultural development strategy. The rural non-agricultural sector in all of those countries has not been able to develop high productivity activities, partly due to demand constraint and partly due to a lack of technology and infrastructure.

There is an urgent need for not only expanding public expenditures on health and education sectors but also redirecting them towards the poor, especially in the rural areas, with an increasing emphasis. There is a need for an innovative mechanism for financing such expenditures, including the rich beneficiaries buying for the cost of their services; while the poor can get subsidy. This is especially needed in view of the heavy financial burden of a considerable expansion of health and education services, especially primary education and health care services.

How to introduce the schemes for targeted food distribution for the poor while maintaining incentive prices for producers, as well as high levels of development expenditures on agriculture, in the context of limited public resources, poses a substantial challenge. Technological change focusing on large farmers in agriculture resulting in an increased output may face a demand constraint as the phase of input substitution is completed. Unless there was a rapid increase in non-agricultural income, the income of the rural poor can be substantially raised, if food, surpluses can be used for undertaking on a large scale labour intensive public works projects.

Unequal ownership of land in rural areas is frequently associated with unequal political power. Land redistribution apart from its contributions towards the alleviation of rural poverty is also likely to help in the growth of viable, democratic, broad based local government as well as rural development institutions with possibilities of popular participation on a wide basis.

Resource constraints will continue to plague the South Asian countries in their effort to mount large scale anti-poverty programmes. How far the international authority is willing and able to allocate resources on the basis of anti-poverty orientation of the recipient countries is an unsettled question, in view of the political and extra economic considerations governing external resource flow. Per capita external resource flow to South Asian countries is related neither to the level of their overall per capita income nor to the extent of poverty within individual countries as shown below.

The role of international community in some of the South Asian countries, where foreign aid is a predominant source of development finance and policy advice, is important. The overall framework of economic policy and programmes which promotes labour intensive or employment oriented development strategy should find a predominant place in policy dialogue between donors and the recipient countries. No less important is the role of external assistance directed towards rural primary health care and education services, nutritional programmes, infrastructure and rural electrification. A shift in the composition of foreign assistance in these directions is more often than not likely to stimulate or initiate a change in priorities of national expenditures; frequently, a corresponding increase in counterpart national resources is needed in order to make an efficient use of additional development assistance.

The alleviation of poverty in South Asia is the primary responsibility of the national governments. However, frequently governments are subject to many pressures from interest groups. Obviously their objectives are often complex and multidimensional: to stay in power to serve particular interest groups and sometimes to enrich themselves. For the governments to be responsive to the needs of the poor, an open multi-party democratic political system in which the issue of poverty alleviation is high on the agenda of the political parties is needed. The resistance to a reduction in the move of the rich and powerful groups in social expenditures is likely to be great while the potential beneficiaries of change generally have little voice or political muscle. That is why the poor need to be organized if they are to articulate their demands and mobilize support for anti-poverty measures.

A massive programme of poverty alleviating measures requires a decentralized political and administrative structure, for not only mobilizing resources but also for designing and implementing, with the help of resources so mobilized, the rural development projects.*

In Asia, gender and rural poverty are inter-linked in different ways. Gender appears to be a principal criterion for the allocation of scarce resources in communities and households. The effects of intra-household and societal gender inequalities leading to women's lesser access to food, health, care, education and skills for productive employment are significant with regard to poverty creation and its perpetuation. Gender inequalities are also exhibited in the process of development thinking.

In Bangladesh, Pakistan and India, the trends in respect of continuing intra-household gender inequalities are reflected in the allocation of scarce resources. Women are less endowed in respect of productive assets that could enhance the returns to their labour.

Women constitute the central agents to the success of poverty alleviation efforts since their income meets the basic domestic needs. There is a lack of data regarding women's contribution in agriculture. The government and donor organizations are not mainstreaming women in agricultural and other rural development programmes. In most countries, women farmers are bypassed by agricultural extension.

Rural women's access to credit is drastically curtailed owing to a number of factors. Women's involvement in non-farm employment is restricted to traditional "feminine" fields, characterized by limited access to credit. In most Asian countries, there persists a lack of apprenticeship non-formal training programmes for women. Their activities are confined to traditional areas like sewing, knitting, embroidery not being linked with any particular demand. Appropriate strategies for poverty alleviation should consider salient gender issues as well as necessary conditions and safeguards for their successful implementation. Moreover, development interventions to alleviate rural poverty need to be mainstreamed by integrating gender issues in all project components.

Gender is, in many ways, interlinked with rural poverty in Asia. In communities and households with very scarce resources, gender becomes a salient criterion for the allocation of these resources. Poor households are forced to adopt short and long-term survival strategies which involve inequitable allocation of resources that treats preferentially members who are deemed to be the best endowed to help the household to survive. Furthermore, while scarce resources are preferentially allocated to men and boys, time consuming tasks and responsibilities are more often allocated to women and girls who work more hours per day than men and boys. Beyond the household, a powerful gender stratification system that places men in decision making positions is responsible for the designation of funds for

---

***Source**: Adopted from Nural Islam, "South-Asia: Those who are Left Behind—Issues and Perspectives", *Asia-Pacific Journal of Rural Development,* Vol. 1, July, 1991.

education and training primarily for men as well as for the designation of profitable employment and training opportunities as "masculine" while women are relegated to traditional, "feminine" training and economic activities with limited demand that do not provide them with adequate means to escape poverty.

The consequences of intra-household and societal gender inequalities that lead to women's lesser to food, health care and education as well as to skills for productive employment are far-reaching in terms of poverty creation and perpetuation in the present as well as in the next generation. Chronically malnourished rural women with often untreated health problems bear children with a high probability for congenital illnesses and small survival chances. Illiterate women with limited access to income cannot take good care of their children with respect to health and nutrition. Poor rural women with a work overload and little or no access to regular income use their daughters' labour for survival and thus deprive the latter of a chance to acquire education and training for escaping the vicious circle of poverty.

Also the lingering notion and poverty alleviation programmes that view at the household as an undifferentiated unit and aim interventions at men only cannot be effective. A poor household can escape poverty when all members, men and women, can have access to food, health care, education, skills training and productive employment. Development programmes aiming at alleviating poverty need to target equally men and women with regard to access to all resources and services. The key to diminishing the pivotal role that gender ideologies and stereotypes play in creating and perpetuating poverty through inequitable allocation of scarce resources is the increase of the economic value of women by providing them with skills in demand and by creating and facilitating their entry into productive paid employment. Furthermore, because the prevailing gender stratification system is powerful and gender stereotypes play a central role in the creation and perpetuation of rural poverty in Asia, there is a need to eradicate these stereotypes by means of valid statistics and data and through the gender training of agricultural and rural development policy makers, professionals and practitioners.

II. Some Important Gender Issues in Asia

A. Are rural women poorer than rural men? Are female headed households poorer than male headed households?

Although rural women in poor households work at least as hard as, if not harder than, men, they have less access to food and health care as well as to education and training and other productive assets than men. Gender inequities in intra-household allocation of resources that favour adult males and boys tend to increase the poorer are the households and to diminish when women have a economic value in the society.

The trends in Bangladesh, Pakistan and India are similar with regard to prevailing intrahousehold gender inequities in the allocation of scarce resources that lead to women's lesser access to food, health care and education but these inequities are more accentuated in Bangladesh and Pakistan. In India, there is abundant evidence documenting such intrahousehold gender inequities with regard to food, heath care and education, especially among the poor with important regional differences (Agarwal, 1986). In Bangladesh and Pakistan, less than 10% of rural women are literate and women and girls of all ages have less access to food and health care than men, these gender inequities being exacerbated by high fertility rates and closely spaced pregnancies and inadequate nutrition during pregnancy and breast-feeding. "Purdah" restrictions further limit Pakistani women's access to the few existing health services in rural areas. Thus, while ill health and premature death is very high among the poor female infant and child mortality as well as because of exceptionally high maternal mortality rates, women in both Bangladesh and Pakistan have by one year shorter life expectancy (at 51 years) than men and the sex ratio is heavily skewed against women. It must be underlined that it is in the poorest households that practically all women work and often carry the greater share of household tasks and responsibilities but still are entitled to a smaller share of food and health care than men. Also women are less endowed in terms of productive assets that could increase the returns to their labour (World Bank, 1989; and 1990a).

In Bangladesh, while 15% of all households are headed by women, 25% of the landless are headed by women. But, whether heads of households, or living in households, there is little doubt that rural women in Bangladesh are poorer than with regard to all poverty indicators (Safilios-Rothschild and Mahmud, 1988; World Bank, 1990a). Similarly, in India, it has been found that the percentage of female headed households with the smallest land holdings and this percentage decreases as the size of the land increases. Also a significantly higher percentage of female heads of household relative to male heads have a low educational level and are illiterate; report unemployment during the reference week; report no participation or no full participation in the labour force; and depend on wage labours versus self-employment in non-agricultural activities (Visaria and Visaria 1983). A household survey conducted in a district in Andhra Pradesh also showed that much larger percentage of female headed households relative to male headed household are below the poverty line and a higher percentage of female than male headed households are among the "poorest of the poor" (Parthasarthy, 1982).

B. THE IMPORTANCE OF WOMEN'S INCOME FOR POOR RURAL HOUSEHOLDS

Women are important economic actors and must be conceptualized as such by all types of projects that aim to alleviate poverty and increase productivity in Asian countries. Women's income is crucial for poor rural households since women are co-bread winners or sole supports of the family. Women's independent income generation helps ensure stability of income for the household. This is particularly important, if men's bread winning ability is problematic. Also in poor households the more women's income is critical for survival, the more women can exert. Influence in household decision-making. Furthermore, in some countries such as Indonesia because of a high rate of divorce and in rural Bangladesh because of a high rate of abandonment, women are quite motivated to secure control over household expenditures and to maintain an independent income (Papnek and Schwede, 1988; Safilios-Rothschild and Mahmud, 1988).

Furthermore, women are central and critical agents to the success of poverty alleviation efforts because they use their income to meet basic household needs and to break the vicious circle of poverty from one generation to the other. For poor households, the women's capacity to work, her health, her knowledge and her skill endowments are often the only resources to be counted for survival. A great number of research studies in different provinces in India have documented that women contribute a larger share of their earnings than men to basic family maintenance and increases in women's income translate more directly to better child health and nutrition. Women's income is particularly critical in landless and marginal landowning agricultural labourer households (Sharma, 1980; Gulati, 1981; and Mencher, 1988). In villages in West Bengal, for example, women consistently contribute a much higher percentage of their income for household expenditures than men because women withhold less than men for personal use (Mencher, 1988). Similarly, in villages in Puri District in Orissa, it was found that increases in women's income benefited more the income available for the household than increases in men's income (Patnaik and Debi, 1986). Also in the Philippines, in male-headed households in which women are working but the women invest more of their income in schooling and health care for the children (1985 Family Income and Expenditure Survey). Finally in Bangladesh, the rural poor women's income is almost entirely used to provide the necessary purchasing power for food security and if sufficient, also for children's (mainly sons') education (World Bank, 1990a).

C. WOMEN'S ACCESS TO AGRICULTURAL EXTENSION

In most countries women farmers are bypassed by agricultural extension. This is due partly to the lack of valid statistics and data about the active role played by women in agriculture as labourers and as farmers who make important agricultural decisions and perform most tasks and partly to the belief that only women extension workers can reach and interact with rural women. In many countries, the latter has led to unsuccessful attempts to create a very limited separate and largely ineffective women's extension service. There is considerable evidence, however, from several countries that in most areas, except the most conservative pockets, male extension workers can effectively reach women farmers, provided women farmers are organized into groups; male and female extension workers are trained to understand women farmers' role in local production systems; and extension directives with a clear message that reaching women is a very important requirement of extension workers' job as well as for agricultural efficiency and productivity (Weidemann, 1987). Furthermore, the Indian experience has shown that the existence of a high percent of women field-level extension workers as is true in Kerala (46%), is not a guarantee for women farmers' access to extension. In the absence of a clear directive regarding the importance of reaching women farmers, women extension workers made no particular effort to select female contact farmers or to work with women producers. Instead, they perceived it to be prestigious to reach men. As a result, there are almost no female contact farmers in the Kerala extension system (Ansuri, 1987).

In Pakistan, there are no women extension officers employed by the Government. The Women's Cell in the Planning and Development Department of Punjab claims to have 38 Lady Field Assistants trained mainly in home economics but only two of them are working in the field. Agricultural training programmes, therefore, consistently train men even for agricultural activities that are clearly the responsibility of women such as, animal care and fruit drying and processing. The Aga Khan Rural Support Programme, however, has demonstrated that it is possible to train and effectively utilize rural women for specific extension purposes. The programme successfully trained 837 women in 382 villages in the North to deliver for a fee, plant protection or livestock vaccine serum to villagers, thus providing profitable employment to the trained women and leading to increased vegetable yields of the women receiving the services (World Bank, 1990b).

In Bangladesh, the situation is quite similar as in Pakistan. While, under the T and V. extension system, only a small percent of all smallholders is reached, women headed farm households are even more rarely visited by extension workers. Starting from the assumption that rural women play only a minor role in agricultural production, as indicated by the official agricultural statistics, reaching rural women with technical messages has not been considered important or relevant for agricultural productivity. Female extension workers who do not have means of transportation, or a transportation allowance and who have been assigned to selected district headquarters and towns. They are not, therefore, able to reach women farmers, except in villages near the towns and rarely poor women. The existence of these few extension women workers is symbolic rather than substantive and is ever further aggravated by the fact that their mandate is to provide rural women with home economics and limited agricultural messages (Safilios-Rothschild and Mahmud, 1988). Evaluations have shown that these women extension workers are less agricultural messages on to women (Halim and Islam, 1988; Safilios-Rothschild and successful in extending extension services to groups of landless and marginal men and arrangements. The model used, according to which young men and women are trained for six months in practical agriculture, they provided them with mopeds and supervised by agricultural specialists, has been quite successful in enabling both men and women to reach landless men's and women's groups involved in crop cultivation on land lease or share cropping arrangements (Safilios-Rothschild and Mahmud, 1988).

D. WOMEN'S ACCESS TO CREDIT (FOR AGRICULTURE AND NON-FARM SELF-EMPLOYMENT)

Poor rural women's access to credit has been severely curtailed by a number of factors, some of which are shared with poor rural men and others which are gender-specific. Barriers shared with men are banks' unwillingness and inability to serve the rural poor who need small loans with corresponding high administrative costs and who often have no collateral, because they are landless or near landless, so that loans have to be made on a collective and potential productively basis. These types of loans require closer supervision that translates into the establishment of rural branches, into loan officers who spend considerable time in rural areas and into the need to train loan officers to understand the needs and potential of poor rural men and women. Gender specific barriers are: (i) poor rural women's almost universal lack of assets that can be used as collateral and their lack of institutional links, such as through cooperative membership; (ii) the gender stereotypic beliefs about women's ability to effectively utilize only small loans and their inability to engage in agricultural production and profitable non-traditional self-employment; and (iii) the resistances of and interferences from male relatives. The reality is, however, that women need and can effectively use as much credit as men; that they save more than men; and that they have higher repayment rates than men.

In Pakistan, rural women have had very limited access to institutional credit. This is due to banks' unwillingness to lend to small borrowers in general and to rural women in particular, who do not own assets that can be used as collateral and who require the existence of women loan officers. Bank officials in Pakistan are, however, aware that a larger proportion of savers are women and although they save small amounts, they have a greater potential role in savings mobilization. While less than 0.1% of the Agricultural Development Bank loans are made to women and the amount of credit disbursed to women is even smaller, one branch (in Gujranwala), introduced in 1985 an innovative Couple Mobile Credit Officer Scheme for promoting agricultural credit for women as well as for men. The scheme, however, is not a success: women have received 10% of the loans and 6% of the disbursement for cottage industries but livestock loans for women have been neglected and there are a number of questions to whether in fact women control the utilization of the loans (World Bank, 1989).

In Bangladesh, in addition to the usual reasons for rural women's limited access to institutional credit, the widespread erroneous perception that rural women are not engaged and cannot be engaged in agricultural production because of socio-cultural reasons has played a crucial role. Thus, even when institutional arrangements were made through the Government sponsored Rural Poor Programme to make credit available to women, such credit was made available only for gender stereotyped non-agricultural income generating activities. Furthermore, the size of the loan was so small that made it possible for the women to engage in profitable self-employment such as buying a cow that could earn profit in one year. Women, thus, were relegated to economic activities such as paddy husking with very low returns and showed no increase in their income as a result of the loans received (Rahman, et al., 1986). When, however, rural women's groups were backed by NGO's or the Grameena Bank, that recognised and supported women's groups for agricultural production, women were able to obtain and effectively use bank loans and to repay the loans at high interest rates. Among Grameena Bank borrowers, 56% of the total share of loans disbursed to individual women members in 1987 were utilized for different types of agricultural production. Also in 1987, 57% of loans disbursed by the Grameena Bank for joint ventures went to collective enterprises of women's groups engaged in agriculture. Two-thirds of these loans were used for crop cultivation on land obtained through leasing or share-cropping and one-third for livestock raising and fisheries. According to available evidence, both within the context of the Government sponsored BRDB Rural Poor Programme and the Grameen Bank (and many other NGO's), poor rural women save more than poor rural men and have better loan repayment records (Saffilios-Rothschild and Mahmud, 1988).

E. ACCESS TO SKILLS TRAINING

The two major barriers to women's access to skills training that could help them escape poverty are: (i) the lingering of "feminine" stereotypes as to appropriate training for women that drastically limits the fields within which women are trained and precludes their training in profitable skills that are in demand because they correspond to basic needs of the local population; and (ii) the availability of vocational training to persons who have a high school certificate that excludes practically all poor rural women. Even the requirement of an elementary school certificate would eliminate most poor rural women. The lack of apprenticeship non-formal training programmes for women in non-traditional skills consolidates women's poverty.

In most Asian countries the story is the same. In Pakistan, for example income generating projects for women are mostly skill-training projects in traditional areas, sewing, knitting, embroidery, which are not linked with any particular demand. While women learn to make their own and their children's clothes, their output is usually not sold and they do not earn any income (World Bank, 1989). In Bangladesh, skill centres for women at lower than college level, although planned within the Vocational and Technical education programme of the Government, were never developed. And there are no provisions for the enrolment of women in any of the important non-formal Vocational and Technical institutions. There is little interest on the part of policy makers in creating opportunities for women to receive non-formal vocational and technical training also (but not only) because women require costly separate hostel accommodation. Women's access to non-formal vocational and technical training is largely confined to programmes under the Ministries of Social Welfare and of Women's Affairs and NGO's that provide traditional, stereotyped "feminine" training that does not prepare women for productive employment. Thus women are confined to low earning "income-generating" activities with limited market demand. NGO's however, such as Gonshasthaya Kendra, that have provided women with profitable mainstream skills have demonstrated women's interest and ability to engage in mainstream productive training and employment (World Bank, 1990a). Other NGO's such as Proshika and BRAC have been providing poor rural women with non-formal non-traditional often on the job training that has been enabling them to undertake profitable collective self-employment in village irrigation schemes or fish ponds (Safilios-Rothschild and Mahmud, 1988).

F. THE ROLE OF NON-FARM EMPLOYMENT

Non-farm employment is crucial for the alleviation of rural poverty since in many Asian countries the rural poor are landless or near landless or have very small landholdings that cannot suffice for the survival of the household. Women's involvement in non-farm employment is, however, besieged by the prevailing double standard of "income generating" activities for women, by gender stereotypes that restrict skills training to traditional "feminine" fields and by limited access to credit, a configuration of crucial factors that confine women to traditional "women's fields of low demand and profits".

The idea behind these training programmes as well as the available income generating activities for women is to supplement the main income which is earned by men as false assumption, as we have seen in the case of poor rural households. These programmes, therefore, do not provide employment opportunities for women with an adequate pay that would enable them and their families to escape poverty. In many countries, the traditional non-agricultural employment opportunities for women, - handicrafts, cottage industry and petty trade, are not remunerative. In Pakistan, the fact that women are mostly trained in traditional "feminine" skills, the lack of market demand for their output and the lack of access to credit, makes it very difficult, if not impossible, for them to engage in profitable non-farm employment. In non-agricultural households, however, which do not own or rent land or in which men are rural non-farm as embroidery, tailoring, crocheting, carpet and duree weaving, handloom production, leather work, pottery and ceramics, as well as construction and food processing. Women's income from these types of non-farm employment, although very low, plays, as we have seen, an important role in the survival of these poor households (World Bank, 1989), despite the fact that the declining size of farms makes it increasingly necessary for rural women to be involved in such employment. Women have less access to non-farm occupational opportunities than men because of men's greater social and physical mobility as well as greater ease to interact with strangers in the non-traditional settings that characterize many of the new employment options. In addition, women's significantly lesser access to non-traditional skills in demand and to credit makes very difficult, if not impossible for women to undertake and sustain profitable micro-enterprises.

III. DEVELOPMENT INTERVENTION TO ALLEVIATE RURAL POVERTY: IMPLICATIONS FOR PROJECT DESIGN

Appropriate strategies for poverty alleviation should take consideration salient gender issues as well as the necessary conditions and safeguards for successful implementation and sustainability. A crucial basis for these strategies is that gender inequities that perpetuate and exacerbate poverty can be weakened by increasing the economic value of women through skills training for productive and profitable employment and through increased women's access to credit and technology. The appropriate strategies are:

1. Gender Mainstreaming of Poverty Alleviation Programmes

Development interventions aiming at alleviating rural poverty need to be mainstreamed by integrating gender issues in all project components if they are to be efficient, effective and sustainable. Rural poverty cannot be alleviated through programmes and projects targeting only men or only women as active actors and beneficiaries. Both men and women must be equally targeted. Women must be targeted because they, as well as men, have a strategic potential as critical actors in the process of moving their families out of poverty. Furthermore, women need to be included in agricultural and rural development projects aiming to intensify agricultural and to improve food security, if the projects are to succeed.

Poverty alleviation projects, on the other hand, are not effective and sustainable when they target only women as active participants and beneficiaries through women specific projects or project components, unless other projects are simultaneously undertaken which offer the same services and resources to poor rural men, these men will take over whatever aspects of the women-specific projects are promising. Furthermore, women-specific projects are cheaper and easier to implement than devising methodologies to integrate women in mainstream large projects but such projects implemented by women-based or women-staffed institutions (NGO's women's national machineries) have little impact on broadcasting women's employment opportunities and chances for escaping poverty (Ruvinic, 1989). This is due to the fact that: (i) they remain small so that they cannot become large investment projects and cannot, therefore, reach many women or afford well qualified staff; (ii) they are not able to stimulate changes in mainstreaming government and private sector institutions that would create a favourable employment environment for poor rural women.

2. The Methodology of Gender Mainstreaming

Gender mainstreaming is more than the integration of women in mainstreaming projects. The gender mainstreaming of agriculture, for example, can be equated with the "rationalization" of agriculture, meaning that the design of projects and the allocation of project services and resources is rationally targeted to the appropriate farmers, men and/ or women, who can maximize the use of these services and resources. Thus, if women are performing some agricultural tasks and make some agricultural decisions, they need to receive the appropriate agricultural training and extension messages.

a. Women's work overload is a barrier to their being able to participate in skills training or to undertake profitable self-employment. When women are offered skills training in non-traditional fields of high demand, they manage to find the time to participate. Attendance is poor when the skills offered have little market value. Also when women are able to engage in profitable agricultural or non-farm employment, they use part of their income to buy fuelwood or to hire help so that they are able to satisfy household needs within the available time.

b. Poor rural women can only cope with small sums of credit; they are not able to effectively absorb larger sums. The evidence, however, from Bangladesh and Indonesia shows the contrary: women are kept at the same poverty level because they are given access to small loans that do not enable them to make the necessary investments that would give them the chance to undertake profitable self-employment and to escape poverty.

c. Women are more motivated by their children's and families' welfare rather than by economic incentives that benefit them as individuals. All available evidence, however, from projects and research shows that women are motivated both by incentives that help improve family welfare as well as by economic incentives that improve their independent income and therefore, not only their autonomy but also their bargaining power within the household.

d. Women are interested in and can cope only with stereotyped "feminine" occupations such as handicrafts, knitting and sewing, pottery, goat and/or poultry raising, but not with new non-traditional occupations that require technical skills. When poor rural women are asked what they would like to do, they often answer in terms of the stereotyped "feminine" activities with which they are acquainted. These answers, however, do not imply that these women are not interested in or capable of engaging in non-traditional activities and occupations, if they are given the appropriate orientation and training, as increasingly projects undertaken in several Asian countries (including Pakistan and Bangladesh) have shown. The upgrading of women's traditional skills to non-traditional skills in demand (e.g. from pottery to brick making skills) also has proven a successful training strategy for women.

In the area of agricultural extension the model successfully used in Bangladesh by an NGO, the Rangpur Dinajpur Rural Services (RDRS), could be adopted and used in most areas in other Asian countries. It is not financially possible to hire and place in the field as many women extension workers as it would be necessary for reaching the large numbers of women producers. In addition, the field placement of women presents a number of practical and logistic problems that is not always possible to solve. At best it is possible to field place young women of rural origin for a limited number of years. It is not, therefore, feasible to visualize that, at least in the near future, the majority of the Asian women producers will be served exclusively by women extension workers. Instead, it is necessary to restructure and reorient the extension service so that both male and female extension workers are utilized to reach women's groups engaged in agricultural (crop and livestock) production. Experiences from other countries have shown that policy directives to extension workers to select women's (and men's) groups as contact farmers followed by incentives for selecting women's groups as well as by gender training in agricultural production for both men and women extension workers are quite effective in reaching women farmers. It is, furthermore, crucial that agricultural research is reoriented so as to provide extension workers with technical messages that are relevant for the different categories of men and women smallholders who may often have different farming systems and different priorities and constraints than larger farmers. In countries, for example, in which rice has been the dominant crop, agricultural research needs to diversify to include vegetables, fruits, livestock and fisheries, that is agricultural sub-sectors in which women are most often involved. Such diversification would allow the development of ecologically sound farming systems rather than the cultivation of single commodities and agricultural research would have to develop gender sensitive technical solutions tailored to local conditions. In addition to diversification, agricultural research needs to: ensure that different categories of women producers (wives, female heads of household) are included in on-farm research and that farming systems research focuses on the complexity of farming systems of female headed households as well as of men's and women's interdependent productive subsystems within the household; and that gender specific constraints and opportunities as well as critical labour bottlenecks of women's labour are assessed and that appropriate agronomic and technical solutions are devised (Safilios-Rothschild and Mahmud, 1988).

In the area of credit, the experiences point to the need to reorient banking and other financial institutions to serve smallholders and the landless, men and women. This reorientation of banking and other official financial institutions involves several steps that need to be guided by the following basic principles: (i) credit projects for women need to move away from small revolving funds for women to mainstream credit programmes implemented through banks and other official institutions that are serving both men and women; (ii) credit programmes aiming to reach the poor men and women, need to include funds for the development of the banks' capability to deal with the rural poor through training of bank officials as well as of loan officers in rural poverty and gender issues and funds to cover initial costs for the establishment and operation of the programme and the establishment of rural branches; (iii) credit programmes for the rural poor must be closely related with the accumulation of savings; (iv) credit programmes for the rural poor must be free of requirements for collateral and be granted to individuals with group responsibility; (v) women must have access to credit for all types of self-employment, including agricultural production and nontraditional technical fields that are in high demand; (vi) the size of loans must be the same for men and women and must be sufficiently large to allow investments for productive self-employment; (vii) men and women must be eligible for several consecutive loans, provided they repay in time their loans in order to be able to build up their self-employment and their assets so that they can escape poverty; and (vii) Credit programmes for the rural poor must include information regarding local profitable self-employment opportunities, basic training in bookkeeping and managerial assistance and support (Safilios-Rothschild and Mahmud, 1988; Safilios-Rothschild, 1990). Such mainstream approach for unforeseen obstacles and inefficiencies in reaching women and in some cases the specification of a target of 33% or 50% of all loans for women.

In the area of skills training for productive self-employment, the following lessons can be derived from Asia, as well as from other regions; (i) skills training for women not be gender stereotyped. Instead, skills training for women needs to prepare women for productive, mainstream and sustainable self-employment with regular earnings that allow them and their families to escape poverty, (ii) skills training for poor rural women needs to be non formal, practical and appropriate for illiterate women, although to the extent possible combined with functional literacy; (iii) agricultural production is an extremely important productive self-employment for women, especially in countries in which food self-sufficiency has not been achieved, that needs to be supported, facilitated and enhanced through extension services, appropriate technical messages, technology and agricultural credit; (iv) skills training for poor rural women must be accompanied with basic entrepreneurial training that enables them to engage in micro-enterprises.

3. Valid Gender-Disaggregated Statistics and Data

The availability of valid sex-disaggregated statistics about economic activity rates and involvement in agriculture as well as detailed data about rural women's participation in agricultural decision-making and their agricultural and nonagricultural income constitute a key instrument for gender mainstreaming. Only through the availability of such data, it is possible to establish the crucial productive and breadwinning role played by rural women in poor households and to mobilize the interest and support of policy makers planners, donors and international organizations. Furthermore, the availability of such nationwide statistics and more in-depth data allows to; (i) prepare effective training materials for the gender awareness training of agricultural and rural development policy makers, professionals and practitioners; (ii) assess the gender –differentiated impact of economic macro policies and agricultural policies and design supportive gender sensitive agricultural and nonfarm employment policies that facilitate gender mainstreaming of rural poverty alleviation programmes and projects; and (ii) institutionalize gender issues training in agricultural and rural development education and training of professionals and practitioners.

In countries, in which valid gender-disaggregated nationwide statistics are available, it is essential that the collection of such data is ensured by; (i) providing statisticians and social scientists responsible for the collection and interpretation of statistics with relevant gender training; (ii) based on experiences from other countries, providing assistance with needed modifications of concepts and methodology used as well as with the appropriate type of training and instructions for enumerators; (iii) develop and test gender modules to be used within the context of different instruments such as Household Surveys, Labour Force Surveys, Farming or Agricultural Surveys and Agricultural Censuses.

4. Institutionalization of Gender Issues in Agricultural Education and Training

Many Asian countries need to be assisted to build local capability in gender training at all levels. This can be achieved through the institutionalization of gender issues in all types of agricultural and rural development training in Universities, Colleges and Institutes. Such institutionalization requires considerable investment with regard to time and funds since in addition to gender training workshops for the education, it is necessary to develop teaching materials that are appropriate for different technical fields (irrigation, forestry, fisheries, horticulture, animal husbandry). Toward this end, gender sensitive teaching modules and research case studies illustrating key gender issues in agriculture in areas with different socio-cultural and agro-ecological configurations need to be developed through gender sensitive farming systems research. Such case studies constitute indispensable teaching materials. There is a need for investment projects to address the institutionalization of gender issues in agricultural and rural development education and training for the development of national gender training capability which is increasingly becoming crucial for the effective training of agricultural professionals and practitioners. Lack of gender skills is creating a bottleneck in the successful and sustainable implementation of agricultural and rural development projects. International organizations and consultants can be of considerable assistance in this area.

REFERENCES

Acharya, Meena and Lynn Bennett, 1982. *Women and the Subsistence Sector. Economic Participation and Household Decision-making in Nepal*. Washington, D.C: The World Bank, Staff Working Papers Number 526.

Agarwal, Bina, 1986, "Women, Poverty and Agricultural Growth in India," *Journal of Peasant Studies*, Vol. 13 (4), pp. 165-220.

Ansuri, Padmasini T., 1987. Present agricultural Extension system and Farm women, paper presented at the National Workshop on Women in Agriculture, New Delhi: India, Ministry of Agriculture, Department of Agriculture and Cooperatives, Directorate of Extension.

Berger, Marguerie, 1989, "Giving Women Credit: The Strengths and Limitations of Credit as a Tool for Alleviating Poverty," *World Develepement*, Vol. 17, pp. 1017-1032.

Buvinic, Mayra, 1989. "Investing in poor Women: The Psychology of Donor Support," *World Development*, Vol. 17 (7), pp. 1045-1057.

Gulati, Leela, 1981. *Profiles in Female Poverty*, New Delhi: Hindustan Publishing Corporation.

Halim Abdul and Md.ShahibulIslam,1988."Women in Homestead Agricultural Production," *The Journal of Rural Development*, Vol. 18, No. 2, pp. 83-96.

Mencher, Joan, 1988. "Women's Work and Poverty: Women's Contribution to Household Maintenance in South India," in: *A Home Divided Women and Income in the Third World*, Daisy Dwyer and Judith Bruce (Eds.), Stanford, California: Stanford University Press, pp. 99-119.

Papanek, Hanna and Laurel Schwede, 1988."Women Are good with Money: Earning and Managing in an Indonesian City," in: *A Home Divided Women and Income in the Third World*, Daisy Dwyer and Judith Bruce (Eds.), Stanford, California: Stanford University Press, pp. 71-98.

Parthasarathy, G., 1982. Rural Poverty and Female Heads of Household: Need for Quantitative Analysis, paper presented at the Technical Seminar or "Women and Employment, Institute of Social Studies Trust, 9-11 April.

Patnik, S.C. and Sailabata Debi, 1986,"An Assessment Women's Economic Contribution to the Farm Sector: A Micro Level Study," *Journal of Rural Development*, 5 (4), pp. 480-490.

Rahman. A., et al., 1986. *Rural Poor Programme - Mid-term Operational Review*, Dhaka, Bangladesh: CIDA Office.

Safilios-Rothschild, Constantina, 1986. Agricultural Strategies and Programmes, the Status of Women and Fertility, background paper for the International Seminar on Women in Agriculture and Rural Development in Asia, Huangxian, China, (FAO/ESH/S86/3).

Safilios-Rothschild, Constantina, 1986b. *Socio-economic Indicators of Women's Status in Developing Countries,* 1970-1980, New York: The Population Council.

Safilios-Rothschild,Constantina, 1990. "Women as a Motor in Agricultural Development: Lessons Learned from Eastern and Southern Sub-Saharan Africa," in: *Beyond Adjustment*. The Hague: Ministry of Foreign Affairs, directorate of Development Cooperation, pp. 153-164.

Safilios-Rothschild, Constantina and Simeen Mahmud, 1989. Women's Roles in Agriculture. Present trends and Potential for growth. Dhaka, Bangladesh: Agriculture Sector Review sponsored by UNDP and UNIFEM.

Sharma, Ursala, 1980. *Women, Work and Property in North West India*, London: Tavistock Publications Ltd.

Tendler, Judith, 1989. "Whatever Happened to Poverty Alleviation?" *World Development*, vol. 17(7), pp. 1033-1044.

Visaria, Pravin and Leela Visaria, 1983. Indian Households with Female Heads: Their Incidence, Characteristics and Level of Living, paper presented at a workshop on "Women and Poverty", Center for Studies in Social Science, Calcutta, 17-18 March.

Weidemann, Jean C., 1987. "Designing Agricultural Extension for Women Farmers in Developing Countries," in William Rivera (Ed.), *Agricultural Extension Worldwide*. London: Croom-Helm.

World Bank, 1989. Women in Pakistan: an Economic and Social Strategy, Volume I: "Main Report" and Volume II: "Supporting Chapters and Annexes," 1989. Washington, D.C., Country Operations Department I, Europe, Middle East and North Africa and Population and Human Resources Department, Policy, Planning and Research.

World Bank, 1990a. Bangladesh. Strategies for Enhancing the Role of Women in Economic Development. Washington, D.C., Population and Human Resources Division, Asia Country Department I.

World Bank, 1990b. The Aga Khan Rural Support Program in Pakistan. Washington, D.C., Operations Evaluation Department.

[**Source**: Adopted from the material *Gender and Rural Poverty in Asia* authored by Rothschild, Volume I, July 1991.]

CHAPTER 5

Field Study Related to the Conditions of the Poor

Though the living conditions of the poor in India and in other countries too are similar in respect to the present study Clinical Approach to Alleviation of Poverty. Two districts have been selected – Kanyakumari in Tamil Nadu, Chittoor in Andhra Pradesh for an intensive and a representative study of the living conditions of the poor. In the following pages we briefly look into various aspects and details in respect to the purposively chosen respondents administering a structured questionnaire. At random 50 respondents from each district as mentioned above were selected and administered questionnaire to them. In the following paragraphs a brief account of the households in respect to Sex, Educational Qualifications and Occupation etc. is provided.

In respect to sex of the respondents, 88 are male and remaining female.

Table I

Sex	Male	Female
No.	88	12

The following table shows the educational qualifications of the respondents

Table II

Educational Qualifications	Below 10th	Inter/ ITI	Degree	Post Graduates	No	Total response
No. of respondents	29	14	26	6	25	100

The respondents are engaged in the following occupations shown in Table III.

Table III

Occupation	Pvt. Job	Social Work	Cultivation	Business	Labour/ Coolie	Government Servant	Total
No. of respondents	33	8	15	19	15	10	100

We just begin whether the respondents own houses where they reside. One of the major problems in respect of the poor is owning of a house. Whatever may be the type (small or big). Out of 100 respondents, 82 own houses and the rest don't. It may be pointed out here that the poor who live in the villages in majority of the cases own houses as against the urban poor who largely don't live in their houses. In villages the poor manage to build a hut with grass and palm leaves.

Owning of House

Table IV

Yes	No	Total
82	18	100

Owning of Land

Since agriculture is the major occupation in villages we look into the ownership of land among the respondents. Table V below shows the numbers who own land and the landless.

Table V

Yes	No	Total
41	59	100

Here the landless is larger than those who own land, that too small pieces of land. One could imagine the plight of the landless poor who live in the villages and most of them invariably engage in labour or in some minor trade.

It is to be mentioned here in respect to the respondents covered in the study are from in Chittoor district. A large number have settled in Tirupati carrying on petty business. Such business does not require much of investment. It is selling of fruits, some eatables, toys and photos of Lord Venkateswara.

The following table shows the sources of income:

Table VI

Employee/ Job	Agriculture	Jobless	Small Business	Social Work	Labour	Total
27	14	4	33	2	20	100

The poor usually try to explore various sources accessible to them depending on their credit worthiness and their use for the lenders, they secure small loans in their neighbourhood and one finds in the villages as well as in urban centres also exorbitant interest charged by the lenders. Usually the interest of the principle amount ranges from Rs.4 to Rs.10 per hundred per month. The borrower even though he borrows small amounts he remains in some cases a borrower eternally. Here, we may point out a meaningful affordable economic measure which would help the poor not to depend for ever on this squeezing money-lender in the rural and urban areas.

Approximate Income (Annually)

The income of the respondents per annum ranges from Rs.4500 to Rs.1,00,000.

Table VII

4500	< 10000	< 15000	< 1,00,000	> 1,00,000
47	3	40	91	

Borrowing Sources

At this level of living the poor invariably go in for borrowing from sources as shown below:

Table VIII

Self-Help Groups	Relatives/ Bank Loans	Neighbours	No borrowers	Money Lenders	Total
5	46	16	9	24	100

The purposes of borrowing are indicated below:

Table IX

Family Mainte nance	Sons'/ daughters Marriages	Sons'/ daughters Neighbours	Agriculture	Small Business	Total
43	10	13	18	16	100

Since they invariably go in for borrowing we look into the range of debt on the part of the respondents.

Table X

< 10000	< 50000	Total
51	49	100

One could find in general extensive dependency among the poor. The following tables shows, the assistance received from different sources:

Table XI

Government	NGOs	Individuals	Not received any help	Total
12	13	29	46	100

Any change in occupation

Table XII

Yes	No	Total
48	52	100

Attempts to change occupation

Table XIII

Yes	No	Total
41	59	100

Since the poor find no better alternative, they feel they are destined to continue with the same occupation whatever may be the gain they get from that occupation. We also find nearly 50% of the respondents making attempts to move in for better sources and remunerative occupation. Here we may point out in such cases it is not only Government or any other NGO assisting these people financially, but providing them with some training which would facilitate their taking to some small business or any productivity activity.

Some more reasons for continuing with the same work:

a) Interest in the present work continuing in the same job, continuing the same business.

b) Some of the respondents are not satisfied with their present occupation and tried for remunerative alternatives.

c) Most of the respondents expect loans to do some business, a small number seek jobs in Government, a considerable number expects the Government to help in respect to their children education.

d) Related to improving their present economic condition majority of them have indicated they would like to go in for small business, of course with assistance from the Government, a small number would like to go in for Government job, still 10% of the respondents would like to improve their agriculture. Most of the respondents who are poor tend to look towards the Government for ameliorating their difficult living in general.

As it is suggested in Chapter 20 dealing with measures to alleviate poverty depending on ethnicity, literacy, educational qualification, interest and affordability on the part of the client system, the development agencies may have to treat each case in the clinical sense and help the poor.

CHAPTER 6

Lessons from Rural Development

In the context of alleviation of poverty, it is relevant to look into the lessons from rural development and other aspects related to the same field.

Rural development under diverse nomenclatures, during the past five decades in most of the developing countries, has been an adventurous effort with models and theories of development, strategies and methods involving policy makers, planners, administrators, scientists, technologists, academics and ordinary workers. It is a programme of developing rural communities with a network of organizations and institutional linkages from the national level to the village level with several layers of administration in between. It is a multi-faceted programme initiated and launched with great hopes and high promises. Some developmental schemes attempted were unchartered explorations. In some respects, it was a trial and error approach. But none can deny the significant contribution of rural development in terms of generation of new schemes, programme planning, programme implementation, organizational set-up, institutional linkages, strategies and methods adopted and the results achieved. Yet, we can draw some lessons from this fascinating journey of rural development.

Approaches and Strategies for Rural Development

With imagination, ideas and new kinds of approaches with all hopes and expectations of development of various segments of population and sectors during the past five decades we have both at the national and at the state level initiated, instituted and carried on diverse type of developmental programmes which are activity-oriented, segment-oriented and area-oriented which are such as the following:

- Multi-subject-matter extension education
- Aided Self-help programmes
- Development of local organizations
- Comprehensive Regional Development
- Decentralized Development Administration
- Intensive Agricultural District Programme
- High Yielding Varieties Programme
- Land Reforms
- Cooperative Development

- Development of Rural Industries
- Farmers' Training and Education Programme
- Small Farmers Development Programme
- Rural Employment
- Rural Artisan Development
- Food for Work Programme
- Area Oriented Development Programme
- Minimum Needs Programme
- Intensive Cattle Development Programme
- Command Area Development Programme
- Integrated Dry land Agricultural Development Programme
- Drought-Prone Area Development Programme
- Hill Area Development Project
- Integrated Tribal Development Projects
- Desert Area Development Programme
- Applied Nutrition Programme
- Whole Village Development Programme
- Integrated Rural Development

It is not a question of pointing out that they have all failed but each one to do justice has achieved something tangible in terms of what was aimed at. But unfortunately, they were isolated and not functionally linked and integrated in terms of planning and delivery of services.

PLANNING

Planning has come to stay as an integral part of rural development activity. But unfortunately, the very act of planning and the plan document were taken for achievement. We realized that centralized planning without the knowledge and proper understanding of the local conditions, resources, needs, capabilities and the socio-cultural milieu of the people was ineffective and so we came up with decentralized or what you call bottom-up planning. But unfortunately, we have failed to strengthen and improve the planning machinery at the lower level with knowledge, skills, resources and decision-making authority. We have also come to realize that it is not merely top-down or bottom-up planning, and that each approach has certain merits and suffers from certain limitations and so it is wise to adopt a blend of both approaches relevant to the magnitude of development and the sphere of its operation.

People's Participation

We came to recognize and realize that people's participation in rural development is a central feature and an unquestionable complement for success and sustainability of any development programme. Despite this recognition, we have largely ignored and failed to facilitate and institutionalize people's participation in developmental activities. We have made a mockery of it. In the name of people's participation, we have exaggerated and inflated the material and labour contributions from the people. We took material and money given by the people as their participation and failed to appreciate and encourage people's participation in terms of ideas, views and moral support.

Weak Grassroots Links

In the organizational structure and hierarchy in rural development, we find in general, a strong top and a weak bottom. Often, we meet with weak links at the grassroots operational level. The crucial part lies at the operational level in terms of understanding people, their problems, needs and motivating and involving them in activities beneficial to individuals and the larger community. Either in respect to expertise, status or recognition accorded, the personnel at the lower rungs of operation are rather weak. We need adequately trained, reasonably paid and highly motivated extension functionaries at the village level.

Ignored Women's Involvement

In general, we ignored women's involvement in rural development activities. It is not a plea on gender issue, but it is a question of maximal utilization of one half of human resources. In the historical evolution of mankind, woman has been an economic partner to man besides her biological and social roles.

The personnel in the various agencies engaged in socio-economic development programmes, especially the extension functionaries in rural development come in contact with and address themselves to the tasks of menfolk in the client community. Seldom are women contacted, their problems and needs looked into, their opinions and views sought, their participation solicited, appreciated and encouraged either because of traditional social restrictions and prejudices or that women are not reckoned with as important entities vis-à-vis the development programmes. The decision-making is not done by man alone though he is in the forefront of most of the business, commercial and social activities. The woman is there behind many decisions that concern social and economic issues of the family. It is a paradoxical situation that though woman is in the background, her understanding and choices influence the kind of decision a man takes and the course of action he pursues. In many a rural development programme, the women are a missing link. Needless to emphasize that the women are to be accorded the importance they deserve and facilitate their involvement as equal, responsive and potential partners in rural development.

TRAINING

Training of extension personnel and non-officials has been a significant and conspicuous activity as a means and as a necessary prerequisite for effective rural development. Thousands of extension personnel and subject-matter specialists needed a new orientation to work with rural people to improve their conditions of life. It is not just specialization in a subject or expertise in a technical field, but it is the right attitude and the conviction on the part of the development personnel that the people in the rural areas are capable of improving themselves to better standards of life. This orientation to a considerable degree was provided by training. Training of diverse nature offered at different levels and at different stages in the career of extension personnel has come to stay as an integral part of rural development.

THEORIES AND MODELS OF DEVELOPMENT

We were overwhelmed by our own and borrowed theories and models of development. We never bothered to understand and appreciate the indigenous knowledge system and integrate the new elements of development with the existing system. Sometimes, we outright discouraged and voted down the age-old functionally well-integrated and useful customs, practices and technology followed by the people. This was an unwise act on our part. We equated economic poverty of the rural people with intellectual poverty. We failed to listen to the people. Seldom we bothered to know the people's image of rural development, what they need, what they think their resources are, the way they think they should fulfill their needs and the kind of assistance they expect from the development agencies.

POOR FOLLOW-UP

Either compelled by targets or to gain entry into the community or to please some people or to meet some genuine needs of the people, with all initial enthusiasm and exuberance, we have initiated several projects and schemes, small and big, but failed to do the follow-up work. It may be a new idea, practice, method, device, technology or an institutional arrangement that has been initiated and introduced by the development agencies and adopted by the people. In such instances, often we failed to provide what may be called after-sale services. We abandoned the projects and schemes and left the people in the lurch to fend for themselves. It does not mean a continuous prop, but some newly initiated projects, individual or community-oriented warrant follow-up by the development agency.

INCREASE IN PAPER WORK

We increased paper work more than tangible, actual accomplishment in the filed, we increased the number of returns, and reports, a chain of reports from the field workers to higher-ups. At one time in Andhra Pradesh, the Village Level Workers (VLWs) presently designated Village Development Officers (VDOs) were to maintain 26 registers of different sorts. They had to spend a large part of their time in filling up the registers, posting figures of achievement, real and false to save their skin under the pressure of unrealistic and unattainable targets. In many cases, actual field work, over a period of time tended to be neat paper work. The work seriousness was lost.

UNREALISTIC TARGETS

Close to increase in paper work and influencing it, is the over-jealously fixing of targets for several activities. Targets are necessary, but they are to be based on time, resources, manpower, interest of people, their capabilities, physical possibility and sometimes, the relevance of targeted activities or items to the client community. Unfortunately, the target fixing in respect to several activities in agriculture, animal husbandry, health, sanitation and family planning for instance was centralized. The officials sitting at the regional or national level fixed the targets to be achieved. Then the targets as if they were funds, were distributed to the lower levels from one development administrative level to another across the hierarchy. Seldom, the lower levels whose burden it was to achieve the targets, questioned the higher-ups, the wisdom and practicability of the targets assigned to them. Since, more often, targets were not based on field reality and feasibility and since there was the tradition of the lower level administrative unit accepting the orders and instructions coming down from the higher level, the situation led to manipulation of figures of achievement and the statistical data as reported, sometimes, became doubtful of their reliability.

EXPECTED SPONTANEOUS RESPONSE FROM THE PEOPLE

The concept of felt-needs and the felt-needs approach has become popular in the literature of rural development. In some cases we assumed the felt-needs of the people in the rural areas and their priorities too. And so, we came up with our programmes and expected people to respond to them spontaneously, which often did not happen. Either, we have not seriously assessed the felt-needs and the people's priorities thereof or we have not prepared and facilitated the people to respond to the programmes.

We expected miracles to take place in a short span of time. Time is an element in growth and development. We became impatient with the pace of people's march towards progress.

Development personnel going to the rural people instead of the other way about was a new and strange experience to the latter. Over a long period of colonial administration and a hard regulatory system of administration, more often, the rural people tended to be silent, passive spectators and receivers. In general, the initiative and action towards development was nipped in them. When development personnel lectured to the villagers on new projects and schemes, either out of sheer respect to the personnel or having not, comprehended the purport of the programmes or finding the programmes irrelevant to them, the villagers remained silent. We misjudged people's silence for their acceptance.

MORE SLOGANS AND PROMISES

Right from the politician and down to the village level extension functionary, we created more noise, came up with more slogans, made more promises to the people, but fell short of actualizing them. Slogans are a part of motivation campaign, a part of movement for development, appealing to the people's emotions, competitive spirit, stirring their unified and concerted action for their betterment. But if the slogans and promises fizzle out as empty sound, the development agency loses its credibility. This has happened in several instances in terms of promised supplies and services to the individuals and to the communities at large.

OVEREMPHASIS ON MATERIAL PHYSICAL DEVELOPMENT

There is no denying the fact that provision and creation of physical and material facilities constitute development, but we took such physical and material things as progress and the end of development. We laid more emphasis on roads, school buildings, toilets, community halls, play equipment, etc., and less on the human side, educating the people, motivating them to higher achievement and facilitating technical and managerial skills among them to increase the production pursuits. We failed to recognize and develop human resources maximally in the rural communities.

More often we thought for the people and acted for the people. In some cases, we made the rural people more dependent on the development agencies, instead of gradually building up and fostering self-confidence and self-reliance at the community level. What is needed is an inner change agency within the community. It comprises the local leadership serving as a positive and leading force for betterment of life in the rural communities. The inner change agency is a stimulant and a human asset.

Wherever we have demonstrated economic gain to the people, such schemes or activities have been successful. More often, short-term gains catch up faster. They serve as motivators to long-term projects. We should appreciate the fact that village people wanted a better way of life; that once the superiority of improved practices and ways of doing things was demonstrated, villagers would accept them; and that once the villagers were assured that the "outsiders" had an unselfish interest in their welfare and advancement, they would accept the outsiders' guidance.

PAMPERED THE RURAL ELITE

There are social and power barriers in the rural communities. When it comes to reaching the poor and the disadvantaged, we have to pass through, in many instances, the rural elite. They are the nodes of power, authority and influence. The local elite pose as barriers as well as serve as stimulants and supporters to the cause of the rural poor. Some programmes are specifically meant to reach the poor in the community. But the extension personnel at the village level, often cannot reach the benefits and services to the poor directly ignoring the rural elite, since the latter perceive it as a threat to their standing and authority in the community and that their hold and influence over the poor would diminish. And so, as a strategy, the extension functionaries had to work through the rural elite, whether they liked it or not, of course with mixed results. In this process, though very much necessary, we tried to pamper and please and keep the rural elite in good humour. We expected the rural elite to work for, encourage and support the welfare programmes meant for the weaker sections. The results have been mixed. Sometimes, the elite blocked the flow of benefits to the poor. The extension personnel felt helpless and they could not either ignore or antagonize the powerful in the community. The encounter, defiance and challenge to the exploitative stumbling Block-the rural vested interests should come from within the community. Further, inadvertently or deliberately, we have contributed to the creation of cliques, factions and divisive forces in the rural communities.

WRONG CHOICES

We, unjudiciously and unimaginatively mixed up regulatory activities with extension functions. This has distanced the people from the extension functionaries. The latter playing a dual role has affected their primary extension role. We tried to plant new institutions and organizations like farmers' forums, youth clubs and women's clubs in the rural communities but most of them withered away soon, since they appeared superfluous in the context of life in rural communities predominantly of extended families and of a broad kinship system. One major lesson from rural development is that we are far from being effective in coordinating development activities.

CONCLUSION

We may conclude that political will, clear-cut policies, realistic objectives, effective organizational and institutional linkages, a blending of planning from below and above, enlightened involvement of the client system, building up and strengthening of local institutions, training of development personnel and people's leaders, implementing programmes with religious seriousness and continuous evaluation of the programmes would facilitate meaningful and sustained rural development.

CHAPTER 7

Programme Planning to Meet People's Needs

Rural development programmes are created and maintained for influencing people to make changes in their way of living and of making a living. The existence of such programmes implies that the present situation of the rural people is not what it should and could be, that something different should prevail, and that it is possible through appropriate action to attain a more desirable status for them. From this assumption another one arises: that it is possible and feasible for a person or group of persons – officials, non-officials or a combination of both – to identify the nature of new conditions that could and should prevail, and devise means for achieving them. Hence, the entire process of planning for rural development implies a need for change. The question then arises: change from *what,* to *what,* by *whom, where* and *by what methods?*

Changes that are important to people are those that help them meet their needs for biological, economic, social, aesthetic and moral well-being. Basically, all programmes for rural development exist to help people meet their needs. If programmes do not do this, people in free-choice societies will not long participate in them. The element of people's needs, therefore, becomes a central concern of planners for rural development. If a society is to find ways to adjust itself so that people meet their needs for an improved economic status, for being more useful citizens and for enjoying a higher degree of social satisfaction, it must identify these conditions and plan realistically to achieve them.

What needs do people have? How can needs be identified? What plan of priority should be set up for meeting people's needs? What resources are necessary to meet people's needs? How should resources be organized and directed to help people meet their needs? These questions give the key orientation and justification for rural programme planning.

THE NATURE AND ROLE OF PLANNING

The controlling objective of India's Rural Development Programmes is to develop in village people the ability to make a better living and to live a more satisfying life as individuals, as family members and as citizens of their community, state and nation. How to attain this objective is the key problem confronting the architects and current leaders of the scheme.

The first step in any systematic attempt to promote rural development is to prepare a useful programme. The term programme indicates focus, priority and design. It assumes the ability among the planners to distinguish important needs from unimportant ones. Such a programme must be based on people's needs to make it significant and on their interests to make it effective. *"If we could but know where we are now, and where we ought to go, we could better judge what to do, and how to do it"*. This statement by Abraham Lincoln lies at the heart of the nature and role of planning for rural development. Effective programmes for rural improvement do not just happen; they have to be built. Planning does not go on in a vacuum, or automatically; it has to be made to happen. Good programmes are not developed merely by wishing for them, but by working for them.

The need for planning arises from the complexity and from the importance of the job to be done. Planning is a necessary aspect of any activity that is too involved to be disposed of off-hand. The use of planning is to discover and prepare the way for action that should be taken. Planning gives meaning and system to action. It prepares the basis for a course of future action. Possibly, the most basic fact-giving rise to planning is that effective rural development results from choice, not from chance; it results from design, not from drift; it results from a plan; not by trial and error. Hence, effective work is an intentional effort carefully designed to attain certain specific and predetermined goals assumed to be important.

The use of programme planning stems from a belief in the need for change that results in progress, and from the view that change in certain directions is good for those affected by it. Planning must, therefore, result in programmes that help people find more satisfactory modes of living and of making a living. Planning assumes that the programme, or the lack of one, followed in the past will not do the job in the present and the future.

Designing programmes for rural development is one of the most difficult tasks confronting rural development workers. This is so because planners must avoid programming that has superimposed characteristics and instead assure programmes that have roots among the people. The problem is complex because the components of rural programming are complex. People, their needs, their interests, useful technology, educational process, analysing situations, making decisions about what should be done, determining useful action, projecting the desired shape of things into the future and such other components of rural programming are rarely simple. Programme planning for rural development has but little research support, a wide range of patterns of approach, and consequently requires great imagination and judgement on the part of the planners.

Good programme planning is primarily an intellectual activity, for it usually involves a study and use of facts and principles. It requires knowledge, imagination and reasoning ability. Often it requires a mastery over special skills and techniques of research. It is basically a process of making decisions that will carry into the future. If these decisions are not made wisely, they may not lead to useful attainment. Decisions have to be made about what the present situation is, how it could and ought to be changed and what means can be sued to accomplish the new and more desirable situation. Finally, good planning for rural development requires the ability to synthesize facts and value judgements in a process of sound decision-making about the objectives the programmes should seek to attain and what courses of action are most likely to achieve them. The ability to plan requires:

1. an understanding of the nature and function of planning,
2. skill in formulating planning procedures,
3. skill in identifying problems and needs,

4. ability to decide on significant objectives and goals,
5. skill to formulating means and wise courses of action to attain objectives, and
6. skill in involving key leaders in the planning process.

The first condition of success for any programme to promote rural development is a widespread belief in the usefulness to a large number of people. Good plans are to the professional rural worker what the compass is to the seaman.

SOME GUIDES TO PLANNING

The broad aims set forth for India's Community Development Programme are great and important. They are complex and far-reaching. They are significant and difficult to achieve. But they are assumed to be worthy of effort, since foremost in the order of things they embody are social, economic and human values to which the new India is committed. The process through which these aims were derived was a long and tedious one involving many people, much study, interpretation of facts and careful application of judgement in arriving at final decisions. In short, a massive programme-planning job was done. Plans for rural development are usually made best when a number of propositions are followed in the planning process.

1. *Effective rural development programmes must have clear and significant objectives.*

An objective is that which a person, group or agency sets before itself as an object or condition to be attained. Programme objectives designate directions of movement. Since that is so, objectives properly become the focus of primary material and human resources for attaining change. Maximum progress can be made only when the objectives are clear, full commitment of resources is made to achieving them and effective use is made of the resources.

If there is to be progress and not mere evolution in the development of people, the objectives of the programme must be clearly and periodically determined in view of progress and changed conditions. It should be kept in mind that not all people need or desire to move in the same direction or for the same distances. Directions have varying degrees of importance to different people. Extension workers must be prepared to offer opportunity for people to move in various directions. This is what is really meant by the term-balanced programme. Thus, a good programme objective is one that provides possible direction for large numbers of people to move some distance, a direction in which they want and need to move, then provide them assistance in travelling in those directions. This is really the essence of extension work for Community Development.

These facts place great importance on the wise choice of purposes. For, if the choice of purposes is not made well, the resources committed to their attainment will be poorly used. This is a mistake the leaders of India's rural development scheme can ill afford to make, especially at a time like the present when the objectives to be achieved are so numerous and so great and resources for achieving them so few and so small.

2. *To achieve the broad purposes of Community Development requires planning at the top level and also at lower levels including the state, district, Block and village.*

Deciding purposes at these lower levels requires a degree of specificity that results in objectives being moved from the level of glittering generality to the level of practical reality. Identifying the most useful purposes, assigning a priority to them and developing effective means of achieving them at the local level is an intricate process which must ebb handled with great skill. If the statement of purposes at higher levels is to be realistic and useful in guiding the programme at lower levels, it must be reformulated at each lower level to align it with varying situations.

3. *There are no unplanned programmes*

Programme development is a relative matter. The quality of a programme is related to the extent to which certain steps are taken that are essential in planning. A number of crucial questions about programming must be asked and their answers taken into account in the planning process. Proper answers to them will improve the preciseness with which programmes are developed. These questions are:

a) To whom and to how many people is the programme important?
b) In what way is the programme significant to people – economically, socially, aesthetically, or morally?
c) What is the relative importance of programme objectives?
d) Who thinks the programme is important – nation, state, district, block, village?
e) Who arrived at the programme objectives?
f) On what amounts and kinds of information is the programme based?
g) Does the programme reflect significant needs and interest of large numbers of people?
h) Who is acquainted with the programme and its purposes?
i) How clearly conceived and understood is the programme by those who are to participate in its execution?
j) What would be the likely consequences in one, five or ten years if work on certain parts of the programme is not carried out?

4. *The most effective rural development programmes result when there is general agreement among village, block, district, state and national officials on three important items.*

Village and block workers in order to plan the most effective programmes need to agree on (a) a basic philosophy regarding programme development, (b) a clear policy that reflects the basic philosophy, and (c) a workable procedure that gives general direction but provides ample latitude for adjustments needed to meet local situations. Questions like the following may serve as a guide for this purpose:

a) What is the relative importance of programme development as a step in the rural development process?
b) Who should participate in programme development and in what way?
c) How much time should be allocated to the task of planning?
d) Should a so-called long-range programme be developed in each village and block?
e) Upon what kinds and amounts of factual information should the programme be based and how should this information be collected?
f) To what extent should procedures provide for participation of people at the village and block level?

g) Should the different phases of a block programme be organized into a single overall unified programme?

h) What is the role of the technical specialist in block and village programme development?

i) To what extent should leaders among the villagers participate and which method is most useful for providing this opportunity?

In relation to these questions there are many different points of view depending on established policy and other factors. But experience and sound principles of good programming suggest that such questions should be considered with care. One point of view suggests that when numerous problems are evident, as in Indian villages, decisions are easily made about what should be done. This argument has validity. But merely making decisions about what should be done is not enough. Also important is how the decisions are made, on what facts are they based, who participates in making them and what priority is to be followed in meeting the needs.

5. *Programmes are most effective when based on adequate and current facts pertaining to local conditions as well as those related to national and regional situations.*

No rural development programme or any of its parts can be any better than the facts on which it is based. A programme must be based on adequate and current facts about the situation at all levels and related factors that influence it in order to be most effective. To be useful, these facts must finally be carefully analyzed and interpreted through the joint efforts of the technically trained staff and progressive village leaders. Facts about the local situation and others affecting it form the foundation upon which the Block staff and village leaders, working on various community development problems, build and carry out an effective programme. When properly weighed on the scales of people's values, these facts reflect local needs and the enlightened desires of people. Moreover, they show not only what people think they want, but also what is best for them. To define rural problems it is necessary to consider both scientific and folk knowledge. Thus, the true basis for a programme lies in the needs and problems of the individual, the home, the farm and the community.

The fact cannot be overstressed that local conditions furnish the basic problems with which rural development programmes must deal. People are most concerned about facts relating to their immediate situation as it affects them personally. Community development workers and local leaders use properly interpreted facts about local conditions to show how these facts directly and personally affect the people. In this way interest is aroused and indications found that lead to the solution to problems. Facts about the local situation help to identify problems and needs with which the people are concerned by pointing out the gaps between what is and what should be, by indicating shortages and by drawing attention to undesirable trends. To have adequate facts about a local situation, data that generally fall into these four categories must be obtained.

a) Current trends and outlook.

b) The people themselves – their needs, interests, knowledge, social organization, etc.

c) Physical factors about agriculture, industry, health, sanitation, etc.

d) Community problems – communication, education, etc.

6. *Selection of a relatively small number of the most significant needs singled out for major attention contributes to the effectiveness of rural development programmes.*

When the resources for promoting rural development are limited, a programme cannot successfully be at the same time all things to all people. To identify problems or needs that are important is a relatively easy task, but it is not enough. Problems must be found that are not only important but that are most important. Consequently, some careful choice-making must be done. Since it is physically impossible to deal simultaneously with all the needs of people in a block or village, it is necessary to sort out for special attention those needs that are of greatest importance at a given time, thus developing a scheme of priority for dealing with items in the programme. Programme elements may then be arranged according to relative amounts of time and other resources committed to them. Research quite clearly supports the idea that no single exposure of a person to a recommendation will usually produce much action. Getting the adoption of new practices generally requires that recommendations be brought to people's attention on several occasions spread over a period of time. It is necessary then, in cooperation with village leaders, to ferret out the most significant problems and weave them into the core of a vital and dynamic village and block development programme. The most significant problems can then be attacked with all the resources of the programme which collectively form a powerful force for economic and social change.

7. *Skilful involvement of progressive village leaders is fundamental in planning rural development programmes.*

A synthesis of experience in planning rural programmes makes it clear that programmes developed *with*, not *for* or *by* the people, stand the best chance of success. Good programmes result from joint efforts of the technically trained development workers and the progressive members of the villages. The key to successful programme development, therefore, lies in weaving the following information together into decisions about what should be done: facts about local conditions, targets set up at national, state and regional levels, knowledge of block and village staff and that of local and village leaders.

This is a vastly complex task and one of the most important jobs and greatest challenges to better programming and, in turn, to more effective Community Development. There are many reasons that make constant work at this task worthwhile. In the first place, "it is not what the programme does for people but what it does *to* them that counts." Secondly, the assumption is very unsound that either the village leaders alone, or officials at the block, district or national level alone, have all the good ideas about what the programme should be. Good programmes should reflect the best knowledge and insights of *both* village leaders and professionally trained workers.

Furthermore, good planning procedures lead people to see beyond the present felt needs to the basic underlying problems. The ultimate performance must be by the people; for it is what they do that is of transcendent importance. It is clear, therefore, that rural development programmes – if they are to have their roots in the social and economic life of villagers – must be planned in villages and blocks around the needs and interests of the people. Programmes planned in this way become programmes of the people, with all the pride of authorship and satisfaction that comes from joint participation in both their planning and in execution.

All village people, of course, cannot be involved in this process. The problem of people's participation is handled by tuning in the masses through carefully selected village leaders. To attain worthwhile goals there usually must be some compromise between the ideal and the practical – between facts and value judgments. Is there any better way of assuring this than by involving village leaders with the block staff in analyzing situations and in making the decision on what should be done to improve conditions?

8. Programmes that are planned for longer periods of time than one or two years tend toward greater effectiveness.

Long-time programming, or identifying objectives that aim into the future, is more likely to be effective for a number of reasons. The important needs of people usually cannot be met in the short period of one or two years. Changing what people believe, what they do, and how they do it, is, at best, a slow process. Long and constant effort is usually needed to accomplish important community development objectives. To assure continued work on the most fundamental needs in a village or block requires provision in the programme for important elements to recur periodically. The formation of long-time objectives is a good technique for assuring continuation of work that focuses on major needs. This point of view suggests that care should be taken in the planning process to provide assurance that the short-term interests of people are also to their long-time advantage.

9. Procedures in rural programming that assure fairly close integration of problems related to the farm, the home and the community appear to contribute to their soundness and effectiveness.

The word integration implies a smooth and efficient operation of a combination of activities or services in the solution of problems. In view of the wide scope of content in a community development programme and the common objectives of its phases, various aspects of the programme should be blended into one effective force aimed at building better rural communities. The primary way to achieve coordination and integration in programmes is through common understanding among officials as well as between them and non-officials. This can be attained most effectively through joint participation in appropriate phases of the planning process.

10. Programme planning must take into account cultural values and the social system.

Rural development programmes cannot be most effective unless they are planned and carried out in harmony with the basic cultural values held by people and the social setting in which they live. Cultural values reflect what people generally think is important. The social system tends to maintain adherence to the scale of established values. In traditional cultures, the social system and prevailing cultural values tend to serve as forces working against social and economic reform. Even in so-called advanced societies these influences are formidable. Programmes, therefore, cannot be most successful when they are too much at odds with innovations the value system will sanction. People's values and their social system must be understood and taken into account by planners of rural development programmes.

11. Programme content must be determined with care and preciseness.

Predictions with a high degree of accuracy can be made about the probable outcome of programmes to promote change by examining their content. Content specifies the subject areas in which change is expected to be made. Consequently, the content of programmes is the most important index to new ways in which people may be influenced to behave. Programme content represents what actually will be attempted in changing people and the situation in which they live. Methods used for executing programmes are merely means to ends, not the ends themselves. The selection of the content of programmes of change tends, therefore, to be a central or basic concern in rural programme planning.

12. *The interpretation of the programme to officials and non-officials and to the general public is an essential step in successful programming.*

It is important that the aims and objectives of programmes become common knowledge among villagers. Interpretation means translating into familiar language or into terms that are readily understood as well as explanation of the meaning of facts as they apply to local conditions. Interpretation is important, for, unless people know what is available to them they cannot know what kind of help to request for.

PROFESSIONAL ABILITIES NEEDED BY PLANNERS

Planning effective programmes for Community Development requires a number of high-level professional skills. Needed abilities include understanding and skill in at least the following broad areas of competency:

1. Understanding of the nature and role of the Rural Development Services.
2. Knowledge and understanding of technology related to subjects with which the programme is to deal.
3. Ability to clarify the objectives of a programme and to state them so that they are useful in guiding its execution.
4. Ability to organize people and things.
5. Skill at seeing the relationship between principles and practice.
6. Skill at inquiry.
7. Skill in human relations.

In the following pages, a brief characterization is made of each of these areas of competency. If the suggestions made here provide some insight and serve as useful guides to further study, they will serve their purpose.

1. *Understanding of the nature and role of the multi-faceted Rural Development Programme.*

Gaining an understanding of the nature of the services extended in India and its role as a national initiative for promoting rural development, requires a knowledge of the following:

a) Development, present scope, philosophy and objectives of Community Development.
b) Organization and administration of the agency at the national, state, district, block and village levels.
c) The role of various categories of personnel at various levels in the hierarchy.
d) Responsibility and opportunity of the agency in a developing country.

Adequate competency in these areas is fundamental to effectiveness and leadership on the part of officials and non-officials in the entire organization. Each officer is a professional person. Knowing about one's professional affiliation is commonly viewed as a primary tool of the trade in any field of endeavour. Without this knowledge one cannot understand one's job, intelligently defend his profession, or suggest action to improve it. Likewise, he cannot effectively communicate opportunities to those who should participate. Effective professional leadership requires competency in this area on the part of all personnel engaged in the programme.

2. *Knowledge and understanding of technology related to subjects with which the programme is to deal.*

Adequate knowledge and understanding of technology appropriate to one's professional job requires the following:

a) Thoroughness of knowledge.
b) Acquaintance with current technology.
c) Knowledge of reliable sources of technology.
d) Understanding of how technology relates to specific problems.
e) Continuous study.

Technology related to the various special fields with which Community Development is concerned constitutes the chief commodity the programme has to offer to people. Whether the subject is agricultural production, social education, cooperatives, home science, youth work or any other, a body of useful technology is assumed to be available. Every successful educational effort requires significant technology appropriate to the problems dealt with. Subject-matter or technology is to workers in rural development what food is to human beings; it is life's sustenance. To attempt to teach others something one does not know oneself is to invite failure from the start. Every official in the community development organization, therefore, should have not only adequate knowledge of appropriate technology in his particular field of operation, but also an understanding of it and its relationship to the problems of villagers.

3. *Ability to clarity objectives of a programme and state them so that they are useful in guiding its execution.*

The importance and role of programme objectives were mentioned previously. The ability to clarify and state objectives for one's work is also important. This task includes:

a) An understanding of the nature of purpose and the role of objectives in educational work.
b) Knowledge of the sources of objectives.
c) Knowledge of levels and interrelation of objectives.
d) Skill in stating and using objectives to guide educational activity.

It has been said that 'to him who knows not the port to which he is bound, no wind can be favourable.' A frequent criticism of workers in Community Development is related to the fuzziness with which objectives are conceived and stated. Too often statements of objectives at all levels can be characterized as glittering generalities. In this form they are not very helpful in guiding the programme. The importance of clarifying objectives and goals is found in two major truths:

a) Subject-matter and methods necessary to attain educational goals can be wisely selected only when the objectives are specific and clearly stated.

b) Evidence of the effectiveness of community development work can be collected only in the light of specific and clearly defined objectives.

Clear objectives, therefore, improve the preciseness with which educational activity is carried on. One important characteristic of the twenty first century is its requirement of decisiveness in action. Clear objectives give direction to action.

4. Ability to organize people and things.

This requires an understanding of:

a) The nature and function of organization.

b) Principles of organization.

c) Techniques of organization.

d) The nature and rolè of coordination and integration in programmes.

The need for organization increases in direct ratio to the growth in the size and complexity of tasks to be performed by an individual or an agency in attaining its purposes. Organization is properly viewed as an arrangement of relationships of persons or functions. It should be looked upon as a means, not as an end. The principle of organization is not limited in its application to people alone, but has a much broader application. People are organized for joint activity. Materials, ideas and facts are organized for common use or for use by one person. Thinking is essentially a process of organizing facts and ideas with a view to taking action. In all cases, the need for organization has its origin in the work to be done. The term organization is properly used when it refers to any collection of persons, materials, procedures, ideas, facts and the like, so arranged and ordered that in each case the parts make a meaningful whole. Good organization then is that which groups activities ideas, facts, materials or persons so as to get the best performance with the least effort. Good organizational ability is shown by definite regularity, predictability and dependability in the everyday performance of persons or groups doing the job expected of them.

The act of organizing requires attention to at least the two following definite and well-established processes:

a) Coordination. Coordination means making harmo-nious adjustment – to give things and actions their proper perspective – to unify designated effort into an integrated whole. Coordination is necessary in carrying out practically any job or assignment. It, therefore, becomes the essence of any effective organization of efforts. There must be coordination in all major community development functions, including administration, supervision, programming, programme execution and appraisal of accomplishments.

b) Procedure Analysis. Procedure is a way of arranging sequences of operations necessary for effective action. Certain definite elements must always be considered and employed in both the preparation and evaluation of procedures. Important facts upon which the success of procedures rests must be discovered, selected and clarified. These are the facts which are of such outstanding importance that they must be given consideration in the design of procedures.

Organizational ability is a high level skill and is essential to the effectiveness of extension workers.

5. *Skill in seeing the relationship between principle and practice.*

The ability to relate principle and practice involves knowledge and understanding of::

a) The nature and role of principles related to Community Development.

b) The nature and role of techniques and procedures for carrying out programmes.

c) The inseparable interdependence of principle and practice in the extension educational process.

Theory and practice always have a relationship. Principles relate to why, techniques to how. One may understand the structure of theory and be unable to apply it in practice. On the other hand, one may be able to use technique skillfully, but be superficial in one's efforts because one does not understand how the technique relates to the whole process of Community Development, or to the specific aspect of the activity one is performing.

The effective extension worker is neither only an abstract thinker nor only an accomplished user of tricks. He is both. He must understand the principle lying behind his technique in order to make the technique most effective. The importance of principles stems from the fact that they are general rules – well established truths – that usually have wide application. They serve as useful guides in a wide range of situations. Extension workers equipped with an understanding of principles applicable to their work are more likely to be creative than those who pride themselves on just being practical.

Rural development, workers sometimes appear to misinterpret the term 'practical'. They infer that to be practical, things must be simple, easy to do, primer-like, not complicated. The basic meaning of the term practical really suggests that whatever technique works well in a situation, regardless of its complexity, is practical. Principles give meaning to technique. Techniques give application to principles. One who glorifies techniques without trying to understand the principles related to them is really a captive of technique. One who paramounts principles without an understanding of the technique necessary to apply them are a captive of theory. An understanding of principles related to techniques and skill with techniques is the height of professional competency. The person who only knows how and the person who only knows why are always likely to have a job, but the person who knows both how and why will eventually supervise both of them.

6. *Skill at inquiry*

Ability at inquiry requires the following skills necessary to help individuals:

a) Identify their problems,

b) Discover focal points of concern,

c) Determine alternative solutions, and

d) Evaluate possible solutions and make decisions about them.

Without this competency, extension workers cannot be effective in helping people analyze their problems. Skill at inquiry is not only basic to planning, but also to guidance. Unless rural development workers are skilful at inquiry they cannot help people discover problems and work out useful solutions to them. It is a relatively easy task to supply answers based on opinion, but a vastly more difficult one to supply leadership that truly helps others analyze their problems and arrive at sound decisions about them. The process of inquiry consists of these four primary steps:

a) Identifying the difficulty or problem or need. Inquiry usually begins with a specific problem that causes people to feel that something ought to be done. Whenever a situation causes people – officials or non-officials – to be disturbed, there is need for inquiry, community-wide, family-wide or confined to an individual. Those responsible for planning rural development programmes should be skilful in discovering these feelings of dissatisfaction in order to further analyze the special aspects of the situation in which ***lies*** the specific concern.

b) Discovering the focal point of trouble. This step requires facts that will pinpoint the true nature of a problem, its scope and its importance. It usually entails careful scrutiny of attitudes, beliefs, values, habits, prejudices and the like, in addition to the scrutiny of the body of information commonly called facts.

c) Determining possible ways to solve the problems. In this step, ideas about plans of action must be developed that offer possible solutions to the difficulty. At this point, community development workers must provide leadership. Often it is easy to supply solutions to problems, but difficult to reach a truly joint decision about how to solve them.

d) Evaluating alternative plans of actions. This step requires the ability to project probable consequences of each suggested course of action if it were taken. It involves determining the probable value of each idea, and a decision about which kind of action is most likely to succeed.

Without skill at inquiring, a rural worker's relation with the people is one of the blind leading the blind, or, even the more disastrous one of the blind attempting to lead those with excellent sight.

7. Skill in human relations

Ability in human relations is necessary for successful work with people in general, and especially with local leaders, co-workers and those in the administrative organization.

Human relations concern how people get along with one another. Since the job of extension workers is ultimately to bring about educational change in people, they have to discover how to get people act in the ways they want them to. If extension workers cannot do this, they must change their goals to those desired by the people. If rural development workers cannot bring what they want in line with what people want, they may as well give up trying to change people in that particular way. One may know the technical answer, but unless one also knows how to work with people one won't know how to get technical answers translated into better farm, home, and community practices.

Man not having been born a social being, these behaviours have to be learned. Fortunately, they can be developed. Human judgement is fallible and mistakes will always be made. But many errors in relations among people can be avoided if fundamentals of the subject are studied and understood.

A CONCEPT OF "NEEDS"

Efforts to promote change in conditions of free-choice participation are successful only to the extent they are focused on the important needs of people and are effective in helping people meet these needs. Under voluntary conditions of participation, people concern themselves with programmes of change only when they think that the programme is valuable to them in meeting personal, family, group or community needs, therefore, becomes a central concern in rural programming.

Since the people in Indian villages are free to participate in community development activity or not to participate, their participation in effect constitutes casting a vote. When they participate, they vote favourably. When they do not participate, they also vote, but unfavourably. They determine their vote on the basis of their estimate of the probable value to them of the things participation may give them. This judgement is made on the basis of satisfaction, or the lack of it – economic, social, aesthetic or moral – which a villager feels he may obtain from participation. In short, people concern themselves with programmes only on the basis of needs as they see them, not as the officials view them. The central problem, therefore, of successful programming is one of identifying accurately what people want, think they need, and actually do need, and then getting these items woven into a realistic well organized and concerted series of forceful activities. This may properly be called a programme. Effective programmes to promote change are developed through an approach to individuals and groups – by finding people's needs and arranging action that helps meet them. Hence, a clear understanding of the nature and role of people's needs in programmes of change is essential to the leaders of such programmes.

The term need is a simple four-letter word and appears rather innocent at a glance. But it is one of the most important words related to rural development programmes. This is so because the needs of people constitute the core around which successful programmes are built. Needs imply conditions including necessity, requirement, urgency, prerequisite, vacancy, scarcity, lack and indispensability. An understanding of the nature and role of people's needs can be developed by gaining a clear concept of the meaning and implications of a number of widely accepted propositions related to the term need. Some basic aspects of need are indicated as follows:

1. *Man is an independent living system surrounded by an environment with which he constantly interrelates.* Man is constantly influenced by his environment and in turn exerts influence over it. His well-being depends on keeping a balance between the internal forces produced by the energy resulting from the food intake and the external conditions produced by the environment. To keep the human system in equilibrium with the external forces, it is necessary that certain needs be met. In this sense every person is continuously meeting his needs – trying to attain those conditions of living that make for satisfaction. To the extent that the relationship between man and his environment goes out of balance, he has needs. People are constantly attempting to attain, maintain or improve this balance.

   The nature and extent of needs depend upon the nature and extent of the imbalance. For example, when a person becomes physically ill, a condition is created in which the affected parts of the body become functionally out of balance with the other parts. Consequently, it is said that the person is sick. To get well, the imbalance must be removed. In a like manner the imbalance between man and his environment in all of its aspects is the source from which people's needs emerge. Man's attempt to attain, and maintain a satisfying equilibrium between internal and external forces represents in a true form his real struggle for survival and economic, social, aesthetic or moral improvement.

2. *People's needs are identified by finding through the programme planning process, the actual, the possible and the valuable.* By the actual is meant *what is;* by the possible is meant *what could be* and by the valuable is meant *what ought to be.* In choosing the things on which to focus programmes, it is necessary to analyze these conditions and possibilities and choose from among them the *most valuable.* Then it should become the objective of programmes to change people and the present conditions in which they live to the most valuable and possible conditions. Making the analyses and decisions necessary in this context is the essence of programme planning to meet people's needs.

3. *People's needs may be defined as the differences between what is, what could be and what ought to be.* Needs always imply a gap between the two conditions as shown in the following diagram:

   W*hat is* can be determined by a study of the situation. Some of the major kinds of information this study should include are important facts about people, their attitudes, knowledge, and what they think their needs are. It should include facts about physical factors, soils, crops, livestock, home conditions, farm implements, production resources and community services. It should include facts about public problems, programmes, trends and outlook.

   What ought to be can be determined on the basis of research findings and value judgements of the people and their official leaders. For example, the results of research may show that the use of recommended practices in rice production will result in a one-third larger yield per acre. The cultivator on the other hand, may not place great value on reaching this level of production, or he may place greater value on spending his available resources on some other goal like better education for his children than on producing extra rice.

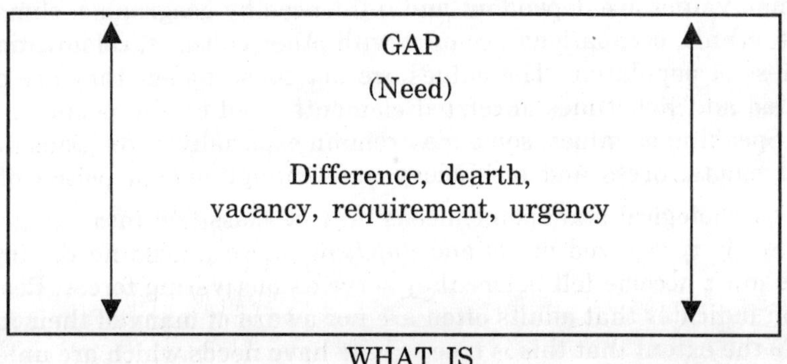

Diagram

It should be recognized that information about *what is* does not make a programme, it only shows the situation. From this point planners have to take another step. This step is that of deciding *what ought to be*- what the desirable situation is. Hence, deciding on *what ought to be* is the process of selecting programme targets, goals or objectives. In setting objectives, care must be taken to assure that the level of *what ought to be* is within the physical, economic, social and mental possibilities of attainment by those who are expected to make the change. Finally, it should be recognized that the nature and extent of the need (the width of the gap)) is an indication of the significance of the problem. The wider the gap, the greater the problem.

4. *People have to recognize the gap between the actual, the possible and the desirable and place value on attaining the desirable condition before they will become motivated to change in desirable directions.* This point poses the crux of the problem in programmes of change. Village people being wedded to custom and tradition, often being illiterate and surrounded by many outmoded cultural norms, are slow to make innovations in what they do and how they do it. When people have been schooled by centuries of experience to satisfy their wants by not having wants, it is difficult to conceive them that they should, for example, adopt new practices to increase crop yields or go through the uncertainties of consolidating several tracts of land into one piece.

   Reluctance by villagers to change is not due altogether to a natural resistance to change, but to an apparent lack of interest in change. They seem to feel satisfied with their old ways even when new ones are demonstrated side by side with the old. When the actual or *status quo* is seen as the ideal, desirable or satisfactory status of things, no need is recognized on the part of people. Consequently, there is in their minds no need for a programme to promote change because there is no need for change in the first place, as they view the situation. To be successful, therefore, a programme must cause people to recognize the gap between the actual, the desirable and the possible, and place a value on attaining the desirable.

5. *Human behaviour and the status of things can only be judged by some standard and the standard can only be derived from a concept of what is valuable and desirable to attain.* Human behaviour and the status of things usually can be placed on a scale of human values.

   The human values are dependant and influenced by geographic, climatic, historical, religious, ethnic, occupational, contact with other cultures, colonization and density or thinness of population. The values are not constant but they are dynamic. They are related and sometimes-unrelated elements lived by the people at a given point of time. Speaking of values, some may remain especially of religious nature constant but food habits, dress and technology may change over a period of time.

   From a psychological standpoint, needs may be classified into two groups, viz., felt or consciously recognized needs and *unfelt* or unrecognized needs. In a free society all needs must become felt before they serve as motivating forces. Research in adult education indicates that adults often are not aware of many of their most important needs. To the extent that this is true, adults have needs which are unfelt. Significant needs of which people are not conscious must be ferreted out and met in order to help them advance toward more desirable economic and social conditions.

One of the problems in rural programming, therefore, is to help people identify important needs they do not recognize. Thus it is not enough to base programmes entirely on what people feel their needs are, because these often may not represent some of their most important needs. Leaders of programmes must dig deep and identify needs people have which they do not recognize, then plan educational effort to convert these into felt needs. Without this, rural development programmes will be less significant and may tend to focus on the everyday short-term interests of people rather than on their more basic long-time needs.

6. *Final decision about the selection, or rejection, of needs to be included in a programme should be made with great care.* In the process of programme planning to meet people's needs, many decisions have to be made. These decisions have to be related to the actual, the valuable and the possible. Ultimately they must become decisions about acceptance or rejection of items to be included in the programme. These are crucial decisions and are highly significant, not only because the future of the people and their conditions will be influenced, but because extensive physical and human resources will be committed to helping people meet the needs accepted by planners and made a part of the programme. Indeed, these needs become the subject-matter or content of a programme. In turn, they are translated into the objectives or targets which the programme will seek to attain in course of time.

In the process of making final decisions about the needs to be included in a programme, some further points should be kept in mind. All people have needs. Needs vary in nature, scope and significance. Needs are often individual in attachment but they also tend to be common among members of groups. Needs change with time and progress. This tends to be true whether concerted effort is made to meet them or whether nothing is done to meet them. The needs of people change with age, growth and with social, economic and family status situations. People's needs arise from lack of harmony between themselves and their environment. The relative importance of needs is influenced by the physical environment, what is possible in it, and by the cultural factors which form a system of values that people hold to be important.

CRITERIA FOR PRACTICE AND PROCEDURE IN PROGRAMMING

The process of programme planning to meet people's needs includes four major elements or key steps that are generally viewed as of primary importance. It appears that the development staff should give proper attention to these elements in planning programmes that are significant and workable. The elements are:

a) A plan for involving local people in the planning process.

b) Procedure in programming planning.

c) The programme – the product of planning.

d) The annual plan of work.

These elements are described briefly in the following pages and a set of criteria for dealing with each of them is suggested. The criteria are attempts to describe the major steps, procedures or conditions that evidence shows to be good practice, involved in dealing with each element. The criteria are selected and designed to specify conditions, procedures, or practices that are conducive to developing the most effective rural programmes.

ELEMENT - A

A plan for involving people in programme planning

Rural programme planning, in essence, is a process of making decisions about important objectives to be attained in an area. One of the most significant problems confronting rural development workers is that of deciding on programme objectives which reflect the primary needs and interests of people. How to do this skillfully is a question of major concern to every professional worker. Decisions about programme objectives are usually best when made neither by the officials alone, nor by the people alone, but when made jointly by the officials and the people.

The contributions of the local people to rural programming are obtained most effectively through some form of organized approach. Research indicates that no one type of organization is best for programming in all situations. There are certain criteria, however, which are usually met when the local people contribute to programme development most effectively. These are indicated below:

1. Representative committees of non-officials are organized by the development staff. These function systematically on a continuing basis in developing and maintaining a current programme for development.
2. The people who function as members of the planning committees at the local level represent major interest groups, various economic and social levels of people, major vocations of the locality and other important elements in the area.
3. Each member of the planning groups clearly understands (a) the purpose of the group, (b) how the group can function in attaining its purpose, and (c) his individual role as a member of the group.
4. Members of the planning groups functioning at the local level are selected by appropriate democratic procedures.
5. Policies or rules formed for maintaining continuity of the planning groups include an appropriate plan for terminating the services of the temporary groups, and membership in the permanent groups, and for selecting new members of the permanent groups and new temporary groups.

ELEMENT - B

Procedure in programme planning

Procedure in programme planning means the process, course of action, methods, or major steps taken in an area to develop a suitable programme. A summary of experience of extension workers and conclusions from research pertaining to procedures used in rural programme development supports the following conclusions.

a) There are a number of essential steps in programme development that must be taken to develop a programme of the highest quality.

b) The basic steps are generally applicable with adjustments to meet particular circumstances in local situations.

c) After the steps are properly executed the basic principles of programme development should be applied.

d) The detailed procedures employed for executing each of the basic steps may vary considerably in accomplishing the purpose of each step.

The following is a list of criteria pertaining to the various steps assumed to be essential in procedures for local programme development.

1. The entire development staff has considered and reached agreement on:
   a) The importance to be attached to programming
   b) The amount of time to be devoted to programming
   c) The time when programming is to be done
   d) The phases of the programme to be developed, and
   e) The general approach to be followed in the area.
2. The development staff, with the help of technical specialists and planning groups, has assembled basic facts about the situation for use in developing a programme including such information as the following:
   a) Sources and levels of family income
   b) Health and educational levels of the people
   c) Needs and interests of the people
   d) Marketing facilities and practices
   e) Farming and home-making practices, and
   f) Community problems and needs.
3. Basic facts about the local situation have been analyzed jointly by the official staff and the planning groups and decisions made on this basis about major needs and interests of people.
4. A long-term programme has been developed and is used as a guide to all major activity in the area.
5. The technical specialists have assisted in developing the long-term programme by supplying specific basic information and recommendations pertaining to their special field that has been considered by the staff and the planning groups.
6. The development staff, jointly with the planning groups, has defined the problem and taken decisions about the long-term and the short-term objectives of the programme in line with major needs and interests of the people.
7. The development staff, jointly with the planning groups, has arranged a system of priority for work on problems included in the long-term programme.
8. The planning groups along with the official staff, has actively promoted coordination of the long-term programme.

ELEMENT – C

The Programme

A rural development programme is a carefully prepared statement written in a form that clearly sets froth the significant changes that are needed in the behaviour of the people and in the conditions in which they live, to be attained over a period of time. Specifically, it is a statement that includes:

a) Primary facts that reveal the situation for each major subject or problem in the area that is to be dealt within the programme.

b) Significant problems or needs.

c) Major means for meeting the problems or needs.

d) Statement of long-term objectives to be attained.

It is of utmost importance that the staff and the people in each area not only develop a basic long-term programme, but also prepare the programme in a written form that is readily understood and is suitable for use as a guide for officials and non-officials. Experience shows that this practice is a valuable guide to the staff and advisory committees and also a very effective means of improving public relations. The criteria listed below represent standards that should be achieved in written statements of a basic long-term programme.

1. The written programme should be suitable for use by the staff, planning groups, and other individuals or groups concerned with the programme.
2. It should state the primary facts that clearly reveal the situation for major subject or problem areas.
3. It should clearly state the important problems or needs identified by the staff and the people in the programming process.
4. It should state both the long-term and short-term objectives for each major subject or problem area that is to be focused on in programme execution over a period of time.
5. It should state the objectives of the programme in a form that:
   a) Clearly reveals the kind of new condition or situation desired
   b) Is meaningful to the staff and the people, and
   c) Will serve as a useful guide to programme execution.
6. It should specify the subject-matter related to each objective that is highly significant to the people, socially or economically, or both.
7. It should include the summary of the long-term programme prepared in a form suitable for public distribution, containing the following items:
   a) Major facts about the over-all area situation.
   b) Brief statement of the organization, statements of major problems, long-term objectives, and major means of achieving them for each of the major subject or problem areas.

c) Brief descriptions of the situation, statements of major problems, long-term objectives, and major means of achieving them for each of the major subject or problem areas.

d) The names of members of the planning groups and the official staff, and

e) Other appropriate information.

8. It should be made available in a summary form to all the members of the planning groups, and the professional staff.
9. It should be circulated by appropriate means so that the general public can understand its nature and objectives.
10. It should be used as the basis for developing annual plans of work.

ELEMENT - D

The Annual Plan of Work

The annual plan of work commonly consists of a definite outline of procedure for carrying out work related to the different phases of the long-term programme. It should indicate specifically the means to be used and the methods of using them. Its basic function is to provide a guide for use in carrying on development work planned for the year in a systematic manner. The annual plan of work should effectively serve the following functions:

a) A specific guide for carrying out systematically all the major aspects of work planned for the year.

b) A guide to the development of plans and procedures for evaluating accomplishments.

c) A guide to the scheduling of activity related to various aspects of the programme.

The following criteria related to annual plans of work are assumed to be important in their development and use.

1. Annual plans of work should be developed and used as a guide to all major activity during the year.
2. They should be developed from the long-term programme in a way that the content and goals are directly in line with the objectives of the different phases of the long-term programme.
3. They should include facts about the current situation pertaining to major subject or problem areas assembled by the development staff, technical specialists, and planning groups. They should also include facts about accomplishments during the past year for consideration in developing the annual plan of work.
4. They should include decisions jointly taken by the staff and the planning group on the major problems to be worked on during the year after a careful analysis of the current facts.
5. An annual plan of work in a written form, prepared by the staff, includes the following kinds of information for each project, subject or problem area:

a) Major subjects or problems to be worked on during the year.

b) Goals to be attained during the year.

c) Brief description of work to be done – methods, materials, etc.

d) Who is to participate in carrying out the plan?

e) A calendar of work which shows the approximate amount of time to be devoted to each major activity, and seasonal distribution of major activities.

f) Who is to be reached with the programme?

6. The annual plan of work is used during the year as a basis for:

   a) Coordinating activities of the different aspects of the area programme.

   b) Developing and coordinating teaching plans for different specific activities.

7. The annual plan of work is reproduced in an appropriate form for distribution and copies placed in the hands of (a) local leaders, (b) planning groups, and (c) other groups and individuals whose support is important for advancing the programme.

8. Means are used to acquaint the general public with the major activities to be undertaken during the year that is specified in the annual plan of work.

ORGANIZATION OF PROGRAMMES

Important changes in human behaviour generally are not produced quickly. Usually, no single learning experience has a very profound influence on people who participate in programmes. Changes in the ways of thinking, in fundamental habits, in attitudes, in interests, develop slowly. In free-choice societies, it is only after months and years that workers in rural development are usually able to see major changes resulting from their educational efforts. In some respects, the effect of programmes involving education is cumulative like that of water constantly dripping on a stone and wearing it away. In a day, or a week or a month, there is no appreciable change in the stone, but over a period of years definite erosion is noted.

Correspondingly, by the accumulation of impressions resulting from exposure to recommendations made by rural development workers, profound changes are brought about in the action of rural people. In order that educational effort produces cumulative effect, it must be so organized as to expose village men and women to recommendations periodically over time and in such ways that the programme elements reinforce each other. Programme organization is thus seen as a very important consideration in the process of rural development.

There are two major criteria for effective organization of rural development programmes. The first of these is continuity. Continuity refers to the provision in a programme for important recommendations to recur frequently, thus giving people an opportunity to come into contact with important ideas again and again over a time, and, if possible, at advanced levels. Continuity in programmes is basic to the achievement of cumulative effects. It is often referred to as follow-up.

For example, meetings of village people are often held with a little or no particular follow-up on important ideas or recommendations presented. Under these conditions little actual change in people's behaviour has to be expected. Research related to the adoption rate of new practices by rural people shows quite clearly that as the number of exposures to any idea is increased up to five or six, the number of people making changes increases. Provision for the continuity or recurrence of ideas and recommendations several times and

SUGGESTED GUIDE FOR DEVELOPING FOR DEVELOPING AND STARTING A VILLAGE OR BLOCK PROGRAMME

(Useful for specialized segments or for more comprehensive programmes)

Description of the situation: Include only significant facts necessary to clarifyconditions for each subject area. Include facts about(1) the people, (2) physical conditions, (3) farm and home practices followed, (4) trends and outlook	*Significant needs:* Using facts about the situation, list conditions in each subject area that show important gaps between what is and what should be. These gaps represent the needs.	*Objectives to be achieved:* Select from column 2 those needs that are agreed upon by the planning group and state them here in the form of objectives.	*Means for achieving the objectives*: Select and list here the primary means of attaining each objective stated stated in column 3. and the dates on which the activity will be performed.	*Calendar of work:* Decide and enter in this column the amount of time to be devoted to each major activity listed in col. 4,
1.	2.	3.	4.	5.

over a period of time is, therefore, a highly important criterion that should guide the organization of programmes.

A second important criterion useful in guiding the organization of rural development programmes is integration. Integration relates to the horizontal relationship of various elements in a programme. It has to do with the relationship of one item with another. Programme organization should be such that it helps rural people increasingly to gain a unified view of major programme elements. To be successful, participants in programmes of rural development must eventually recognize all the elements as a whole, and how each one relates to others and to their problems.

For example, the objective of developing an understanding of the value and need for village latrines should also convey the idea of cleanliness and order throughout the village. The idea of integration implies the concept of transfer of learning. It recognizes that people should eventually see ideas, needs and action in relation to the total task of Community Development. Integration implies the opposite of developing ideas singly as isolated behaviours or activities to be applied only at a single place, in a given time, in certain forms. The total capacity of people for Community Development must eventually be developed. Integration helps the officials and the people to see how one item is related to another and how each one is affected by others. Thus, increased breadth and depth of people's educational development and increased unity in their action in relation to important elements in the programme are made possible.

After considering the two major criteria for organizing programmes, questions arise about an organizing structure. Many structures may be used for organizing programmes. These include specific subjects or projects like animal husbandry, cooperatives, small industry, home science and social education. A second common way of organizing programmes is according to problem areas like health, income, agricultural production, housing, home conveniences and farm equipment. A third used structure for organizing rural development programmes is on the basis of broad fields of content, usually designated as production and marketing, family living, youth development and community services.

A clearly developed structure of programme organization helps to assure proper continuity and integration. It helps one to recognize the kind of activity that fits into a programme and that which seems relatively inappropriate. Those engaged in programme planning to meet people's needs, both officials and non-officials, must think and plan together. It is this kind of action that helps assure programmes that end in unity, rather than in a series of separate sets of knowledge, skills and activity. It is only when each element in programmes reinforce others that they make maximum contribution to Community Development.

Some of the devices for assuring continuity and integration in programmes are carefully stated objectives that are well understood by everyone engaged in programme planning and execution, joint planning between officials and non-officials, especially at the local level, long-term planning, annual plans of work, preparation of programmes in written form, and wide distribution of the written programme among officials and the people who are to participate.

CONCLUSION

The development of programmes that harmonize the local needs as people see them and the national interests, with which a country as a whole must be concerned, is a significant responsibility of local non-officials and officials at each level in the hierarchy of publicly sponsored programmes to promote rural development. Any procedure that takes into account the basic concept of needs and meets a set of criteria that will assure that the programme focuses on the significant needs of the people is a good procedure. The measure of success achieved in free-choice societies by public programmes to promote rural development is in direct ratio to the extent to which the programme is built around people's needs and consequently, is an effective influence in helping meet their needs.

To accomplish these desirable ends effectively requires a carefully structured programme at the village and block level that meets the following criteria:

1. It must focus on the felt needs and interests of the people.
2. It must be developed through joint participation of village leaders and block staff, taking into account recommendations from district, state and Central Government personnel.
3. It must be in line with local as well as state and national needs.
4. It must focus on problems that are most important since it cannot be all things to all people at the same time.
5. It must be flexible, but with a 'backbone' that gives it stability and continuity.
6. It must provide for a system of priorities in line with local needs, interests and resources.
7. It must be balanced, that is, contain items of assistance for all major social, economic, age and sex status groups.
8. It must have objectives that are attainable within the economic, social and mental capacities of the people through education with a minimum of government aid.
9. It must be highly significant economically, socially, aesthetically or morally to a relatively large number of people in each village or block.
10. It must be developed, understood, conducted and judged as an educational instrument for helping people learn how to help themselves.
11. It must provide satisfaction for the people who participate. The central objective of India's National Extension Service programme is to help each individual, each family and each village achieve the highest level of living that is capable of economically, socially, and culturally by means of aided self-help through education. Those responsible for developing a programme to achieve this objective must ferret out and perpetuate only the useful from the past, exercise concern only for the promising in the present and focus skillfully all available resources on the significant elements in the bright future. This is the formula for achieving the new India.

SELECTED REFERENCES

Department of Economics, *Seminar Papers,* University of Madras, Madras, 1956-57.

Dube, S.C., *India's Changing Villages,* Routledge and Kegan Paul Ltd., London, 1958.

Harrison, George Russell, *What Man May Be—The Human Side of Science,* William Morrow & Co., New York, 1956.

Kelsey, L.D. and C.C. Hearne, *Cooperative Extension Work,* Comstock Publishing Associates, Ithaca, New York, 1949.

Krishnamachari, V.T., *Community Development in India,* Publications Division, Government of India, New Delhi, 1958.

Loomis and Allen, *Rural Social Systems,* Prentice Hall Inc., New York, 1950.

Mayer, Albert and associates, *Pilot Project in India,* University of California Press, 1958.

Ministry of Community Development and Cooperation, *Guide to Community Development,* Government of India, New Delhi, 1957.

Penders, J.M.A., H. Veenman and Zenen, *Methods and Programme Planning in Rural Extension,* Wageningen, The Netherlands, 1956.

Planning Commission, *First Five-Year Plan,* Government of India, New Delhi, 1951.

Planning Commission, *Second Five Year Plan,* Government of India, New Delhi, 1956.

Ruopp, Phillips (ed.), *Approach to Community Development*, W. Van Hoeve Ltd., The Hague, 1953.

Spicer, Edward H., *Human Problems in Technological Change,* Russel Sage Foundation, New York, 1952.

[**Source**: Adopted with grateful thanks from J. Paul Leagans, *Extension Education*, Publications Division, New Delhi, 1960].

CHAPTER 8

Each Village as a Unit of Development

Though as stated earlier, the focus is on the poor, but it is not possible to totally isolate from the relatively better of people in the various approaches and measures suggested here. These measures relate to the total community. In a limited sense, as a kind of analogy if it rains, it rains for everyone. Poor as the target, some of the measures and efforts made by the administration will benefit the entire community. Keeping in view this object some of the discussions in the work assume a general character. We do discuss the situation in detail in respect of the poor.

The process of organizing rural communities for their participation in development involves working and interacting with the people in the communities. The prerequisite for effective interaction with the people in the rural communities is a knowledge of the characteristics of the rural communities, their way of life, the value systems, traditions and customs, the network or relationships and the kind of changes taking place among them. In the clinical approach, there is a need to consider each village as a unit of development. In order to do this we should have a comprehensive and detailed data pertaining to the village. This will help us in identifying the historical background of the settlement, its natural resources, the kind of avocations people are engaged in, the kind of infrastructure, the topographical details and the human resources the community is endowed with. Further, we may also look into the community common needs and in some cases individual needs also. Treating each village community as a unit of development is a necessity in carrying out gradual sustained development activities in each village. In this context, we may briefly look into the characteristics of the rural communities as a kind of background to understand the general nature of rural communities in India.

Rural communities are not identical in every respect. There is a considerable diversity among them. They could be ranged along a continuum. At one end, we have the sacred-folk societies and at the other end the secular ones, varying in terms of simplicity and complexity. In folk-sacred societies, established practices and ideas are taken for granted. There are few contacts with persons outside of the local geographic areas. Kinship relations are dominant. There is little formalized education; teaching is by means of family training, conversation, preaching and ceremonial. Occupations are learned by apprenticeship. The older men, who have lived longest and whose experiences and memories reach back farthest, are respected and relied upon for advice and guidance. Such societies are relatively changeless; they, in fact, quite generally resist change.

In a highly secular society, means and methods of communication and transportation are ample and ready. Persons are highly mobile both physically and mentally. Formal education is universal occupations and professions are learned as technical sciences. Most social relations are impersonal. Even kinship relations are loose in terms of duties and obligations. Changes of all kinds are prevalent, rapid, and generally welcome. Individuals are members of many groups and live by a number of different value systems.

To be completely bound by folk customs and traditions would mean stagnation. To be completely secular would be inhuman or non-social. No present day society is completely either of them. Those which are nearer the folk end of this continuum are working, some rapidly, toward the secular end of the continuum. The results of too rapid a movement in this direction have been discovered by the study of the most mobile part of the people who live in large cities. The results of little or no movement in this direction are illustrated in a number of countries where a thin layer of wealthy, educated, elite at the top of the social and political structure purposely sabotage change in the large folk segments of their society.

CONCEPT OF COMMUNITIES

Territorial boundary and the sentimental bindings are the essential factors in a community. The group of people that live within a geographic region have the uniformity or similarity in many customs and habits, such as food, clothing, occupation etc. These matters depend upon the availability of material, climatic conditions, nature of soil, etc. The above factors bind the people together.

Another factor, which is the outcome of face-to-face, intensive functional interaction, is the community sentiment. This sentiment that makes them feel that they are one, or the "we" feeling is the life of the community. The sentiment gives rise to responsibility, makes the members of the communities conscious of their rights and duties. Rights and obligations implicate inter-dependence of the members.

A community then means a group of people living in a given area with common interests, bound by a sense of and common mode of living. A village satisfies the requisite to form a community. It gives the inhabitants a common area of land, common past that brings about a sharing of experience and standard of behaviour and attitudes. They share some degree of common activities or some degree of common life, irrespective of their social and religious differences. It is not confined to any of the various restricted fields of community life on the basis of religion, caste, race, language or profession but one that envelops the whole life of the total community. Whatever affects the villages, affects the whole population. A community may be settled or an unsettled one. It may be migratory having come from another area in search of livelihood or it may belong to the new village where they live for centuries, or they might be newcomers.

Some of the distinguishing features of rural community are:

1. Occupation is mainly agriculture and/ or allied professions.
2. People live closer together and closer to the natural environment. This makes their life and attitude simpler and unaffected.

3. Smallness of the size of the community brings the members closer together in everyday life. This and the common occupational interest make the people know each other better than the urban people do.
4. Lesser density of population is caused by the nature of occupation. People in the rural areas can move more freely.
5. There is greater homogeneity of life than in urban areas; because the people are bound not only by common occupation, but also are bound by common traditions, customs and common heritage.
6. Relatively, there is very little social mobility in the community. They live in the same land generation after generation, by the same occupation, follow the same old customs and habits and maintain the purity of their ethnic identity by avoiding inter-caste and communal marriage or any other type of social intercourse.

Hundreds of local communities in folk societies have been studied by anthropologists. Based on these studies, the characteristics of communities of folk societies can be broadly generalized as follows:

1. Each community is something approximating a complete society in terms of both geography and people.
2. No external forces other than the physical environment enter the community. Few strangers ever come to the community.
3. Each community is composed of families and other kinship groups, the systematic relations between which constitute the social structure of the community.
4. The rights and duties of these groups are passed down from generation to generation and maintained by a value system which consists of the mores of the community. They are accepted by everyone.
5. There are no written constitutions or contracts. Relations between groups are monitored and even enforced by the elders of the group.
6. The community perpetuates itself by teaching each on-coming generations its old way of doing and thinking. Apprenticeship in occupations and initiation into each age group by various types of ceremonial guarantees that each new generation shall know and do as the old generation did.
7. The natural resources with which the people used to sustain their economic life are generally owned by the whole community. Each family sustains itself economically by participating in the development and utilization of these resources, and participates in the economic returns from the resources.
8. The economic relations of the community are the accepted division of labour between groups rather than by trade or even by barter. The economic and social security of all is, therefore, a total community responsibility.
9. There is thus less possibility of change in the status of groups, much less of individuals in the community.

To the degree that simple communities manifest these characteristics, they are whole societies, in terms not only of social, economic and political structures, but in terms of value systems. Each person growing up in one of these communities believes and practices these values, plays his assigned roles without questioning, and as a person is pretty much a complete reflection of the community as a whole.

In the present societies some new types of behaviour develop, but by no means do all the old characteristics of folk society disappear. The total or relative social and cultural isolation of the peasant communities is on the decline. The outside world has moved in on them. Due to multiple factors of influence such as, planned and guided community development efforts on the part of the government, increase in transport and communication, the gradual process of urbanization and industrialization, the emergence of new political and economic institutions, the rural communities in general are in the process of change and the situation in the past few decades may be summarized as follows:

1. The first thing was that trade and commerce entered the village.
2. As contact with trade centers, either with merchants located in the village or with trade towns, developed, at least on the part of a few of the village people there, a knowledge of the outside world in terms of activities about which they had previously known very little. What they learned naturally became matters of gossip within the village and, therefore, some understanding of marketing , prices, and things of that kind developed on the part of all village people.
3. Government had entered all of these villages many years back, but modern government of the type which brings services and assistance to villagers was fairly new in all of the villages. Agents of the government had come in and promoted development and welfare activities. When this once began there was a new basis for forming new parties, and often new factions developed.
4. Government servants, located in or serving the village were seldom local villagers themselves, therefore, new persons, generally persons with more education and receiving higher incomes than the villagers, introduced a new type of person and, in some ways, tended to introduce new social status among the other statuses of the village.
5. Government made incursions in all cases, sooner or later, in terms of establishing and helping to maintain schools. School teachers were new citizens of the community and in some cases, played quite different roles than any outsider ever played in the village.
6. As some youth of the village received considerable education, they became capable of making contacts and did make contact outside the village and thus became a channel of cultural traffic in and out of the village.
7. In a few cases, persons with a degree of education took up new occupations different from those which they had traditionally followed, and moved away from the village. This has led to occupational and territorial mobility.
8. As the price and market economy entered the village, some persons began making more money. Those who had made more money or had better contacts with outside agencies became money-lenders. Some of them began purchasing land previously owned by peasants who now lost the ownership of their land. Thus a whole new elite developed in the village, sometimes quite a powerful group.

9. In the case of contacts with the market town or with outside sources of income, some of the villages began to attend picture shows and other recreational events outside the village.
10. A new kind of formal and informal leaders emerged. The youth or the younger generation began influencing the developmental activities in the village. In some cases, government servants began to be looked up to rather than feared.
11. In most villages a degree of individualism developed. Some persons were paid special attention by the development agencies. They gained new importance and they tended to form a group which protected the group against the large owners.
12. In most villages, the lower classes, that is, the lower income people, were paid special attention by the development agencies. They gained new importance and they tended to form a group which protected the group against the large owners.
13. It may be stated here, that the same old reverence for elders, and for the set class structure, and even for the villagers' values, had been considerably diluted.

The rural communities are, however, far from having lost all their old folk characteristics. The following such characteristics, though somewhat modified, are still maintained, (Taylor).

(a) The elders, while they no longer constitute the village government, are highly respected and are still counselors in many types of issue.

(b) The village community's organization is perpetuated by each new generation tending to follow the family occupations of previous generations.

(c) There is in all of the villages some division of labour between the families, this division being fixed by the traditions of the community.

(d) Families, generally extended families, are more integral social groups than are the villages as a whole.

(e) Sentiment for the land, pride and tenacity in the ownership of the land, is still very strong.

(f) There is relatively little tolerance for new ways of thinking and doing. If the people were asked to choose between tradition and progress, tradition would perhaps be their instinctive choice although a second choice might induce them to take a few hesitating steps in the direction of change.

REFERENCE

Taylor, Carl (n.d), *Community Mobilization for Group Formulation*.

CHAPTER 9

Local Institutions as Primary Agents of Social Change

People's participation in the sense of sharing their ideas, interests, needs and views with the development agencies could be direct and indirect. Direct people's participation in any development activity is constrained, besides other community factors like its size, its geographical spread, and in other words the population in the community and its social composition. One logical, practical and simple mechanism for people's participation is institutional representative participation wherein people's elected, selected, nominated representatives, of diverse people's bodies (organizations/institutions) from the village to national level participate on behalf of people and for expressing their views. These are formal statutory bodies like village panchayats (India, Nepal), Tambon Committees, Mandals, Samithis, Unions (Thailand and India) and Upazillas in Bangladesh (suspended after General Ershad's exit) and Zilla Parishads in India. Apart from the above statutory bodies which are the administrative and institutional products of decentralization we may also cite voluntary and feeder organizations such as Youth Clubs, Women's Clubs, Farmer's Forums and all forms of cooperative societies facilitating institutional representative participation of the people in the promotional and developmental activities.

Decentralization at the district and sub-district level in terms of policy formulation, planning, resource mobilization, allocation of resources and implementing development programmes is a measure and a means to bring down development administration close to the people for their active involvement. Democratic decentralization is a facilitating factor in representative people's participation and this takes us to look into the various facets and dimensions of decentralization.

DECENTRALIZATION: ISSUES, EXPERIENCE AND POLICIES

Decentralization means decreasing the role of central government, and augmenting the authority of responsive local institutions. It is concerned with increasing accountability between people who provide local services, and the people who use these services. Above all, it is about the improved management of some of the development activities in the rural area. There are many forms that decentralization can take, including transfer of authority from central to local government, from provincial government to community and non-governmental organizations, and to the private sector. It is a tool for better rural management, by changing the institutional framework to include a significantly greater role for local and community institutions. Decentralization is official policy in many countries of the region. It is no longer an issue whether local governments will assume greater responsibility, but how they will perform the functions statutorily devolved and entrusted to them.

Whether the formal or constitutional structure of the state is federal or unitary, governmental functions are performed in most countries at several levels. While responsibilities for some of the crucial functions such as defence, external relations and macro-management of the economy rests with the national government, several other functional and technical services in agriculture, education, health care and social welfare are usually the responsibility of the administration at the sub-national or local levels. In some Asian countries, the administrative structure is made up of more than two tiers, with the second tier looking after subjects like law and order and justice, and the planning and execution of development programmes at the regional or provincial level, while government bodies below them are entrusted with the responsibility for providing basic civic services. In developing countries, although forces favouring centralization have usually been strong, a common tenet of policy has been to decentralize governmental functions and foster the growth of local government.

It is universally acknowledged that certain functions of the state are best performed at the local level for the simple reason that decentralizing the provision of basic civic services (eg. Sanitation, public health, primary education and social welfare activities) maximizes welfare by responding efficiently to public needs. Local governments responsible to the people from the locality are in a better position to respond to the preferences and needs of the people than governments functioning at a distance. To a developmentalist the decentralization of the powers and functions of the government among different levels, which essentially underlies the rationale for federalism, helps to reconcile the aims of achieving unity in the midst of diversity. From the economic point, optimal provision of public goods calls for both centralized and decentralized decision-making in the appropriation and allocation of resources in the public enterprises.

In the developmental context, decentralization acquires special significance in view of the fact, given the requisite authority, local bodies can generate activities suited to the resource endowment and needs of the local people. Local government units can undertake more effectively activities like improving local infrastructure, such as roads, transport and communication facilities, water supply, electricity and energy, apart from delivering social services in the area of health, nutrition, sanitation, housing, and so on. Local governments can also make valuable contributions to irrigation and land utilization, the protection of the environment, animal husbandry, household industry, public works and the supply of inputs for agriculture and cottage industries. Excessive centralization in planning and implementation of development programmes often causes needless delays and wastage while stifling local initiative. It is increasingly recognized that real grassroots development can take place only with the active participation of local government bodies in these activities.

Local units are also perceived to be in a position to tap resources, which centrally administered revenue, instruments cannot reach. Participation of the people in the government at the local levels makes it possible to tap resources in ways which may not be acceptable if imposed from above.

The healthy growth of local government units together with the representation of the people also helps inculcate participatory government and development. The units can serve as a training ground for the people and their representatives in responsible decision-making and meaningful participation in national life. Above all, it helps to impart a sense of fulfillment among the people as citizens and thereby strengthens the foundations of a democratic polity. These considerations, as well as the widening resource gap of the public sector in many developing countries, which underscores the urgency of developing more resources and ensuring their efficient use, have impelled many governments to look to decentralization as a partial answer to their problems.

Despite recognition of its merits, however, and the resolve to decentralize governmental functions in planning and management, the process of decentralization is yet to strike roots in most developing countries. Planning has to be decentralized if idle resources are to be utilized optimally and local needs and aspirations are to be met efficiently. Diseconomies and other costs of over-centralization coupled with advances in technologies, particularly in the field of information and telecommunications, have made decentralization both imperative and feasible.

The term "decentralization" in the context of governmental organization is generally taken to mean the transfer of authority from the national or central government to its field offices, local authorities or other local bodies. Decentralization in the economic sense implies the transfer of responsibility for planning, management, resource raising and allocation of resources in the public sector. Such resource transfers can be effected through the devolution of powers and functions of government to lower-level bodies with a degree of autonomy, by the deconcentration of central government offices, and by deregulation, and with the setting up of public enterprises.

If the benefits of local participation and involvement in deciding the use of national resources for public purposes according to local preference are to be derived, decentralization has to aim at what is implied by "devolution". Such devolution should proceed to the lowest possible level where the people can effectively participate in development and have direct access to the benefits of growth as well as civic and social services that governments provide to their citizens. It follows that to be meaningful, devolution carries with it the need for introducing an element of self-governance or some representative character in the lower-level government bodies to whom responsibility for specified functions, along with requisite powers and autonomy, is transferred. Fiscal decentralization, which essentially implies a greater access to national resources with increased powers to mobilize and use them for meeting local wants, provides the real content of functional decentralization.

While decentralization has been attempted in developing countries in all the forms distinguished above, the picture that emerges from the close scrutiny of the countries shows that progress in devolution has been rather slow and halting. Seldom was the intention to devolve matched by necessary action, and even where action was taken in the form of legislation or creation of necessary institutions, other conditions for devolution to be effective were not met with. While there are more than two tiers of government in all the countries, few have succeeded in devising local government institutions which could involve the people in the function of government and in its various activities. At this point, we may at length look into, in a larger sense, a revolutionary change in India – democratic decentralization and Panchayati Raj.

Panchayati Raj

The institution of Village Panchayat is as old as Indian history and is part of Indian tradition. The ancient Panchayats discharged most of the functions affecting the life of village communities and were effective units of administration until the eighteenth century. With the advent of the British, however, they got relegated to subservient place in the colonial administrative setup. Even during the British rule, particularly after Ripon Resolution of 1892, attempts were made to revive these village institutions. Accordingly, Panchayats and Local Boards were set up in the Provinces of British India.

The Need for Panchayati Raj: The Constitutional Sanction Behind It

The Panchayats, the Taluk and District Boards and the Municipalities established after Ripon, were either purely nominated or containing some members elected by narrow electorates. Under Montague-Chelmsford Reforms, Local Self-government was made a transferred subject and the State Ministries concerned attempted to broaden the foundations of these local bodies.

In some States, Village Panchayats were sought to be established on a wider scale. But all these efforts were half-hearted and the establishment of Village Panchayats and reconstruction of other local bodies on a truly democratic basis figured prominently on the platform of the Indian national Congress.

After Independence, the importance of revitalizing the Village Panchayats and assigning them a specific role in administration was recognized and it was laid in the Indian Constitution as a Directive Principle of State Policy that "the State shall take steps to organize village Panchayats and to endow them with such powers and authority as may be necessary to enable them to function as units of Local Self-Government" (Article 40).

Its Relevance to Community Development in India

The first organized effort to tackle the problems of rural India was through the Community Development Programme, which was launched in fifty-five selected projects on October 2, 1952. The programme, based on an integrated approach to the various aspects of rural development, emphasized from the beginning the importance of working through the people's institutions like Village Panchayats, Cooperatives etc. to ensure their involvement in the planning and implementation of development programmes and to secure the fullest possible public participation. A great deal of consultation and development work was done under the National Extension Service Schemes. The Planning and Development Committee set up in each Block was merely advisory.

After the Community Development Programme, which was gradually expanding to cover larger areas, was under implementation for about four years, in January 1957, a Study Team under the Chairmanship of Balwantray Mehta was appointed by the Planning Commission to review the working of the Community Development Programme and also to examine the question of reorganization of district administration to provide for popular organizations between the Village and State levels.

The Study Team recommended, *inter alia,* the setting up of elected and organically linked democratic bodies at the village, block and the district levels and the entrustment of all planning and developmental activities to these bodies. This recommendation was accepted by the National Development Council in 1958. The Central Council of Local Self-Government in its fifth meeting at Hyderabad in 1959, took stock of the action taken by the States to implement the decision of the National Development Council and recommended that "while the broad pattern and the fundamentals may be uniform, there should not be any rigidity in the pattern. In fact, the country is so large and Panchayati Raj (democratic decentralization) is so complex a subject with a far reaching consequences, that there is the fullest scope of trying out various patterns and alternatives. What is most important is the genuine transfer of power to the people. If this is ensured, form and pattern may necessarily vary according to conditions prevailing in different States".

All States have accordingly undertaken to establish Panchayati Raj. Thus we find the ideology and the objectives of Community Development and the concept of Democratic Decentralization-building or extending democracy to the grassroots are fused together, and christened as "Panchayati Raj". The new statutory institutions have become the agencies of Community Development Extension Programmes. In essence, this was further growth in the previous programme designed to strengthen the people's own democratic, elected organization by opening new avenues of opportunities for their development. This new device offers the villagers a share in their own direction and self-development which is indeed a new and a novel departure in their lives. In this programme the people under their own organizations at the Village, Mandal, Block and District level were given equal share and status in the working of the whole community development block. Village Panchayats are constituted through elections and given democratic powers and responsibilities. The Sarpanchs or the Presidents of all the Panchayats formed a Panchayat Samithi, the Panchayats formed a Samithi at the block level and Samithis constituted the Zilla Parishad at the district level. The functions of the Rural Development Agency and the people's organizations at all levels up to the district are to further strengthen and make the rural development programme more dynamic and its structure more complex.

"The Community Development approach has to be an essentially democratic approach as this will draw large masses of the people as active partners in the tasks of developing the vast country. For, only thus can this gigantic task be accomplished. The Community Development approach, while it will depend on the democratic process, will at the same time also help to strengthen it. There is, therefore, complete inter-relationship between Community Development and the progress of democracy; they are two sides of the same coin. Both are processes of human development. It is for this reason that the Community Development Programme came to focus attention on the importance and urgency of democratic decentralization. Democratic Decentralization must not be understood as merely the creation of Local Self-Governing Institutions of the people at different levels or as transfer of real power to the people. Its object is to give vitality to the whole democratic process and to provide to a new born democracy a wider and firmer base" (Mukerji, 1961).

Basic Elements of Panchayati Raj

The term "Panchayati Raj", which is popularly used in the country includes the two words Panchayati and Raj. Panchayati means "of the Panchayat", which consists of a group of "Panchas" who are representative leaders of people at the village level. What is emphasized is the representativeness of Panch, irrespective of how this element of representativeness is determined. The word "Raj" in this context means Government. The term "Panchayati

Raj" therefore, literally means "Government of People's representative leaders". In this sense it is an expression of the essence of democracy as internationally understood. The Balwantray Mehta Committee Report expresses this categorically in these words: "in the ultimate analysis, the establishment of the Panchayat Samithis with a wide devolution of powers by the State Government has to be an act of faith-faith in democracy".

The fundamental or basic principles of Panchayati Raj emphasized in the COPP Report are:

(a) It should be a three-tier structure of Local Self-Governing bodies from the village to the district, the bodies being organically linked up.

(b) There should be genuine transfer of power and responsibility to them.

(c) Adequate resources should be transferred to the new bodies to enable them to discharge these responsibilities.

(d) All development programmes at these levels should be channeled through these bodies.

(e) The system evolved should be such as will facilitate further devolution and dispersal of power and responsibilities in the future.

The primary objective of Panchayati Raj is to establish an integrated structure of local democratic or self-governing bodies linking the village within the district and to make the Village Panchayat as a unit of planning and execution of all schemes of rural development. Secondly, Panchayati Raj aims at developing the initiative of the local people and create conditions for maximum popular participation. Thirdly, it seeks to develop sound leadership at all levels in the district necessary for the success of democratic institutions. And finally, it seeks to provide at the instance of Panchayati Raj bodies, a development-oriented and efficient administration.

In terms of organization or structure, the programme of Panchayati Raj, as mentioned earlier, envisages three tiers of the Government from the village up to the district level. These three tiers are:

1. Panchayat at the village level consisting of elected representatives of the people with provision for the co-option of two women members and one member each from the Scheduled Castes and Scheduled Tribes.
2. At the Mandal or block level, an elected Self-Governing Institution to be called Mandal Parishad Panchayat or Samithi. Membership in this to be by indirect elections from the Village Panchayats. Its jurisdiction to be coextensive with a Mandal or Community Development Block.
3. At the district level there is a body called Zilla Parishad. In order to ensure necessary co-ordination between the Mandal Parishad or Panchayat Samithis, Zilla Parishad was constituted which consists of the presidents of the Mandal Parishads or Samithis, and elected political representatives of the area namely MLAs, MPs and district level government officials.

In recent years there has been changes in the size, nomenclature and mode of election to the above bodies one example is Andhra Pradesh.

Three tiers viz., Village Panchayat, Panchayat Samithi and Zilla Parishad when constituted and operated simultaneously make up the structure of Panchayati Raj in a district. Functionally, Panchayati Raj is assumed to be operative to the degree that it results in the community understanding its problem, realizing its responsibility, exercising the necessary powers through its chosen representatives and maintaining a constant and intelligent vigilance on local administration.

Progress of Panchayati Raj

Panchayati Raj, as mentioned earlier, is an institutional arrangement for decentralized planning and plan implementation. It was brought in to enhance and facilitate people's participation, even though it was representative type of participation. Panchayati Raj was first introduced in Rajasthan and Andhra Pradesh in 1959. This was on the recommendations of Balwantray Mehta Committee on Committee on Plan Projects (COPP) appointed in 1957. This was followed by the Ashok Mehta Committee in 1978 which made vital suggestions for restructuring the Panchayati Raj bodies. It recommended three-tier system of Panchayati Raj institutions and direct elections to Chairpersons of all the three tiers. It also recommended election of women to Zilla Parishads and the Mandal Panchayats, and in case no women were elected to these bodies, they are to be co-opted. Ashok Mehta was followed by three Committees i.e., G.V.K. Rao (1985), L.M. Singhvi (1986) and Bommai (1989). Amongst other recommendations of these Committees was reservation of seats for women in these bodies to a tune of around one-third.

Though the spirit and objectives of democratic decentralization are the same in all the States in India, there are a few variations in terms of number of tiers, their structure, nomenclatures, levels of their operations and provision in them for women representation. The lowest tier is called Gram Panchayat, the middle tier is variously known as Panchayat Samithi, Panchayat union and Mandal Parishad, and the tier at the district level predominantly goes as Zilla Parishad and in a couple of cases as District Council. The idea here is only to indicate the institutional structure and not to go into the details of their constitution and mode of elections, co-options and ex-officio membership at the middle and the upper tiers.

As of December 1992, the following States have a three-tier structure of the Panchayati Raj system: Andhra Pradesh, Bihar, Gujarat, Himachal Pradesh, Karnataka, Madhya Pradesh, Maharashtra, Orissa, Punjab and West Bengal. In case of Haryana, Kerala and Tamil Nadu, it is of two-tier structure at the village panchayat levels and block levels which were earlier community development blocks.

TOWARDS FUNCTIONAL DEMOCRACY

Panchayati Raj is in our making. Statutory changes alone do not bring in the desired changes and transform the human elements. Slowly, patiently, and methodically the statute must be translated into action. For a planned social change towards a richer and meaningful life for the masses in the countryside, an inter-disciplinary approach is the means. A scientific approach to the problem is the answer. Hit and miss methods may not pay higher dividends in the long run. Panchayati Raj must become more a way of life of the rural people.

In a democracy the individual is no more than a spectator; he is actually one of the spectators. He cannot play his part unless he is properly informed as to the processes of democratic government at all levels. Planned public relations are essential to inculcate civic spirit, civic pride and civic unity in villages, as the percentage of literacy is low, a judicious selection of the media of public relations will have to be made. The radio, the film, civic exhibitions, civic weeks and civic *melas* are some of the useful tools of public relations in rural area. Civics with due emphasis on rural self-governments should be made a subject in the curriculum of schools, colleges and universities.

In a greater measure, the people's representatives are to deliver the goods. On them depend the development of the local community the strengthening of the democratic institutions and largely the success of the Panchayati Raj. This development of local leadership and responsible and responsive citizenry could be achieved only through Social Education Programmes apart from economic measures. The community must be mobilized, interest groups identified and organized into responsive and dynamic groups. This mobilization of the community into institutions, interest groups and associate agencies will create the conditions necessary for the emergence of leadership at the local level.

It is only by educating the general public, could we expect awareness, leadership and initiative among the elected members of the Panchayat or of higher tiers, we cannot neglect the general mass and merely concentrate on the elected representatives. A massive adult education movement is desirable to educate the general mass. Literacy Programmes should find a predominant place in the adult education movement. All illiterates below 40 years must be made functional literates within reasonable time. Further, radio-forums and reading rooms-cum-libraries could be organized for dissemination of knowledge.

It is needless to emphasize that the elected representatives should be trained and educated in all aspects of Panchayati Raj. In the course of the Panchayat term, the Panches (or the sarpanches and up-sarpanches as the case may be) should be trained at least twice-once soon after their election to the office and for the second time, in the middle of the term. The stress must be on utilizing the institutional facilities available and not on merely creating institutions.

In educating the sarpanches and the panches the Extension Personnel in the Community Development and more especially the Extension Officers, panchayats could play an effective role. At least once in a quarter or six months, the Executive Officer of the Panchayats may convene a meeting of all the sarpaches and panches of one or two gram sevaks circles at a convenient place and arrange for talks by special invitees – officials and non-officials on Panchayati Raj. This may help understanding and motivating initiative on the part of the elected representatives.

There is no element of force or coercion in making people do things. The means are constant persuasion and education.

Multitudinal problems arise in the working of the Panchayati Raj Institutions. These problems need scientific treatment and solutions arrived at on empirical studies. Action research with an interdisciplinary approach to the problems is a must in the field of planned social change. Under such a built-in action research programme the social scientists and the administrators have to devise ways and means to ensure effective and active participation of the elected representatives in the working of the Panchayati Raj.

An attentive study of the process of decentralization in various countries suggests a few impeding factors in decentralization.

ABSENCE OF LEGAL FRAMEWORK

The disappointing progress of efforts to decentralize can be attributed to a lack of adequate constitutional and legal backing and a weak fiscal base that is fundamental to such a process. We may say that India is an exception in this kind of lacunae. In many instances, local bodies have failed to come up with legal support provided through constitutional recognition or separate legislation. This is true irrespective of whether the country in question is federal or unitary. In Pakistan, a federation, several attempts were made in the last forty years at the initiative of the central government to set up local governments throughout but none has been of much avail. In Thailand, a unitary country, the local level bodies with elected assemblies have been created through specific legislation laying down the structure as well as the powers and functions of the local bodies at different levels. Local governments are, however, not in a position to perform more than a few functions assigned to them by the laws which brought them into being (Cohen and Uphoff, 1977).

LACK OF FISCAL AUTONOMY

A more serious impediment to the functioning of local autonomy is the financial dependence of the local bodies on the central and provincial governments. Almost invariably, the bulk of the financial needs of local governments are met out of the share of the national taxes, and / or subsidies from the center or grants, and the dependence seems to be increasing.

The domination and control of local bodies by the central and provincial governments, which is partly attributable to their financial dependence, has also been responsible for stifling local autonomy and blocking decentralization. In most cases the central government is unitary type and the central and provincial governments in federal structures exercise control over the local bodies in various ways, direct and indirect. In Thailand, while the degree of control varies between different local bodies, all are subject to close control by the central government. Central control is maintained in Thailand through a system that allows the Ministry of Interior directly to control the administration of all local bodies in the kingdom. Supervisory powers over local bodies are delegated to the provincial governors, who are also assigned responsibilities to monitor the activities of local governments. The statutory authority of the local bodies to raise certain taxes and incur expenditure is subject to the rules and regulations of the central government.

China is perhaps the only country to have seen substantial decentralization. Although a country with "unified leadership and government", China has in practice allowed considerable latitude to the local government entities, the provinces and the municipalities, in their function. Even though the country has a unified national budget, the provinces and municipalities have their own separate budgets and run enterprises often on a large scale. Decentralization gathered momentum in the 1980s and in fact the pace appears to have been too rapid for the country to adjust. It may, however, be fair to say that much of the freedom which the local governments enjoy in China despite a monolithic political structure stems from their relatively strong financial base (Cohen and Uphoff, 1977).

FISCAL MISMANAGEMENT

In country after country what has prompted higher level interference is financial mismanagement. In Thailand, the financial weakness of the local bodies is attributable partly to the inefficiencies of the local governments themselves and their inability (or unwillingness) to make full use of whatever tax powers they have under the law. The poor yield of the house and building tax which constitutes the most important component of local taxation in Thailand is due both to deficiencies in the structure of the tax as well as inefficiencies in its administration. While liberal exemptions undermine its base, administrative inefficiencies have also stood in the way of its effective implementation and tackling evasion practiced in various ways by landlords. Tax rolls and maps are not updated and cadastral maps of even resourceful local authorities like the Bangkok Metropolitan Administration are 40 to 60 years old. The system of billing and maintaining tax rolls is outdated. According to a recent estimate, computerization and regularization of the tax-payers would alone double the yield of the tax. While with urbanization one would expect a rise in the revenue from this tax, its contribution to local revènue has gone down (Jurgen, *et.al;* 1989).

ADMINISTRATIVE WEAKNESS

In many countries, especially at the district and municipal or village levels, there is lack of trained manpower to levy taxes efficiently and mange their affairs. The elected officials or representatives furthermore do not always display the sense of responsibility or dedication required for fulfilling the objectives of the local government and often engage in intrigues for power, seeking personal gain to the detriment of public interest. Supersession of local bodies in several countries has also often followed from their mismanagement and the failure of the democratic system to work at the local level (Cohen and Uphoff, 1977; Jurgen, *et. al;* 1989).

STRATEGY OF PLANNING FOR DEVELOPMENT AND EFFICIENCY ARGUMENTS

An important factor impeding the process of decentralization in the developing countries is the adoption of planning as a strategy of development with considerable involvement of the public sector. A degree of centralization is inherent in a strategy of planning, with the government taking a lead role and laying down the basic programmes and priorities at the national level to ensure consistency and efficiency although decentralization might lead to faster development of better-endowed but less developed areas, central intervention and allocation of resources were often thought necessary to bring about the balanced development and provision of public services at a minimum level in all parts of a country. Modern technology with the vast economies of scale spilling across regions in areas like power and communications also have reinforced the trend towards centralization. A lack of expertise in and familiarity with modern techniques of harnessing and managing natural resources also have strengthened the case for a certain degree of centralization. In addition, there are the gaps in technology, resources and skills at the local levels which cannot be made up without help from above. The creation of specialized agencies or authorities to undertake specific tasks like metropolitan planning and development is often motivated by considerations like these.

Considerations of efficiency also argue for centralizing certain important functions, as do the centralized collection of the major taxes like the income tax, which unavoidably created a vertical fiscal imbalance in the system and so the dependence of the local bodies on higher level governments. This is compounded by their lack of managerial and technical skills. Denuding the central government of its command over resources also undermines its capacity to even out regional imbalance, as is now being witnessed in China.

RECENT TRENDS

Experience of the last three decades has, however, cast doubt on the efficacy of centralized planning in promoting growth and spreading the benefits to all sections. Moreover, disenchantment with over-centralization has led to a search for other ways of decentralization apart from devolution. Given the will, it is argued, solutions can be found for the problems and dilemmas or at least these can be rendered manageable. Although decentralization often gets stalled because of a lack of managerial skills, there are examples of good results achieved by associating the people in governmental activities at the lower levels. The involvement of the local population in some of the States in India where elections to panchayats were held in recent years seems to have activated hitherto untapped energies and resources and made tangible contributions to improving public services and activities in those regions. There have been several instances of positive gains from the association of local people and organizations like village cooperatives in the past in Thailand, Pakistan, India and Malaysia. Besides, not all the weaknesses of the local bodies of their own making. As already mentioned, their fiscal powers are often constrained by central control exercised in various forms.

As is to be expected, decentralization, even when acknowledged as desirable, encounters resistance from those for whom it implies a loss of governmental power and authority. A striking example of how the central authorities tend to shackle the autonomy and initiative of local bodies, even when the involvement of local government is sought, is provided by the guidelines issued to district councils in India to implement an employment programme in the rural areas in the late 1980s. Rodinelli and others conclude their discussion on what impedes decentralization with the following observations:

"Untimely however, decentralization is an ideological principle, associated with objectives of self-reliance, democratic decision-making, popular participation in government, and accountability of public officials to citizens. It is a political decision, and its implementation is a reflection of a country's political process and maturity". (Rondinelli *et al.,* 1983).

These observations are equally valid even after a decade and a half. The recent experiences and trend show that there is now greater political awareness of the need for decentralization than before. Hence, the search for solutions to the problems encountered in its implementation and the urge to draw lessons from the past.

Decentralization with its full complements of vertical geographic devolution of powers, administrative control, financial and resource raising authority, freedom of allocation of resources and mandate and responsibility to development planning and plan implementation at local levels, by itself is a great leap forward in the governance of public interest and welfare. People's and people's representative leaders' participation in all the above functions will strengthen the roots of democracy and ensure enduring people-oriented development.

REFERENCES

Cohen, J M and Uphoff N.T, (1977). *Rural Development Programmes: Concepts and Measure for Project Designing: Implementation and Evaluation*. Rural Development Monograph Series No.2, Cornell University, USA.

Jurgen, Ronald (1989). *Local Governments in South East Asia*. HSD Working Paper, Asian Institute of Technology, Bangkok (Thailand).

Mukherji, B. (1961). *Community Development in India*, Orient-Longmans, New Delhi.

Rondinelli, D., *et al.,* (1983). *Decentralization and Development*. UNCRD Regional Development Series, Japan.

CHAPTER 10

Local Leaders and Their Participation in Alleviating Poverty

There is a close relationship between the leadership in a rural community and the nature and degree of their participation in rural development activities. The local leaders may be instrumental in mobilizing and motivating people to participate in development activities or they may sometimes be barriers inhibiting and subtly or deliberately discouraging participation for their selfish ends and or do so out of ignorance, misinformation, avarice, or trying to keep their followers as marginal and occasional beneficiaries of development programmes and not as active participants in decision-making or authors of any policy issues.

Participation in development programmes as a product or function depends on the structure and type of leadership and the ethnic, social and class composition of the rural community. Sometimes, the numerical strength of the ethnic, occupational and professional groups are factors to be reckoned with when we speak of local leaders as stimulants or barriers to people's participation in development programmes.

We may have a brief look at the rural leadership and some instances wherein local leadership was a deciding factor for any initiative for promotional or developmental programme or the local people accepting a project, innovation or participating in a communal activity.

The village community world over, despite its social, ethnic, religious and lingual composition, is a social entity. It has its structure and traditions. The diverse activities of the community, both individual and communal are carried on and regulated by some individuals from within and outside the community. The individuals who guide, who are sought after to guide and shoulder the affairs of the people in the village may be called leaders. Sometimes, the pattern of leadership and its functions vary from community to community. It is interesting to look into the principles that control human relations and how a social group organizes and lives its life. More often, the burden of village responsibility rests on the leaders just as family responsibility rests on the head of the household.

AREAS OF LEADERSHIP

Leaders emerge and function in diverse fields. The areas of leadership and the number of leadership and the number of leaders functioning in each area and one leader functioning in several areas depend on the size and social structure of the rural community and, as mentioned earlier, on the occupations and profession of the population, their literacy and intellectual levels, and also on the degree of their interaction with the outside world.

In a broad sense, when we think of rural-traditional communities, the following activities may be considered as areas wherein the question of guidance and consulting arise and the local leadership centre around these functions.

1. Coordination of village communal undertakings.
2. Liaison between the people and governmental personnel.
3. Guidance in times of epidemics.
4. Guidance in religious magical matters.
5. Financial problems – monetary matters.
6. Political matters.
7. Guidance in legal matters.
8. Financial help for marriage and death ceremonies.
9. Settling quarrels-disputes outside the village.
10. Settling quarrels-disputes inside the village.
11. Agricultural matters.
12. Guidance in educational matters.
13. Guidance in warding off the effects of witchery and sorcery.
14. Guidance in employment opportunities.

As communities progress, with the increase in skills and literacy rate and change in the value system the nature of needs, degree of dependency and also leadership change. Leadership is a social phenomenon and it is subject to change and will in some measure, in some areas persist forever.

Leaders as Facilitators and Blockers

One comes across innumerable instances in rural communities and equally in urban settlements too wherein local leaders function as motivators and facilitators encouraging and enthusing people to participate in development activities concerning their community and as blockers discouraging the people in participation. The local leaders have been instrumental in accomplishing several projects for their communities. Participation by significant individuals in the community secures the projects as a sanctity, approval and acceptance by the generality of the community. We may look into a few cases wherein the weight and significance of local leaders manifest itself.

PARTICIPATION FOR A NATIONAL CAUSE

During the Indo-China War in the last quarter of 1962, over the border dispute which lasted for a short period, the Government of India had to mobilize its resources and a fund raising campaign was started all over the country. It was called "War Fund". The State Governments were asked to raise funds from the people and they acted through several of their line and development agencies. During this period what were then called Community Development Blocks were given each a certain target of amount to be raised from People's

Contributions towards the War Fund. As usual (we mean the target distribution downward in the hierarchy) the Block Development Officer (BDO) assigned each Village Level Worker (VLW) a certain target of amount to be raised in his circle comprising households ranging from 1,500 to 1,800.

During this period the author happened to be a VLW and the target of raising money for the War Fund fell on him. Inclusive of hamlets he had around twenty villages under his jurisdiction. Indo-China war was a distant cry for the people in the area. Many of the villagers had no idea of China, its geographic location and its borders with India and the disputed borders. It became a big problem to explain the situation to the simple but intelligent villagers. We had to approach the local leaders for help in raising the amount. Through the initiative taken by the local leaders, we were able to raise small amounts of money ranging from one to twenty rupees or so, from each household.

In this context the author would like to cite one instance pertaining to a community of shepherds in one village, most of them poor and landless, mainly thriving on rearing sheep and goats. We told them that the millionaire-farmer and politically influential leader of a higher caste community from the neighbouring village was visiting their village on such and such a day and he expected them to contribute their mite for the War Fund.

The day the leader visited the shepherd community, one could see the spontaneous and enthusiastic presenting of old silver bangles, rings, waist-strings made of silver, the only valuable ornaments some of the families possessed. Most of them had no money to give. Some of the silver ornaments given by them can be considered antics, for they were of old-fashioned and some may be called of tribal-wear. Later, we sold the silver ornaments to some well-to-do families and passed on the proceeds to the BDO. The participation of the people in this instance was overwhelming and largely it was to be attributed to the respect the villagers had for the leader and his very visit to them seeking their humble contribution. As mentioned earlier, to a large measure, the people's response and their contribution, as a symbol of their participation for a national cause was not a response to Government nor to those skirmishes taking places at the international border between India and China, but for the influence and initiative of the local, small leaders and the big wealthy leader from the neighbouring village.

The following two cases reflect the spirit of healthy competition amongst the rural communities and the significant and appreciable role-played by both, by the formal and small informal leaders in effecting popular participation in mobilizing resources to start a high school and forming of approach roads to the villages.

Small Informal Leaders Collecting Contributions from the Villagers for a Large Educational Project

Rampur is a fairly big village with a population of around three thousand at the time of this incidence and is located in Chittoor district, Andhra Pradesh, South India. It is a multi-caste community. It is a market center for the main villages and hamlets within a radius of 15 km. The population of the cluster of villages around Rampur in 1960s was around 30,000, but there was no high school in the whole area. The majority of the population comprised small farmers, landless labourers, artisans and petty traders. Since there was no high school within the walkable distance and many families could not afford sending their children to distantly located high schools and keep them in hostels, many children had no chance of going beyond primary education.

As a contrast to the conditions of the commonality of the communities under reference, one family of the dominant caste-Hindus in Rampur was rich. This family and its clanfolk and kin in the neighbouring couple of villages and other districts were traditionally affluent. The head of the rich family in Rampur is a graduate, well-informed, with high connections, wielding influence with the administration at the district and at the State level too. He is a big farmer, moneylender and most of the farmers in the neighbouring villages were to borrow money from him and so they were captive sellers of their groundnut produce to him only. He was politically powerful and whether the people like it or not he had a sway over them and there was no opposition to him. He could send his children to expensive public schools and colleges and so he had no felt-need for a high school in the village. The neighbouring villagers felt an acute need for a high school in their area. It was reported that some of the important people in the area approached this rich man and raised the question of a high school for the area. His response was evasive, with excuses and explanations of impractibility of opening a high school in the village to serve the village and the neighbouring communities. A high school was a long felt-need. The neighbouring villagers sensed and realized that the big man was not interested in a high school in his area, may be thinking that if the children of poor families received higher education, his importance and his family status will go down, when poor get educated and become rich it is a threat to the already rich.

A few leaders in the neighbouring villages took initiative, went around the villages, discussed with local leaders the prospect of raising money from each family after the harvest of paddy and groundnut, the principal crops in the area. This silent campaign for raising contributions was done without the knowledge and approval of the big man of Rampur. It was a successful fund raising campaign. Obviously, the message of popular concerted efforts, mobilization of small resources in cash and kind and the community's solid social action reached the big man as a shock and threat to his eminent position. He realized that he could not stall the starting of a high school for the area, for the people were determined, have raised considerable amount from the people to approach the government for sanctioning for opening a high school in their area. They were to offer their collections as a matching contribution to government's grant. The big man realized that it was already too late and even if he opposed subtlety or diplomatically the opening of the educational institution, it would come with the popular force. And so, not to be left behind and sidetracked he sent invitation for a grand feast to all-important leaders in the neighbouring villages. Some of the invitees knew that it was a face saving mechanism. A large group gathered on his spacious mango garden and after treating them with a rich feast, he gave a small speech, how, for a long time, he had been pondering over the need for a high school for their area and that he was glad that some initiative was taken by the local leaders and the people in the area and announced with a flourish that he was donating three acres of prime land close to the main road in his village for the high school and certain amount in thousands and wished that the high school may be named after his late father.

After a few months the high school was sanctioned by the government. From then on the big man assumed the lead position. The buildings came up. The high school was opened and for the past forty years now the children of this area have access to higher education.

It is the small informal and formal leaders in the rural communities, who initiated the movement and secured popular participation. We should acknowledge the help rendered and boost given by the big man in Rampur whatever might have been his initial attitude and intentions for a high school to serve the needs of the common people in the area.

Participation is Contagious

When an occasion arises, when proper climate is created, when people's competitive spirit is kindled, when people perceive the tangible benefit for them and when properly guided by the local leaders people's participation in promotional and development activities becomes contagious. The term "contagious" is used here in the sense of exciting enthusiasm from one to the other for a positive course of action.

It was Andhra Pradesh in India which was the first State to introduce Panchayati Raj system in September 1958, in the Community Development Blocks that were in operation during this period. In order to celebrate the first anniversary of the Panchayati Raj system in the State, a grand programme of multiple development activities viz., kitchen gardens, soak pits, drainage, mass environmental sanitation and formation of earthen approach roads to the villages where they did not exist then was initiated. Of all the above programmes, the formation of cartable and suitable approach roads to villages was given the place of primacy.

The present case refers to the former Chowdepalle Community Development Block in Chittoor district, Andhra Pradesh. The approach road campaign in particular was carried on for a couple of weeks by the Community Development Workers and local leaders. Prizes were established for the best people's participation in terms of their labour contribution in forming the roads. For a few weeks it looked like a massive festive activity in dozens of villages, people engaged in cutting, digging, forming and aligning the earthen approach roads to their villages. One could see the spontaneity and enthusiasm among the people. It was really contagious. Later, the VLW circles which had the best performance were selected and the concerned Village Level Workers were awarded the prizes by the Block Agency. Here the credit goes to the people and their leaders.

What happens when a Leader is Ignored?

As mentioned earlier in this chapter, participation by significant individuals in the community secures the projects of a sanctity approval and a legitimacy. The local leaders are the gate keepers and one can visualize the role of these gate keepers in rural communities. We may look into the case wherein an educational institute as a development agency failed to contact a local leader and solicit his involvement in a housing project for the cobbler community, a constituent of the village. The failure to contact the leader by the development agency was not deliberate or negligence, but it was out of ignorance of the personnel of the development agency, and local communal dynamics and the leader's influence over the cobblers. The non-involvement of the local leaders of different caste and religion acted as a stalemate to the project in the beginning.

Servaipuram

Servaipuram is one of the villages in what is called Achampatti complex of villages, close to Dindigal town in Tamil Nadu. The complex comprises around ten villages which used to be the service area of Gandhigram Rural Institute. The institute had several extension and service activities such as pre-school education, women's clubs, agricultural societies (for access to credit), leather tanning and housing for the weaker sections. The institute was receiving funds from a German voluntary agency and this was the only source of funds for the institute for its extension service activities. These activities served as a field orientation to the students of the institute.

Servaipuram is fairly a large village with a population of 2,500 persons. The majority comprised of Servai Christians and there is a church in the village with a priest who was an outsider and a local leader as the manager of the church. Obviously, the manager of the church was a Christian and was religious and secular leader in the village. Nothing in the village should happen outside his knowledge. He had a grip over the Hindu minority groups in the village.

The Cobblers

One such minority group was cobblers, the leather workers comprising 45 households. All these families were living in hovel like huts, crowded in a small area outside the main settlement of Servaipuram. The most immediate need for the cobbler community was housing. The institute's faculty (the author was one of the faculty) on deliberations with the cobbler community arrived at this priority of housing for them. The housing project required acquiring of land for house sites and building the houses for the 45 families. The leaders in the cobbler community were asked to choose some land around the village (private or government land) so that preparations may be made for formal acquisition of land for housing.

The faculty from the institute used to meet the cobblers periodically in order to know the progress in their selection of land. Thus, the faculty spent ten months without getting any indication from the cobblers. Whenever the faculty assembled the cobbler leaders and discussed the question of their choice of house-site, the response was silence or some vague and evasive answers. The faculty was at a loss as to why the cobblers were not coming forward with any indication of their choice of land for their new houses. After ten months of futile meetings with this clientele group, the faculty at one point asked them as to what was holding them in making a decision. The leader of the cobblers came out in an hesitant way and in a faltered tone informed the faculty that they better consult the manager of the local church. Later, it surfaced that the manager of the church felt that he was not consulted by the institute's faculty and he was ignored though he was also a secular leader of all segments in Servaipuram. He had kept vigilance on what was going on between the cobblers and the service agency. It came to be known that he mildly and indirectly warned the cobblers that he was not happy about what was going on between the cobblers and the service agency. The cobbler leader threw a hint at the faculty that better they discussed the house site affair with the manager. The faculty realized the lapse on their part that they have failed and did not bother to know the nexus of relationship between the cobblers and the majority Servai Christian community and more importantly the influence of the church manager. He blocked the activity, since he felt that his importance was not recognized and the programme did not go through him.

After a few days this lapse was remedied. The faculty went to the manager, apologized for having been ignorant of his status and his importance as a local leader and arranged a big meeting of the community including the cobblers and the manager was requested to preside over the meeting wherein the housing for the cobblers and other programmes (a community hall, loans for draught bullocks, a kindergarten) were discussed. Later on, the housing project for the cobblers was routed through the manager. We cite this case in order to emphasize as to what happens to development programmes in rural communities, when individuals do not participate in the development activities.

Further, it is not only a question of enthusing, motivating the existing local leaders to encourage and induce participation among the people, but it is also cultivating new leadership in the local communities to generate and institutionalize more and more of people's participation in development activities. Activities or programmes are the means to build new leadership and strengthen the existing leadership. Local leadership is an invaluable human resource and energy to build up healthy rural communities on the plank of participation.

CHAPTER 11

Role of Youth in Alleviating Poverty

Youth constitute a potential and a rich human resource in any community. The youth with the vigour of their age, most often bubbling with enthusiasm for change for better ways of life look for opportunities to fulfill their psychic, social and economic needs. It depends on how the youth is motivated, mobilized, organized, facilitated and utilized in building newer and progressive communities. The programmes should satisfy them and should also be contributory to community development.

When we speak of the rural youth, we meet with a diversity in their case, literate, illiterate, people with some social and technical skills, rich and poor, employed and unemployed. And so the rural development programmes are to be satisfying and challenging to them so that we can secure and ensure their participation. The youth are involved in development programmes as adults in general and there are special schemes like the National Service Scheme (NSS) in India wherein the students of colleges and universities, volunteer and contribute their labour in forming approach roads, digging irrigation canals, and other kinds of manual work beneficial to rural communities.

Youth development or involvement of the youth in development forms a department in the Ministry of Education, Human Resources Development in some countries (e.g., India) or a separate ministry as in the case of Bangladesh. We may focus on twin objectives in this chapter-developing the youth and the youth developing the family and the community which may be called "Family-based Integrated Youth Development".

FAMILY-BASED INTEGRATED YOUTH DEVELOPMENT

Developing the youth is of prime importance in all societies. Ministries of Youth Development and in some cases the Departments of Youth Development have been attempting the development of youth in creative, constructive and productive activities. But it has been realized that by focusing on youth alone, the desired kind of development changes among the youth are not encouraging and commensurate with the efforts made. It is found necessary that youth development should be an integral part of family and community development. At least in the initial stages, there is a need for an intensive coordinated approach and effort in developing the youth and their families simultaneously- the youth contributing to the parents and the family and the parents and the larger community guiding, helping and giving moral and socio-economic support to the youth and involving them in constructive and productive activities.

Such a desirable youth-family development could be achieved only through a systematic approach which may be termed as "Family-based Integrated Youth Development".

Objectives

The main objective of family-based integrated youth development is to take each family as a unit of development, study its material and human resources and help the members in the family in their developmental pursuits and assist them in utilizing their physical, material and human resources for increased productive activities. In other words, in the programme, we look at each family, take stock of what its resources are, how the resources are utilized today, how best they could be utilized, the kind of support they need, develop initiative and motivation among the youth and the adults in the family in order that they mobilize their own resources. In addition, technical and managerial guidance and marginal monetary assistance is extended to them so that each family attempts a maximum level of resource utilization, physical as well as human.

Programme Content

In the proposed scheme, the activities will comprise moral, spiritual, social and economic programmes for the youth for their own progress and for the betterment of their families and their communities. The on-going programmes in the Ministry or Department of Youth Development will be carried out intensively involving each family as a unit of development.

Basically the scheme will comprise social and economic components. The emphasis in the scheme is maximal utilization of the internal resources of the family and the community, mobilizing the youth as instruments of change.

The programme may comprise:

1. Collection and processing of family-community data.
2. Identification of small enterprises, self-employment avenues which may be taken up by the youth ad their families.
3. Preparation of feasibility studies on small enterprises.
4. Training of the youth to take to small entrepreneurial activities.
5. Organizing the youth into viable associations.
6. Involvement of the youth in community development activities.

Coverage of the Pilot Scheme

In view of the clinical-family community-intensive integrated youth development, initially as a pilot measure two units each comprising 5-8 villages may be taken up under the pilot scheme. Preferably one pilot project may be selected in a better off area and another in a backward region. The two pilot project schemes will lend themselves for comparison and future replication of the programme. The criteria for selecting the pilot project areas may comprise:

(a) The cluster of villages or the blocks/unions selected for the pilot project are neither too close to an urban center nor too isolated.

(b) The units selected currently carry on satisfactory youth development activities and have the response and immediate potential for intensive development; and

(c) The units enjoy minimum transport and communication facilities and some infrastructure for small enterprise development.

Institutional Arrangements

The existing organizational set-up of the Ministry or Department of Youth Development at the district level may be utilized for planning and implementing the programme in the pilot area with a small staff to keep in touch with and monitor the youth and a small staff to keep in touch with and monitor the youth and family development activities. A small information-monitoring center in each village of the pilot area may be established which will have in its office the family resource and development cards pertaining to all the families in the communities. In addition to the youth development agency, the other promotional agencies may be involved in planning and implementing the activities. The data and information system will be maintained at the pilot project headquarters concerning all the villages in the area. It can be envisaged that each family will have a "Family-Resource and Development Card". This card will contain basic data about the family; its members, their age, educational attainment, how they are occupied, means of livelihood, how their present assets are utilized, their income and expenditure, their needs, the way they would like to improve their conditions and potential and scope for further development with external guidance and assistance. The data from the family cards will be aggregated both at the community level and pilot project level. The data could be classified in different ways both at the village and the project levels for purposes of planning and implementation of programme.

Organizational Setup

The overall functioning and administration of the pilot project will be under a "pilot project committee" comprising elected or nominated youth representatives from each village in the pilot project area. There may be one or two representatives from each village and wherever there is response women also may serve on the committee. The committee will elect a chairman from amongst themselves to head the committee.

The committee will be entrusted with powers to decide, formulate, implement and monitor all activities under the"Family-based Integrated Youth Development". The committee will be assisted by an executive wing consisting of an executive officer and field and secretarial staff. The executive officer may be the Assistant Director of Department of Youth Development or any officer with a different title but with a similar function. He will guide and assist the committee in its deliberations and decision-making. It is envisaged that the pilot project committee and the executive wing are complementary to each other and they are to work in unison.

Staff of the Pilot Project

1. *Project Executive Officer:* He will be in overall charge of the project.
2. *Rural Social Analyst:* A qualified person in social sciences with experience in social surveys and human resource development. He will be responsible in assisting data collection, processing of data etc.
3. *Field Investigators (two):* They will assist the Rural Social Analyst and most importantly the youth volunteer investigators who will collect data pertaining to families and the community.

4. *A Secretarial Assistant*: A steno-typist-cum-cashier.
5. *An Office Attendant*.

It is envisaged that the secretarial and transport assistance will be provided by the Department of Youth Development.

Approach to the Implementation of Pilot Project

To begin with, detailed data as mentioned above, in respect of each family will be collected by the youth in the community as volunteers with the assistance of the project officials. The *Family resource and Development Card* will be so designed that it will contain basic data about the family and also will have provision to record subsequent development activities etc. A copy of this *Family Resource and Development Card* as mentioned earlier will be with each family and one at the village center and another at the project headquarters. At any given time it is possible for the family, community and project to know the present position and what is happening and what should be done at three levels; family, community and project. A monitoring system of to and from informal dissemination will be developed, sometimes using computer facilities where necessary. The *Family Resource and Development Card* will serve as a reminder and as a progress card of the youth and family developmental activities. It involves initial information gathering and recording of the data and coding the families, the activities and the communities in the project area. In the monitoring system, there will be regular and periodical feed-back and evaluation in respect of each family and community. In the total process of planning, implementing and evaluating the activities, the youth will be the principal participants.

Time Frame

The first cycle of the two pilot projects will have a two-year period. During this period the basic data of the families and the community will be prepared and aggregated at the community and project levels. Programmes of action will be formulated. Youth organization and other institutional arrangements will be made. Programmes of immediate and long-range activities will be planned and scheduled for implementation.

The pilot scheme suggested above could be extended to all the rural areas depending on the success gained in the pilot schemes and with improvements too. The youth involved in the programme could be those educated, high school dropouts looking for employment or self-employment and those who are still doing their studies in secondary schools and colleges. The objective is to benefit the youth and at the same time make them active participants in rural development.

CHAPTER 12

Janmabhoomi in Andhra Pradesh – A Clinical Approach to Multi-sectoral and Segmental Development

Janmabhoomi is a movement imbued with principles of democracy, self-reliance and concerted coordinated community action for all round development in rural and urban areas. The programme carries with it an emotional and patriotic tone. It aims and stands for comprehensive community development, a massive people's planned movement with the stimulus provided by the Government. It works towards realizing the VISION-2020. It is not a one-time operation and one sector development but it is envisioned as a continuous and periodic collective activity focusing on one sector at a time.

During the past five decades there have been several programmes under the generic name of rural development. Though these programmes covered, of course, several development sectors and segments of population and despite efforts made, the results have not been encouraging. It was not only due to limited funds, lack of detailed planning and organization, but in a way the official machinery both at the planning, administrative and delivery level was not streamlined. The people also at the receiving end of the dividends of development were not properly mobilized in order to secure their participation in planning and carrying out development activities as partners with the administrative machinery. Based on the lessons learnt from the previous experience, the Government of Andhra Pradesh has come up with an innovative idea of sectoral and segmental development in a focused and concentrated way. They have christened the programme as Janmabhoomi. The first round was initiated on the 1st of January, 1997. In the beginning there were four rounds in a year, later on it was reduced to three and now it is two rounds per annum in January and July lasting for ten days. We may briefly go through the philosophy and imperatives of Janmabhoomi and the achievements of the programme.

Prior to our spelling out the Imperatives of Janmabhoomi, it is relevant here to briefly look into the historic impetus behind Janmabhoomi.

Our freedom struggle is an epic saga of unparalleled martyrdom and a relentless battle of truth and non-violence fought under the leadership of the Father of the Nation, Mahatma Gandhi. A non-violent struggle aimed at political freedom, reinforced by tireless effort at social reform, represented a defining moment in the annals of world history. The Vision of an independent India, a strong committed leadership, and the fusion of the masses were the unique characteristics of India's freedom movement. Our struggle for freedom was a true example of mass mobilization cutting across the barriers of class, community, caste, creed, or occupation.

The mass mobilization of the people in the freedom movement constituted only the first phase of democratic development. The founding fathers envisioned that democratic development has to bridge the gap between political equality and economic equality with social justice as mandated by the constitution.

What have we achieved?

While celebrating the Golden Jubilee of our Independence, we cannot but bow with gratitude and reverence to all those who fought selflessly and valiantly for our freedom. The leaders of the pre-independence era believed that political freedom would herald economic and social emancipation. To what extent have we achieved these aims? Do we stand up to their expectations?

We can justifiably feel proud of having preserved the democratic framework, as also the unity and integrity of the country despite several threats. We have tripled our agricultural production which has made us self-sufficient in food despite the pressures of growing population. Industrial production has grown manifold. We have built up a vast reserve of scientific, technological and managerial skills. After Independence, we undertook planned economic development through the instrument of five-year plans to fulfil the needs and aspirations of the people. Many welfare schemes were introduced to improve the living conditions of the people. When the 'trickle down' effect of the overall growth of the economy did not benefit the disadvantaged, we made special efforts, in recent years, to formulate programmes specifically directed at them.

But, when we evaluate our achievements against our expectations, we realize, to our dismay, that despite notable successes in certain sectors we are still extremely backward in several areas like literacy, health, employment-generation, etc. Even in sectors where we have achieved a measure of success, the fruits of success have been uneven and have not been distributed equitably. There is a wide gap between the aspirations of the people, particularly the poorest of the poor, and the achievements made so far.

The level of human development is an important indicator of the development of a Society. At the global level, the Human Development of the UNDP for the year 1996 ranks India as 138th out of 174 countries and classifies India as a country with "Low Human Development". This contrasts sharply with the remarkable progress made by and the enviable ranking of countries such as Japan (rank 7), South Korea (rank 32) and Malaysia (rank 61).

Countries that attained independence around the same time as we did have, overtaken us in improving the living standards of their peoples. For example,

- Japan, which was reduced to shambles in the Second World War, has emerged as a premier world economic power by dint of hard work, discipline and by the innovative adoption of technologies. Through a strong sense of loyalty, devotion to the nation and a keen urge to excel, the Japanese have succeeded in making their country an economic dynamo and a byword for quality and 'values' in an age of technology.

- Malaysia, which is also an agro-based economy like ours and which became independent ten years after us, has become an industrial giant in a span of 40 years mainly due to the team spirit of its people and a strong and visionary leadership.
- South Korea, which was backward and underdeveloped until the sixties, has been able to attain sustained economic growth through rapid strides in industry and exports. This was achieved through an innovative mass mobilization strategy that focused on internationalization of the core values of diligence, self-help and cooperation among the people and provision of intensive training.
- China, despite its large population, is poised to emerge as the economic giant of the 21st century, thanks to the spirit of hard work of its people and also the commitment of the Chinese Diaspora across the world.
- Israel, which is a small country, has successfully illustrated how innovative approaches and appropriate technology can contribute to progress even in the face of several natural and man-made adversities.

Within India, the position of Andhra Pradesh is unfortunately below the national average in several key development indicators such as per-capita income, literacy and health status. The brunt of poverty and adversity is borne by our women and children and their condition continues to be a cause of serious concern for all of us. Environmental degradation has been posing a serious threat to sustainable development. Abysmal sanitation in the villages and towns is posing a serious threat to health.

This scenario in the human and physical development front is particularly distressing given that the State is endowed with rich natural and human resources. Our people, who have gone abroad, have achieved commendable success in their respective fields. However, here on native soil we have been unable to provide an environment whereby our people reach their full physical and intellectual potential.

What have we learnt?

What are the causes of this distressing scenario? Government institutions and local bodies could not succeed to the extent expected. The common man perceives the government as inaccessible. We have not succeeded in effectively harnessing the latent creativity of the people in formulating and implementing schemes for their own development. Instead of becoming 'partners in development', the people, particularly the poor, have become 'passive beneficiaries'. As the government acquired the role of 'doer' and 'direct provider', its paternalistic approach has driven people further towards dependency on government, even for small and sundry interventions. Lack of information about government programmes and procedures has made people dependent on intermediaries to intercede on their behalf in the Government.

Even though a few government programmes have specifically sought to enlist people's participation, the effort got diluted in practice. The excessive centralization in planning and decision-making has dampened the initiative of the people. Access of people to government has been neither direct nor adequate. Government programmes and activities have remained largely ineffective in fostering the naturally positive elements of collective good, teamwork, honesty, dedication and hard work.

Values and principles, which once formed the core of the Indian ethos and which were so forcefully reflected in our freedom movement have got deeply eroded. The malaise we find ourselves in, today, is a result of this loss of values.

What should we do now?

The individual well-being of each one of us lies in restoring the health of the society and in promoting a healing process. No individual or group can prosper in the long run, at the expense of the society. As in the freedom struggle, each citizen is required to join hands with fellow citizens in finding a lasting solution to this crisis. The enemy is within. The fight should be directed at eradicating our internal enemies such as lethargy, despair, dishonesty, corruption, inequality, and moral degradation. We need wage another freedom struggle. This is the time to liberate our people from morass and despair, restore the lost values and build an egalitarian society based on the principles of equity and sustainability.

Towards a people's movement

The struggle to be waged today by each one of us, individually and also collectively, is an important and perhaps more difficult one than the freedom struggle. Janmabhoomi is a people's movement for reconstruction and revitalization of the society. It is aimed at helping each one of us internalize the time-tested values of sacrifice, hard work, diligence, discipline, honesty, self-respect and the quest for excellence. Through this movement, every institution internalizes the guiding principles of participation, equity and equality, transparency and accountability, organizational excellence and sustainability. These principles will guide the policies, programmes and the day-to-day activities of all institutions.

Janmabhoomi - Values

The effort to be made by each one of us, individually and collectively, should be for restoration of these timeless values and for internalization of these values by each of one of us. Rejuvenating these core values is the pre-requisite for succeeding in our quest for excellence. Let us see how these values assume critical importance in our Janmabhoomi philosophy.

- ***Spirit of Sacrifice***

The spirit of sacrifice, which was the dominant quality that spurred the people of our country during the freedom struggle, needs to be revived. The Gandhian thought of simple living and high thinking will help every individual to lead a happy life devoid of greed and also enthuse him to contribute to the welfare of his fellow beings. The idea of living for others and for a cause, by sacrificing the 'self' should be the guiding principle. It is through the spirit of sacrifice that team spirit is nurtured and teamwork built up.

- ***Diligence***

Everybody should work hard. Anything is possible through hard work, dedication, determination and consistent effort. Consistent effort leads to success and sustainable development. Diligence coupled with dedication plays an instrumental role in achieving one's goals and ideals in life.

• ***Honesty***

Honesty and integrity are the two cardinal principles of life. Honesty means no contradictions or discrepancies in thought, word or deed. To be honest to one's self and to the purpose of a task earns trust and inspires faith in others. Honesty is the basis for cooperation between individuals and institutions. It is also the basis for transparency.

• ***Self-help***

The spirit of self-help enables one to solve one's own problems with one's own efforts. Solving problems with one's own efforts imbues one with a sense of pride and achievement. It also gives dignity of life.

• ***Self-respect***

To know one's own worth and to honour the worth of others is the true meaning of self-respect. Self-respect and belief in one's own ability are essential for achieving one's goals. Self-respect also means respect for honest labour. Physical or manual labour should be looked upon with respect..

• ***Quest for excellence***

Quest for excellence should be the motto of every individual in his or her respective filed of activity. Only then will the society advance. One should never be satisfied with one's current standards of achievement but constantly strive for perfection. There should be pride in doing a job well. A scientific outlook can make a significant contribution towards our pursuit of excellence. Scientific progress is a harbinger of change in the modern world. Imbibing scientific temper promotes excellence.

• ***Sense of fulfillment***

One can attain a sense of fulfillment through achieving something useful. A person with a sense of fulfillment is at peace with himself. Acquisition of wealth or achievements on the material plane does not necessarily lead to happiness. One should therefore aspire for spiritual fulfillment.

Janmabhoomi – Principles

In addition to rejuvenating values, Janmabhoomi seeks to radically reorient the way we do things. Such a shift is essential not only to accelerate the pace of development but also to sustain the same through equitable distribution of benefits. Towards this end each one of our institutions should be restructured and realigned with the core principles of Janmabhoomi, namely, people's participation, equity & equality, transparency & accountability, innovation and sustainability. The institutions will then be able to promote Janmabhoomi values among every citizen in the Society. These basic principles have the potential to enrich the life of every citizen irrespective of gender, age, profession, status, caste, creed, community or location. Let us see how.

Operationalisation of Janmabhoomi

The conduct of Prajala Vaddaku Paalana, Sramadanam and Janmabhoomi has positively reaffirmed the power of these time tested values and basic principles. Armed with exemplary grit, determination and commitment, our people have demonstrated the immense potential of Janmabhoomi.

Janmabhoomi essentially means a people centred participatory development process. The institutional framework for Janmabhoomi should therefore facilitate such a process wherein the Government, the democratic institutions of the people, the grassroots people's institutions, the facilitating agencies (including NGOs, academic institutions, etc.) and the people themselves can participate as equal partners. All these Institutions would be imbued with the core principles of Janmabhoomi to enable them to carry out their tasks effectively.

We are conscious that a movement of this magnitude would have wide ramifications for all of us. Accordingly we should gear ourselves through the following interventions:

- Environment building
- Promotion of grassroots people's institutions
- Strengthening local bodies
- Training and orientation
- Administrative reforms

- **Environment building**

A massive environment building will be one of the activities for sensitization and for inculcating the values and principles of Janmabhoomi. The philosophy of Janmabhoomi would be widely disseminated, through all the institutions – academic, government institutions, youth associations, women's organizations, voluntary organizations, grassroots people's institution, local bodies, industrial establishments, etc. Eminent citizens, freedom fighters, professionals and experts in various fields will be requested to take an active part and lend their time and effort in this process. Voluntary Organizations will play an active role and their services will be fully utilized, particularly in training the grassroots people's institutions and community volunteers. The media, industrial establishments – private and public, financial institutions, research bodies will be motivated to define a clear role for themselves and participate in the Janmabhoomi processes.

- **Promotion of grassroots people's institutions**

Janmabhoomi will induce, develop and nurture social mobilization of people, particularly the poor, organizing the community around specific interests such as women thrift and credit groups, youth groups (CMEY), Vana Samrakshana Samithis, water users associations, watershed development committees, village education committees, etc. This will be achieved through sensitization, awareness building, organizing grassroots people's institutions (GPIs), organizing women into thrift and credit groups (self help groups), building up the capability of the leaders of these people's institutions and promoting the consolidation of the groups on a sustained basis. Janmabhoomi will provide for capacity building of these groups to enable them to access and manage the resources, to articulate their requirements in the Gram Sabha, to sensitize them on issues affecting the people and to train them to take up participatory planning. Janmabhoomi will build up people's skills through intensive training. Janmabhoomi will foster leadership at the grassroots level and the grassroots people's institutions shall act as the nurseries for the growth of leadership.

Janmabhoomi will develop appropriate support structures for achieving social mobilization and capacity building. The support structures are intended to provide necessary training and technical guidance, exposure, as well as to develop suitable literature for different sectors. There will be a system of regular feedback and discussions in the workshops where the best experiences within and outside our State would be considered for adoption. At the State level, appropriate structures will be established for overseeing this as well as to look after the training needs including development of literature.

- **Strengthening local bodies**

Janmabhoomi will strengthen local bodies through a policy of decentralization and develop a framework for a larger role for the local bodies. The guiding principle will be that what can be done at the grassroots level would be done only at that level. For this, each department will analyze and draw up a list of activities in each sector that can be decentralized, including the powers necessary at appropriate levels for effective decentralized decision-making. Necessary financial devolution will also be made. At the same time, full accountability to people will be ensured. Janmabhoomi will build up the mechanism of an active and vibrant Gram Sabha, which will not only decide on various issues but also monitor development programmes. Janmabhoomi will also develop a system by which information and knowledge are constantly made available to people.

Janmabhoomi will enable participatory planning at the grassroots level. Towards this end, individuals, members of the local bodies, representatives of the grassroots people's institutions will be sensitized about the significance and modalities of participatory planning. The Gram Panchayat would be the unit for planning in those sectors where it can act. For other sectors, the Mandal or the District will be the unit for planning. Suitable units will be identified in the urban sector. Training would be provided to enable the grassroots level institutions to take up planning and preparation of action plans. These will be implemented by the people and monitored constantly by the Gram Sabha, which would also take up evaluation of the programmes at their level.

- **Training and orientation**

Training shall be organized for government functionaries, elected representatives, voluntary organizations, representatives of grassroots people's institutions, community volunteers and all those involved in the implementation of Janmabhoomi at various levels. Expert groups constituted at various levels shall prepare training modules. The existing training infrastructure available shall be utilized for providing training. Similar training programmes shall be organized at the village level in schools and colleges.

Academic institutions will participate in the Janmabhoomi movement, as part of socially useful and relevant work experience. It is proposed to integrate the Janmabhoomi experience into the academic programme by allotting a specific number of hours for this purpose. The Janmabhoomi philosophy will be incorporated in the curriculum. The daily Assembly time in schools and colleges will be utilized for inculcating the values of Janmabhoomi. Specialized training for staff and students will also be given.

- **Administrative reforms**

In contrast to its current role of a 'provider' and 'doer', the Government's role would be transformed into that of a 'facilitator' and enabler of self-governance. Towards that goal of a transparent and people friendly Government, administration would be simplified and demystified through a comprehensive set of reforms. This would include a thorough reorientation of the government functionaries to enable them to adopt their redefined roles and make the system service oriented. Janmabhoomi will institutionalize the process of the governmental actions being transparent and the government machinery being accountable to the people. All activities of public bodies shall be subjected to Social Audit. Each Department shall have a Citizen's Charter presenting the standards of services to be provided to the citizens.

Emphasis will be laid on building awareness among the people. Janmabhoomi will also develop a process by which information and knowledge are constantly made available to the people. Janmabhoomi will seek to provide the people with all the relevant information through appropriate channels.

The task ahead....

Janmabhoomi is a people-centred development process aimed at establishing an ideal society, which embodies and cherishes the principles of people's participation, equality, transparency and accountability leading to sustained economic development and excellence in all walks of life. The goal is an enhanced quality of life for every man, woman and child in the State.

As the children of this beloved land, 'Janmabhoomi', it is our privilege to be proud of our heritage. At the same time, it is our responsibility to contribute our might to enhance the glory of this land. Janmabhoomi is our collective effort for achieving and sustaining such a glory.

Janmabhoomi - Rural Development

Janmabhoomi as conceived and introduced by the Hon'ble Chief Minister Nara Chandra Babu Naidu, though primarily relates to Shramadan (Gift of Labour) on the part of the people, it is to be reckoned as significant movement with economic, social, cultural and psychological ingredients educating, appealing, inviting and encouraging people to plan, organize and develop in order to accomplish community needs and infrastructure on their own. It is not simply educating one individual but it is a very effective education to the entire community which is to become a tradition and value system of the community for its development. Janmabhoomi as a movement goes with emotional tone instilling activity and pride on the part of the members of the community. In the course of the last five years it has drawn the attention not only of the people but the entire administration, and the personnel at different levels. The Janmabhoomi as a people's movement initiated and augmented by the Government is expected to be a continuous periodic movement towards development. The expectation is that this movement should become a part of the socio-cultural value system to be observed and carried on in action for all-round development in the rural and urban communities. It is envisaged that it should be something sacred as in the case of certain traditional and religious observances.

It is interesting to see that the concept of Janmabhoomi is akin to 'SAEMAUL UNDONG' a South Korean model of community development. It may be relevant here to briefly look into SAEMAUL UNDONG as it was adopted by the South Korean Government. This has been a nation-wide development movement under the slogan of diligence, cooperation and self-help. The first nation-wide community development programme in Korea was launched in the late 1950s after the Korean War another trial was made in 1960s under the name of National Reconstruction. But these two attempts were not much of success and so in 1970s SAEMAUL UNDONG succeeded in achieving the people's voluntary participation and active public support. The community development projects in Korea were carried out by community people themselves who were led by elected SAEMAUL leaders. Integrated planning (Bottom-up and Top-down mixed) were made democratically. Adequate administrative and financial support and supervision were made with the priority of hardworking communities.

Generally speaking, integrated community development projects are designed to improve the standard of living and social welfare of people living in communities through effective cooperative utilization of all available physical and human resources. Every community has a different historical, social and economic background, which must be taken for project planning and implementation. The community development in the name of SAEMAUL UNDONG can be largely divided into three categories: spiritual reform, social development and economic development. SAEMAUL UNDONG based its action on the following principles: Firstly, the movement relied on integrated participation of the whole nation. Everyone in the community can take part in its development plans and programmes with common agreement by the community members. Secondly, the SAEMAUL spirit of diligence (self-help) and cooperation has to reflect people's aspirations and visible in the everyday life. Thirdly, all the activities must be undertaken in the interest and for the benefit of the community. The members of the community should be involved directly or indirectly in the increase of production and income. The Korean model of community development though emphasizes on community action it is always to be encouraged and supported by the State.

As one could see, in the case of Janmabhoomi, it is being initiated by the State Government, mobilizing all the administrative resources and soliciting, motivating and encouraging the people to participate in the chosen programme. As mentioned earlier, the communities though they are interested in their development, may not maintain the same momentum of spirit and seriousness in their efforts to meet their needs. A constant and a periodic awakening of the community is essential to carry on self-help community development. More often, a community may not realize its own resources, the potential it has and the way in which the potential could be utilized for its development. There is need for some body like the State authority to remind the people what they could do for themselves with partial assistance from the government. In this kind of development, the people play a major role and the state a supportive role. It should become an established tradition of continuous improvement in the quality of life in rural and urban communities. The Janmabhoomi as a popular and pragmatic movement is committed to generate enthusiasm and action on the part of the community for its overall and comprehensive development towards a richer life.

A BRIEF REVIEW OF JANMABHOOMI PROGRAMMES

The Janmabhoomi Programme as a people's movement for development is highly imaginative in motivating and stimulating action on the part of the people towards bettering their way of life. And thus for the following have been the focal areas:-

1. Micro Level Planning

2. Health and Sanitation
3. Education
4. Community Organization
5. Artisan Development
6. Empowerment of women
7. Decentralization of Administration
8. Development of Local Bodies
9. Constitution of People's Functional Associations
10. The environmental protection
11. Upgrading of Artisans
12. Focus on aged and disabled and
13. The focus on Farm Development, in terms of increased production and profitable marketing of produce within and outside the country

It is needless to say that all the programmes initiated thus far under Janmabhoomi are quite relevant for the overall development of rural communities. In one sense, some of them are initial motivating activities. Some try to meet solve certain local problems and local needs. Some needs are of a perennial nature. In a larger sense, the major objective of Janmabhoomi as a People's Movement is to build self-reliant, self-generating, progressive little dynamic, democratic communities.

In brief, the Janmabhoomi movement has created awareness among the people, it drew their attention to the basic minimum needs of life. And in a sense, made them aware of the physical, natural, material and human resources they are endowed with. It also made them feel their own potential, what they could do and accomplish if they want to. The periodic programmes to a considerable extent, tapped new human resources, talents of the leadership and initiative among the various age groups in the villages and organized several self-help associations to manage certain sectoral and segmental needs of the rural community. These are newly organized social, operational, functional sub-systems within the rural community. The credit goes to Janmabhoomi Programmes in motivating, mobilizing and organizing these individuals both men and women. The programmes have created social support systems, and social infrastructure to initiate and manage certain interests of the community. We may mention here the rejuvenation of the Grama Sabha by the Janmabhoomi movement. Though it has been the statutory, people's association at the community level, in many cases, the Grama Sabha has been dormant and non-functional. The Janmabhoomi movement through its stipulated programmes activated and regenerated the periodic assembly of the Grama Sabha. The Janmabhoomi programmes educated the people and drew their attention to the Grama Sabha, how it is the statutory fundamental forum of the community wherein the development ideas, needs, issues and problems could be discussed and to forward the needs and plans of action to the Grama Panchayat which may be described as the executive wing of the Grama Sabha. Further, interestingly and very importantly, Janmabhoomi drew the attention of the community and all wings of administration at the state, district and mandal level to the primacy of women welfare. It does not mean women's development did not figure in the earlier movements but Janmabhoomi specifically devoted to what is called Mahila Janmabhoomi and also focused attention on the minorities and of course on the larger segment of the society the farmers. Creation of awareness and reinforcement through motivation and practical programmes of action are necessary and this has appreciably manifested in the Mahila Janmabhoomi.

The officials operating at the village level promoting developmental activities may acquaint themselves with the indigenous knowledge system which has been developed over a period of time for meeting local needs and solving local problems. The indigenous knowledge system comprises the ways, the means, the methods and the techniques which the rural people have been using for decades in the past. At the operational level, one may make use of the indigenous knowledge system also along with new ways of development. Sometimes, in our enthusiasm we introduce new methods and technologies, ignoring the norms and the mechanisms, people have developed in solving their political, economical and social issues. By now, 14 rounds of Janmabhoomi programmes have been carried out and it has been recently decided by the Government that hereafter there will be 3 rounds, one devoted to Farmers, and the second one to Women, and the third one to the Minorities.

We may briefly focus on the 14th Janmabhoomi aptly called Rythu Janmabhoomi (Farmer's Janmabhoomi) 2-8, January, 2001, since the farmers and agriculture are the backbone of India or any other country.

The commitment, dedication and hard-work of the farmer who toils year-round in the field often does not get appropriately rewarded in the market. Farmers are not adequately compensated, and they do not get competitive prices for their produce.

Therefore, the government of Andhra Pradesh has stepped forward to strengthen the agricultural sector and empower farmers by helping them fetch the highest possible prices for their produce; and to also provide solutions to all their problems.

Since the farmer is the mainstay of progress of the State, the government has dedicated this Janmabhoomi to them.

To alleviate the hardships faced by the farmers during the summer season, the government has launched **Neeru-Meeru** Programme. Despite cyclones and other natural calamities which befell Andhra Pradesh last year, it is creditable that the State nonetheless recorded an increase in agricultural production as a result of the previous Janmabhoomi's agriculture development programmes.

The government understands the needs, limitations, trials, and tribulations on the part of the farmers and the Government is with the farmers.

Rythu Janmabhoomi targeted on the following activities:

- Improving the water levels of canals and ponds,
- The use of dry crops during the Rabi Season
- Keeping the shortage of electricity in mind
- Timely decisions to be taken in all related matters
- Creating awareness about the harmful effects of using spurious pesticides.

The farmer is the base and the foundation, there will be no State, no progress, no promise for a better future without the farmer.

We may just mention here the priority issues that have been covered thus far during the past Janmabhoomi Programmes:

- Neeru-Meeru
- Veterinary Camps
- Distribution of Revolving Fund to DWCRA Groups
- Eradication of Superstitions
- Health Camps – Special emphasis on Prevention of AIDS, Pulse Polio
- Awareness about sanitation
- Distribution of Pensions
- Akshara Sankranthi
- Distribution of Gas Connections

GRAMA SABHAS

- Grievance redressal
- Problem solving

The 13th round of Janmabhoomi programme focused on distribution of 4 lakh LPG connections under 'Deepam' Scheme, granting of revolving funds/matching grants to thrift groups, pension distribution to various groups like Old age, Widow, Landless, agriculture labour etc; distribution of smokeless Chulhas, formation of new thrift groups, construction of 'DWCRA' Bhavans, distribution of Bank Loans to 'DWCRA' groups, free health camps, enrolment of girl children in schools, campaign for equal wages for equal work etc., was held from 1st August to 7th August, 2000, all over the State.

In the 14th round of Janmabhoomi, 886 proposals for works at an estimated cost of Rs 15.47 crores were sanctioned under 50:50 pattern. The Government share for these works comes to Rs 7.73 crores and an amount of Rs. 2.19 crores has been released by the Government so far. Out of 886 works sanctioned, 807 works have already been grounded.

Evaluation of the Gram Panchayat / Ward / Mandal / Municipality is done to introduce a system of incentive for the local bodies linked to their performance. The Nodal Team is also being evaluated. Achievement during last financial year will be the basis for evaluation.

An elaborate analysis is made to identify the pending Grievances department-wise. The mandal register is updated and computerization of the grievances is done at the mandal/ municipality level.

Feedback workshops were organized from 15th to 20th June 2001 at the Mandal level for village / mandal officials and at the district level for Nodal Officers, Divisional Resource Persons and District Level Officials to identify the problem areas of the last round of Janmabhoomi for improvements in the future.

The fifteenth round of Janmabhoomi was conducted for ten days, for the first time in the history of Janmabhoomi. Two gram Sabhas were conducted per day. 1263 Nodal Teams were constituted to conduct 26172 Gram/Ward sabhas. 25787 Gram / Ward sabhas were actually held during this round of Janmabhoomi. Only 385 (1.47%) Gram / Ward sabhas could not be held due to various reasons like drinking water problem, electricity problem, non-redressal of pending grievances and extremist activities. The number of boycotts in this round is the least in the last five years.

ACTIVITIES THAT HAVE BEEN COVERED UP TO THE SIXTEENTH ROUND UNDER JANMABHOOMI PROGRAMMES

Round	Period	Theme
First Round	1-8 January, '97	Janmabhoomi Concept and Micro Level Planning.
Second Round	1-7 May, '97	Constitution of HLCs/WLCs, Community Infrastructure Development Works.
Third Round	1-7 August, '97	Janmabhoomi Janachaitanyam – Immunization and Health Camps
Fourth Round	1-7 October, '97	Clean Village/Town Concept. Free Veterinary Camps, Campaign on Save Energy and Small Savings
Fifth Round	1-7 January, '98	Participation of Students and Lecturers along with the Habitation/Ward Level Committees and the people in activities promoting Clean Village/Ward concept and creation of Community assets.
Sixth Round	1-7 May, '98	Free Health Camps with focus on TB and Blindness control. Works Programmes through Self-Help Groups.
Seventh Round	1-7 August, '98	"Cheyutha" for Disabled. Pollution Control in Urban Areas.
Eighth Round	3-9 October, '98	Free Health Camps with focus on AIDS, TB, Eye Care, Dental Care and Reproductive health care.
Ninth Round	2-8 January, '99	Micro Level Planning Free Health Camps with focus on curative and preventive aspects of AIDS, TB, Eye Care, Dental Care and Reproductive health care.
Tenth Round	1-7 May, '99	Mahila Janmabhoomi
Eleventh Round	3-11 Jan., 2000	Micro Level Planning & Evaluation of Gram Panchayats/ Wards and Nodal Officers.
Twelfth Round	1-7 May, 2000	Neeru – Meeru – Focus on Health Drought and Water Conservation.
Thirteenth Round	1-7 August, 2000	Mahila Janmabhoomi
Fourteenth Round	2-8 January, 2001	Rythu Janmabhoomi
Fifteenth Round	1-10 June, 2001	Mahila and Sishu Janmabhoomi
Sixteenth Round	2-11 Jan, 2002	Welfare of the Weaker Sections

JANMABHOOMI-CUMULATIVE ACHIEVEMENTS FOR THIRTEEN ROUNDS

(FROM JAN 1997 TO AUG 2000)		
1.	Habitations And Wards Covered (in every round)	58,753
2.	No. of Teams Constituted	1,347
3.	A).No. of Grama Sabhas Held In Each Round	53,625
	B).No. of Grama Sabhas Held In Twelfth Round	25,762
4.	PRIMARY EDUCATION	
	Additional enrolment in Primary Schools during 1997-98	6.31 lakh
	No. of children identified for enrolment in 1998-99	7.90 lakh
	Additional enrolment in Primary Schools during 1998-99	5.71 lakh
5.	PRIMARY HEALTH AND FAMILY WELFARE	
	No. of eligible couples motivated for Family Planning Operations	9.84 lakh
	No. of Free Health Camps organized	3.16 lakh
	Patients Treated	147.49 lakh
	Malaria treated	43,953
	AIDS awareness Camps conducted	2.07 lakh
	Dental Camps organized	11,876
	School Children Treated in Dental camps	3.64 lakh
	Women Medical camps conducted in Mahila Janmabhoomi	10,062
	Women examined under reproductive health care	7.12 lakh
	Children Immunized	8.11 lakh
	No. of TB patients identified for treatment	69,240
	No. of persons identified with eye problems	2.25 lakh
	No. of operations done	1,70,541
	• Conventional	1,00,491
	• IOL	70,050
	No. of persons with cataract	4,44,542
	Free Spectacles distributed for refractive errors	83,201

(contd.)

	Glaucoma cases identified	1,644
	Glaucoma cases operated	77
	No. of cases identified for GE treatment	2,430
6.	ENVIRONMENTAL CONSERVATION	
	Trees planted	1087.06 lakh
	Individual Sanitary latrines sanctioned	19.50 lakh
	Individual Sanitary Latrines completed	12.27 lakh
	Repairs to Soak-pits and Platforms of drinking water sources	62,130
	Cleaning and Chlorination of drinking water sources (no. per round)	89,390
	Adoption of Smokeless chulhas	1.76 lakh
	Special sanitation driver under taken in public institutions (no. per round)	40,948
	Pollution check-upNo. of vehicles	25.16 lakh
	P.V.C. Certificates issued	15.97 lakh
7.	REDRESSAL OF FELT NEEDS (1st – 12th rounds)	
	INDIVIDUAL FAMILY NEEDS (Nos.)	
	Received	42.43 lakh
	Solved	16.18 lakh
	Ineligible	24.52 lakh
	Balance	1.73 lakh
	NON-FINANCIAL COMMUNITY NEEDS (Nos.)	
	Received	1.78 lakh
	Solved	1.14 lakh
	Ineligible	0.57 lakh
	Balance	0.01 lakh
8.	**COMMUNITY WORKS**	(Rs. in crores)
	Received in Grama Sabhas - 1,22,572	1937.47
	Grounded - 1,18,194	814.53
	Completed - 1.01,539	1627.85
	Government share required for works grounded	1337.34

	Funds released (including those released in April, 2000)	1117.03
	Expenditure	1091.12
9.	FREE VETERINARY CAMPS (1st – 12th rounds)	
	No. organized	3.45 lakh
	Animals treated	1294.13 lakh
	Sheep Dewormed (Jan '99 round)	127.16 lakh
	Sheep Dewormed (Jan '2000 round)	90.89 lakh
	Cattle vaccinated against Foot & Mouth Disease (Jan'99 round)	15.68 lakh
	Calf Dewormed (May '99 round)	19.69 lakh
	Farmers assisted in 12th round	15.68 lakh
10.	DISABLED WELFARE (Distributed upto May 2000)	
	Marriage Incentives issued	6,173
	Scholarships	99,374
	Pre-Matric	34,248
	Post-Matric	17,558
	Aids/Appliances distributed	62,583
	No. of persons economically assisted	31,873
	Issue of Certificates (Non-Financial benefits)	8,06,087
11.	MICRO LEVEL PLANNING DURING ELEVENTH ROUND OF JANMABHOOMI	
	Total No. of students drafted	1,26,852
	No. of students actually participated	1,22,216
	No. of GRPs attended	22,854
	No. of WRPs attended	3,985
	No. of Mandal/Municipal Resource Persons attended	1,299
	No. of households surveyed (excluding part of Hyderabad city and other urban areas)	1,71,50,761
	ANNAPURNA SCHEME (During 12th Round)	
	Beneficiaries covered	58,843
	Rice distributed (in M.Ts.)	160.75

(contd.)

DROUGHT – INPUT SUBSIDY (During 12th Round)	
Farmers covered	32,28,806
Amount distributed (Rs. in lakhs)	2421.14
PENSIONS DISTRIBUTED DURING 12th ROUND	
No. of pensions distributed	8,55,233
Amount distributed (Rs. in lakhs)	1270.98

Note: The detailed figures of achievements under various heads are available upto 13th Round of Janmabhoomi and in respect to the 14th, 15th and 16th Rounds, a brief description as to what has been achieved in general is provided below.

This round of Janmabhoomi provided an excellent opportunity for effective convergence of Self Help groups and Gram Panchayats. The participation of women was quite encouraging. It resulted in increased awareness among the people on health, education and small family norms. The distribution of assets was done in a transparent manner. During this round, JANANI for women and children (integrated health care) was launched.

Village level exhibitions were organized for the first time. The themes covered in the exhibition were women and child welfare, Neeru-Meeru, population control, literacy and agriculture. The exhibition mainly focused on the achievements made in the village on the above-mentioned themes and inters comparison with other villages.

Funds amounting to Rs. 340 Crores were sanctioned for carrying out various activities in this round of Janmabhoomi. Rs. 52 Crores were released towards revolving fund to DWCRA/DWCUA. A provision of Rs 30 Crores was made for girl child protection scheme and Rs. 37 Crores for distribution of pensions. Funds to the tune of Rs. 120 Crores were earmarked by the SC/ST/BC/Minorities/Women Finance corporations out of the marginal money available with them for group based economic support programmes for the women. An amount of Rs. 46 Crores (Rs. 2 Crores per district) was released for decentralized planning to fill the gaps as untied funds. Rs. 40 Crores was released for giving 4 lakh as connections under DEEPAM Scheme.

41673 DWCRA/DWCUA groups were sanctioned revolving funds. An amount Rs 45 Crores was distributed as pensions to 12.31 lakh beneficiaries. 36695 women were provided assistance under National Maternity Benefit Scheme and 3365 beneficiaries under National Family Benefit Scheme. 20521 'girls were provided assistance under Girl Child Protection Scheme. 1.91 lakh gas connections were released to women beneficiaries under Deepam Scheme. 34420 beneficiaries were provided assistance under Cheyutha and 7649 aids and appliances were distributed to disabled beneficiaries.

During the 15th round, the total number of grievances received under IFN and NFCN are 2,22,351 and 16,522 respectively. Including the number of grievances pending before 15th round, the number pending redressal under IFN and NFCN are 2,36,097 and 17,241 respectively.

Free Health Camps organized during this round were 28052 in which 20.45 lakh patients were treated. In addition, 6607 Special Camps were conducted for women and 2.11 lakh patients were treated. Medicines worth Rs. 107.84 lakhs were given to the patients in these camps.

Free Veterinary Camps organized were 36587 and 89.98 lakh animals were treated. The total number of farmers assisted during these camps is 16.01 lakhs. Medicines worth Rs.191 lakhs were used during these camps.

Proposals for .12309 works at an estimated cost of Rs.198.65 Crores were received during 15th round under the sharing pattern of 70:30 pattern. The Government share for these works amounts to Rs. 139 Crores where as the people's share comes to Rs. 59.59 Crores. So far, Rs. 68 Crores has been deposited by the people and there is an assurance for depositing Rs. 25.77 Crores. In addition, 171 proposals costing Rs. 5.13 Crores under 50:50 pattern were received. Only Rs. 1.81 lakhs have been deposited so far. There is an assurance for depositing Rs. 2.08 Crores.

The Sixteenth Round of Janmabhoomi was conducted from the 2nd of Jan to the 11th of Jan 2002, focusing on the welfare of the weaker sections.

By now 19 rounds of Janmabhoomi were carried out through out the state focusing as mentioned earlier on women, children, minorities and farmers. Janmabhoomi focuses on several development and welfare activities, it will take time for some of the programmes to bear fruits. It may be briefly mentioned here apart from sensitizing and motivating people, Janmabhoomi has to its credit tangible results in physical and material development. Though, the official machinery is there, it is the people and the people's leaders who have to move forward and shoulder the responsibility as partners in development. One can easily say that it is a failure, that so much of time and lot of money and large amount of human resources both on the administrative side and from the people have been invested during the last rounds of Janmabhoomi. Development is time related. One cannot expect instantaneous results. Janmabhoomi is not a miracle or a magic to bring about instantaneous changes for better. No one can call the past 19 rounds of Janmabhoomi as total success, because as mentioned earlier you are dealing with diversity of people at different levels of motivation, potential and capability and even in the case of officials who are drawn into the Janmabhoomi programme as Nodal Officers and others are not just stereo type of human tools doing exactly what was expected of them. In the case of the officials also you find differences in terms of commitment, sincerity, knowledge and skills in planning and in working with the people. There is mild criticism also. The creation and the support provided to self-help groups in the rural communities is highly desirable and it has gone in the right direction in organizing the community into viable functional units. Though, it was a desirable kind of community organization in terms of specific activities, it has rather minimized the importance and the role that is expected of the village panchayats.

The State of Andhra Pradesh has started the journey of comprehensive rural development with Janmabhoomi as an emotional, motivating factor. And it is a long way to go for accomplishing the overall development of rural communities wherein every individual is ensured of the basic minimum needs and leads a happy life. In this context, while we refer to the journey of development one could recall the famous lines of Robert Frost, the National Poet of the United States of America,

> ***"The woods are lovely dark and deep***
> I have promises to keep
> And miles to go before I sleep
> **And miles to go before I sleep".**

REFERENCES

1. Setty, E.D., "*A Model for Securing People's Participation in Janmabhoomi-Rural Development*", published by Dr.MCR HRD Institute of AP, Hyderabad, Govt. of Andhra Pradesh, 2001.
2. www.andhrapradesh.com

CHAPTER 13

Caste Dynamics Influencing Alleviation of Poverty

Of several affinities that foster unity, bonds of enduring relationship, solidarity and concerted social action on the part of the people such as territorial, regional, racial, ethnic, political, ideological, religious, sectarian, lingual, occupational and professional, the social institution of caste is a strong and enduring one. The institution of caste is unique in India. It is an unchanging ascribed status and identity for an individual. One may change his political and ideological views and change his religious faith and move from one region to another, but one's caste identity does not change. Caste is both a unifying and divisive force. The forces of caste for and against are apparent in every field. One could witness the caste dynamics operating in the villages creating enmity, cliques, factions, and rivalries, one caste group fighting against another. Caste generates competition, both subtle and vibrant with expression of emotions. Competition by itself is not negative. It promotes improvement and advancement. A healthy competition is a welcome factor in order to make the caste groups in the villages compete with one another and excel and improve their lives.

When it comes to helping people caste promotes favouritism helping the group that belongs to the political leaders and administrators although we have all the rules, regulations and specifications as to whom the help should reach yet caste factors influence the delivery of goods and services to the deserving minority caste groups.

It is well-nigh impossible to eliminate the negative and detrimental caste born attitudes from some caste groups. The problem with caste system is its rigidity in attitude. Caste discriminations are more visible and active in rural areas. One may come across instances wherein numerically dominant and politically influential caste groups are barriers in assistance reaching the lower caste groups or downtrodden ones. One may speak at length about the dynamics and the historical tradition and hereditarily inherited patterns of behaviour associated with different caste groups. As we discuss below there are positive and negative elements in the institution.

In the context of rural development with multiple development and welfare programmes, the development workers at the field level should have some understanding of the caste dynamics. They have to keep in mind the forces that are in operation and manoeuvre over these forces to see that help reaches the deserving and they should also work as effective social change agents to bring about harmony in the rural communities to work towards development of the entire community.

Here, we may mention that it is not only the field workers who are to be sensitive to these forces but the entire administration in the field of rural development should be sensitive and wise-enough to operate in such a way that over a period of time we succeed and gradually reduce the prejudices and stereotypes attributed to different caste groups. In this context, a brief understanding of the emergence operation and slowly declining caste system in India is relevant and interesting.

It is much easier to say what caste is not than what caste is. It is not class, for it consists of rich and poor, literate and illiterate and of high and low mental calibre. It is not colour. An upper-caste man may be black and a Harijan quite fair in complexion. It is not Aryan and non-Aryan, conqueror and conquered. It is not even occupation. Many occupations, mostly of artisans, overwhelmingly identify themselves with particular castes, but the main occupation, agriculture is open to all. Hundreds of castes and sub-castes live on the plough. So occupation alone has not caused caste. Occupational distribution is not now based on caste.

Caste is not exclusively Hindu or exclusively Indian. It obtains elsewhere too in a modified form. Nor does the present caste structure bear much relation to the traditional four *varnas*.

> Each caste embodies in itself its rites, taboos, do's and don'ts in food, drinking and matrimony.

Whatever sets off a group in any way may be sufficient to make it a caste in India. If groups diverge within an established caste they become recognized as sub-castes, perhaps finally to develop into wholly separate castes. Caste is a way of thought that the Hindu has tried to universalize.

CASTES ARE ENDOGAMOUS

All Indian castes are in theory strictly endogamous; intermarriage is intolerable. All possess an intrinsic, unchangeable worth. Thus they automatically rank themselves. Caste embraces one's life activities in their entirety from cradle to grave. Each possesses an occupation, a mode of life and customs, a set of prescribed rituals, inherently peculiar to it. The greater the restriction and prohibition incumbent upon it, the less it relaxes to comfort and indifference, the more spiritual it is, the higher its grade. In consequence it is also more pollutable, and so its restrictions are drawn closer. The wider the gap with the lower classes, the greater becomes its purity.

Life cannot be lived in parts or compartments; it is an integrated whole. So, religion, man's spiritual food, is fused with caste or the other way about.

The *Rig Veda*, the most ancient and sacred of Hindu hymns, does not talk of the caste system. Caste existed during the epic period. Caste is a hierarchy and has no bearing to the original four *varnas* in its content and functions. Hundreds of castes are sub-divided into sub-castes and sub-castes run into thousands. Among Brahmins alone there are over two thousand sub-castes and even among the so-called untouchables, over five hundred. It is the sub-castes which give Hindu society its character. Each caste embodies in itself its rites, taboos, do's and don'ts in food, drink and matrimony.

Caste not only governs one's manner of life, it also fixes the place in society in which one lives. Caste structure, to a larger extent, conditions human relationships and sentiments. "Caste gives its directions for recognition, acceptance, consecration, and sacramental dedication, and *vice versa*, of a human being on his appearance in this world. It has for infancy, pupilage, and manhood, its ordained methods of sucking, sipping, drinking, eating, and voiding; of washing, rinsing, anointing, and smearing; of clothing, dressing and ornamenting; of sitting, rising and reclining; of moving, visiting and traveling; of speaking, reading, listening, and reciting; and of meditating, singing, working, playing, and fighting. It has its laws for social and religious rights, privileges, and occupations; for instructing, training and educating; for obligation, duty, and ceremony; for errors, sins and transgressions; for intercommunication, avoidance, and ex-communication; for defilement, ablution, and purification; for fines, chastisements, imprisonments, mutilations, banishments, and capital executions. It deals with death, burial and burning; and with commemoration, assistance, and injury after death. It interferes, in short, with all the relations, and events of life and with what precedes and follows . . . life".

> This winding has been going on for centuries and to unwind the whole thing in a span of few decades would demand a basic change in people's attitudes.

Caste hierarchy was built on inter-caste relationships. It was the elaborate proliferation of the rules governing inter-caste relationships and the meticulous enforcement of them that guaranteed the separateness and integrity of each caste. It was this complete separation of the various social strata which made India's class structure unique.

Caste grew with the sanction of the society. Conditions such as geographical isolation, static society, foreign aggression, rural social structure, influence of the religion, differences of races, and lack of education, have favoured the continued existence of the caste system. However arbitrary it is, it was spontaneous in the growth. It has played a positive cementing role. It has been a unifying force. In the long chequered history of India, it has held together the fabric of Indian society. Caste in unison with Hinduism resisted the onslaught of successive foreign invasions and centuries of alien rule and preserved the content of Hindu culture.

Caste reveals itself most obviously and most rigidly in everyday life, through the concept of pollution, a concept fundamental to the Hindu way of life. Caste which begins with pollution develops into a way of life. The concept of pollution is simply maddening, carried to meaningless, illogical and incomprehensible extremities. How fantastic are its magnitude and ramifications! There is pollution by sight, pollution by approach, pollution by touch, pollution by drink, pollution by food, pollution by matrimony, pollution by travel over sea and so on. The faith or the belief works in this way; God has ordained everything and caste too is His making and so preserves and live the tenets, rituals, taboos and everything that go with each caste.

Caste functions in a multitude of ways, diet regulations for every occasion; ritual bathing, caste deities, the manner of worship, fasts, the colour of one's clothes, the colour of the flowers one wears, the shape of one's ornaments, the pattern of one's rituals, decoration, ancestral worship etc. Further we have the Indian village structure and during festive and ceremonious occasions the distribution of work or division of labour is assigned to each sub-caste and each attends to a specific item of work arranged in gradation underlying prestige and privilege.

CHANGES DESPITE RIGIDITY

Despite the rigidity, conservatism and complexity of caste, changes have been taking place in the system. Many forces opposed the evils of caste system, Jainism, Buddhism, Lingayatism, Sikhism, Christianity and the movements of Arya Samaj and Brahma Samaj and social reformers have proclaimed their opposition to caste. Modern education with its democratic ideals and values, industrialization and urbanization, money power, various movements of social emancipation, increase in the means of communication, political awakening, the emergence of legal machinery, appearance of new social classes and most important the universal adult franchise have tended to weaken the caste system.

Opposition to the caste system works in two ways. People do not believe in either predestined superiority or predestined inferiority. With all these things, the change in the villages is obviously very slow. Caste breathes quite healthily even today in the rural areas.

But, on the other hand, by the very nature and composition of the social structure in towns and cities, caste is ineffective; it does not raise its head, does not make much ado and is fast sinking. Here, no segregation, no discrimination in buses, trains, restaurants and other public places is possible. It is dying a slow and a natural death.

The villager's contact with the town slowly undermines the hold of caste on his thought. As a result of modern education and industrialization, the sanctity of caste has begun to be questioned. The caste hierarchy is slowly crumbling down.

The Constitution forbids the practice of untouchability and does not recognize caste. Though law holds itself against caste and untouchability, yet does not operate by itself but in a social environment. Transformation must take place in the attitude and beliefs of people.

The political parties in their own pursuit for power are reviving the disintegrating caste system. The slow dying embers of casteism are kindled by the politicians at every level during the elections.

The process of democracy is changing the old order; the old structure is being restructured, the functions are changing, power is redistributed, and the whole fabric of the socio-economic order is reconditioned, in a manner unthought of and unheard of before.

Caste differences were accepted as cultural and social norms. So long as it was not challenged, it flourished. Had it been challenged in the earlier centuries, it would have crumbled long ago. Many factors made this institution thrive for a pretty long period. This winding has been going on for centuries and to unwind the whole thing in a matter of few decades would demand a basic change in people's attitudes. For caste lies in the mind of man. Let us hope that at least in the years and decades to come it will become a thing of the past and a primitive institution.*

***Source**: E. Desingu Setty, "Caste Hierarchy: The Crumbling Edifice", *Social Welfare*, Vol. XXV, No.9, December 1978, New Delhi.

CHAPTER 14

Specific Focus on Dalits Development

A large number of programmes under the generic name rural development are meant for the poor and the people below the poverty line (BPL). They are the main target population in terms of ameliorating their living conditions. The intentions are fine, the programmes are appreciable, but the problem always arises in regard to the manner of delivery and extension of services to the target population. The scheduled castes who are now known as Dalits constitute the majority under the BPL. When we are speaking of clinical approach to rural development there is a need to understand the present status and the dire needs of these poor segments of the population. We cannot simply think of the Dalits as a numerical number, but one has to understand their social history and their psychology when attempts are made to better their lives.

Dalits in India numbering around 800 distinguished groups who go by several ethnic names and titles constitute about 15% in India's population. Their lives in millennia have been poignant psycho and social suffocation. The discrimination meted out to them, the humiliation they have suffered for centuries, the hardship they have endured, the servitude they were subjected to and their earlier deep pathos of life runs into volumes. Even today despite constitutional and legislative safeguards and measures providing them some reservations and extending to them incentives exclusively, they have not wriggled out of their psychic social feeling of subordination and sense of inferiority.

Excepting in a few cases, the majority of the so-called higher caste Hindus appear to be reluctant and unwilling to treat the Dalits with equal respect and extend help to them and also see that assistance reaches them. Because of the long discriminatory tradition, a large number of higher caste groups appear not psychologically prepared to accept the Dalits as equals and extend help to them to bring them up to the level of the better off people. On the other hand the Dalits also make hesitant moves. One can find the pattern of behaviour among the elder generation and the younger generation in case of Dalits as well as non-Dalits. One could see today the younger generation among the Dalits, as a retaliatory measure to the past-untold discrimination meted out to their generations of ancestors, is demanding and aggressive in their behaviour. The only analogy to the turmoils undergone by the Dalits is the institution of slavery perpetrated by the white settlers in America.

We bring in the question of Dalits here in the context of clinical approach to rural development. Here it is relevant and interesting to have a comprehensive and yet brief anthropological account of Dalits in India. The statistical data relate to 1981 census.

The details furnished below cover 751 communities and their segments. Many scheduled castes have plural identifies and for an anthropologist the task of listing and studying them poses a dilemma. None of the identities can be ignored, for some of them may be transitory, but a majority is permanent. Indeed the plural identities of these people are largely due to the processes of fission and fusion that plagued the Indian caste system and the reform movements that have changed community names many times over. In retrospect and in the final analysis it is to be believed that every identity has a specificity to itself which is not traceable in another identity. Adi Andhra and Mala are not synonymous, nor Adi Dharmi and Chamar. In some cases, certain communities with similar names and even spelling were treated separately for their distinct cultural features and occupational diversity, such as the Kadaiyan from Kerala and Tamil Nadu, and the Turi from Gujarat and other places. The size of scheduled-caste communities is an important factor. Some of these communities consist of more than a million people, whereas others number fewer than 1000 persons. Out of the total population of the scheduled castes in the country, their largest concentration is in Uttar Pradesh (22.39 %), followed by West Bengal (11.46%), Bihar (9.68 %), Tamil Nadu (8.48 %), Andhra Pradesh (7.60%), Madhya Pradesh (.7.02%), Rajasthan (5.57%), Karnataka (5.34%), Maharashtra (4.28%), Punjab (4.31%), Orissa (3.69%), Haryana (2.35%), Gujarat (2.33%), Delhi (1.07%), and in the remaining states/union territories their proportion is less. The smallest number of scheduled casts is found in Mizoram (135 persons). The scheduled caste communities perceive themselves mostly as local and regional communities. One hundred and five communities (13.8%) perceive their distribution at national level.

The scheduled caste communities are non-vegetarian except such sections of them as have been influenced by bhakti movements. The number of scheduled castes who are regular non-vegetarians is 404 (53.8%). A number of them consume cow beef – 104 communities (13.8%), whereas 117 communities (15.6%) consume ox beef; others eat pork (358 communities, 47.7%) and carrion (27 communities, 3.6%). Meat is their source of protein. Eighty-nine per cent of the communities reportedly consume milk. In all these communities alcoholic drinks are occasionally consumed; by men in 457 and by women in 284 communities. These alcoholic drinks are purchased mainly from the market, as only 20.8% take home brewed drinks. The transition from non-vegetarian to vegetarian food habits is observed among 101 communities. The incidence of beef-eating has gone down. With the rise in family income there is a marked increase in the consumption of fruits (18.2%), pulses (35.8%) and vegetables (39.9%).

Divisions also exist in terms of sub-castes or subgroups (178 communities) in the case of major scheduled castes. Differentiation among the subgroups is reported at social (428 communities), occupational (125) and religious (63) levels. Stratification has emerged with the rise of elites who have benefited from developmental programmes. Polarization and inequality have increased among various strata of the scheduled castes.

Scholars hold the view that the scheduled castes generally lie outside the chaturvarna system (avarnas). There is the Panchama cluster of communities in Andhra Pradesh who consider themselves the fifth varna. A number of scheduled castes do not recognize or place themselves within the varna system, particularly in Andhra Pradesh, Tamil Nadu, Karnataka, Kerala, Madhya Pradesh and Goa. In Maharashtra and Rajasthan between 25 to 33 per cent do not recognize varna. However, the data also suggest that a substantial number of scheduled caste people (80.2%) are aware of the four-fold varna system and a substantial number of them (70.2%) even place themselves within it. About 70.2 per cent recognize themselves as Sudra, 7.6 per cent as Kshatriyas. This corresponds by and large to the self-perception of scheduled castes. For example, 72.2 percent of the scheduled castes perceive themselves as occupying low, 23.2 per cent as middle, and 4.4 per cent as high positions. Other communities see 91.2 per cent of the scheduled castes as occupying low, 7.9 per cent as middle and 0.3 per cent as high positions. This shows the very long way that the scheduled castes have to go in achieving a measure of equality with others and in getting their equal status recognized. A large number of scheduled castes are endogamous (96.3 %). The incidence of hypergamy and hypogamy is negligible.

The women among the scheduled castes have a role in all economic and income generation activities, as well as in social functions (89.1%) and ritual matters (89.5 %). But they have generally a lower status (73%), and only a few have decision-making powers. The traditional institutions of social control are fairly active in as many as 82 per cent of the communities. The scheduled-caste communities are substantially represented in statutory panchayats which have come into existence. The traditional caste councils decide social maters and impose punishment for crimes and offences like adultery, elopement, disputes over land and water, disrespect for traditional norms, etc.

The scheduled castes are mainly landless (69.6%), with little control over resources such as land, forest and water. However, the distribution of land among them, besides other factors, has led to an increase in the number of landholders (28.5%). There has been a marked rise in the number of agricultural labourers (49.1%), casual labourers (72 %), industrial labourers (17.3%), plantation (6.1%) and fishing labour (2.5%). Child labour exists in 58.7% of the communities. Unlike the scheduled tribes, the scheduled caste-communities have followed a wide range of traditional occupations, usually more than one. Many of these, however, are rapidly disappearing. Prominent among the traditional occupations are skin and hide work, carrying carcasses, scavenging, drum-beating, playing music and singing. There were also acrobats like the Bazigar, magicians like the Bhanumati, devil dancers and exorcists like the Nalkadaya, the Pambada and the Malayan. The Bangali in Haryana and a few adjoining states, and the Garudi, were snake charmers, while the Baori prepared mohra (seal) and the Sindhuria manufactured vermilions. The Barar and the Kunchi Korava made combs for pit looms and the latter also did fibre-twinning to make ropes for peasants. The Mangan and the Turi are genealogists and bards. Some communities, like the Beda Jangam, the Kuruvan, etc., were soothsayers while the Singhiwala eked out a livelihood with their skills in traditional medicine. The Dhoba in many states of north India and the Velan and the Mannan in the south are washermen.

Service to the village community was rendered by the women of a few communities, like the Hari, who acted as midwives. Some communities like the Bhand, earned money by mimicry. The Sindhollu of Andhra Pradesh lived by performing street drams (veedhibhagavatamulu) based on mythologies of the great tradition, and the Sillekyata by performing leather picture shows. The Gandhila were horse and ass traders, while the Sauntia were animal breeders. Communities like the Byagara, the Thoti, etc., were traditionally village servants, and the Kotegar guarded forts in olden days. The Bhoi, the Keot, the Kahar and a few others were palanquin-bearers. The Bindla of Andhra Pradesh had a role in the traditional system of invoking and appeasing village deities. Communities like the Darai and the Patni are traditionally ferrymen. A scheduled caste by name, the Kanda of Tripura supplied flowers to the royal palace (which then existed). An analysis of the occupations among scheduled castes suggests that some occupations like leatherwork, scavenging, etc., were considered degrading. However, in some areas certain groups are considered untouchable, whereas the same occupational groups are not considered so in other areas. If fishing communities are untouchable in eastern India, it is not the case in the western coastal areas or in the south except for the Bharatar of Tamil Nadu. The potters of Madhya Pradesh or Manipur are untouchables, but not in any other area. The washermen in Andhra Pradesh are not untouchable, whereas in many other areas they are, and there they are notified as scheduled castes.

With the degradation of the environment and the depletion of forests there has been a sharp decline in many of the traditional economic activities of the scheduled castes (represented by percentages), such as hunting and gathering (43.86%), the trapping of birds and animals (17.64%) and shifting cultivation (20%). There has been a considerable involvement in modern occupations like horticulture (50%), settled cultivation (31.92%) and terrace cultivation (13.64%). However, there also has been a sharp rise in animal husbandry (32.84%) and wage labour (43.62%). There is increased involvement in activities like business (79.82%), trade (65.84%) and small-scale industry, which is reported from 23 communities. There is a phenomenal rise in white-collar employees (399 communities) and in private service (324) and self-employment (443). There has been a perceptible decline of crafts like dyeing (11.12%), weaving (9.28%), salt making (33.34%), weapon-making (33.35%), and metal work (10%). Specialized categories practising the traditional occupations mentioned above have also suffered. However, a category of skilled labourer has emerged, registering an increase of 64.04 per cent. There is increased involvement in woodwork (51.52 per cent).

Though untouchability has been abolished by law, the study shows the persistence of untouchability, particularly in rural areas, in relation to the exchange of water and food with communities considered to be higher in the social hierarchy, even though commensal norms have generally weakened. Scheduled castes in every region and area in the country have their own hierarchy which prohibits the acceptance and exchange of water and food. For a Mala, a Madiga is an untouchable, and for both of them a Thoti is an untouchable. For a Meghwal, a Regar and a Bhangi are untouchables, whereas among the later two the Bhangi is an untouchable. Even the subgroups in a larger generic category have these distinctions. Among the Chamars, the Jatav, the Mochi, the Satnami and many others have their own sense of superiority. So, there are a few scheduled castes from whom the other scheduled-caste communities accept neither food nor water. However, the data on the exchange of food and water show that there is a substantial number of communities with whom such exchanges do take place. There are also many scheduled castes, particularly those comprising professionals, who are not considered untouchables and with whom an exchange of food and water takes place. Further, the data also show that 42.3 per cent of the communities have putative kinship relations across communities, and 79.8 per cent of the communities share water sources and crematoria (66.2 %) with other communities. Ninety-one per cent of them visit the same religious shrines. As many as 681 communities (90.7%) participate in the traditional festivals and festivities, and 132 scheduled castes (17.6 %) have a specific role to play in these festivals.

That education has made an impact and promoted mobility is evident from the fact that a class of public servants (250 communities), teachers (364), administrators (155) and entrepreneurs/businessmen (286) has emerged among them. Political leadership has emerged at the village (39.4%), regional (18.5%) and national (4.5%) levels. One of the features of the degraded social status of scheduled-caste people has been the role of myths which explained their lowly origin, and even rationalized it. But there has been a sea change in recent years in the perception by scheduled-caste people of themselves; a new sense of self-respect. Part of this is due to the sanskritization of those sections of these communities which abstained from drinking liquor, eating non-vegetarian food (especially beef and pork)- in fact non-vegetarianism of all kinds. This also involved giving up names which were considered derogatory and assuming names which were considered respectable, e.g., the Chuhras called themselves Balmiki, Lalbegi; the Chandals became Namasudras; the Julaha called themselves Kabirpanthis; the Mala and Madiga named themselves Adi Andhra; the Pallan and Parayan claimed to be Adi Dravida, the Holeyas in Karnataka are now Adi Karnataka; the Chamar and Chuhra, after conversion to Sikhism, called themselves Ramdasia.

A new strand in the self-perception of the scheduled castes are the Neo-Buddhists who stress their identity as members belonging to an order that stands outside the varna system. In fact theirs is a newfound sense of dignity in their identity as members of the scheduled castes *in situ* without associating themselves either with the sanskritization process or various protestant reformist movements. In fact a new sense of self-respect is in the air. The old myths which legitimized degradation are being discarded. Colonial ethnographic surveys were replete with stories of degradation caused by beef-eating and that arising out of functions such as removing carcasses. These are either being ignored now or are referred to very weakly. Instead there is a new sense of dignity and self-assertion symbolized by Dalit literature. The Dalits now not only question the varna system and the ideology underlying it but consider their movement a larger struggle for equality. In this respect they have not only continued with Babasaheb B.R. Ambedkar's struggle for equality and self-respect but have taken it into new areas. The new leadership has articulated a radical counter-ideology, powerfully expressed in a burst of creative writings. The Dalit sahitya is in vibrant form today. The Dalit poetry states the stark truth and calls upon Dalits to act:

As mentioned earlier, the Scheduled Castes are a heterogeneous category. Most of the sections of the scheduled castes have generally lived in symbiosis with other sections of the general population. They have been, and are being, closely integrated with the country's larger society. This fact, and this process, is also reflected in economy, culture and politics.

The Madiga of Andhra Pradesh are also referred to as Arundhatiya, Jambavalu, Jambhavanthulu, Adi-Andhra, etc. There are many legendary accounts of the origin of the Madiga. The Madiga and Mala have common legends that speak of their origins. Many legends say that the divine cow, Kamadhenu, was killed by two watchmen of Eswara and as a consequence they were cursed by him. The descendants of these two watchmen were the Madiga and Mala. Most Madigas live in their own hamlets (Madiga Palle) segregated from the main village. According to the 1981 census, the population of the Madiga in Andhra Pradesh is 3,572,072. They are predominantly found in rural areas. However, a considerable number of them, i.e., 477,596 persons (13.37 per cent of the total population) are returned from urban areas. The Dravidian language, Telugu and the Telugu script are used for both intra-and inter-group communication. The morphometric features of the Madiga in Andhra Pradesh fall between the tribal communities and the agricultural and economically dominant castes and, in general, are similar to the average physical features of the state's population. The Madiga are predominantly round-headed, of below medium to short height and have a broader facial profile. They show a higher occurrence of gene B (27-35 per cent) than gene A (13-14 percent). In the Tirupati area they were found to have an excess of gene O (73 per cent) than in the north-western parts of A.P. (61 per cent). The presence of Sickle cell trait, low levels of Hp^1 allele, relatively low levels of Rh-negative cases (4 %) and low frequency of colour-blind males, indicate their similarity with tribal groups of the area. The Madiga are non-vegetarian and they are in the habit of taking alcoholic drinks frequently. It is stated that their untouchable status was due to their habit of eating beef. Rice is the staple cereal consumed.

Malas are settled in every Andhra village and constitute the backbone of the agricultural labour force. Out of their total population, 49.59% are returned as workers (58.50% males and 40.44 % females). Of them, 67.64 % are returned as agricultural labourers, whereas only 18.41% are cultivators; 1.10% of the workers are engaged in livestock and forestry. The remaining 12.85 % of the workers are engaged in various other services. Intercommunity linkages between the Malas and the other communities are characteristically limited to the economic sphere. Of late, particularly in urban areas, there has been an increasing interaction between the Mala and other caste communities in terms of exchange of food and water. Many changes of greater importance can be witnessed among the Malas in their socio-economic life, mainly due to the government's interventionist and protective developmental programmes. They avail of all the facilities extended to them for the improvement of their quality of life. There has been considerable progress in the field of education. Their literacy rate, according to the 1981 census, is 21.23%. The sexwise literacy rates for male and female, according to the 1981 census, are 29.72 % and 12.51%, respectively.

At present, some Malas are employed as clerks, administrators, doctors, engineers, teachers and defence personnel. They forge and establish intercommunity links at various levels, though only in a limited way. Some of them have improved their economic condition by availing of different developmental programmes. Their literacy rate is only 12.75% (1981 census). The Mala in the Union Territory of Pondicherry call themselves Adi Andhra and are distributed all over Yanam. Their population, including Mala Masti, in Pondicherry, according to the 1981 census, is only 11. It appears that in the 1981 census, they mainly returned themselves as Adi Andhra who numbered 2148. In addition to their mother tongue, Telugu, they are conversant in Tamil. As Pondicherry was a colony of the French, the elderly people of the community can understand and speak French. The script commonly used for writing is Tamil. In terms of food habits, social division and customs, they do not show much variation.

Neo-Buddhist / Nav Buddhist:- Also referred to as Nav Buddhist, they are the new converts to Buddhism. Baba Saheb Ambedkar initiated these conversions to the Buddhist faith and the first conversion took place in 1956 at Nagpur in Maharashtra. Dr. Ambedkar believed that only by leaving the Hindu fold could the depressed castes free themselves from the burden of untouchability. Conversions have since taken place in different states. A large-scale conversion took place in 1981, the silver jubilee year of the first conversion, when a large number of Jatavs in Uttar Pradesh were converted to Buddhism. Neo-Buddhists are distributed all over the country, but they are largely concentrated in Maharashtra, Uttar Pradesh, Karnataka, Gujarat, Andhra Pradesh and Punjab. In Uttar Pradesh, most of them live in Bareilly, Badaun, Moradabad and Agra districts. The Hindi language and the Devanagari script are used for both inter-group and intra-group communication. They are occasionally non-vegetarians. Of late, there has been a shift to vegetarianism.

Neo-Buddhists use surnames like Gautam, Bodh and Ashok for boys and Gautami for females. Marriages are contracted within the community beyond blood relations. The usual form of marriage is monogamy, and adult marriage is the norm. Glass bangles, the vermilion mark, toe-rings, etc., are the marriage symbols for women. There is no dowry. After marriage, the patrilocal rule of residence is followed. Divorce is not permissible. However, levirate and sororate are permissible. They usually live in nuclear families. Inheritance is in the male line and the eldest son succeeds to the familial authority. Their women share the tasks of bringing potable water, collecting fuel and fodder and assisting their men in agricultural operations. Besides, they are also proficient in embroidery. A pre-delivery ritual known as gabb-mangal is performed, in which panchsheel is adopted and a bhikshu recites the dhammapada and performs the jai managal asthagatha. The bhikshu or bodh acharya names the infants. The first feeding of cereals (annaprasan) is performed at the age of five months. The tonsure ceremony (keshkampan) is initiated by a bhikshu but the Nai is given cash and grains for performing the tonsure. The ear-piercing ceremony (karan vichedan) and initiation to education (vidhya arambh) are performed at the age of five years. The religious course of prabajya is taken by both married and unmarried persons. The jal kriya or samarpan rituals have replaced kanyadan and haldi is performed three days prior to the marriage. The marriage is solemnized at the bride's place. The important marriage rituals are oathtaking, panchsheel, jal kriya and jai mangal asthagatha. Marriages are registered with the Bhartiya Bodh Parishad. On death (parinirvan), the corpse is either cremated or buried. On the fifth day after death, the paaritrana path is performed.

In addition to their traditional occupation of shoe making and leatherwork, they are also engaged in sharecropping as well as wage labour. Nowadays, some of them are employed in government and private services and a few of them are in industry.

The Bharatiya Bodh Parishad to which their community is affiliated takes care of their social disputes. They believe in the original granth, Tripitak. A bhikshu performs their different life-cycle rituals. They observe the general festivals of the Buddhists and also celebrate the birth and death anniversaries of Baba Saheb Ambedkar. They are experts in shoe making and in embroidery on cloth and leather.

Traditional intercommunity linkages with the different untouchable communities are still maintained. They share the same water sources and cremation grounds with other communities. They continue to cultivate the fields of upper caste Hindus as sharecroppers and also work for them as labourers. The scholars, teachers, doctors, engineers and administrators from amongst them promote modern intercommunity linkages. Some of them have emerged as political leaders at the national level.

The Adi Hindu Movement which propounded the theory that the untouchables are the original inhabitants of India did not find favour with the Arya Samaj and its followers like the Jatav, some of whom identify themselves to be Nav Buddhists. In Swami Atma Ram's *Gyan Samudra* it was mentioned that according to Lomash Ramayana found in Nepal, the

Jatav race was traced to a gotra of Lord Shiva. Thus, it was stated that the Jatav are Kshatriyas. Now after their conversion to Buddhism in 1956, they have begun to assert that they are indigenes of the soil, who were once Buddhists before they adopted Hinduism after Aryan migration.

Their attitude towards formal education is partly favourable for both boys and girls. For curing their ailments, they use both modern and indigenous medicare systems. Their attitude towards family planning is positive and they have adopted modern methods of family planning. They make use of irrigation and electricity facilities. Their children avail of the midday-meal scheme in schools. Their attitude towards saving is encouraging.

In Karnataka, most of the Neo-Buddhists are converts from Mahar, Chalvadi, Holeya and Madiga communities. They are largely concentrated in Bangalore, Mysore, Tumkur, Bidar, Gulbarga, Dharwad, Belgaum and Kolar districts. The different linguistic groups speak their respective languages at home and use Kannada for inter-group communications. The Kannada script is used. They are non-vegetarians who consume beef and pork. Rice, wheat and jowar are their staple cereals and tur is the main pulse consumed. Their men occasionally consume alcoholic drinks purchased from the market. Smoking beedis and cigarettes and chewing betel leaf are common habits that are encountered amongst them.

They place themselves in the Sudra category of the chaturvarna system. Marriage with one's father's sister's daughter, mother's brother's daughter or elder sister's daughter is permissible. Adult marriage is the norm and marriage is arranged through negotiation. The thali and toe-rings are the marriage symbols for women. Monogamy is the form of marriage. Divorce is not permitted, but widow and widower remarriage is allowed. Vertically extended families are predominant, however there has been a decline in the number of extended families. Their women participate in economic activities like agricultural operations and animal husbandry, besides participating in social, ritual and religious spheres. Birth pollution lasts for eleven days. A few of them observe the initiation ceremony (sila) which is related to the observance of the five principles of Buddhism, i.e., panch sheel (abstention from killing, stealing, adultery, telling lies and drinking of liquor). Puberty rites (pushpavati) are performed on menarche. Marriages are solemnized at the bridegroom's house. The marriage ritual starts with an exchange of garlands followed by the tying of the thali to the bride by the bridegroom. The marriage feast is hosted by the bridegroom's parents. The dead are either buried or cremated and death pollution is observed. On the sixteenth day after death, a mortuary rite known as tithi is performed. Ancestor worship is observed.

In Andhra Pradesh, Dr. Ambedkar's teachings have inspired several communities, which have converted to Buddhism. They are now called Neo-Buddhists and are found in Visakhapatnam, East Godavari and West Godavari districts. They speak Telugu and use the Telugu script. They recite the Panchasheel and Trisaran in the Pali language during the puja. The Neo-Buddhists are non-vegetarian. Their personal names are suffixed with Gautam, Buddha, Vikas, Ashok, etc. Sometimes they are also named after characters in Buddhist literature. They are largely drawn from various scheduled castes like the Mala, Madiga, etc., who, after their conversion, do not strictly follow the earlier caste distinctions. They follow surname (intiperu) exogamy and marry either the mother's brother's daughter or the father's sister's daughter. Sororal polygyny exists among them. Their women wear a thali (mangalasutra), vermilion (kankanam) and toe-rings (Mettelu) as marriage symbols.

They follow patrilocal residence after marriage. Divorce is not permissible, but widow and widower remarriage is permissible. The majority of their families are of the nuclear type. All the male children inherit an equal share of the ancestral property. The eldest son succeeds as the head of the family. Women have a role in socio-religious functions and claim to have a secondary status. The tonsure ceremony is performed in the ninth month of the child. Puberty rites (Mangalasnanam) are performed for girls. Marriage rituals take place at the bridegroom's house or at Buddha viharas. A Bhikshu or an Upasak imparts Trisaran and Panchasheel to the bride and the groom before a picture of Lord Buddha. Then their names are registered in the Bharatiya Bodh Parishad. They either cremate or bury the dead. Death pollution is observed for five days. They do not perform ancestor worship.

Agricultural labour is the main occupation of the Neo-Buddhists. Some of them work as daily-wage labourers at construction sites, factories, etc., and a few other are employed as doctors, lawyers, teachers, etc., in government establishments. The Buddhist Sangam settles their disputes. The elderly monks of the Neo-Buddhists follow the Mahayana sect of Buddhism. After their conversion, they started observing Buddha Jayanti or Buddha Poornima, Ambedkar's birth and death anniversaries and Vijaya Dasami (Dussehra). Vijaya Dasami is specially observed because Dr. Ambedkar embraced Buddhism on that day. They have their own Bhikshu to conduct socio-religious functions. A fast is observed on full-moon days, as Buddha was born, received enlightenment and died, i.e., attained Mahaparinirvana on a full-moon day (Poornima). They accept food and water from all Hindu castes. The Brahman, Kshatriya and Vaishya communities accept only sidha food from them. In Andhra Pradesh, the Hindus do not treat them as equals in spite of their conversion to Buddhism. They receive the services of a barber (Mangali) and washerman (Chakali). They have their own viharas where religious teaching is imparted. They share public amenities like cremation/ burial grounds and schools with other communities. Their attitude towards the formal education of their boys and girls is positive. Modern methods of family welfare are being adopted. They are also availing of financial assistance from institutions like the Andhra Pradesh State Financial Corporation and from banks. Since 1990, the government has extended the facility of reservation in jobs to the scheduled-caste converts to Buddhism.

Panchama: The term Panchama means the fifth one, alluding to a non-existent fifth varna. All these groups later came to be called Harijans, scheduled castes and Dalits. It is often pointed out that the Panchama include many other groups. Panchama should be regarded as a varna, because Manu declared that there could never be a fifth varna. Panchama is, in fact, a generic term encompassing different endogamous groups. These are further subdivided by surnames (intiperu). The surnames, besides being exogamous groups, are also meant to indicate descent and ancestry. They also place themselves above the Jambavulu and below the Brahman, Raju, Komati, Kapu, Setti Balija, Gowda and Golla. Some of them consider themselves Sudras in the chaturvarna order. Group endogamy and surname exogamy are the general marriage rules observed. The Panchama are largely landless and only a few own cultivable land ranging from half an acre to five acres. Traditionally, they are agricultural labourers. Toddy-tapping, plucking coconuts, government service, cycle-rickshaw-pulling, etc., are the other occupations tht are pursued. According to the 1981 census, 51.07 per cent of them are workers (62.81% males and 39.13% females). Of them, a majority are agricultural labourers (71.41%) and cultivators (9.57%). The rest (3.32%) are engaged in mining and quarrying, 2.35% in the household industries and 13.35% in other services.

Paraiyan/Parayan: Bishop Caldwell is of the opinion that the name Paraiyan is from the Tamil word parai, a drum, as certain paraiyans act as drummers at marriages, funerals, village festivals and on occasions when government or commercial announcements are proclaimed (Thurston, 1909).

Pulayan, along with the Izhavas and some other high-castes, participated in the Vaikom Satyagraha, which was started in 1924. In 1907, they started the Sadhu Jana Paripalana Sangham (SJPS) and Pulaya Mahasabha. In Perinad in Quilon district, the Pulayan began a movement against the traditional practice of their women wearing bead necklaces, which was considered a sign of degradation. This was strongly resented by the Nairs. Finally, the Pulayan women won the right to throw away the beads.

Santia: Distributed in Kota and Jhalawar districts of Rajasthan, the Santia are a migrant community from Raipur district in Madhya Pradesh. They are notified as Santia, Satia and their population, according to the 1981 census, is 5372. They are a predominantly rural-based community and more than 91 per cent of their total population is returned from rural areas. They speak the Indo-Aryan language, Gujarati, among themselves and Hindi is spoken with others. The Devanagari script is used. Both male and female wear a ceramic bead necklace. They are non-vegetarian and consume beef, pork and carrion. Their staple cereals are jowar and maize. Alcoholic drinks, purchased from the market, are occasionally consumed. There are both Hindu and Muslim segments among them. The former do not practise consanguinity whereas the later does. Village exogamy and monogamy are the marriage rules observed.

Sapela / Sapera: Known as Sapela, Sapad or Sapera, they are snake charmers. The word Sapera is derived from sap, meaning snake. Rose (1919) mentions Sapela, Sapera or Sipada as a snake-catcher, like the Sapela. The Sapela or Sampela claim to be an offshoot of the Jogi. They are distributed all over Haryana and their population, according to the 1981 census, is 4716 (2722 males and 1994 females) and they are primarily rural-based community. They are also returned from Punjab, Himachal Pradesh, Delhi and Chandigarh. In different parts of Haryana they use the Indo-Aryan language, Haryanvi, for both inter- and intra-group communication. The Devanagari script is used,. Their staple food constitutes pulse (dal), unleavened wheat bread (roti) and vegetable (sabzi). They prefer wheat to rice. They are more or less regular non-vegetarian and occasionally consume alcoholic drinks. The income generating activities are snake-charming, selling of snake venom and rearing mules for sale. To supplement the family income, they play on a gourd-pipe and dance in marriage parties. According to the 1981 census, 15.92 per cent of their total population (25.94% male and 2.26 % female) is returned as workers. Out of them 13.59 per cent are engaged in manufacturing, processing, etc. and 41.41 per cent are in other services which include workers engaged in playing on the gourd-pipe and those who dance in marriage parties. However, a considerable number of them, i.e., 39.28 per cent, are returned as agricultural labourers, 2.53 per cent as cultivators and 3.19 per cent as engaged in various other services.

While the study undertaken by the Anthropological Survey of India has covered the scheduled castes above a population of 10,000 in all the states and union territories of India, it has left twelve communities in a few states and one union territory, whose major components are listed below. These communities along with the state/union territory of their distribution, their population (1981 census) and an explanation for not studying them, are all appended below:

Sl.No.	Community	State / UT Explanation
1.	AD DHARMI	Himachal Pradesh (15,098) Reported as a synonym for Chamar
2.	ADI ANDHRA	Andhra Pradesh (698,857) Being a generic group, its constituent communities have been studied.
3.	BARAHAR, BASOD	Madhya Pradesh (60,789) Studied as Basor in Madhya Pradesh
4.	BHANGI	Delhi (21,752) Reported as a synonym for Chuhra and Balmiki.
5.	CHAKKILIYAN	Kerala (29,001) Studied as Arundhatiyar.
6.	HOLAYA, HOLER	Maharashtra (14,927) Reported as a synonym for Holar
7.	KABIR PANTHI or JULAHA	Haryana (31,503) Studied as Julaha.
8.	MADARI	Tamil Nadu (346, 899) Reported as a synonym for Chakkiliyan.
9.	MALA	Maharashtra (11,890) Reported to be untraceable.
10.	MALLAH	West Bengal (38,101) Reported as a synonym for Deshwali Majhi.
11.	MOGER	Kerala (19,665) 'Real' Moger are untraceable.
12.	PALLAN	Tamil Nadu (993,070) Studied as Kudumban.

CONCLUSION

The details of data that are provided above would, it is believed, help the development agencies and the change agents in the field to understand and recognize the way to go about extending help to bring the Dalits to the surface, to the level of other groups who would enjoy respect, recognition and politico-economic advancement. Even though it may take several generations to bridge the gap but genuine attempts are to be pursued to do justice to the Dalits in terms of their overall development.

A list of those unstudied communities, whose population is below 10,000 along with the states and union territories where they were not studied, and their population figures (1981 census or as in the case of Assam, 1971 census) is appended below:

Sl.No.	Community	*State / Union Territory and Population*
1.	Adi Dharmi	Chandigarh (1431), Haryana (698), Rajasthan (780)
2.	Adi Andhra	Kerala (7353), Pondicherry (2148)
3.	Adi Dravida	Kerala (2458)
4.	Adi Karnataka	Kerala (1087)
5.	Ager	Gujarat (151), Maharashtra (3846)
6.	Agria	Delhi (1139)
7.	Ajila	Karnataka (1301), Kerala (155), Tamil Nadu (35)
8.	Arwa Mala	Karnataka (171), Maharashtra (241)

Sl.No.	Community	*State / Union Territory and Population*
9.	Arunthathiyar	Karnataka (899)
10.	Audhelia	Orissa (15)
11.	Bagdi	Tripura (239)
12.	Baira	Tamil Nadu (431)
13.	Bakad, Bant	Gujarat (303), Maharashtra (736)
14.	Bakuda	Tamil Nadu (198)
15.	Bandhela	Himachal Pradesh (30)
16.	Bandi	Kerala (24)
17.	Bangali	Chandigarh (49)
18.	Bansphor	Arunachal Pradesh (152), Meghalaya (212), Mizoram (8)
19.	Bantar	West Bengal (2086)
20.	Barar, Burar, Berar Barar, Burar, Berar	Haryana (957), Himachal Pradesh (416)Chandigarh (200)
21.	Basor, BurudBasor, Burud, Bansor, Bansodi, Bansphor, Basar	Orissa (178)Madhya Pradesh
22.	Bathada	Kerala (46)
23.	Batwal	Chndigarh (41), Haryana (524)
24.	Bauria, Bawaria Bauria or Bawaria	Himachal Pradesh (87)Chandigarh (791)
25.	Bavuri	Orissa (50)
26.	Bediya, Beriya	Rajsthan (2361)
27.	Bellara	Kerala (45), Tamil Nadu (44)
28.	Bhangi	Dadra and Nagar Haveli (44)
29.	Bhanjra	Chandigarh (207)
30.	Bharatar	Kerala (1892)
31.	Bhuinmali, Mali Bhinmali or Mali Bhuinmali or Mali	Meghalaya (201), Arunachal Pradesh (36), Mizoram (3)
32.	Bindla	Karnataka (194), Maharashtra (303), Meghalaya (303)
33.	Brittial-Bania or Bania Brittial Bania, Bania	Arunachal Pradesh (102), Mizoram (2), Meghalaya (115)
34.	Byagara	Maharashtra (356)
35.	Chakkiliyan	Karnataka (2831)
36.	Chalavadi Chalvadi, Channayya	Tamil Nadu (131), Gujarat (58)

Sl.No.	Community	*State / Union Territory and Population*
37.	Chamar, Muchi	Kerala (298), Tamil Nadu (165)
38.	Chambhar	Andhra Pradesh (520, Daman and Diu (22)
39.	Chanal	Chandigarh (90), Haryana (293), Punjab (139)
40.	Chandal	Rajasthan (1105)
41.	Chandala	Andhra Pradesh (184), Karnataka (175), Kerala (90), Tamil Nadu (37)
42.	Chaupal	West Bengal (37)
43.	Chenna Dasar, Holaya Dasar Chenna Dasar, Holaya Dasar, Holeya Dasari	Gujarat (139), Maharashtra (631)
44.	Chohra (Sweeper)	Delhi (3272)
45.	Dabgar	West Bengal (460)
46.	Dagi	Chandigarh (4), Haryana (50), Punjab (54)
47.	Dakkal, Dokkalwar	Karnataka (141), Maharashtra 342)
48.	Dandasi	Tripura (57)
49.	Darain	Chandigarh (23), Haryana (55), Himachal Pradesh (656)
50.	Dhanak	Himachal Pradesh (34)
51.	Dhaogri, Dhuai	Himachal Pradesh (793)
52.	Dhogri, Dhangri, SiggiDhogri, Dhangri or Siggi	Haryana (438), Punjab (265), Chandigarh (21)
53.	Dhor	Andhra Pradesh (2443)
54.	Dhor, Kakkayya, Kankayya	Gujarat (877)
55.	Dhupi or Dhobi Dhupi, Dhobi	Arunachal Pradesh (353), Mizoram (33), Meghalaya (313), Manipur (186)
56.	Domban	Tamil Nadu (8482)
57.	Dome, Dom	Rajasthan (3692)
58.	Dum	Tripura (283)
59.	Dumna, Mahasha or DoomDumna, Mahasha, Doom	Chandigarh (112), Haryana (9248)
60.	Dosadha	Orissa (455)
61.	Dugla or Dholi Dugla, Dholi	Arunachal Pradesh (7), Mizoram (4), Meghalaya (22), Assam (4013)
62.	Gagra	Chandigarh (37), Haryana (58), Himachal Pradesh (6)

Sl.No.	Community	*State / Union Territory and Population*
63.	Gandhila or Gandhil Gondola Gandhila, Gandil Gondola	Chandigarh (22), Himachal Pradesh (6)
64.	Garoda, Garo	Karnataka (1219), Maharashtra (352)
65.	Gharami	Uttar Pradesh (615)
66.	Ghasi	Tripura (443)
67.	Ghasi, Haddi, Relli Chachandi	Andhra Pradesh (1872)
68.	Godagali	Kerala (37), Orissa (24), Tamil Nadu (24)
69.	Godari	Orissa (225)
70.	Godda	Kerala (186)
71.	Gosangi	Karnataka (7474), Kerala (769), Tamil Nadu (157)
72.	Halalkhor	Bihar (5463), West Bengal (1348)
73.	Halleer	Gujarat (28)
74.	Halsar, Haslar, Hulasvar, Halasvar	Gujarat (154), Maharashtra (123)
75.	Hari	Uttar Pradesh (2121)
76.	Hira	Arunachal Pradesh (9), Meghalaya (48), Mizoram(3)
77.	Holar, Valhar	Gujarat (170), Karnataka (1190)
78.	Holaya, Holer-Holeya	Gujarat (92),Andhra Pradesh (664)
79.	Holeya Dasari	Andhra Pradesh (620)
80.	Jaggali	Karnataka (229), Tamil Nadu (1248)
81.	Jalkeot	Arunachal Pradesh (34), Meghalaya (8), Mizoram (2)
82.	Jambuvulu	Karnataka (4082), Pondicherry (237)
83.	Jhalo, Malo, Jhalo-Malo-Jhalo, Malo or Jhalo-Malo	Meghalaya (1052), Arunachal Pradesh (75), Mizoram (1)
84.	Jolaha	Jammu and Kashmir (371)
85.	Kabir Panthi	Delhi (4334)
86.	Kadaiyan	Karnatka (172)
87.	Kaibartta or Jaliya	Arunachal Pradesh (764), Mizoram (6)
88.	Kakkalan	Tamil Nadu (66)
89.	Kalladi	Karnataka (511), Tamil Nadu (409)
90.	Kanakkan, Padanna	Tamil Nadu (176)
91.	Kanjar	West Bengal (1067)
92.	Karimpalan	Tamil Nadu (9)
93.	Katia, Patharia	Maharashtra (3207)

Sl.No.	Community	*State / Union Territory and Population*
94.	Kavara	Tamil Nadu 3711)
95.	Khangar, Kanera, Mirdha	Maharashtra (858)
96.	Koch	West Bengal (9714)
97.	Kooch-Band, Kuchband	Rajasthan (1509)
98.	Koosa	Kerala (268), Tamil Nadu 41)
99.	Kootan, Koodan	Tamil Nadu (147)
100.	Kori or Koli	Chandigarh (1889)
101.	Kotal	Tripura (43)
102.	Kudumban	Karnataka (140), Kerala (3368)
103.	Kurariar	West Bengal (1416)
104.	Lalbegi	Arunachal Pradesh (20), Assam (45), Delhi (134), Meghalaya (30), Mizoram (3)
105.	Madari	Delhi (?), Karnataka (3434)
106.	Madiga	Orissa ((1314)
107.	Mahar-Mahar, Taral, Dhegumegu	Dadra and Nagar Haveli (83), Rajasthan (7635)
108.	Mahara	Arunachal Pradesh (13), Assam (899), Mizoram (6), Meghalaya (Not available)
109.	Mahayavanshi Mahyavanshi, Dhed-Mahyavanshi, Dhed, Dheda, Venkar, Maru Vankar Mahayanvashi, Dhed, Vankar, Maru Vankar	Goa (119), Dadra and Nagar Haveli (943), Rajasthan (1868), Karnataka (719)
110.	Maila	Tamil Nadu (47)
111.	Mazhabi	Himachal Pradesh (221)
112.	Mala, Jhala, Malo, Zala	Orissa (6118)
113.	Mala Dasari	Karnataka (2193)
114.	Mala Dasu	Andhra Pradesh (8384)
115.	Mala Jangam	Karnatakka (291)
116.	Mala Masti	Karnataka (34), Maharashtra (60)
117.	Mala Sale, Netkani	Karnataka (21), Maharashtra (437)
118.	Mang	Goa (686), Daman and Diu (16), Orissa (273)
119.	Mang, Matang, Minimadig	Gujarat (2765), Rajasthan (241)

Sl.No.	Community	*State/Union Territory and Population*
120.	Mang Garodi, Mang-Garudi Mang Garudi, Mang Garodi Mang Garudi	Rajasthan (177), Karnataka (2339), Gujarat (1184)
121.	Mangan	Orissa (983)
122.	Manne	Karnataka (174), Maharashtra (1752)
123.	Mavilan	Karnataka (51)
124.	Megh	Chandigarh (338)
125.	Meghwal Meghval, Menghvar	Delhi (1481), Karnataka (22)
126.	Mehtar or Bhangi Mehtar, Bhangi Mehtor	Arunachal Pradesh (209), Mizoram (10), Meghalaya (621), Orissa (2332), Tripura (1279)
127.	Mitha Ayyalvar	Maharashtra (202)
128.	Moger	Tamil Nadu (89)
129.	Muchi, Ravidas Muchi or Rishi Muchi, Rishi	Manipur (193), Arunachal Pradesh (328), Meghalaya (1204)
130.	Mukri	Gujarat (26), Maharashtra (74)
131.	Mundala	Andhra Pradesh (853), Tamil Nadu (26)
132.	Musahar	Orissa (29)
133.	Nadia, Hadi	Karnataka (118), Maharashtra (249)
134.	Nalakeyava	Karnataka (4928), Kerala (269), Tamil Nadu (7)
135.	Namasudra	Arunachal Prdesh (540), Manipur (2423), Meghalaya (1112), Mioram (6)
136.	Nat Nat (Rana)	Chandigarh (21), Himachal Pradesh (232), Uttar Pradesh (?) Delhi (?)
137.	Nayadi	Karnataka (1434), Tamil Nadu (360)
138.	Od	Chandigarh (35)
139.	Padannan	Tamil Nadu (Not available)
140.	Paky	Pondicherry (42)
141.	Pallan	Karnataka (745)
142.	Palluvan	Tamil Nadu (151)
143.	Pambada Pambada, Pambanda	Tamil Nadu (624), Andhra Pradesh (2333)
144.	Pamidi	Orissa (64)
145.	Panchama	Karnataka (785), Kerala (134), Orissa (269), Tamil Nadu (76)

Sl.No.	Community	*State/Union Territory and Population*
146.	Panika	Orissa (?)
147.	Panniandi	Karnataka (97)
148.	Paraiyan, Paraya	Karnataka (2307)
149.	Pasi	Chandigarh (928), Gujarat (1164), Himachal Pradesh (226), Rajasthan (943)
150.	Pathiyan	Tamil Nadu (23)
151.	Patni	Arunachal Pradesh (11), Manipur (2293), Meghalaya (54), Mizoram (4)
152.	Perna	Chandigarh (18), Himachal Pradesh (21)
153.	Pherera	Chandigarh (12), Haryana (24)
154.	Pulaya Vettuvan	Kerala (1008)
155.	Puthirai Vannan	Kerala (280)
156.	Raneyar	Kerala (148), Tamil Nadu (4), Andhra Pradesh (1845)
157.	Samagara	Andhra Pradesh (1845), Tamil Nadu (37)
158.	Samban	Karnataka (71), Kerala (2486), Pondicherry (16)
159.	Sanbhai	Chandigarh (89)
160.	Sanhai	Haryana (59), Punjab (73)
161.	Sansi	Maharashtra (531)
162.	Sansoi	Chandigarh (138), Haryana (68), Punjab (32)
163.	Sapela	Chandigarh (138), Himachal Pradesh (23)
164.	Sarbhangi	Rajasthan (613)
165.	Sarera	Chandigarh (215), Haryana (51)
166.	Shenva, Chenva, Sedma, Ravat	Maharashtra (501)
167.	Sidhollu, Chindollu	Karnataka (41), Maharashtra (181)
168.	Sirkiband	Chandigarh (178), Delhi (566), Himachal Pradesh (15)
169.	Sutradhar	Arunachal Pradesh (100), Manipur (11), Meghalaya (270), Mizoram (Not available),
170.	Tamadia	Orissa (238)
171.	Thoti	Karnataka (1184), Kerala (411)
172.	Tirgar, Tirbanda	Karnataka (173), Maharashtra (1154)
173.	Turi	Mahrashtra (275), Rajasthan (2041)
174.	Vallon	Kerala (431), Tamil Nadu (104)
175.	Valluvan	Karnataka (1002)
176.	Velan	Tamil Nadu (318)
177.	Vetan	Pondicherry (307), Tamil Nadu (774)
178.	Vettuvan	Tamil Nadu (143)

Add I, born to be a carrier of carrion, am now the lowly one to whom the Brahmans come and lowly bow. They seek the shelter of my name, Servant of the Sun, Whose service is the service of the Lord.

—*Raidas*

(From Sources of *Indian Tradition*, ed.William T. deBary, trans. J.S. Hawley and M. Juergensmeyer, New York, Columbia University Press, 1982).

The *Brahmin* who flies into a rage at the touch of a *mahar*
- That's no *Brahmin*.
The only absolution for such a *Brahmin*
Is to die for his own sin.
He who refuses to touch a chandal
Has a polluted mind.
Says Tuka, a man is only as chaste
As his own belief.

—Tukaram

(Says Tuka, trans. Dilip Chitre, New Delhi, Penguin Books, 1991).

Source:- *The People of India*, *The Scheduled Castes, National Series*, Vol.II, edited by K.S.Singh, Anthropological Survey of India, Oxford University Press, Delhi, 1995.

CHAPTER 15

Rural Sanitation: Need for a Perspective Plan

"The causes for the bad sanitary conditions in the villages are physical, economic, socio-cultural and psychological."

The sanitation in most of the villages in India presents a dismal picture. It has been a perennial problem, so complex in its character posing a threat to public health. The situation deserves utmost attention and consideration of every individual, local institutions, corporate bodies and the Government at large, for it affects our health and living.

The Japanese are said to be meticulous in their personal and environmental cleanliness. They take as much care of the precincts of their dwellings as they do in the case of their drawing room and bedroom. After a picnic party is over, the Americans do take pretty care to see that they do not leave any litter behind. They leave the place as clean as it was before. What an appreciable civic sense it is! And what do we do here? And what is the environmental sanitary condition in the Indian village?

By sanitary environment we mean a place or village where the residential quarters, cattle sheds, the village precincts, lanes and streets, are regularly swept and kept clean, free from open ditches, pools or slushes, dungheaps or garbage and faecal matter fouling the whole surroundings. A clean village is one free from the above and enjoying drainage facilities and arrangements for regular disposal of refuse. But today most villages in India present a dismal picture. Indiscriminately deposited dung and garbage heaps in various stages of decomposition, ditches and unwanted dirty water pools, ugly looking lanes and streets are some of the characteristic features of the villages. The insanitary conditions pose a constant threat to public health, being the root causes of innumerable diseases and spread of epidemics.

THE MULTIPLE CAUSES

The causes for the bad sanitary conditions in the villages are physical, economic, socio-cultural and psychological. In regard to the patterns of settlement of Indian villages, there are mainly three types – the dispersed or scattered type, the nucleated or the cluster type and linear type i.e., houses built on either side of a road in rows. The nucleated or the cluster type poses many sanitary problems in regard to space for drinking water wells, drainage, bathing and lavatory facilities, disposal of refuse and for sinking of soakage pits. Many of the villages were unplanned houses clustered together with narrow lanes or no lanes at all. Some ancient villages are walled around as a measure of protection from wild animals and thieves. And there will be fields around the village narrowing down the residential quarters. Where the houses are congested and where the villages are situated in low-lying areas, drainage is a problem. So, the very pattern of village settlements, the narrowness and physical or spatial limitations on the expansion of some villages, the topographical features of villages lead to bad sanitary conditions.

In a broad sense, occupation or economic activities of the people also decide the type of environment they live in. India is predominantly an agricultural country. Agriculture in India means use of cattle for draft, milk and manurial purposes which mean housing the cattle in separate sheds and the collection and depositing of dung and other waste materials. Lack of improved cattle-sheds and sheep-pens is a problem in the villages. Either as a matter of convenience or due to socio-cultural and religious attitude of the villagers, the cattle sheds are located near the living quarters and there may not be any wall separating the living quarters and the cattle shed. In many cases the cattle dung and urine are not properly collected. The droppings of cattle, sheep, goats and of poultry strewn all over are usually not taken care of. Even though each household attends to its own immediate surroundings, the village lanes and streets are nobody's responsibility. The villagers also dump indiscriminately cattle dung and all waste material of considerable manurial value around the house and the immediate surroundings of the village. This is due to congestion of space, feeling of difficulty in carrying the matter over a long distance to the fields or outskirts of the village. The indiscriminately dumped dungheaps are seldom covered as a measure to conserve the nitrogenous content in the matter or to prevent foul or stinking smell emanating from them.

Lack of drainage facilities in the villages and the habit of open defaecation on the part of the villagers are other common causes for disgusting sanitary conditions. The open defaecation is a psycho-cultural problem. The villagers are used to it. A change in this habit is long overdue. Either the villagers could use sanitary type of latrines or the centuries old habit of open defaecation persists. The simple fact is that over 90 per cent of the villagers were not used to a flushout latrine in their lives.

Illiteracy, poverty and lack of contract with the outside world contribute to the low civic sense among the villagers.

Another source of insanitation is the drinking water well that lacks raised platforms and causes cesspools making the place dirty.

THE BLEAK BACKGROUND

Illiteracy, poverty and lack of contact with the outside world contribute to the low civic sense among the villagers. Further, the places where shandies and weekly markets are held, when not maintained properly, add to the insanitation of the area. Chewing and indiscriminate spitting is another common social phenomenon.

Having been used to a bad sanitary environment, the villagers do not shudder at anything dirty. The tendency is to take things easy.

There are over 5,80,000 villages in India – just one village per two square miles over the surface of this sub-continent. Now all the villages in India come under the village Panchayat administration. The Panchayats vary in geographical, topographical and economic conditions and cultural practices. Each area in view of its diversity needs a special treatment to solve the problem of environmental sanitation.

In the case of those panchayats which have adequate income, water facilities and have a permanent establishment for sweeping and scavenging, the question of village sanitation is not serious. But the problem becomes acute only with the minor panchayats which cannot or do not have sweeping and other facilities, nor do the villagers in such panachayat areas attend to general sanitation of the village.

Thus we find small villages suffering from (or enduring) a distressing and disease-producing sanitation. Most villagers are aware of the problem, but a remedy is beyond them.

Rural sanitation finds a prominent place of importance in Gandhiji's constructive programme. He often emphasised the magnitude and importance of village sanitation. He practised what he preached. He himself swept the streets and cleaned the latrines. He introduced the ***wardha*** latrine (trench type) which is beneficial in two ways – preservation of night soil (for manurial purposes) and preventing the fouling of village surroundings through indiscriminate defaecation.

LOW PRIORITY

Civil amenities and environmental sanitation are statutory functions of the village panchayat. But apparently the order of priority goes to items like water supply and street lighting and mostly sanitation is not accorded the importance it deserves.

Programmes to improve rural sanitation find a place in the Five Year Plans. Individual and mass sanitary drives were targeted items in the community development extension programmes. These drives in the initial stages were effective and successful and attained a great degree of publicity. The villagers and the school children participated in the drive enthusiastically. Local leaders, officials, men, women and children held brooms in their hands and cleaned the streets. In this, an attempt was made to drive home the dignity of labour and to create among the villagers a new awareness as to the prime importance of the upkeep of the village.

Civil amenities and environmental sanitation are statutory functions of the village panchayat. But apparently the order of priority goes to items like water supply and street lighting and mostly sanitation is not accorded the importance it deserves.

Allied to the sanitation programme are the propagation of sanitary type of latrines, sinking of soakage pits where there are no drainage facilities, construction of *kacha or pucca* drains, improved cattle yards, urinal trenches, scientific methods of compost making, provision of refuse bins, pavement of lanes and streets. This integrated approach is aimed at promoting sanitary conditions in the villages.

Some of the officially sponsored programmes could not make any headway. There were certain inherent shortcomings. Strictly speaking there was no scientific approach on the part of the extension and public health personnel in introducing innovations. The rural workers dictated by a conceptual frame of modern sanitary amenities and accessories as provided by the agencies tried to implant new ideas and habits in the rural communities. For instance, the construction of public lavatories (flushout latrines) in the villages at a considerable public cost was a thorough failure. First, there was no sufficient involvement and commitment of the villagers in this programme. There was the problem of water scarcity. While we discuss the question of rural sanitation water should not be treated as an isolated factor. Above all, the failure in the use of the public latrines was mainly due to the villager's attitude and habits. An attitudinal change is what is desired.

The second factor is limited governmental allocations for programmes connected with village sanitation. Thirdly, poor and inadequate finances of the panchayts and lastly the general apathy of the villagers towards sanitary measures.

As observed earlier, rural sanitation is a complex problem warranting a perspective plan and short-range specific measures to promote better sanitary conditions. The rural Development Agency, the village panchayat, the village school and the voluntary organizations such as youth clubs and mahila mandals could play a significant role in this respect.

The supply of technique, personnel and funds depends on the Government. The programmes towards better sanitary conditions in the villages should be flexible enough so that they could be modified in accordance with the local conditions. A survey of attitudes, felt-needs and specific problems of the villagers should precede on scientific lines before the programmes are formulated. In introducing innovations, the approach should be scientific and institutional. The techniques of group-involvement, group-commitment, propaganda, publicity, demonstration, etc., must be made use of. In other words, the extension methods must be fully employed so as to motivate the villager to use a sanitary latrine and keep the precincts of his house clean. This is a slow, painstaking process. It must be gone through. There is no short cut to it.

In each rural area the vulnerable areas of insanitation and the factors causing unclean conditions are to be located, studied and remedied. The dungheaps should be taken care of. If the villagers are educated on scientific lines of compost making, the ever exposed heaps will not foul the village with stinking odour and become a breeding source for flies and insects. Wherever possible a common compost yard a little away from the village could be established. This could be done by the village panchayat. Drainage depends mainly on two things – the physical feasibility of constructing drains and financial resources. Wherever these two are positive, depending on the size of the village, *kucha or pucca* drains could be constructed as a phased programme. Areas where either of the two is absent, soakage pits are better substitutes. It falls to the lot of the individual householder. Sinking of soakage-pits is cheap and is within the capacity of the commonest man in any village. The only limitations in digging soakage pits are availability of space within the housesite and the composition of the ground soil in the house site. In case of loose soil the soakage pit is not to be located close to the draw-well because of percolation of impure or contaminated water from the soakage pit to the draw-well.

Strictly speaking, the panchayat is responsible for ensuring better sanitary conditions in the panchayat area. In the budgetary allocations of the panchayat enough provision must be made for water supply, drainage, public latrines and refuse bins and recurring expenditure towards sweeping, scavenging, etc. Every panchayat has its annual and Five Year Plans. The panchayats which could not afford full-time sweepers for daily sweeping of the village, could at least appoint either a less number of full-time or more number of part-time sweepers, in order that the villages are kept clean at lest once a week. It is desirable that this minimum programme is carried out by every panchayat.

In regard to the using of sanitary type of latrines by each family, the panchayat should take the initiative and lead in their introduction not only as a civic measure but as a persuasive step creating facilities and favourable public opinion in the use of latrines. In achieving the above-mentioned ends the panchayat can enlist the cooperation of the village school, youth club and mahila mandal and work in unison with them.

The voluntary organizations in the villages could take up village sanitation as one of their main activities and arrange periodical mass sanitary drives. The mass sanitation drives, if carried out sincerely over a period of time, are bound to influence the general public and change their attitude, make them sane to keep their surroundings clean.

The village school as one of the three basic institutions in the village could take the lead and function as a pioneer and model in sanitation programmes. It could function as an experimental and demonstration centre for a soakage pit, a lavatory, a compost pit and for environmental sanitation. The school children could be very easily trained to make use of a sanitary latrine, providing one at the school. They carry their ideas and habits to their homes and it may result in a flush-out latrine in their homes. Further, under the guidance of the school teacher the children learn the importance of environmental sanitation and could even participate in the periodical mass sanitary drives organized in the villages.

PUBLIC HEALTH CESS

Some of the corporate bodies at present are engaged in rural developmental programmes. It is a welcome sign that they have assumed this role as partners in rural development. Their role in rural uplift will become more significant and pointed if they could concentrate on rural sanitation. They may take up programmes such as provision of drinking water, sanitation which will include drainage, latrines and gobar gas plants. The Government may also consider income tax relief to the corporate bodies in respect of the amount they spend towards rural sanitation. Further, the nationalized and scheduled banks which have adopted some villages for development may lay emphasis on programmes of rural sanitation. The Government may also bring in legislation towards what may be called public cess. The public health cess as a certain percentage of land revenue will go to the village panchayat and the amount will be utilized exclusively for rural sanitation.

Thus, we see the problems of rural sanitation in India today are deep-rooted, complex and important demanding the attention, cooperation and coordination of the Government, statutory bodies, educational institutions, voluntary organizations and above all the understanding of the general public.

[Source: Dr. E. Desingu Setty, 'Rural Sanitation – Need for a Perspective Plan', *Social Welfare*, April-May, 1981]

CHAPTER 16

Integrated Approach to Water Supply and Sanitation Management

We may consider water and sanitation as perennial issues. They are the life savers. We have discussed the question of rural sanitation in the previous chapter. In the present one, the focus is on harvesting and conserving rainwater. While discussing conservation of water we also focus on sanitation. Though it may sound a little repetition of what we have already discussed in the previous chapter. The sanitation is brought in here as an organically linked factor with water.

While focusing attention on harvesting and conserving rainwater and going in for various devices for percolation of rainwater in order to have rise of groundwater table, we may have to pay attention to the day-to-day use of water. Further, environmental sanitation is closely associated with the availability and use of water. Conserving water is one thing, utilizing and managing the use is another. The following pages outline an integrated approach to water supply and sanitation management.

I. Water supply and sanitation and their management are an integral part of a rural community and they cannot be isolated from the culture or way of life of a people. An integrated approach to WSS management raises a series of questions before one can think of what the approach should be. Some of the questions are:

   i) What are the conditions and problems prevalent in a rural community with respect to WSS?
      - the physical nature of the problems, cluster, linear, dispersed type of dwellings
      - nature of the soil
      - sources, adequacy, distance, and means of supply, storage and use of water
      - size of population, its ethnic and class structure and social stratification
      - sanitary conditions

   ii) What is the present nature and level of WSS in the community?

   iii) What is the community's perception of sanitation?

   iv) What do they consider as insanitary?

   v) The causes they attribute to insanitation?

vi) What is their level of awareness of insanitation?

vii) What have they done to improve sanitary condition?

viii) Assuming that the people are aware of sanitary problems, what are the reasons for their not alleviating the situation?

ix) How does the community organize and manage WSS?

x) What are the physical, economic, social, technological, organizational and managerial requirements to ensure a better/ satisfactory level of WSS?

xi) What are the kinds of resources available within the community?

xii) What are the kinds of resources that need come from outside?

xiii) What are the external agencies that are to provide/ facilitate with the requisite resources?

xiv) In what manner have the WSS activities been carried out by the development agencies thus far?

xv) What is the experience and attitude of the residents of the community *vis-à-vis* the WSS activities of the development agencies?

xvi) What is the level and nature of integration of WSS activities that obtains now?

xvii) What are the missing links? Where does the lacuna lie?

II. Keeping in view the ensuring of general health and welfare of the community through WSS, what kind of an integrated approach is necessary?

III. The elements in the integrated approach:

i) Physical housing, use of the precincts of the house, cattle shed, kitchen, backyard, disposal of waste, the environs, the source, supply, protection, adequacy and use of water, and its disposal.

ii) Technological improvements/innovations and their maintenance in respect to WSS.

iii) Economic: the cost of improvement, maintenance, the local resources, the anticipated external support, the individual/community affordability

iv) Cultural values attached to WSS, habits of people in the use of water, Defecation and waste disposal, attitude towards environmental sanitation and level of tolerance to insanitary conditions.

v) Organizational: who will organize and manage the WSS activities at the community level? Who from external agencies?

IV. What should be integrated at the community level?

- needs
- interest
- initiative
- activities
- groups

- resources
- leadership

V. What is to be integrated at the external agencies level? How to integrate and the problems of coordination?

- programme planning
- programme implementation
- programme evaluation

VI. The suggested approach is a holistic, integral, composite one linking physical, technological and institutional components: housing – environs – water – sanitation – toilets – waste disposal – the user.

VII. The organization and management of WSS at the community level is dependent upon and influenced by the following aspects of the community:

i) Awareness
ii) Pressure of the need
iii) Resources – material, human
iv) Composition of the group
v) Size of the group
vi) Social structure
vii) Structure of power and authority
viii) Kind and strength of existing organizations / institutions in the community
ix) The kind and strength of local – institutional leadership
x) The degree of influence from outside the community
xi) Channels and pattern of inward and outward communication
xii) Cultural orientations, values, attitudes of people towards sanitation, use of water and maintenance
xiii) Economic level and affordability
xiv) Occupations and professions of the groups

In this context it may be relevant to briefly look into community organization the concept, objectives, benefits and some of the organizations at the rural community level. We may remember that an existing organization may be utilized for a specific new activity. An organized community, in terms of groups, institutions, functions and responsibility is a machinery that may be used for diverse purposes. It does not deny the need for a specific organization or special organizing for a specific activity. The thrust of the question is on organizing the community and revitalizing the existing institutional infrastructure at the rural community level.

(i) Community Organization[1]

It is important for a worker to have a complete understanding about the community with which he works. By making a sociogram of the community, he can work out the pattern of communication and then understand who influences whom and to what extent. The question is often raised as to how best agency workers can assist the people in dealing with recalcitrant individuals and groups whose sole purpose is to block progress. This needs a careful examination and it brings us to the question of skills involved in working with groups and communities. The worker has to understand what exactly is, the cause and the real cause may be different from what appears on the surface. The worker may have preconceived notions. He can look for the answer by studying the power structure within the community and the vested interests it upholds. It has also its processes such as decision-making, communication, social and cultural linkage and boundary maintenance. A social compass would provide valuable guidance to the extension worker and if he understands the elements and processes operating in it, he will very easily map out the interrelations of various factors. The components of the social compass comprising of such things as community, governmental structures, education, religion, family, social class, health, communication, etc., can be analyzed in terms of its elements and processes.

Community organization is a method by which an individual is influenced through the group in which he works. This group provides him the "fields" and it is by understanding the "field forces" that affiliations and alignments of individual members are identified and interpreted.

(ii) Community Concepts

The word community signifies different things to different people according to their interpretation. In some places ethnicity and religion may come to the mind whereas in other countries various social communities are mentioned. Community refers to a group of people inhabiting a given geographical area and having some kind of common activities or some degree of common life, irrespective of their social, religious or social differences. It is not confined to any of the various restricted fields of community life on the basis of religion, caste, race, language or profession but one that envelops the whole life of the whole community.

(iii) Definition

Community organization has been defined as a process initiated to bring about and maintain an adjustment between social welfare needs and social welfare resources in a given geographical area. As a disciplined method "community organization seeks to bring about a social climate in which it is easier to resolve group conflicts and initiate cooperative activity for the common good of the community".

Community organization work concentrates its efforts in narrowing down the areas of conflict and enlarging the areas of cooperation. In short, the negative and destructive aspects of competition is sought to be replaced by the positive and constructive aspects of cooperation.

(iv) Central Objective

The objective of "community organization" as a method of social work activity is, one of helping the communities to recognize and realize their needs and aspirations. First, there has to be awareness about their problems and secondly there must be willingness to work together towards these common objectives.

In any area, there will be problems of some sort and resources both in men and materials and "community organization" seeks to rouse the latter for the solution of the former. There is invariably a gap between what facilities a community has and what it would like to have, in other words, between achievements and aspiration. It is the task of "community organization" to narrow down and bridge this gap between social welfare needs and social welfare resources of a community.

(v) Specific Objectives

(a) *To obtain consciousness of community:* For harmony and progress of the community, a sense of "we" feeling, a sense of belongingness is to be fostered among the members of a given community. Such a sense of "we" feeling and interrelatedness make the members feel that they constitute a unit by themselves, a social entity as distinct from other communities. Just as self-consciousness is essential for the individual so its importance to the community. The process of integration rests primarily upon definite self-consciousness of the community.

(b) *To Satisfy unmet needs:* Common needs which individuals and groups are unable to satisfy for themselves could be met by the collective action of the community. It may be in any sphere, political, economic, social or cultural. Collective action is the basis for community integration and community mobilization. Determination of the needs of the community is therefore one of the first steps.

(c) *To obtain social participation as a means to socialization:* The ultimate goal of all human association is the development of better personalities by the individuals concerned. A community is composed of various groups in which its people associate. One of the chief handicaps to community action is the number of families and individuals who do not belong to any formal organization, who live a relatively isolated social life associating with their own families and neighbours. The best index of the socialization of the members of a community is the degree of their participation in its organizations.

(d) *To obtain social control:* Community organization is to obtain social control through community spirit and loyalty. Social control becomes possible by the development of community spirit, by loyalty to the community and by symbols which express the common objective of community activity. Sociologists have called these three factors – morale, collective representations and *esprit de corps* (common spirit pervading the group).

(e) *To coordinate groups and activities:* In a given community there may be several interest groups and their interests and activities may come in conflict. Community organization is necessary in order to prevent conflict and promote efficiency, cooperation and coordination. This is important in a small community. Proper adjustments are necessary. Efficiency may be promoted and ends attained if coordination can be carried out to the point of active cooperation.

(f) *To prevent the community from the introduction of undesirable influences and conditions:* It is not enough to promote community betterment from within, for the community must be able to defend itself from the aggression of undesirable influences. Many a community has found that it can work together for the elimination of a drinking place or any other nuisance to the physical and social health of the community.

(g) *To cooperate with other communities and agencies to obtain common needs:* Frequently, the community is too small a unit to achieve certain desired ends on its own. To obtain them, it is necessary to cooperate with neighbouring communities to obtain a bus line, water facilities, schools, colleges, etc.

(h) *To establish a means of obtaining consensus:* As for having their needs accomplished, it is easily done by coming to a common understanding. In a small rural community, it is obtained by gradual crystallization of public opinion through casual conversation at any shop or public place where people gather usually. Sometimes hearsay, gossiping distort the facts and promote disagreement rather than consensus.

(i) *To develop leadership:* Leadership for any group or collective activity is a must. Potential leaders in the community are to be identified, their talent recognized and developed. Local initiative and local leadership are essential for building up a self-reliant and self-confident community. It is not a question of spoon-feeding, the external agency alone functioning, but creating opportunities so that the local leadership is fully developed and employed for the growth of the community.

Benefits of Community Organization

(a) Group thinking and common good,

(b) Division of labour and responsibility,

(c) Recognition of individual merit,

(d) Community work, and

(e) Group efforts are more effective than individual efforts.

A MEASURE OF COMMUNITY ORGANIZATION

Community organization should not be conceived as a relationship which can be set up and which can be abolished. It is rather a process of establishing relationships which will always be in a state of becoming analogous to the growth of personality or character in the individual. One measure of community organization is the degree to which organizations and interests are willing to cooperate in activities or objectives for the betterment of the common welfare, for which they are not primarily responsible and in which others will take the lead.

Another measure is the ability to have competition in politics or business without conflict and the ability to discuss matters with a division of opinion but with tolerance and with united support for the objectives sought.

The degree of socialization of the community is the best measure of its organization. The better a community is organized the more it serves the needs not only of its adult individuals but also of its potential members.

It has been very well summarized that the goal of community organization is enlisting everyone in the community activities so that each individual shall register effectively, that is, shall achieve self-expression and status in community service.

From a behaviouristic standpoint the measure of community organization is the degree to which the members, individuals or groups of the community act collectively for common welfare.

Statutory and non-statutory organizations like Village Panchayats, cooperative societies, special interest groups like DWACRA, Self Help Groups, Vana Samrakshana Samithis, Vidya Committees, Water Users Associations, Water Shed Development Committees etc., constitute some organizations at the rural community level..

FACILITATING COMMUNITY ORGANISATON[2]

A generic description of the process of facilitating community organization in a population group is depicted in Fig.1. Each step in the critical pathway is needed for achieving stated objectives.

- Meeting population leaders: The critical entry point for the worker at which the process of confidence building begins.
- Gathering information (community diagnosis): Demographic, socio-cultural, topographic, and health data may all form a part of the information gathered. Information also serves to broaden dialogue and include women.
- Identifying existing structures: organizations capable of serving as vehicles of community development are identified and the worker seeks to strengthen, mobilize and coordinate them for the subsequent steps. Most communities present several candidate organizations, such as councils of elders, development committees, or saving and /loan associations.
- Selecting priority problems: The worker assists the new organized group to agree on a set of problems of greatest importance to the population. Community diagnosis also helps to define these problems.
- Choosing one problem to work on: From the problem set the group selects the one to attach first of all. Usually the problem chosen will be the most pressing to the dominant faction or the most amenable to local solution.
- Informing the people about the problem: By means of explanation, demonstration, and auxiliary materials the workers and others seek to raise the level of knowledge of, and sensitivity to, the problem and its ramifications.
- Assessing local resources: Money, labour, materials, and technical expertise may all be needed to adequately address the problem selected. The extent to which they can be obtained locally is ascertained.
- Setting staged objectives: The solution to the problem, whatever it may be, can usually be divided into several stages and to each attached a concrete objective, a time for achieving it, and a sense of what it takes in labour, materials, and expertise to reach it.
- Setting responsibilities and time schedules: The staged objectives, attached time frames, and resources requirements, are identified with individuals and groups within the population, to whom are given the responsibilities for execution.
- Implementation

- Evaluation: Achievements are matched against objectives. Problems are identified as well as success and used as platforms for launching a new critical pathway.

THE GENERIC PROCESS OF FACILITATING COMMUNITY ORGANIZATON: A CRITICAL PATHWAY

Each step is necessary to achieve objectives

Meeting Population Leaders

↓

Gathering Information

↓

Identifying Existing Structures ←

↓

Selecting Priority Problems

↓

Choosing One Problem To Work On

↓

Informing The People About The Problem

↓

Assessing Local Resources

↓

Setting Staged Objectives

↓

Setting Responsibilities And Time Schedules

↓

Implementation

↓

Evaluation Of Results → (back to Identifying Existing Structures)

Figure: 1

It may be noted that "with each successful organized community effort the cooperative and collaborative attitudes and practices of the community are broadened and deepened. Likewise, unsuccessful efforts have profound demoralizing effects".

RATIONALE

The appropriateness of the community organization process to water and sanitationprogrammes resides in two conditions for the success of these programmes:

- If water supply and sanitation facilitates are to function properly they must be maintained and repaired in a timely and correct manner. Maintenance and repair can be assured in most rural communities of developing countries only by an organized and trained constituency.
- If the health and social benefits of improved water supply and sanitation facilities are to be obtained, then the population must participate in an organized way to properly use and protect water, and to incorporate essential personal and domestic hygiene associated with excreta disposal, food handling, and infant and child care.

Maintenance and repair of facilities

The appalling rate of breakdown of water supply and sanitation facilities in rural areas of the developing world is well known. Few developing countries are able to provide sufficient numbers of maintenance personnel or the institutional and material support needed to maintain a widespread network of water supply and sanitary installations. Most water supply ministries are seriously hampered by shortages of trained personnel, lack of transport facilities, deficient material supplies and overly centralized organizations. Ministries of Health, the usual repositories of responsibility for sanitation, suffer even more in the usual case from these organizational maladies.

Responsibility must therefore, devolve upon communities themselves at least for the long-term maintenance and repair of facilities. Women must necessarily play important roles in this regard. The success of community maintenance programmes is dependent on how well communities are organized. Community organization is in turn conditioned by a number of other factors.

Achievement of Health and Social Benefits

Even if the water supply is safe and in working order, and the excreta disposal facility properly installed, a host of behavioural factors may intervene to mitigate potential health and social benefits.

In the case of water supply, factors associated with water drawing, transport, and storage may bring about contamination of the source or the household supply. Even more importantly, use of excreta disposal facilities needs to be reinforced by personal hygiene: hand-washing, bathing, and washing and protecting food after preparation. A sustained approach to these matters depends on organization of supportive community structures, and networks of peer support for behavioural change.

Conditions for Successful Facilitation of Community Organization

Ideally, community organization goes on without the influence of the worker or any other external assistance. In fact, population groups may quite properly be said to have their own intrinsic organization, i.e., the innate ability to deal with defined problems. Yet in practice normal social structures of many communities may have deteriorated and function very poorly at best when challenged with such matters as technological change. Colonial policy, leadership factors, urbanization, disease patterns, and traditional systems of assigning status have been cited among those correlated with variations in adaptive community behaviour.

For water and sanitation the conditions for successful facilitation of community organization need to be made more explicit. Four conditions appear relevant:

(a) Trained personnel

(b) Information about the community (community diagnosis)

(c) Integrated approaches among sectors

(d) Available technology and information.

Trained Personnel

Personnel need to be armed with skills of three types: diagnostic, supportive, and evaluative. Diagnostic skills relate to the ability to delineate the communities within populations that represent the main social units. Leadership, decision-making and communication patterns, as well as the physical, demographic, economic and health characteristics of the population should be assessed. The worker should be enabled to gather data that will be immediately useful in guiding his/her action without spending undue time or effort in doing so. In essence what a worker needs to know is how he/she can operate within the resources and constraints of a given community to generate optimum participation in the planning, installation, maintenance, and repair of water supply and sanitation facilities. The categories of what information is needed are explained below.

Supportive skills extend from establishing trust to guiding and facilitating group discussion, and providing continuous support and empathy to individuals and social structures until they become independently viable. We may think of a list a number of subsidiary supportive functions:

- Creation of favourable group settings for community leadership to emerge and develop.
- Reconciliation and mediation of conflict or potential conflict, where there is a threat to continuity to community organization.
- Maintaining contact between community structures and their progress on the one hand and external government or agency action on the other.
- Acting as a resource link for village and external resources.
- Knowledge and appropriate use of technical back-up resources.
- Assurance of a continuity of surveillance and monitoring of water and sanitation facilities.

Evaluation skills pertains particularly to understanding the relevance of programme evaluation to continuous programme improvement and effectiveness, and to stimulating the participation of the people of the community in the design and application of evaluative procedures as a means of developing greater commitment on their part to the programme. Community workers should also be able to do simple process evaluation of events, activities, and the characteristics of local participation as well as simple outcome evaluation of change in knowledge and behaviour.

Information about the community

By means of simple observations and selected interviews the community worker should be able to gather a modicum of data sufficient to make the diagnosis of community capacity to participate mentioned earlier. Data items selected from the following categories should be incorporated into a simple instrument feasible for use by community workers.

i) Physical features of the community
   a. Topography
   b. Types of soil
   c. Water table
   d. Types and location of water sources
   e. Meteorological and climatic features
   f. Availability of natural resources

ii) Biologic features
   a. Water quality
   b. Common disease vectors
   c. Prevalent water and excreta-related diseases

iii) Economic features
   a. Assets
   b. Access to resources
   c. Liabilities
   d. Economic infrastructure

iv) Demographic features
   a. Distributions
   b. Ethnic composition

v) Socio-cultural features
   a. Beliefs about water and excreta
   b. Water use
   c. Excretion patterns
   d. Local skills
   e. Existing local organizations
   f. Relationships to outside organization
   g. Leadership patterns
   h. Communication patterns
   i. Decision-making patterns
   j. Previous self-help experience

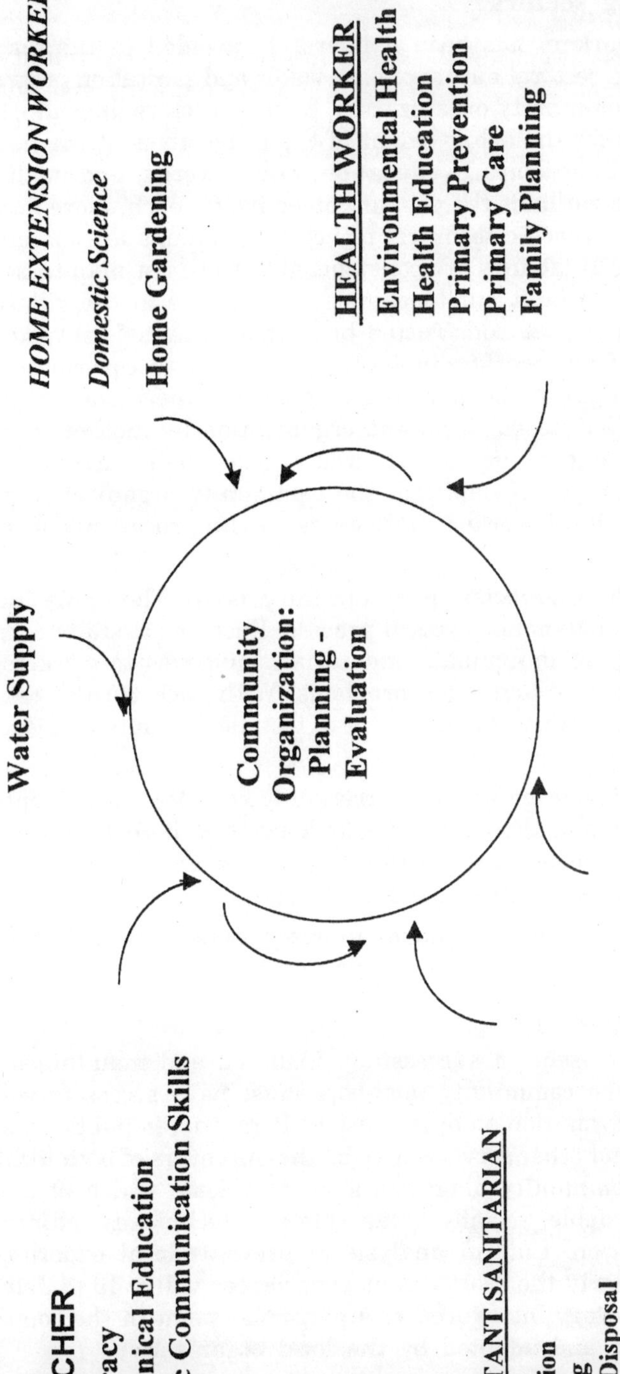

Fig. 2. THE COMMUNITY ORGANIZATION PROCESS: Community Organization: Planning -Evaluation

Integration of approach among sectors

Specific reference to health workers has been deliberately avoided in the discussion above in order to emphasize the intersectoral nature of both water and sanitation programmes and the concern with facilitating community organization. Several sectors depend upon the success of community organization for the achievement of their objectives at the periphery of the population. Among them are agriculture, education, public works, and health. In a sense, facilitating community organization is the primary objective for each, more important in the long run than achieving any specific technical objective. If pumps are installed but break down, whom do they benefit? If latrines are constructed but are not maintained, who will use them? If a primary school is built but teachers refuse to live in the village, how will the children be taught? A feeder road constructed but not maintained may not result in increased access to markets. If one worker undermines or fails to contribute to the success of the community organization others may not be able to achieve their objectives. Workers need to be able to refer "felt-needs" from one organization to another to another and to feel a sense of accomplishment in success achieved outside their particular sector. Figure-2 illustrates these relationships. As depicted, the community organization process is at the centre. Each community level worker contributes to the process while making specific technical inputs.

These inputs need to be made at appropriate points in the process. The figure indicates that the community organization is a dynamic cyclical process. Each successfully completed project in fact enhances the ability of individuals and social structures to work together and strengthens local ability to analyze and solve problems. With each turn of the cycle, as it were, the capacity of the community to absorb new technical inputs and face new adaptive challenges increases.

Thus a community at one point may be able to successfully complete and maintain an open well with a bucket and pulley and though what was learned in both a technical and organizational sense, be able to move on later to the installation and maintenance of a handpump, or even later to the maintenance of a feeder road.

These interrelationships need to be operationalized in joint intersectoral policy-making, joint middle level management, and joint training programmes.

Available technology and information

If community organization is to issue in successfully installed and maintained water supply and sanitation facilities, then community members must have access to adequate and appropriate technology, and information on how to use it. Personnel in public education, public works, health, agricultural, and other services may be the purveyors of both technology and information. The results of community diagnosis should indicate which of available technologies are economically affordable, socially acceptable and technically maintainable for both water supply and sanitation. Careful analysis of previous local experiences of organized problem solving, particularly the most recent experiences will help to determine whether the information and technology introduced at a particular point in the community organization cycle can be absorbed and adapted by the local organization.

A good case in point is that of villages in the South Cameroon, which at the onset of efforts to stimulate community organization installed temporary protection of springs using strictly local materials, but later were able to commit funds and labour to a more permanent protection. The introduction of more sophisticated technology close on the heels of the initial success was a key strategy. An important element in this transfer of technology was the introduction of a technique of splitting rock. The project chauffeur, who had learned the technique on trips to another region of the country, taught the villagers how to pour cold water over a heated rock. This technique facilitated spring box construction.

Information on the use of the many varieties of water supply and sanitation technology is unfortunately in short supply. Most available manuals are written in English and use language and images too technical for practical use by community members. Needed are manuals generously illustrated with non-technical drawings and a minimum of written explanation.

Greater emphasis needs to be placed on the development of demonstration models.

Outcomes of Successful Facilitation of Community Organization

Case histories drawn from Africa illustrate three major benefits of effectively stimulating or facilitating the local community organization process:

1. Reinforcement of local management capacities
2. Enhancement of participation
3. Increased probability of programme success

The first, taken from a village in the South Central Cameroon, illustrates the catalyzing effect or efforts to facilitate community organization on local ability to manage water and sanitation facilities. This village with about 1500 inhabitants in five hamlets, was one of four selected as pilot villages in the AID/OCEAC Public Health Training Project (1972-76). Four years prior to the onset of the project, this village had experienced a remarkable reversal of what had been a deteriorating relationship between the older and younger generations. Through the establishment of dialogue between the generations on a number of important issues, a reconciliation took place which the Project inherited.

A village health committee took shape readily in the central hamlet. Despite having no technical experiences with the protection of springs or the construction of latrines, the committee was able to organize the temporary protection of one spring and the construction of over 40 properly covered pit latrines. Later the spring was protected in a permanent manner, and plans were laid for pumping water from the spring to an elevated reservoir and thence by gravity to a community standpipe. In all, 43 pit latrines were constructed (out of 50 households) and in use. At a later date, the committee had calculated the costs of putting in similar systems in the other hamlets. The health committee had become a community water and sanitation planning board.

A second South Cameroon village presented in 1972 a distressing picture of a predominantly/ dependent population (elderly or very young), widespread endemic disease, and virtual absence of water source protection or excreta disposal installations. Leadership was confined to the hands of a few clan leaders surrounding a rather weak elderly traditional chief.

Community leaders agreed to form a health committee, but spring protection and latrine construction progressed little beyond the talking stage, except for a single pit latrine at a clan leader's.

The committee, however, provided a forum in which many others besides village elders participated. Discussions of issues surrounding environmental protection, direct health education presentations, and the baseline medico-social survey, exposed many, including women and youth to new technology and new information. In the second year of the project, with continued efforts to strengthen the committee, other latrines began to appear and protection of four springs moved ahead apace. Facilitation of community organization had a salutary effect on both the characteristics and the extent of participation.

We may think of a framework for analyzing participation as an impact of the community organization process described above. In simplest terms, this framework cossets of two parts: (1) the *dimensions* of participation in terms of what it consists of, who participates and the characteristics (the how) of participation; and (2) the *context* of participation, comprising characteristics of both the *project* and the environment in which the project is implemented.

One could be sure of a steady reduction in the prevalence of intestinal parasites as community leaders took hold of the long-term management of latrine construction and use, albeit and the incentive of periodic vermifuges played an important role. In the same Cameroonian village reported earlier community leaders on the basis of their success with the management of the water supply, took advantage of a change in Cameroonian land tenure laws that allows for optional individual or communal ownership of land, to develop a community-wide landholding. The Malawi enhancement of organization at the community level was prelude to a successful long-term maintenance programme.

Thus whether one is speaking of health or social benefits or simply the proper functioning and use of water and sanitation facilities, improved organization at the community level appears to be an essential ingredient in the mix.

CONCLUSION

Experience to date points, therefore, to community organization and to whatever can be done to stimulate and enhance this process intrinsic to local population groups, as an imperative to the success of water supply and sanitation programmes among most rural populations of developing countries. Organized individuals and social structures appear to be essential for both the proper function of facilities and the achievement of health and social benefits. Certain conditions, however, are needed for facilitation of the process: *personnel* trained in community diagnostic supportive, and evaluative skills, *information* about the community to guide facilitation, integration of approach among services standing to benefit from successful community organization, and *technology and information* the continuous cycle of local development. Finally, successful facilitation of community organization produces in practice certain benefits: improved local management of water and sanitation facilities, enhanced participation by community members, and increased probability of project success in both an operational and an outcome sense.

NOTES

1. Setty, E.D. 1970, *Community Development and Extension in India*, Gandhigram Rural Institute, Gandhigram, South India.
2. WASH *Technical Report No. 7*, June 1981, WASH Coordination and Information Centre, 1611, N. Kent Street, Room 1002, Arlington, VA 2209, USA.

CHAPTER 17

Model For Securing People's Participation in Their Development

People's participation is a central feature of present thinking about alleviating poverty and rural development. There appears to be an increasing consensus that participation is essential for any effective development. From this pre-supposition arise the attendant questions of how best it can be operationalized on the assumed grounds that more of it is beneficial. In what activities, in what manner and shape, can the participation be maximized? Can participation be perceived in this way, as an ingredient to be injected into target groups as though they were ill and, as though, this was somehow the panacea? Can participation even be institutionalized? Or legalized? Or must be perhaps be forever on the margins of official policy prescriptions and in that way provide a vehicle for countervailing explanations and organizations that are so necessary in the struggle against entrenched orthodoxy.

In these latter terms, participation provides a potentially powerful tool, together with communication, education and conscientisation. Present concerns with participation are rooted in a complex historical context. People's participation has been a constant theme since the beginning of rural development in all the Asian and African countries that have emerged free from the colonial powers.

Further, we need to ask ourselves a few basic questions and lay emphasis on some aspects of people's participation in rural development. They are:

1. What constitutes rural development?
2. What is people's participation?
3. Objectives of people's participation.
4. Why should people participate? (the philosophy and assumptions behind people's participation)
5. The range and variety of participation
6. Why people fail to participate?
7. Magnitude of people's participation.
8. The mockery of people's participation.
9. Enabling and facilitating people's participation in multiple ways in organizing the community and through decentralization, extension educational process and statutory measures.

In the analysis that follows, the terms "rural" and "community" are used in the same sense, denoting a rural settlement as distinct from towns and urban centres with large population and diversity in social structure and social and economic interactions.

Before we look into the various aspects of people's participation in rural development, there is a need for a definition of what constitutes rural development which would indicate the scope, the limitations and the manner in which people could participate in their development.

Rural development, in general, is a strategy designed to improve the economic and social life of people in a rural settlement and, in particular, it focuses on the rural poor comprising the small-scale farmers, tenants and the landless. Since rural development is intended to reduce poverty, it must be clearly designed to increase production and raise productivity.

Rural development recognizes, however, that improved food supplies and nutrition, together with basic services such as health and education, cannot only directly improve the physical well-being and quality of life of the rural poor, but can also indirectly enhance their productivity and their ability to contribute to the national economy. It is concerned with the modernization and monetization of rural society, and with its transition from traditional isolation to integration with the national economy (World Bank, 1975).

The objectives of rural development, therefore, extend beyond any particular sector. They encompass improved productivity and increased employment, and thus, higher incomes for target groups, as well as minimum acceptable levels of food, shelter, education and health.

Rural development, in a comprehensive sense, is a process of social action in which the people of a community organize themselves for planning and action, define their common and individual needs and problems make group and individual plans to meet their needs and solve their problems, execute these plans with maximum of reliance upon community resources, and supplement these resources, when necessary, with services and material from governmental and non-governmental agencies outside the community. Thus, we see that rural development is focused on the development of the people. It is a dynamic, unified problem-solving approach and the education of the people could be said to be one of the end products of rural development. It is recognized as a social process of directed change.

Further, the essentials of the rural development process are the stimulation of local initiative, location and development of local leadership, and fuller utilization of local resources. In addition to these, self-help and self-reliance, sustained interest and co-operation are other aspects of significance in the concept of rural development. The thrust in rural development is people's participation in the total process and in the entire gamut of rural development, and simultaneous development of people, their conditions and quality of life.

WHAT IS PEOPLE'S PARTICIPATION?

People and their participation. Who are the people? The people in general comprise the target population, the clientele, the beneficiaries, the men and women, the old and the young, the formal and informal leaders in the community, people of different segments and strata of the community, depending upon the specific development programmes and activities.

Rural development programmes comprise: agriculture, animal husbandry, cooperation, rural industries, rural engineering consisting of minor irrigation, roads, buildings, health and sanitation including family welfare, family planning, women's welfare, child care and nutrition, education including adult education/social education and adult literacy, youth welfare and community organization. In each of these areas of development, there are several programmes, schemes and activities which are additive, expanding and tapering off, covering the total community, some segments, or specific target populations such as small and marginal farmers, artisans, women and, in general, people designated as weaker sections – the people living below the poverty line.

The programmes or the activities, by their nature, determine or limit the scope, shape and manner of people's participation. The development programmes could be classified into three broad categories: 1. individual-based wherein the target or the beneficiary is the individual and the participation is restricted to the individual (e.g. agriculture, livestock, poultry, family planning, nutrition, adult literacy); 2. community-based, the projects or programmes that cover the total community or some segments of the community (e.g., irrigation, plant protection, contour bunding, roads, buildings, schools, community centres, mid-day meal programmes, environmental sanitation and activities of community-wide nature; and 3. individual-cum-community based programmes. Some of the programmes mentioned above, fall both under individual and community categories. Such programmes cannot be successfully initiated and accomplished without the response and support from the individuals and the community at large.

The question that arises at the outset is who participates with whom? And for what purpose? All development plans and all strategies for assisting the poor and the needy necessarily should have the community as its central focus and starting point. All other resources, techniques and expertise are of relative importance compared to the community. Begin with the community and build with them. In the context of development programmes, the agencies and institutions cannot be the prime factors in the dynamics of participation. If community's growth and development is the vital and ultimate concern then the community necessarily assumes the prime status in the relationship between community and agency. The healthier and meaningful approach would then be not people's participation in agency's programmes but agency's participation in people's programmes. It has to be remembered that agencies, programmes, expertise are all secondary resources restricted to the role of assisting the community, they do not form in any way the major content in the development process.

The ultimate goal of providing for people's participation in the programmes is imparting the community with skills, strategies, opportunities and support to enhance its own functioning towards self-sufficiency and self-development. In concrete terms, the goal of people's participation in programmes could be helping people to build their own organization and institutions equipped with and capable of accelerating their own development. This implies that the community which is continuously being provided with opportunities for participation in the programmes will one day take on itself the role hitherto played by the agency of enhancing its own capacities to meet its needs. Further, it follows that all agencies and their programmes have a time-bound role in their intervention for the development of the vulnerable sections.

People's participation is a challenging concept; a review of its understanding, use and practice by numerous agencies often betrays a superficial commitment to it. The agencies and development workers who are seriously concerned about the development of the community need to do a thorough heart searching to find out whether there is a feeling of insecurity preventing them from expressing and demonstrating their real concern for people's participation. It could be like a leader who enjoys leading, though expressing concern for the development and progress of his followers, frequently experiences insecurity of being overtaken by the ones whom he leads. People's participation, if it achieves its desired goal, would necessarily make the patron agency obsolete beyond a given point of time. Of course, the agency can still renew its relevance and role if it identifies new areas to continue in its helping intervention. An attempt is made in this chapter to critically look into the various facets of people's participation in development activities not as an embellishment but as a functionally necessary component to build a healthy, egalitarian, democratic society.

CONCEPT AND OBJECTIVES OF PEOPLE'S PARTICIPATION

People's participation, in a broader sense, means their total involvement with development agencies in deciding the programmes and activities, fixing up of priorities, taking initiative and carrying out the projects as partners by the contributing of their ideas, interest, material, labour and time. The scope of people's participation depends upon the nature of the activity, the duration of its execution, its technical nature, the clientele it covers, whether it is an individual project or concerns the total or some segments of the community, its location, the amount of funds it involves and, above all, what the development agency stipulates about the kind of participation at different stages of activity and the quantity and quality of participation it expects from the people.

Of late, several terms have come into development terminology in respect to involving people for their betterment. Terms like people's participation, popular participation, community participation, target group participation, public community participation, citizen's participation and so on are in current use meaning almost the same thing that people as partners in their development. Participation is a comprehensive concept embracing all the facets and phases of development beginning with people's initiative and unto their sustaining the activity.

In view of the nature of rural development programmes, most of them initiated by the development agencies, the participation of people could be as diverse as follows:

1. Responding to the programme, accepting the process and adopting technology and innovations;
2. Extending moral support;
3. Participation in decision-making, cooperating in implementation;
4. Contribution of money, material and labour;
5. Taking initiative, mobilizing people and resources; and
6. Assuming leadership and ownership of projects.

People's physical and monetary contributions also irrespective of the nature and degree of people's involvement in the development programmes are recognized as people's participation. This kind of contribution of material, money and labour, rather modest in quantitative and qualitative terms depends on the affordability on the part of the people. In other words, people's economic participation depends upon their affordability.

People's participation is a question of values, giving importance and recognizing individuals and groups in communities as equally important and significant in the overall development and welfare of the total community. People's participation is not just complementary to what the development agency does, allocates, spends, but it is more than that. Social participation in terms of policy support in decision-making, adoption of strategies and implementation of development programmes depends on the social structure, social status, traditional role expectations and role boundaries of members in a rural community.

Participation is a process and it could be viewed as a means to an end and in one sense as an end in itself. In a broader sense, people's participation is beyond rural or urban development. It is organizing, building responsive, active and democratic communities. Participation is a learning process. It is transferring knowledge and skills to the people while they participate in development activities. It is a non-formal education and education through activity. Participation is a democratic process and it provides equal opportunities and strengthens democracy.

Participation of the clientele in the development activities throughout the life of a project will prepare people knowledge-wise and skill-wise to sustain the activity after the development agency withdrew from the scene of action. Participation is people's response, a matching support from the people and their local institutions. It is activating dormant groups, enabling them discover their talent, potential, capabilities, resources and strengths. It is participative planning, development and management of development activities. Rural development is instrumental to people's participation. Community organization is a means and a measure to facilitate and secure people's participation. Participation is a contributing and stabilizing factor to community organization and its strength.

People's participation in activities that concern them, is providing them equal opportunity to share their ideas, views, plans and other material and non-material resources. Most of the developing societies are ridden with economic and social disparities, racial, ethnic and religious. They stand stratified with graded inequalities and suffer from social and cultural communication and restrictions. Some of these graded social structures with privileges and denial of these privileges are centuries and decades old. In such a social structure wherein economic and social inequalities operate in varied degrees, people of all segments participating in the individual and community promotional activities would work against social and ethnic barriers and rigidity gradually breaking down the graded compartmentalized sanctions for and against participation.

Enabling and encouraging the disadvantaged and the poor people to participate in the programmes that affect them and the local community at large is one way of empowering them. It is legitimizing the diverse roles that may be played by different groups standing at different distances in respect to social positions and interactions. People's participation is bringing people together functionally. It is physical, psychic and emotional involvement of the clientele with the development activities. It is training and organizing the community for self-reliance, responsiveness and leadership. Process-wise, people's participation is drawing people from periphery to the center of action, widening their sphere of thinking, contacts and contributions. It is bringing people from relative to total isolation to mutual interaction.

OBJECTIVES OF PEOPLE'S PARTICIPATION

As mentioned earlier, people's participation in rural development is an educational process. It is a training for development involving people in the projects, making them their own. It is to create a sense of awareness, a sense of participation, a sense of belonging, a sense of possession and ownership. It is to develop self-reliance, self-confidence, competence and managerial capacity. It is to train people to take initiative, accomplish and sustain their activities. It is to build up and reinvigorate communities and generate social action. It is to enable people to discover their strength, increase their aspiration level, mobilize and channelize their resources for productive purposes. Participation is bringing people to the core from the periphery, to activeness from passiveness, and to be thinkers, decision makers, doers and implementers from acceptors.

Further, participation facilitates discovery, promotion and encouragement and utilization of new ideas, views, talents and new resources. It is sensitizing the people. Participation creates a sense of individual and group worth, creating awareness of rights, duties and obligations on the part of the members in a community. In a larger sense, society with its culture and civilization is a product of people's social, economic and political participation.

People's participation is not restricted to rural development but it has far greater implications. It is building a new social order, wherein every individual and group will be active participant in community-wide activities, and thus contributing to a certain degree of minimization in social distinctions and differences. Paradoxically, though caste differences and social distance are apparent in the Hindu society, there is to a larger extent smooth running of family and community affairs at the village level.

One could go at length speaking of the objectives and effects of people's participation. It creates *esprit de corps* and ensures dignity of labour when it is labour contribution by the people. It is a means to foster social responsibility and community ownership among the people, and it is organizing and reorganizing groups and community. As a human resource development, people's participation facilitates utilizing and adopting indigenous knowledge system for new programmes. It is a measure to understand people's interests their nexus of relationship with other groups in the community and it also functions as an aperture to understand the ethos, the strengths and limitations on the part of the clientele community. Involving people in development activities is a kind of political education.

To participate is to identify with a cause, purpose, self-interest and interest in the good of the larger community. It is to legitimize, he or she being a member of a group, to make one's presence felt, his or her contribution recognized. It is common interest and common concern that bring people together fostering collective social action especially at the grassroots level. In people's participation, in several of the development activities, new grouping and new alignment emerge and the participants are to learn new ways of adjustment, contribution and coordination which may be termed as re-socialization or neo-socialization.

Some of the development projects on their completion are to be taken over and sustained by the people and so there is a need to involve them in the project activity all through or at crucial stages, so that there is a smooth change over of management of such projects to the people from the development agency (e.g., roads, school buildings, community toilets, minor irrigation projects).

In the ultimate sense, the whole purpose and process of people's participation is Human Resource Development (HRD) – the development of human and inner material resources, with stimulus and support external to the community. Unless we create this culture of people's participation, democracy will not grow.

PHILOSOPHY AND PSYCHOLOGY OF PARTICIPATION

Why should People Participate?

There is no controversy as to whether there should be people's participation in the development programmes designed to meet the basic needs of the people. In fact, governments and development agencies have learnt at a great price as to what happens when programmes have overlooked this important factor of "People's Participation" in their planning and implementation. The *postmortem* of many unsuccessful programmes has shown that they have invariably failed when they failed to provide an adequate place and importance to people's/ target group's role at various stages of implementation.

We are all aware today that there are no plans which do not allot a role to people's participation. In fact, all agencies involved in the field take great care to speak about people's participation repeatedly in all their project plans, annual reports and periodic meetings. It is an all too frequent fact that this term has received abundant lip service rather than convinced practitioners.

There is a body of philosophy and a set of assumptions behind people's participation in rural development. We may briefly look into them.

1. The whole philosophy of rural development is based on one very simple and apparent assumption that the government machinery, however big and efficient it might be, is grossly inadequate by itself to achieve the economic and social revolution needed for ensuring a better and richer life for the vast masses of humanity living in the rural areas. The rural development personnel were to function merely as "catalytic agents". The idea was that a programme started as a government programme with people's participation should gradually and eventually shape itself into people's programme with government's participation.
2. Communities can develop their own capacity to deal with their problems (we assume that people do want and can change).
3. People participate in giving direction to social change in their communities. Change which is brought about by sharing of an effort and social participation, possesses democratic vitality and is also realistic. Self-imposed changes have permanence as compared to those imposed from outside and above.
4. Holistic approach is better than fragmented approach, because the life of a community is itself a whole and any attempt to tackle one aspect of the whole is bound to affect others.
5. People must learn participative skills in democracy because, unless they themselves share responsibilities and participate in fulfilling them, they do not strengthen the democratic structure of their society. Democracy will weaken, if not perish, unless the supporting institutions are created. The basic plank of community development is the growth of the democratic idea. Democracy does not function unless there is

a decentralization of power to be shared very widely at various levels of the social strata.

6. People need help in solving their new problems. External help provides stimulus to inner resources of the community. Communities are like infants who need a prop while they learn to walk. This is rationale for agency functioning and agency support.
7. The tendency of sub-groups, developing themselves as separate entities inside a community, produces social tension and has, therefore, to be channelized and their energies to be diverted to common initiatives.
8. The barriers that prevent active participation by individuals in the direction of social change inhibit personal development. The process of community development is, therefore, to be so organized that the community functions for the good of the individual and the growth of the community. The communities have to be so organized that they promote the growth of individuals.
9. The process of urbanization has destroyed the feeling of belonging to a community and it is necessary to revive this feeling in rural area where the masses of agricultural populations of the developing nations dwell. The contractual relations of an urban society do not work well in a rural society. The problem of developing and maintaining common and shared values, which form the basis of cohesion in a community, is made vastly more difficult by industrialization (Setty, 1970).
10. Beneficiary or target community consists of people who are adults and thinking human beings. They are also intelligent and pragmatic in their own way just as the patron or the helping agency.
11. If given the opportunity, people can organize and draw out solutions to the problems.
12. The community is in the best position to understand its own problems in all their dimensions and complexity.
13. The best resources for their progress and development are they themselves who, if assisted and supported, could be the vital and effective inputs for their own growth and development.
14. Outside assistance, support and expertise are only secondary though important resources provided within time-bound frame.
15. The role of the community cannot be substituted or taken away, however great the vulnerability of the community may be.
16. The apparently most helpless community can be an active factor in helping itself.
17. People always have their own wisdom of meeting their basic needs, however antique and tedious the mechanism of doing so appears to be.

The above assumptions need to be convictions of all those agencies and people who believe in people's participation in development programmes, lacking which no agency can meaningfully provide for the participation of people in any venture (Pinto, 1982).

Further, in a historical perspective, in ancient times, the primary face-to-face group of the communities were knit in a close everyday relationship of togetherness with one another. The "we" feeling was dominant. In the social structure of the rural communities of ancient times, depending upon the value systems of those days, the individual sub-served the needs of the community and the community, in turn, gave him services, environmental freedom, and congeniality to grow to his maximum stature. It was out of this concept of mutual interdependence of the community, the individual and the state, that the welfare of the subject was considered as a primary function of the state. Like two halves of an arch the citizens and the state were supported by and supported each other. The ancient village communities, relatively speaking, had more harmony and community cohesiveness.

By passage of time, the village communities tended to become closed, isolated and limited in functioning, having little intercommunication among them. For instance in India, in medieval times, the Moguls developed a system of feudalism, which increased the distance and tended to diminish the close contact between the ruler and the ruled. The intermediaries acquired symbols of authority in their status and roles, and applied sanctions according to the delegations of authority operating in the system.

In the colonial regimes which most developing nations have passed through, the emphasis shifted to urban centres of trade and it suited the colonial powers to evolve a system of administration which bestowed patronage on certain classes. This naturally ignored a bulk of the villagers and their participation in the administration and their development.

A witness to this fact is the colonial past, the civilizing efforts of the colonizers, the dependency psychology they have created and the legacy they have left behind. The self-centred, urban and elite-oriented administration and development created a sense of alienation among the rural communities. They tended to withdraw. Sometimes, the natives were bewildered, frightened, awestruck, unwilling, uninvolved spectators of the civilizing efforts, and schemes of the colonial administration and the so-called development. In the name of humanitarian work and to serve his purpose, the master did attempt to improve the imagined facilities and needs of his subjects. But the subjects were seldom involved. It was not their programme. They did not and could not appreciate the purpose behind them and so they were not involved and were not participants in the programmes meant for them. This tendency of uninvolvement in government initiated and sponsored programmes continued even after the people became free. The sense of alienation and un-involvement, looking to the government initiative and action, and a tendency to underestimate their abilities, capacities and inner resources, grew over the centuries and decades. These trends had to be remedied, reversed, and a need arose to make people enlightened and full-fledged participants in their development.

In a large sense, the whole civilization and culture of a society, its social organization and institutional apparatus are the product of people's participation. When the people are convinced that a project or a programme is beneficial to them, they are likely to participate and involve themselves in the activity. People more often look for immediate material/ tangible benefits. The gestation period for the programmes to yield results tangible or intangible varies depending upon the nature of the programme. The onus of carrying conviction to the people for their involvement depends on the development personnel and the local leadership, and the way people's participation is facilitated and received. Motivation is a factor in participation.

Participation may sometimes decide your social status – high, middle or low – or your status or rank will influence the nature of participation. Asking for participation is recognizing one's (individual or group) existence and importance. One gets recognition by participation.

For instance, when we approach marginal people in the economic and social sense, and women in some communities who are seldom consulted for their ideas, views and opinions, for their participation in planning and implementing any development activity, there would be a gradual transformation in their behaviour. They feel important. It is according recognition and dignity to them. On the other hand, you cannot ignore the elite in the community, who normally (in some programmes which would benefit them and enhance in their eyes their prestige and status) expect the development agency invite them to participate in the programme. Their participation, as we shall discuss further, may be in terms of policy decisions and monetary support.

People tend to participate (take part) as a social conformity, not to stand excluded from community activity. Prestige is a factor both for participation and non-participation. Participation in a group comprising general, social and economic strata, engaged in a development activity reduces individual and group prejudices. In a philosophical and psychological sense, people's participation in development programmes, meant for the people, is endowed with several virtues, economic development, optimal utilization of human resources, healthy environment and social harmony.

FAILURE, ABUSE AND MOCKERY OF PEOPLE'S PARTICIPATION

Why People Fail to Participate?

People's participation, as we have observed earlier, depends upon the social and class structure of the rural community, the patterns and traditions of decision-making and carrying out communal and individual activities, the way people perceive the programmes and projects initiated by the development agencies, and people's own ability. Further, and importantly it depends upon what the development agencies expect from the people with respect to participation, the stipulations they make and the manner in which the agencies mobilize, motivate, encourage and facilitate people's participation.

People's participation sounds like begging the question. When programmes are meant for people, for their benefit, welfare and advantage, the paradox is why people fail to participate. Ignorance and lack of motivation is a factor of non-or negligible participation. When matters are of technical nature beyond the understanding and outside the experience of the people, participation is less. People look for immediate and tangible benefits. For instance, the problem of population explosion and, consequently, the need for the family to participate in family planning programmes, is a distant cry for the individual or the family. The individual does not feel the urgency of it, its immediacy, and he or she does not visualize the magnitude of the problem, does not see the population explosion within the family and so does not respond. The tendency is to accept a situation as given and live with it.

Sometimes, group rivalry, cliques, conflicts within the community, vested interests, conflict in values, opposition to the programmes, resistance to change and poor local leadership are factors as to why people fail to participate. We just cannot blame the people for their poor response or their failure to participate in rural development activities. The responsibility lies equally on the part of the personnel of the development agencies. Centralization of authority weakens popular participation. Effective implementation of rural development programmes could not be achieved so long as decision on matters concerning them are taken by a super agency. A decentralized system, which allows participatory development from below, is necessary for a healthy society. Sometimes, you have to sacrifice the quality in the works (e.g., roads or buildings) that are accomplished through people's participation, mostly in terms of labour and unskilled work.

We do not question the enthusiasm and good intentions of the planners, administrators and field personnel in rural development but, at the same time, we have to appreciate the fact that people are not ready to tune in to our development programmes, our expectations, and targets in terms of their participation. Often, participation sounds like a rare material, ethereal in nature, difficult to grasp to have a strong grip on, or to secure enough of it and blend it with government initiated programmes. Despite limitations, and though poor in quality and quantity, instances of people's participation abound in number. It provided the impetus to popular enthusiasm, channeled their ideas and energies and brought in an element of sense of integration in rural development activities.

When it comes to participatory planning and development, people are to be placed first. It is not as a political slogan, but as an indispensable factor of real, acceptable and sustainable development. People for whom all the development is meant may not be all wise but they are important. Sarvodaya leader Vinobha Bhave likened the people to numeral '1' (one) while the government is '0' (zero). The values of zeros, he said, placed after 1 increases but no value for the zeros without numeral '1'. Vinobha stressed the importance of people through this analogy.

When it comes to the poor in community for their participating when the programmes affect them or the programmes are of general nature covering the entire local community, they lack affordability for economic participation and at the same time do suffer in the social sphere, since they are marginalized socially and hence not invited and involved in participation. Another paradoxical and unfortunate situation often is, even in areas where the poor could decide for themselves they leave the decision-making to the elite in the community, ethnically and economically so-called superior and dominant groups. Though the poor are the beneficiaries, sometimes, the choices and decisions for them are made by the development personnel or the local elite or the two groups together. In such instances, the poor out of respect or fear or being uninformed or unaccustomed to such decision-making and exercising their freedom of choice, give the decision-making unto the elite and the development personnel or the latter arrogate to themselves what the poor should be doing at their end.

Often we come across situations in the rural communities where the elite's stand runs as follows:

> "We take decisions on our behalf and on behalf of the poor in our community. We expect and let the poor to be silent and just contribute labour to projects where it is required. The poor are an ignorant lot; they have no ideas. We have to think and act for them".

Similarly, if the development agency is more bureaucratic in its style of functioning, there is likely to be less involvement of the people and their participation, especially of non-material nature will be less. The "after all" attitude and notion on the part of the development personnel in respect to the villagers, meaning that people do not matter much, is highly regrettable. We are to seriously ponder over questions like: What prevents people from participation? Who prevents people from participation? What are the issues to participate? What are the opportunities to participate?

The responses to these questions would aid in mobilizing and motivating people to participate. One has to look into the poor or negligible participation and the problems and barriers thereof and whether the poor participation is an internal problem or related to the way development agency has operated the project. Participation should not only be a nexus of relationship between the target population and the development agency, but it should be the responsibility of the client system (target population plus the larger community) in securing and ensuring people's participation. It should become an internal affair and responsibility of the clientele. Such a response and responsibility on the part of the clientele would be an hallmark of real people's participation.

People's participation in terms of their giving ideas, opinions, methods and solutions to certain problems may indicate their status, rank and intellectual capacity; material and monetary contributions, their economic status and affordability and mere physical labour contribution, people's economic poverty. It is a rough kind of categorizing the people based on the type of their participation. It is a common phenomenon to observe in rural communities that factions, cliques, rivalry and group hostility are the factors obstructing participation. Interestingly, pride and status both operate as barriers and stimulants to participation. When people sense that they are brushed aside by the development agency and / or the elite in the community; when their material and non-material contributions are treated as inconsequential, when they had negative experience at the hands of the development agency, when they have not been accorded any recognition by the development agency, when people's requests for help were not properly responded to, there is all likelihood of people not coming forward to participate.

In the name of "participation" often the rich and the powerful in the local rural communities exploit the poor in labour contribution. There have been instances wherein contractors of roads, culverts, school buildings, and other kinds of earthwork exploit the local community in the name and guise of people's contribution, make profit, showing on records, that they have spent money on those parts of the work which were accomplished by people's contribution, in terms of labour and material.

It is not sometimes, the poverty of ideas that prevents the poor from participation, but it is the social distance, isolation from decision-making, and a notion that their ideas, views may not be worthy of consideration, the poor holding a low image of themselves and their ideas, the decay and death of initiative among the people, in general, especially among the weaker section. No attempt is made here to generalize the situation. The upsurge of initiative and action for progress among the poor on the other hand, is quite evident. The presence or absence of initiative and action, the degree to which it obtains, depends on the social composition and economic levels of the people in the rural communities.

Another social phenomenon of interest is the old and the youth playing leadership and influence roles. In a group where old age is respected, experience and wisdom associated with or attributed to the old, the old dominate and the youth are deprived of participation in discussions pertaining to development issues and on the other hand, during recent times, in some communities, as a result of education, urbanization, change in the values, the youth dominate and the old are relegated to the background. Whether it is the old or young, men or women, the barriers to participation are cultural, social, psychological, religious and political. There are many genuine reasons why a lot of agencies and people do not actually provide for people's participation in their programmes.

a) Some development workers, agencies, planners and experts do not seriously believe that the beneficiaries of the programmes have anything important to contribute. They think that the clientele are people who need to be helped but cannot help themselves. Thus being ignorant and incapable how can they contribute to or participate in plans aimed at helping themselves?

b) Some believe that programmes that are minutely drawn up by experts and planners cannot be exposed to the risk of being messed up by the beneficiaries. They feel that the agencies know best what their beneficiaries need.

c) Others feel that once access is left open to the beneficiary community to participate in planning and implementation of the programmes, then results will take too long to come. It is very tedious to work with unqualified people. Agencies want to see material results in the quickest possible time.

d) Allowing for people's participation necessarily implies complex dynamics and a readiness to be very flexible. It also implies getting down to the beneficiaries' level and following their pace to develop. Agencies often experience a cross-culture conflict in this regard and ultimately circumvent involvement of the beneficiaries.

Some organizations and workers who claim their belief in people's participation have their own way of expressing it in practice. It is obvious that in spite of their supposed motivation and efforts, their kind of expression of people's participation is far from what it should be. There are reasons why agencies and people shy away from the genuine practice of people's participation. If one understands the dynamics which controls the operation and functioning of these agencies, it could possibly point out to the reasons why people's participation in its true sense is not within the capacity of these agencies.

People's participation is differently understood and implemented in as many different ways. It is also a fact that all those who claim to value people's participation in programmes and services do not always mean it seriously. Fortunately however, there are numerous agencies who are genuine believers in the need for emphasizing people's participation in programmes and are as serious to give scope to this in their actual operations.

THE MOCKERY OF PEOPLE'S PARTICIPATION

Since it was stipulated and emphasized as a necessary component (on the material and monetary side), people's participation led to blowing and boosting up of figures under people's contribution to community projects. In cases such as approach roads, culverts, irrigation works, school buildings, and community centres, the people were expected to contribute to the extent of 25 percent of the estimated cost of the project. In the absence of such a contribution or when it was only a part of the stipulated amount, the personnel at the mandal and district level had the works executed within the 75 per cent of the government grant, and the local contractors who were entrusted with these works managed to have their profit too. In realistic terms, the works were executed within fifty to sixty per cent of the estimated cost. In such cases, the quality of work suffered. The roads, culverts and tank bunds were washed away and the buildings collapsed. It was not only a physical loss and damage but it created a bad image among the rural people and it became increasingly difficult to get their involvement in newer projects.

The tendency to manipulate and blow up figures under people's contribution (as symbolic of people's participation) in order to show achievement of the targets, and to satisfy the higher-ups in the hierarchy, corrupted the people. The morale of the officials was affected and the people's participation was not taken seriously. With a nod, it was accepted, it was taken for granted. It became nominal. It lost its significance.

In some instances, people's participation meant and was taken to be the physical kind such as labour, and monetary contribution while the people's involvement in the choices, decision-making and programme planning was lost sight of by the development agencies. It became a mockery. There were several instances wherein the community toilets and bathrooms constructed were a total failure, for, in these cases, the local people were not involved, they were not consulted, their habits were not taken into account, the availability and supply of water was not given any thought, and the people were not educated and motivated to use the toilets and bathrooms. The whole project was unimaginative and was carried out in a mechanical way. We took the needs of the people for granted. We never bothered to know the people's views, and the way they would like to have things. We were under the pressure of heavy and unrealistic targets; we were in a hurry to accomplish the targets. The casualty in this hasty process (pursued, of course, with all good intentions) was people's involvement and their participation.

THE RANGE AND VARIETY OF PARTICIPATION

A village community consisting of men, women and children of the village, is the best agency for organizing people's participation, on a systematic basis, for working on projects of common benefit. As mentioned earlier, participation is at various levels and it is of various kinds and modes. It is at the people's level at the grassroots, and it is through people's representative leaders from the village council to the parliament, and through voluntary organizations, advisory bodies, consultative committees, seminars, workshops, conferences held at various levels. The formal and informal organizations at various levels that function as machinery and instruments of rural development, are expected to facilitate and increase people's participation.

Participation at the village level depends upon the social structure of the community, the class composition, social stratification and status hierarchy of groups, the distribution of power and authority, and traditionally determined decision-making patterns and participation. In some groups, women and children are excluded. In some decisions, that concern the total community (community projects), the weaker sections and the less influential are ignored or left out. When participation is voluntary, it depends upon self-interest, obligations to the community and socio-economic conditions of the family. Sometimes, the participation, mostly in terms of labour, material or money, is compulsory or is done under social pressure. In such cases, the individuals have no choice and they have to meet the social expectations or the obligations. Outwardly there will be participation but without the psychological and emotional involvement. It may happen when a programme is not apparently of interest to some individuals and groups, or if the programme does not show any immediate benefit, or meet their needs, or solve their problems.

When we look at people's participation at the rural community level, the following common pattern emergences (refer Fig. 1.). The pattern of participation shown in Fig. 1 is illustrative of the kind that generally obtains in rural communities.

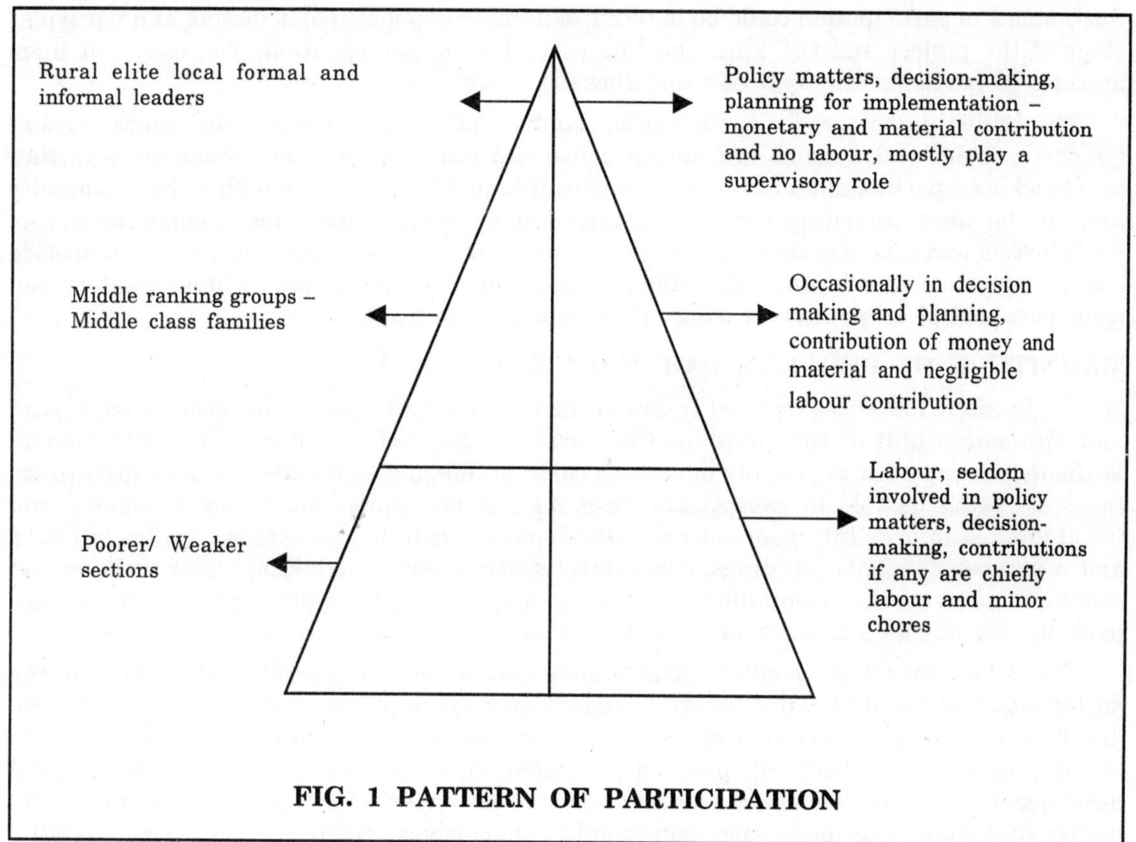

FIG. 1 PATTERN OF PARTICIPATION

Participation of the people in the programmes could be right from the formative stage or at some point in the course of the life of an activity. The question is how important or significant is that stage in the life of the project wherein the people participate. Participation depends on the nature of the activity, and the areas, activities, issues and problems that are of common interest and concern of the larger community and interest groups within the community. Further, there could be variations and fluctuations in the people's participation overtime. In terms of typology of participation it could be voluntary, obligatory, induced, mandatory, under coercion, occasional, once-in-life time, recurring, continual and what may be called supportive participation.

There could be in the initial stages of an activity almost nil and negligible participation of the people, and over a period, it may have gradual increase and depending on multiple factors, especially when people think that the activity is beneficial to them and it is in their long-term interest, their participation would be stable and enduring. On the other hand, people in the initial stages of an activity imbued with exuberance and euphoria may participate in large numbers with intensity, and the participation may decrease as the initial enthusiasm dies out. Further, the other kind of phenomenon is very little participation in the beginning, its significant increase for some time and then its tapering off. These fluctuations in participation could be in terms of number of people participating at a particular stage of the project and the kind and intensity of their participation. You may call them as tides of participation with ebb and flow.

The motivating factors for participation could be self-interest, concern for others, concern for environment and a sense of common cause and public good. The participation further is of two kinds: participation in the programmes initiated by the people within the community and in the ones introduced by the external development agencies. People to people participation and people to development personnel. In terms of activities, people's participation could range from sanitation to disaster management, from irrigation to immunization and from pest-control to poultry rearing. This is just illustrative.

MAGNITUDE OF PEOPLE'S PARTICIPATION

In many instances (related to India) the people's participation in terms of cash, kind and *shramadan* (gift or contribution of labour) has exceeded the share of the government. While there is no limit to people's maximum contribution, a rough scale has been prescribed, the scale being flexible in exceptional cases e.g., in its application to the scheduled and tribal groups. In over fifty years of rural development in India, hundreds of miles of roads, and a number of school buildings, community centres, parks, drinking water wells, water sheds and several other community projects, or assets, have been accomplished, in full and part, by the villagers by dint of their labour and contribution in cash and kind.

The other aspect is people's direct participation at the operational level and the participation of people's representative leaders at various levels in the hierarchy of rural development set-up, in formulating policies, in decision-making and in the implementation of the programmes. Above all, people's participation, as a necessary component of rural development, has created an awareness, provided an opportunity and made people think, realize that they have ideas, they can mobilize themselves, mobilize their scarce material resources, and can build their homes and communities. The real measure of people's participation is their involvement in development activities, which has not been in a desired measure earlier. While we should give credit to the personnel of the rural development agencies for their accomplishment in securing people's participation, we cannot ignore the negative side of it.

In a broader sense, there is no realm in the life of the community wherein people's participation does not arise. It is energy and technique with massive potential to build healthy societies.

ENABLING AND FACILITATING PEOPLE'S PARTICIPATION

People's participation in rural development has short-term and long-term goals. The former deals with the involvement of people in the current programmes and development activities, and the utilization of local material and human resources, while the latter aims at building self-initiating, self-reliant and self-managing rural communities. It is a continuous process of democratization. In this process, two basic things draw our attention: community mobilization and group formation. At the rural community level, two human groups that are universal in all societies and which have been and still are the generators and preservers of primary group, are families and the local communities themselves.

We need to have trust and faith in the ability of the people in rural communities, provide them with the opportunity for participation, however humble and insignificant it may be, respect their ideas and views; channelize and integrate their energies and resources for improving the quality of their life. Even at the cost of repetition, it may be mentioned that the process of working with people demands understanding, appreciation, respect, patience and, above all, wisdom. One effective methodology for channelizing people's participation is through community organization and, cooperative development. Participation shows the ethos and the pattern of behaviour on the part of the people. We may think of several core and marginal factors in a contextual sense either facilitating or inhibiting participation.

FACTORS INFLUENCING PARTICIPATION

1. Awareness on the part of the individual as to the nature and details of the activity and his own abilities to take part in the activity.
2. Self-interest.
3. Motivation to participate.
4. Encouragement provided by the people, leaders in the community and personnel in the development.
5. Authority vested in the individual and exercised by the individual and individual's response to authority within and outside the community.
6. Knowledge and skills on the part of the individual or group which are relevant to the activity.
7. Attitude on the part of the individual or group vis-à-vis the activity and the sponsors of the activity.
8. Ideas that people think which would enrich or improve the activity.
9. Availability of time, money and materials.
10. A felt-need.
11. Interest in the welfare of the community.
12. The cost of participation i.e., how much does the participation cost people.
13. The monetary and non-monetary value of participation.
14. The extent to which individuals and small groups are answerable to the community than to external development agencies.
15. The extent to which the client community is cohesive and organized.
16. The nature and quality of the client community.
17. Internal nexus of relationship and social structure of the community.
18. Easy implementability of the programme.
19. Uniformity.

20. Absence of social, cultural, physical and psychological barriers.
21. Easy to monitor.
22. Within the economic, social and cultural framework and capabilities of the target population.
23. The programme having a good demonstrative effect.
24. Quick results.
25. People could easily understand, respond and adopt.
26. Effective local leadership and leadership on the part of the development agency.
27. The kind of approach made by the development agency.
28. When people are recognized.
29. When you have started the programmes from where people are.
30. Individual/family/ethnic status and prestige.
31. Sex and age.
32. Division of labour in various functions in the community.
33. Hereditarily and traditionally assigned roles to individuals and social groups in the community.
34. Traditionally ascribed/expected participation in social, religious and secular activities.
35. Primary group values.
36. Role of functional specialists in the community.
37. Pattern of local internal communication.
38. Influence of culture and religion.

The above list of factors and situations in a community either facilitating or inhibiting people's participation is only illustrative but not exhaustive.

AN OPERATIONAL MODEL FOR SECURING AND ENRICHING PEOPLE'S PARTICIPATION IN DEVELOPMENT ACTIVITIES

Participation as such is not new in any community. There is always certain kind and degree of participation at certain levels in certain activities. Participation takes place as an economic, social, cultural and psychological functional necessity but participating in activities introduced by development agencies is new. Principally, this was because the government and the bureaucracy have distanced themselves from the people and so the emphasis on encouraging and securing people's participation in the activities that are meant for their welfare and progress. The model that is presented here is a series of methods, measures and approaches based on physico-economic and socio-psycho-cultural factors and characteristics of the client community.

1. Identify the target population and their views on the project.
2. Appraise them of: the nature and details of the project, the benefits they would have from the project, the role of development agency in the project, the kind of participation expected from the client group.

3. Assess what the people could contribute towards the project.
4. Motivate, encourage and facilitate and utilize people's participation (material and non-material).
5. Provide space for participation.
6. See at what stage and in what manner the people can participate in the project now and in the future.
7. Identify the leadership behind the target groups.
8. Assign the responsibility to the groups/leaders.
9. Gradually institutionalize people's participation.
10. Develop channels and channelize people's participation.
11. Gradually delegate and transfer the management of the project to the people/their local institutions.
12. Organize people into groups, assign roles and responsibilities to the existing groups. Organize new groups based on knowledge, skills, affordability and capability and based on residential locality and interests and prepare them to be active participants in the project. Build up a sense of responsibility and accountability on the part of the client community.
13. Let the people come up with their ideas, solutions and strategies.
14. Allow people to work initially on their own and having accomplished that, come up with your improved ways and methods and throw them up as a challenge to the people.
15. Make people's participation their responsibility.
16. Start with initially responsive individuals and/ or groups however small and modest their participation may be. Later, people including the recalcitrant individuals and groups will come to know why they should participate and the manner in which they could do it.
17. Create a sense of pride and competition among the individuals and groups in their participation and contribution to and accomplishment of projects. This could be among various age groups, residential groups and even between men and women.
18. Demarcate the respective functional jurisdictions of individuals/groups for them to play their respective roles.
19. Draw in and legitimize the participation of non-participating and seldom participating groups such as women and weaker sections.
20. Encourage participation in the programmes and issues that arise from within the community so that it may become easy and set a pattern for people to take part and contribute to the programmes initiated by the external development agencies.
21. Make people literate so that you can increase their participation.

ROLE OF A DEVELOPMENT AGENCY

The onus of providing space, encouraging and facilitating people's participation lies on the part of development agency. The development agency (multiple agencies in the field for that matter) may have to indicate, open up, solicit and encourage people to participate in large number of programmes at different stages in the process of development activity. It may be a school lunch programme, adult literacy, an approach road or provision of drinking water facilities.

The right attitude and orientation is required on the part of the development personnel, people's elected and informal leaders and the dominant groups in the community. There are some programmes which are pre-determined and in such cases, there is no question of people participating in policy or decision-making and so the programme by its nature and the type of clientele determine the quantity and quality of participation. Sometimes sacrifices are to be made in terms of time and quality of people's participation, especially in terms of skilled labour and material contribution. Getting labour, money and material symbolizing people's participation towards a project is one thing, but involving people in the process of identifying, formulating and implementing a project is another. The material contribution is for a specific project, but the non-material participation is of far more great significance.

WORKING WITH THE PEOPLE

In order to involve people, we should work with the people. It is the field level functionaries in the filed of rural development, agriculture, livestock, public health and medicare, education etc., who are supposed to have more close and frequent contact with the community. People's participation depends to a large degree on how the field level personnel manage the involvement of the people in the development activities. Involving people and securing their participation depends on the attitude, patience, skills, wisdom, commitment and leadership on the part of the development personnel. Working with people is an art and it is human relations and it is an essential part of human development.

In order to maximize people's participation in rural development and build strong, viable rural communities, the following ten questions may be borne in mind:

1. How can the maximum number of villagers be mobilized for undertaking both village and national improvement projects?
2. How can village communities be helped to develop into self-perpetuative units of social action, many of which will become permanent units of local governments?
3. How can solidarity of, and loyalty to, local groups and local communities be developed without developing resistance to outside guidance and possible resistance to outside assistance?
4. How can old established local groups be used to further the prescribed objectives of national development?
5. How can the levels of aspiration (the standard of living) of both individuals and local groups be raised?
6. How can the local group participation of traditionally low-status persons be increased in undertaking local improvement?
7. How to dissolve, or in some way make constructive use of, local factions or other divisive local community groups?

8. How to develop hundreds of thousands of local small groups and leaders who can help develop local responsibility and initiative?
9. How can overhead (Center and State) governments make maximum contributions of money and personnel to local group undertakings without diluting local group initiative and responsibility?
10. To what extent, and by what means and methods, can the highest degree of traditional "village culture" be preserved, and at the same time, a concern on the part of the villagers be developed for problems and issues which, in the past, have been beyond their social and mental horizons (Taylor).

The knowledge about group and community processes cannot be passed down to others in terms of gadgets, which they can use like material tools. The only common denominators to various and varying types of groups are the social processes of group formation and group functioning. In the use of technical, sociological knowledge, each person, who attempts to catalyze and guide group behaviour, must understand these processes. Elton Mayo, a great production efficiency expert, describes the capacity to apply sociological knowledge as a "social skill". Each director of a programme who works with and through human groups, should possess this skill. He cannot, as is done with scientific material knowledge, depend on engineers. He must himself be a social engineer.

The use of these social skills is needed in all societies, because in no country is it the solution to the problem of preserving community values to let, or help, local communities to revert to their old isolated local community self-sufficiency. The solution is to understand and use the known methods by which people who live and work in small communities can, by organized effort, exercise responsibility for the improvement of every aspect of personal and community living. If encouraged and assisted to do so, local leaders will emerge effective; purposeful regrouping of local residents will occur; and communities will grow rather than stagnate or be completely lost in secular organizations and interests. In this process of working with people, organizing, encouraging and enabling them to participate in their development, their participation occupies a place of pride in rural development.

CONCLUSION

People's participation is a necessary component in rural development. Its essence lies in the proper coordination of individual and group efforts, in fully utilizing the potential of the local institutions, the higher level statutory bodies, the village cooperatives, the village school and other associate organizations such as farmers' forums, youth clubs, women's clubs, and in proper harmonization of individual needs with group needs and group needs with national needs.

REFERENCES

Pinto, Gerry, 1982: "People's Participation: The Spurious and Genuine Concern", *Social Welfare*, New Delhi; Central Social Welfare Board.

Setty, Desingu E, 1970: *Community Development and Extension in India*, Gandhigram, Gandhigram Rural Institute, pp.7-9.

Taylor, Carl C., *Community Mobilization and Group Formation*, New Delhi, Ministry of Community Development and Cooperation (n.d.) p.42.

World Bank, 1975: *Rural Development Sector Policy Paper*, Washington, D.C., World Bank.

CHAPTER 18

The Valayar of South India (A Case Study Depicting Their Poor Living Conditions)

The Valayar constitute as one of the castes in the Hindu social system and as such they are part carriers of Hindu culture. They belong to an ancient stock in South India. Their original home is said to be Piranmalai in Ramnad district in Tamil Nadu. They speak Tamil. In terms of complexion they range from very dark to dark. Occasionally we come across people with a little fair skin. In terms of stature, tall, medium and short people are found among them. This distribution obtains within a Valaya settlement. Most people, men and women, look slender and active. Obesity is rare phenomenon among them.

The Valayar claim and believe that they were especially created by Lord Siva and the Lord, their creator was a companion of the first Valayar. This belief in them gives them a sense of importance and superiority *vis-à-vis* other caste groups, despite their relative social and economic backwardness. As a people they are proud, active, industrious and are not ashamed of or constrained by any inhibitions in respect of their occupations, professions, social practices, and their dietary habits. They are a freedom loving people with a very strong sense of community consciousness. This solidarity of the community works out finely through their active, functional kinship organization and religious practices. The strength of kinship organization or the religious beliefs and practices are not exclusive to the Valayar. It is common in varying degree among other caste groups also. But what is unique and that which distinguishes the Valayar from the other caste communities in the region is their enduring, mutually supporting kin obligations ever reinforced and sustained by their social and religious practices. This group unity and solidarity among the Valayar is recognized by the local caste groups and this is a strength to them despite their economic weakness. The other caste-Hindu groups in the region may look down upon the Valayar, ridicule and despise them over their eating rats, other animals and insects but normally could never try to subjugate them.

Sub-divisions and their spread

The Valayar are an ethnic group comprising several major divisions, sub-divisions and the sub-divisions further divided into sub-endogamous groups. Table 1 shows the above divisions among the Valayar and their territorial distribution.

As shown in Table 1, the major divisions among the Valayar which go as separate castes today comprise the Mutracha, the Muttiriyans, the Ambalakarans, the Uralis, the Vallambans and the Valayar. Further, Vedans, Kurivikarans, Vetuvans and Servaikarans are said to belong to the same parent stock. In the case of Mutracha, Muttiriyans, Ambalakarans, Uralis, Vallambans and the other above groups, the term Valayar is not attached to their caste names, though they belong to the stem stock "Valayar". Over centuries by virtue of their caste honorifics, occupations, economic advancement, geographic, economic and social isolation, they have branched out and emerged as distinct endogamous groups though essentially sharing the same basic social and cultural characteristics. The subject of the present study is one such major division of Valayar in whose case the term `Valayar' is attached to their caste names as a suffix. These sub-endogamous divisions of the Valayar are: Karupasi Valayar, Vannia Valayar, Chembasi Valayar, Saragu Valayar, Chettinad Valayar, Aya Valayar and Mukuthipodadhe Valayar. And some of these sub-endogamous groups are sub-divided further into sub-endogamous groups as shown in Table 1.

In respect to the distribution of different ramifications of the Valayar in general, the Mutracha are distributed in the districts of Coimbatore, Tiruchirapalle, Tanjore, North Arcot, Chingleput, Nellore, Chittoor, Anantapur, Cuddapah, Kurnool and Krishna; the Muttiriyans in the districts of Tiruchirapalle, North Arcot, Tanjore and Chingleput; the Ambalakarans in Ramnad, Coimbatore, Tiruchirapalle and Madurai, the Uralis in Madurai, Tiruchirapalle, Travancore and Wynad; the Vallambans in Tanjore, Tiruchirapalle and Madurai; and the Valayar in the districts of Ramnad, Madurai, Tiruchirapalle, Tanjore, Tirunelveli, Coimbatore, The Nilgiris and North Arcot. In regard to spatial or territorial distribution, it is the Mutracha who are widely spread covering four districts in Tamil Nadu and six in Andhra Pradesh followed by the Valayar,

Ambalakarans, Muttiriyans, Uralis and Vallambans in the descending order. Some of the branched out groups like Vedans and Vetuvans are said to be found in Karnataka and Kerala States besides their spread in Tamil Nadu.

In respect to the Valayar in particular, out of 256 community development blocks (Panchayat Unions) in the eight districts in Tamil Nadu, Valayar live in 118 blocks which comprise 1868 villages. Of these villages, 351 are exclusive Valaya settlements, called isolates the remaining 1517 are constituents in multi-caste village communities. The size of the Valaya settlements under the above mentioned two types of settlement, varies from below 10 households to over 1,000 households. Nearly 30 per cent of the Valaya settlements consist of below 10 households in each settlement and most of them are constituents in multi-caste communities. We find that three-fourths of the Valaya settlements are small communities comprising each below 10 to 30 households. In respect of the distribution of the Valayar in the eight districts in terms of number of blocks, villages and population in the descending order, the following is the position. The descending order in respect to number of blocks is 1. Ramnad, 2. Coimbatore, 3. Tanjore, 4. Madurai, 5. Tiruchirapalle, 6. The Nilgiris, 7. Tirunelveli and 8. North Arcot, in terms of number of villages : 1. Ramnad, 2.Tanjore, 3. Tiruchirapalle, 4. Coimbatore, 5. Madurai, 6. Tirunelveli, 7. North Arcot and 8. The Nilgiris and in terms of population distribution the order is 1. Madurai, 2.Tanjore, 3. Ramnad, 4. Tiruchirapalle, 5. Coimbatore and 6. North Arcot (and no Valayar were returned from the districts of Tirunelveli and The Nilgiris in 1921 census which was the last census which used caste as a variable in the census enumeration). Thus we find that the districts of

TABLE 1: Types, Major, Divisions, Sub-divisions and Sub-endogamous groups among the Valayar and their Territorial Distribution.

Types of the Valayar with Major endogamous divisions	Sub division	Sub-endogamous divisions	Territorial divisions in terms of Districts, State of areas
I. The Valayar who add their caste honorificas suffix (covered inthe present study)	i) Karupasi Valayar	i) Ettaraikoppu	Ramnad, Madurai,
	ii) Vannia Valayar	ii) Tanambanadu	Tanjore
	iii) Chembasi Valayar	iii) Veluvadi	Tiruchirapalle
	iv) Saragu Valayar	iv) Nadunattu or Asal	Tirunelveli
	v) Chettinad Valayar	v) Kurumba	Coimbatore
	vi) Aya Valayar	vi) Vannia	North Arcot &
	vii) Mukuthipodadhe Valayar	vii) Ambunadu	The Nilgiris.
		viii) Punal	
		ix) Vedan	
		x) Sulundukaran	
		xi) Ambalakaran	
		xii) Vellamputtu	
		xiii) Karadi	
		xiv) Kangu	
		xv) Pasikani	
		xvi) Karaikatti	
II. The Valayar who do not add their caste honorific as a suffix (Not covered in the present study)	1. Mutracha (also known as mutturasan) Mutracha, Muthurajulu, Talayari, and Palayakkarans	—	Coimbatore, Tanjore, Tiruchirapalle, North Arcot, Chingleput, Nellore, Chittoor, Anantapur, Cuddapah, Kurnool and Krishna.
	2. Muttiriyans	—	Tiruchirapalle, Tanjore, North Arcot and Chingleput
	3. Ambalakarans	—	Ramnad, Madurai, Coimbatore Tanjore, Tiru-chirapalle, Salem and Tirunelveli
	4. Uralis	—	Madurai, Tiruchirapalle, Travancore, Wynad and Karnataka
	5. Vallambans	—	Tanjore, Tiruchirapalle, and Madurai

Ramnad, Madurai, Tanjore and Tiruchirapalle emerging as the strongholds of Valaya population with the highest concentration in Madurai and Tanjore districts followed by Ramnad and Tiruchirapalle.

In respect to the sub-endogamous groups in whose case the term 'Valayar' is attached to their caste names, basically there are no differences in their social and cultural life save minor ones, while the Karupasi Valayar and Vannia Valayar distinguish themselves as separate endogamous groups by their use of black-bead necklaces, the Chembasi Valayar do it by red-bead necklaces, the Aya Valayar are distinct by the way they address their mother as 'aya'; the Mukuthipodadhe Valayar go as an endogamous group by their women not wearing nose-screw and the Chettinad Valayar have become distinct by virtue of the territory where they live. Some minor differences are found in the case of divorce fee. Thus we find the social structure and the cultural idiom of all the sub-groups of Valayar covered in the study are the same and the sub-group and regional variations in certain practices are discussed wherever they are met with.

Population of the Valayar

It may be noted here that 1921 census was the last census enumeration wherein the name of a caste was used as a variable and so the latest census figures available on the Valayar and the other major divisions among the Valayar are of 1921 census. The Valayar as a part of the Hindu population as per the Census of India, 1921 were 345,501 (167,735 male and 177,766 female). The population of the Valayar as per 1911 census was 358,848 (172,554 male and 186,294 female). The population of the Valayar has been fluctuating since 1891 to 1921. There has been increase and decrease in the percentage of population. Table 2 shows this fluctuation.

TABLE 2: Fluctuation in Valaya Population between 1891-1921

Year of Census				%age of Variation		
1921	1911	1901	1891	1911-21	1901-11	1891-1901
346,000	359,000	360,000	286,000	-3.7*	-0.4	+25.8

*Minus sign indicates the decrease and Plus sign indicates the increase.

Though there has been a decadal increase of 25.8 per cent from 1891 to 1901 there is a marked fall in the percentage of population growth from 1901 to 1911 and from 1911 to 1921.

It may be mentioned here that the actual Valaya population returned in 1921 was 352,503 and of this the Valaya population described as Hindu in the 1921 census (Vol. I, Part II, Tables p.159) is 345,501 =, it is estimated that the Valaya population now would be around 600,000. And when the Ambalakarans, Mutracha and Muttiriyans are clubbed, the population of those who claim Kannappa Nayanar, one of the Sixty-three Saiva devotees as their castesman would be around two million.

On the other hand, the Ambalakarans, Mutracha and Muttiriyans were returned in the 1921 census as shown in Table 3.

TABLE 3: The population of Ambalakarans, Mutracha and Muttiriyans in 1921.

Category	Persons	Male	Female
Ambalakarns (Madras)	164,748	81,150	83,598
Mutracha Hindu (Madras)	465,198	223,131	243,067
Muttiriyans (Madras)	100,331	50,662	49,709
Total	**729,277**	**353,903**	**376,374**

Of the four sub-divisions among the Valayar, Mutracha are numerically larger with nearly half a million in 1921 both in Tamil and Telugu areas followed by the Valayar, Ambalakarans and finally the Muttiriyans restricted to the Tamil districts.

The total population of the Vallayar, Ambalakarans, Mutracha and Muttiriyans as per 1921 census is 1,074,778 (Valayar 345,501 plus the total population of the other three 729,277). If this population is estimated to be around two million now in Tamil Nadu, ignoring the Mutracha population in the Telugu districts, the Valayar in general (including the other three) constitute 4.76% of the population in Tamil Nadu. That is, approximately for every 10,000 population there are 476 persons either belonging to Valayar, Ambalakaran, Mutracha or Muttiriyan community. Further, in regard to the census returns in the case of Ambalakarans, Mutracha and Muttiriyans in the former Madras Presidency since 1901 to 1921, there have been marked fluctuations – fall and increase in respect of the three groups. These fluctuations may be attributed to dual caste titles and changing or in a way nebulous nomenclature of the communities. We may further look into the population figures of the Ambalakarans, Mutracha and Muttiriyans as returned in the census of 1901, 1911 and 1921 and the figures are shown in Table 4.

TABLE 4: Population of Ambalakarans, Mutracha and Muttiriyans as Returned in 1901, 1911 and 1921 census.

Category	1901 Census	1911 Census	1921 Census
Ambalakarns (Madras)	162,471	185,177	164,748
Mutracha Hindu (Madras)	176,060	153,422	227,536
Muttiriyans (Madras)	65,717	86,856	100,324
Total	**404,248**	**425,455**	**92,608**

The census report describes that Ambalakarans rose in 1911, but fell in 1921 to the level at which they were in 1901. Mutracha fell in 1911, but in 1921 have risen by 48 per cent, while Muttiriyans have increased steadily at each census. Further, it reports that, a Mutturaja Sangham (society/association) started in early 1920s in Tiruchirapalle may be the cause for popularizing the caste title 'Mutracha'.

The figures for the districts, the report adds, are even more remarkable, Ambalakarans, for example, have quadrupled in Salem, they have nearly doubled in Tanjore, while in Tiruchirapalle they have decreased by nearly 50 per cent. The chief increase of Mutracha is in Tiruchirapalle, when none were returned in 1911 and now (1921) over 50,000. there has also been a large increase in Anantapur balanced by a fall in Cuddapah and Kurnool, they have increased in Chingleput and in Chittoor, but have lost ground in North Arcot, Muttiriyans show a decline in Chingleput and a rise in North Arcot and Tiruchirapalle.

It may be noted here that though the Valayar, Ambalakarans, Mutracha and Muttiriyans enjoy similar cultural and social characteristics forcing an ethnologist to group them under one head, they have been returned as distinct caste groups till 1921 census.

However, the data collected for the purpose of the present study show that the Valayar are distributed in Tirunelveli and The Nilgiris districts also.

TABLE 5: District-wise Distribution of Valayar Population as per 1921 Census

Name of the district	Population
Tiruchirapalle	73,018
Coimbatore	13,975
North Arcot	7,790
Ramnad	80,600
Tanjore	88,517
Madurai	88,605

Field of Study

As said earlier, the present study covers the Valayar living in eight out of fourteen (Number of districts at the time of the Study) districts in Tamil Nadu. It may be mentioned here that the Valayar in these eight districts live and interact with several caste-Hindu groups, Scheduled Castes and Tribes and occupational caste-groups. The main caste-groups with whom they live and interact are Kallar. Thevar, Servai, Vellalar, Nadar, Konar, Maravar, Naidu, Vallambar, Padayachi, Vanniar, Naicker, Gounder, Vakkaliga, Odayar, Devanga Chettir, Kammalar, Achari, Barber, Washerman, Pariaher, Chakkiliar, Boyar, Pannikar, Paliar and Badaga and several others.

Since the study is designed to be the first systematic and detailed monograph on the Valayar, two Valaya communities – Valayapatti in Madurai district and Sendhi Udayanathapuram in Ramnad district were selected for intensive and in depth study besides a few Valaya communities in Madurai and Ramnad districts for a comparative study of the sub-groups among the Valayar. These Valaya settlements comprise Chittarevu, Anjukulipatti, Alagar Koil, A.Valayapatti, Pallapatti, Kutladampatti, Konapatti, T.Kallupatti, Melur, and Madurai City in Madurai district and Pasangarai, Sivaganga, Karaikudi, Piranmalai and Rameswaram island in Ramnad district. Besides brief visits were made to Sathyamangalam in Coimbatore district and Tiruchirapalle. The above Valaya communities represent Vannia, Karupasi, Chembasi, Mukuthi Podadhe and Aya Valayar which are the sub-groups, among the Valayar. For the data on the population of Valaya households and their occupations, all the eight districts in Tamil Nadu, Madurai, Ramnad, Tiruchirapalle, Tanjore, Tirunelveli, Coimbatore, the Nilgris and North Arcot where Valayar live are covered.

We may give a brief account of Valayapatti and Sendhi Udayanathapuram which constitute the nucleus for the study.

Valayapatti

Valayapatti is one of the hamlets of the revenue village known as Keelakottai. Its other hamlets comprise Chettiapatti, Samiarpatti, Muthanamapatti and Gandhigram. The Gram Panchayat called Chettiapatti Gram Panchayat constitutes Chettiapatti, Samiarpatti, Muthanampatti, Gandhigram and Valayapatti. Valayapatti is located about 6 kilometres to the west of Sirumalais (hills) and is served by the Police station located at Ambaturai, about 3 kilometres to the southwest of Valayapatti. Valayapatti as a hamlet of Keelakottai and as a constituent of Chettiapatti village Panchayat comes under Athoor Panchayat Union, Dindigul Taluk and sub-division in Madurai district. The details relate to the time of field study 1971-74. Subsequently, new districts were formed with change of names. The nearest town Dindigul is located 16 kilometres to the north of Valayapatti and the district headquarters Madurai city is located one and a half kilometers to the east of the highway that runs from Madurai to Dindigul and 3 kilometres from the Ambaturai railway station. The Chettiapatti Panchayat has an area of 1,250.50 hectares, 662 households and a population of 4,028 (male: 1988, Female: 2,040)

Valayapatti is an exclusive Valaya settlement comprising 50 households and a total population of 272. Of this population 153 (49.64 %) are male and 137 (50.36%) are female.

The Valayar at Valayapatti are known as Karupasi Valayar (those who use black bead necklaces), but the same sub-group is also known as Vannia Valayar. Both the terms Karupasi and Vannia are used interchangeably.

Valayapatti as mentioned above is an exclusive Valaya settlement and in this restricted sense it is called an isolate as opposed to or different from a Valaya settlement which is a constituent in a multicaste community as in the case of Sendhi. The Valaya settlement at Valayapatti is nearly 150 years old. The first settlers at the habitat were the Muthandi brothers who had migrated from Kutladampatti, 20 kilometres from Valayapatti. A primary school and a Balwadi (kindergarten) are located in the hamlet. Chettiapatti, Chinnalapatti and Dindigul are the nearest centers for them for buying their consumer goods and selling their farm products, firewood and other wild products.

The caste-groups that inhabit in the Chettiapatti Panchayat area and with whom the Valayar come in varying degrees of interactions are : (1) Kurumba Gounder, (2) Kapilia Gounder, (3) Pariaher (4) Vellalar, (5) Thevar, (6) Kallar, (7) Dhobi, (8) Cobbler, (9) Goldsmith (10) Nadar, (11) Nayar, (12) Vanniar (13) Naidu (14) Pallar, (15) Boyar, (16) Kannadiga (17) Devanga Chettiar and (18) Barber.

It may be mentioned here that Valayapatti as said above is the only hamlet in Chettiapatti Panchayat which is an exclusive Valaya settlement whereas the main village Chettiapatti and other hamlets are multicaste communities.

Sendhi Udayanathapuram

It is the main revenue village and a Gram Panchayat (village council) located in Sivaganga Taluk, Ramnad District. The revenue village and the Panchayat comprise Sendhi, Karambavoor, Meenakshipuram, Mudigandam and Kumarapatti. The Panchayat office is located at Kumarapatti, Sendhi is about 19 kilometers from Sivaganga which is the nearest town, block, taluk and sub-divisional headquarters, and Sendhi is about two kilometers to the north of Madurai-Sivaganga road and it is about 60 kilometers from Madurai, which is the nearest city. The district offices of Ramnad including the District Collectorate are located in Madurai city for the sake of administrative convenience. Sendhi is a multicaste community comprising (1) Valayar, (2) Pariaher, (3) Kallar, (4) Konar, (5) Pannikar, (6) Dhobi (7) Servai (8) Vani Chettiar (9) Achari and (10) Barber. It has an area of 1348.14 hectares and a population of 1703 (male 862 and female 841).

The Valayar in Sendhi are known as Vannia Valayar. They live in a separate locality in Sendhi. They comprise 44 households and a population of 203. Unlike in Valayapatti the female Valaya population in Sendhi is larger than male population. The male population consists of 44.82 per cent (91) and the female 55.18 per cent (112).

The Valayar of Sendhi are a constituent in a multicaste community and this way they differ from the Valayar of Valayapatti. The Valaya settlement in Sendhi also is five generations old as that of Valayapatti. The first settlers came from Vendavasi. It was during the beginning of the British rule (East India Company) in India. The lands at Sendhi then, were under the Sokkendi Zamindar. Under the patronage of this zamindar, the first Valaya settlers at Sendhi formed the irrigation tank now called Sendhi tank. The zamindar allotted two-thirds of the land under Sendhi tank ayacut to the Valayar and to the servai of Karambhavoor (close to Sendhi). The zamindar retained one-third of the lands for his personal cultivation. After a few years, the zamindar withdrew the right of cultivation of lands from the Valayar and the Servai paying each cultivator some monetary compensation. It was on account of the Servai having indiscriminately felled some trees in the lands of the zamindar. But the Vallayar pleaded with and appealed to the zamindar, they returned him the compensation they received and got their lands back. Motivated by this, the Servai of Karambhavoor too approached the zamindar, but their request was turned down.

During this period, the zamindar wished to have a Brahmin priest and the Valayar at Sendhi brought a Brahmin astrologer-purohit from Pudukottai and he settled at Sendhi with his family. This Brahmin family was the nucleus for the *agraharam* (an exclusive Brahmin residential area away from the non-Brahmin residences) that grew later at Sendhi. The *agraharam* was located in the lands belonging to the zamindar. The Brahmin priest was assigned 1.50 acres as a 'gurukula' manyam (free land assigned in return to some services). The remaining lands under the direct control of the zamindar were given to one of the daughters of the zamindar. The Brahmin settlement when it grew in size and sound economically, the Brahmin purchased the lands at Sendhi from the Zamindarini.

Further, the Brahmin in order to meet their dairy requirements invited a Konar family (shepherd) from the neighbouring village of Meenakshipuram. The Konar desired that he should be assigned some land close to the Valayar's. the first Konar family was assigned one acre of land.

Some time later, the Valayar brought a Pariah by name Sangili Karuppan from Nelakottai, 15 kilometers from Sendhi. The Paraiah family was assigned 0.75 acre. The Valayar being the first settlers at Sendhi, further invited on the request of the Brahmin, a Kallar family to settle down at Sendhi and this family too was allotted one acre of land by the Brahmin community. The Kallar family was supposed to take care of the security of the Brahmin.

The lands cultivated by the Valayar were not clearly defined in extent and demarcated. When the Brahmin grew stronger and when the lands came under the control of the East India Company, after Veerapandiya Katta Bomman was killed by the British, the Brahmin land owners at Sendhi, approached the East India Company authorities at Thirumayam, the regional headquarters of the East India Company then and negotiated with them and secured the *Patta* (right of ownership) for the lands that were under the cultivation of the Valayar of Sendhi. Overnight the owners became tenants; the Valayar were allowed to cultivate the same lands on lease.

Though the Valayar were deprived of their ownership of the lands, their farming became prosperous. This has created jealousy among the Brahmin and they began dominating over the Valayar. Since 1958, the Valayar stopped paying the *melvaram* (the landowner's share in the produce) to the Brahmin landlords. This was a result of organization and leadership provided by A.R.Ayyadurai, a communist leader from Kumarapatti. It turned to be a long drawn civil dispute between the Brahmin and the Valayar and finally as per the verdict of the court, the Valayar got back their ownership right over the lands they cultivated. Gradually, the entire Brahmin community at Sendhi has migrated to several places in Madurai and Ramnad districts. The Valayar now live at Sendhi along with nine other non-Valaya caste groups.

The foregoing brief history of the Sendhi Valayar has resulted in one singular change in them; they had to become sympathizers or supporters of communism which of course will not be a permanent feature with them.

In Sendhi, numerically the Valayar are the major group, but to a considerable extent dominated by the Kallar and Konar in the village.

It is in order here to provide a brief account of the society and religion among the Valayar of South India.

Mythological and Historical Background

The Valayar are a very ancient people in South India. They trace their decent to Lord Siva, Kannappa Nayanar, one of the sixty-three saivite devotees who offered his eyes to God is claimed to be their ancestor. The Valayar have historical links also. Contemporaneous to Pallavas and Cholas (600-1400 AD) some of the Valayar were warrior groups and ruled over small territories as chieftains in Tamil and Telugu parts of South India. "Valayar" is a generic name and it subsumes castes such as Ambalakarans, Mutracha, Muttiriyans, Servai, Vedans, Vallabhans and Kurivikarans. They have branched out in earlier centuries with shifting caste nomenclature and honorifics. The Valayar go with diverse caste honorifics such as Moopan, Moopa, Moopanar, Muthuraja, Valayan, Ambalam, Ambalakarar and Servai. Some of these caste titles are regional in nature.

Life Cycle: Birth and Childhood

A pregnant Valaya woman observes certain taboos in respect to her movements and diet. She should not go out of the house during the hours of lunar and solar eclipse. During the pre-natal period certain magical and medical treats are given to the expectant mother.

In fifth or seventh month of the pregnancy the family deity of the conjugal family is worshipped known as *pala puja* (milk ceremony). In the seventh month of her pregnancy the woman is served some special dishes by her natal family. The first confinement takes place at the residence of the woman's natal family and the subsequent deliveries at the conjugal family.

The barber woman called *dai* attends to the delivery of the child. The placenta is buried at the place where the mother bathes and the child is washed. It is believed that the water when it percolates and wets the placenta the mother will have enough of milk to feed the child. The umbilical tissue that falls off after a few days, is put in a casket and tied to the cradle, crèche, or around the neck of the child. The pollution after the birth of child lasts for thirty days after which the mother accompanied by the child visits the family shrine.

Most of the Valaya names are after their deities. Some of the Valayar have the practice of making horoscopes of their children. Of late, some of the Valayar are taking to surgical contraceptive measures to prevent births. Children are protected from evil eye, evil spirits through spells, talismans and magico-medical treatment.

The tonsure in the case of the first born is done at the shrine of the family deity and in some cases at the shrine of community deities. For the children other than the first born, it takes place either at the shrine of the family or community deities. Tonsure and ear-piercing take place normally before the third year between the first and third year. These twin ceremonies though common among all the Valayar, there is some divergence in terms of details in the ceremonies.

The period of childhood for Valaya children is relatively short. Their levels of living and attitudes and social practices make Valaya children assume adult roles and responsibilities right from their fifth to seventh year. There is considerable juvenile labour among Valaya children in the age group of five and sixteen.

Adolescence and Young Age

Both boys and girls work together and there is no segregation of girls from the boys. There is uninhibited development and growth of sex knowledge among the Valaya children, the Valaya community does not value so much for the virginity of a girl before marriage. There is considerable incidence of sex adventures on the part of both the sexes before and after marriage.

A girl reaching nubile age – her first menstruation is publicized. The girl after the first menses and until she takes the purificatory bath, remains in a hut put up by her mother's brother. The mother's brother plays a very significant part in the puberty rites. The woman during the period of flow remains outside the house and after the purificatory bath enters the inner precincts of the house.

Graduation of a Valaya individual from childhood to adulthood as a member of a group is smooth and gradual. Sexes are not isolated. Boys and girls are equally active right from their teens in supplementing the family's income. This to a considerable measure ensures equality of sex and freedom to the girls. In the life-cycle of a Valaya boy or girl, getting married early in life is an unfailing feature. Hardly a girl remains unmarried more than a year after her puberty. Marriage in the case of an average family does not involve much expenditure. There are traditional types of marriages performed with all paraphernalia and rituals, marriages performed at the *mandai* (an open public place) and marriages by elopement. Though monogamy is the order, the caste tenets permit bigamy, polygamy and there is the practice of levirate and sororate marriage. There is a considerable incidence of pre-marital relations resulting either in marriages or the couple being fined by the caste council for the marital offence.

Marriage

The Valayar marry their sister's, paternal aunt's and maternal uncle's daughters on a preferential basis. Some of the Valaya groups have the practice of comparing horoscopes or consulting local purohits and astrologers on the compatibility of the boy and the girl based on the *namanakshatras* (based on Hindu calendar, relating nakshatras, 'stars' to that of the first letter of the name of a person). The formal initiative for negotiating an alliance is taken by the groom's family. They visit the bride's home and negotiate the alliance. When the parties do not come to a spontaneous decision and also as custom, either of the party visits a local Valaya shrine and look up for a favourable sign from the wall-lizard for the alliance.

Once the alliance is settled, it is followed up by the betrothal ceremony done at the bride's residence during which the consent of the bride's mother's brother is important and so also the agreement of the groom's mother's brother. Bride-price is universal among all the Valaya groups. In most cases it is Rs.10.25. The bride-price is paid either on the betrothal day or on the day of marriage.

On the day previous to the marriage function, *shanty* (purification-sanctification) ceremony is carried out for the groom and the bride at their respective residences. In certain cases, marriages take place at the bride's residence and in some others, at the groom's residence. Two decades ago among most Valaya groups and now among some, it is the groom's sister that ties the *tali* (marriage badge made of gold) around the neck of the bride, while the groom remains at his residence. The actual pattern of *tali* tying is subject to certain variations. After the marriage ceremony, the groom's sister brings the bride to the groom, along with other kinsfolk.

The distribution of betel-nut and betel-leaves to the invitees soon after the tying of the *tali* is a significant feature among the Valayar since the Valaya community claims it as a matter of right. Among some groups of Valayar, even though the marriage takes place at the bride's residence it is the groom's family that arranges marriage feast at the bride's residence and in the case of marriage taking place at the groom's residence it is the groom's family that hosts the invitees.

On the second day of the marriage, the groom and the bride meet the caste elders in the village and seek their blessings and also visit the local Valaya shrines and worship the deities. On the same day, the couples return to the groom's village and they are received by the groom's family ceremonially. The couples stay for a day at the groom's village. On the second day of their stay, they visit the local Valaya shrines and meet the caste elders as they did at the bride's village and seek their blessings. On the same day, the groom's family presents the bride with a measure of rice and a hen. She takes the rice and the hen to her natal family accompanied by her husband. Again on her return to her husband's family after a short stay at her natal residence, her parents present her with a new palm-leaf basket, a measure of rice and a hen. With these presents, the couple return to the groom's village. This completes the ritual and the ceremonial part of the marriage.

Subsequently, the couples are invited for the *Thalai Adi* (first Adi festival after the marriage) by the bride's natal family. Similarly, the couples are invited for the first *Deepavali* (festival of lights). Further, during the first pregnancy either in the fifth, seventh, or ninth month special dishes are brought to the woman while she stays at her conjugal household, by her parents.

Family Life and Kinship

The Valaya couple after the marriage enters the threshold of married life that encompasses economic, social and familial responsibilities and obligations. Usually after marriage, the newly wedded establish their household at the man's village. A married Valaya woman supplements her family's income by engaging herself in some economic activity of the group, besides her keeping the house and rearing children. A married woman enjoys considerable freedom and support from her natal family. The woman's brother plays a significant role in her case and in the case of her children, the natal family among the Valayar assumes greater responsibility in view of considerable incidence of divorce.

The Valayar do not consider marriage to be a sacred bond between a man and his wife and this has a bearing on their family, specifically conjugal life which is not always smooth sailing. It is disturbed now and then with domestic quarrels, money, and interference and bossing over by the mother-in-law. Another important factor that brings in disorganization in the family life is the incidence of extra-marital relations.

Men and women in the age group of 20-55 mostly figure in extra marital cases. They comprise single, married, divorced and widowed of both the sexes. These extra marital relations relate to the Valaya men and women going for Valayar and non Valayar and *vice versa*. The cases end in fines imposed on the guilty party or parties, dissolution of marriage and sometimes a forced marriage which ends in immediate annulment of the marriage. A Valaya woman who cohabits with a non-Valayar is excommunicated. But in terms of value or status, premarital or extra-marital relations of a Valaya woman, within the caste circle does not earn the offender a stigma nor does it impair the chances of her marriage.

Incest taboos are universal among the Valayar as among other people. Divorce among the Valayar is institutionalized and the divorce fee ranges from Rs.7.50 to Rs.350.00. The tendency among some groups is to enhance the divorce fee in order to discourage divorce. The age of divorcing couple usually ranges from 20 to 50 and the dissolution of marriage may take place within days or after ten to fifteen years of marriage. Roughly speaking, one in ten marriages ends in divorce among the Valayar. It is a safety valve and in most cases it is a smooth glide over persons and places in the shifts of matrimonial bonds. But the children are affected and sometimes they become the victims of divorce.

Nuclear family is the order among the Valayar. Father or the husband is the head of the family, but women enjoy considerable freedom and their influence on family matters is to be reckoned with. Avoidance exists in the case of mother-in-law and father-in-law. Yet there have been cases of fathers-in-law having extra-marital relations with daughters-in-law and marrying them on the death of their sons as they stand in the relationship as potential mates. The Valayar are a patrilineal and patrilocal group,

Old Age, Disease and Death

There is intensive economic and social interaction between the old and the young among the Valayar. There is the mutual dependency of the young and the old. Hardly one comes across any generational gap among the Valayar in belief systems and religious matters. The old are respected, loved and cared for. The old and the aged are economically active until they are physically healthy. A Valaya man or woman, has a long old age and his or her economically productive period in the life span, comparatively speaking, is longer and the economic conditions prolong it.

The Valayar are tradition-bound and generally believe that diseases are caused by supernatural powers and that these powers could be propitiated in order to cure a disease. Their behaviour toward the treatment of the sick comprises invoking the gods, spells and formulas suggested by the local mantric or demonologist, the home made remedies, the services of the indigenous medical practitioner and an allopath and a modern hospital. But they tend more to propitiating deities through sacrifices and rituals to cure a disease.

Death is mourned. It is a factor among the Valayar that keeps the kin-bonds strong and sustained. Drum-beating is arranged during the lying-in-time and the journey to the burial ground. The women sing mourning songs. Some Valayar engage professional mourners also. Before the body is lifted on to the bier, it is given a ritual bath and dressed with a new cloth supplied by the mother's brother and other affinal kin. It is the in-laws and affinal kin that carry the bier. The funeral rites consist of the ones performed at the *mandai* by a daughter of the dead or his wife. The milk ceremony takes place on the third day and the last rites on the sixteenth day. A woman technically becomes widow on the day of the last-rites when she discards her *tali* and glass bangles. Disposal of the dead by burial is the practice largely prevalent.

They believe that untimely or sudden death by murder, through drowning, suicide result in the spirit of the dead turning into a ghost and the ghost leading an astral life until it would have lived its normal mortal life. The Valayar believe in rebirth after death and in the existence of heaven and hell. They also believe in the theory of Karma. The practice of ancestor worship obtains among the Valayar.

Social Organization

The Valayar as an ethnic group and as a segment of Hindu population are organized into sub-endogamous groups such as Mutracha, Ambalakarans, Muttiriyans, Vannia or Karupasi Valayar, Chembasi Valayar, Saragu Valayar, Chettinad Valayar and Aya Valayar. Each endogamous group is further divided into inter-marrying exogamous clans and clans into families, which are the basic units of Valaya social organization. Further, the Valayar are organized into occupational, religious groups and into village communities. These are units of social action with specific functions. Though the sub-divisions among the Valayar consider themselves as distinct endogamous groups, in essential occupational, social and religious characteristics, they are similar to one another. One unifying and a common feature among all sub divisions, is their caste affinity to Kannappa Nayanar, a great Saiva devotee.

We come across a few Valaya village communities having been converted to Christian faith (Roman Catholic) who have developed a separate social network even though they are affiliated to their non-Christian kin.

A clan among the Valayar known as *kootam, veedu or vagaira,* is based on patrilineal rule of descent. The size of the clan varies from clan to clan. A clan may live in one village or may be scattered over a cluster of villages but generally in the same territory. Each Valaya village comprises two or more than two inter-marrying clans. Family among the Valayar is predominantly nuclear and is well knit in terms of division of labour and functions among the members in the family. Occupational groupings with mutual assistance and dependency are found in farming, fishing, collection of firewood and wild products and farm-labour. A clan constitutes a religious group when it celebrates its deities. A clan's affinal kin join it when it celebrates the clan deities, and all the exogamous clans in a village settlement join together and collectively celebrate the common communal deities. Thus, a clan, inter-marrying clans and all clans resident in a village constitute different religious groupings. One significant thing among the Valayar is their group solidarity. When the interests and name of a local resident community is in jeopardy, the whole community stands as one, meets the challenge and safeguards its interests.

Caste council is a traditional social institution among the Valayar. It is a regulator of their social and religious life. It consists of all male heads of households headed by the *kambili* and who in turn is assisted by the *Thandal.* These two offices are hereditary. The Kambili is also known as Ambalakarar, Natami, Peria Veettukarar and the Thandal as Nattampillai and Valayapillai. The caste council is a democratic institution serving the community as a public forum, an assembly and as a court of justice. Consensus is the principle and practice. Its decisions are not arbitrary, and they are binding on the members. It decides the celebration of community deities inquires into and settles all cases of pre-marital and extra-marital relations and divorce issues.

Besides the local caste council there is the area or regional caste council comprising a cluster of Valaya settlements. It serves as a court of appeal. In the case of Valayar living as constituents in a multicaste village community they are part of the traditional village council and they come under its purview.

As an effort to bring all the Valaya sub-groups together and to bring in some changes in their customs and practices and to promote their well-being, a few conferences comprising representatives from various sub-groups and regions were held. The first conference was held in 1939 in Thirupparakundram, Madurai district. As a result of the efforts of the community leaders, a Valayar association under the name, "Vanni Kannappa Kula Valayar Munnetra Sangham" with its office in Madurai has come into being in 1958.

In the social organization of the Valayar, they have a network of economic, religious political and social relationships with the non-Valayar in the respective regions. As producers and sellers of farm produce, fish, firewood and wild products, the Valayar interact and enjoy economic links with the non-Valaya caste groups. Similar is the interaction in their being the consumers of goods and services supplied and rendered by other groups. The economic relationship between the Valayar and the non-Valayar relate to selling, buying, borrowing, lending and hiring themselves as farm labourers.

In multicaste communities, the Valayar join the other caste groups in celebrating the village deities. The Valayar as residents in multicaste village communities and as constituents in the village Statutory Panchayats and as voters in the elections to local bodies, State Legislature and Parliament, they influence, share power, and interact with other caste groups.

In terms of social relationship, they occupy an intermediary caste ranking *vis-à-vis* other caste groups. They have commensal relations with all caste-Hindus and they do not dine at the houses of servicing castes and Scheduled Castes. Most of the higher and intermediary caste groups do not dine at the houses of the Valayar. They admit and are admitted to the living houses of all caste groups with the exception of Brahmin.

The Valayar do not admit members of Scheduled Castes into their houses. They have joking and respect relationships with intermediary order castes such as Vellalar, Gounder, Konar, Thevar, Kallar and Servai. In respect to social distance between the Valayar and the non-Valayar caste groups in general, the degree of acceptance of the non-Valayar by the Valayar is less than that of the other by the former. The Valayar have a sense of superiority over the non-Valaya groups, though it is far from acceptance by the other groups.

Religion, Festivals and Magic

Coming to their religious life, it may be observed that one significant feature that distinguishes the Valayar from the rest of the Hindu population is their religious life and practices. The Valayar are polytheistic and they worship a plethora of deities. Most of the deities they worship are the local versions of Sanskritic deities. As Hindus, at a conceptual level, they believe in the concept of Supreme Being, but this concept and belief is not reflected in their religious behaviour. Their sacred geographical world is limited mostly to their settlements and their stem villages in the case of migrants who have settled in other villages. They keep themselves close to the abode of their deities. The Valayar, traditionally, worship twenty-one deities, but these twenty one deities are not the same for each Valaya community. Nevertheless, some deities are common in all the groups.

The Valaya deities comprise male and female, benevolent and malevolent, with form and without form, seen and not seen, deities with diverse locale of abode, deities vegetarian and non-vegetarian, i.e., those receiving non-animal sacrifices and animal sacrifices and deities that are exclusively worshipped by the Valayar and the ones worshipped by both Valayar and non Valayar. Male deities slightly out number female deities, but there is no difference in the status and importance attached to the male and female deities. Majority of the deities are meat eaters. The meat-eating or non-meat eating characteristic of a deity is not universal. Benevolent deities outnumber malevolent deities and majority of the deities have some form. Further the deities could be classified as clan deities and community deities.

The chief offerings they make to the deities comprise animals-rams, he-goats and cocks and coconuts, camphor, incense, vermilion, turmeric and flowers. The animal or non-animal offerings are made by individual families and collectively by the entire community. The sacred specialists among the Valayar are called *pujaris*. The office of the *pujari* is institutionalized and is hereditary. There is an interesting institution of *samiyadis* among the Valayar. They are the media of the deities. They could be men or women. Usually, men are the media of male deities and women the female deities. The samiyadis don a set of ceremonial dress.

The family deities and the community deities are celebrated annually or every alternate year. The celebration of family (clan) or a community deity involves elaborate preparations comprising consultations with their deities through their media-samiyadis, obtaining their approval for fixing a date for the celebration, publicizing the date of celebration, inviting kinsfolk, drum-beaters, Urimikaran and celebration of the deities. The celebration of family and community deities among the Valayar is a cementing force in terms of kin-bonds and community solidarity.

The Valayar believe in supernatural elements, spirits and in the efficacy of magic and spells in treating human and animal diseases and warding off effects of evil spirits. They practice white magic and this practice is universal among them.

Festivals observed by the Valayar may be classified as religious, agricultural and national. The intensity is more in the celebration of their religious festivals and the intensity tapers off when it comes to agricultural and national festivals. Of the religio-agricultural festivals *Adi* is of paramount importance to the Valaya community. The Adi festival is celebrated in the months of July-August. It consists of *Thalai Adi* (first day of Adi Tamil Month). *Nadu Adi* (the middle of Adi the eighteenth day) and *kaluvadi* (the last day of Adi month). The celebration of *Thalai Adi* is marked by the worshipping of their clan and community deities. Animals are sacrificed. Sons-in-law and daughters are invited for the *Adi* celebrations.

Festivals associated with hunting are not universal among the Valayar though hunting has been a characteristic activity of the Valaya community. It is observed by some groups -- Valayar of Sendhi and Piranmalai for instance.

Of the agricultural festivals *Pongal* (14th January) and cattle festival are universal among all Valaya groups. In the cattle festival, *jallikattu* (an Indian version of bull fighting) is unique. *Masi Pachchai,* a Valaya version of *Sivarathri* is observed by all the Valaya groups. It is a community festival and at that, it is an agricultural festival marked with the ceremonial offering to deities and eating of newly harvested grain and pulses. The observance of the Tamil New Year Day (Vershaporappu) and Deepavali, are nominal. *Karthikadeepam* (in November) which follows deepavali is significant for the Valayar. Celebration of national days such as Independence Day, Republic Day, Gandhi Jayanthi (Gandhi's birth day) Children's Day (Jawaharlal Nehru's birthday) are nominal and peripheral in the case of the Valayar.

Material Culture of the Valayar

A study of the material culture of the Valayar is as significant as understanding of their social, political and economic life. The totality of their material culture reflects their levels of living, belief system, social practices and the degree of tradition that persists today. The material culture as such comprises patterns of physical settlements, type of dwellings, ceremonies associated with construction and occupation of houses, personal care and decorations with clothing and ornaments, patterns and quality of diet and the use of stimulants and intoxicants. The dwellings of the Valayar are simple, and clothing is also of a similar nature. They are meat-eaters and go in for a variety of games. The Valayar share the regional characteristics in the State and in their material culture they are more close to the Thevar, Kallar (denotified tribes), Pariaher and other socially and economically backward castes in Tamil Nadu.

Habitation and Dwelling Pattern

The Valayar mostly live close to hills, forests, sea coast, river banks necessitated by their occupations. They live in streets of their own in multicaste communities, or in settlements outside the village or in exclusive Valayar settlements. The spread of the Valayar in Tamil

Nadu, excluding Mutracha, Muttiriyans, Ambalakarans extends from North Arcot in the North, Tirunelveli in the South from the coast of Bay of Bengal in the East and to the boundaries of Kerala and Karnataka in the West and North-west. Because of the topographical, ecological and cultural diversities in the areas Valayar live, the patterns of their habitations, the dwellings vary in design. The Valayar of Rameswaram island have put up their huts along the coast on sand; the Valayar of The Nilgiris district have their settlements in the hilly forests; far from any hill or mountain; the Valayar of Valayapatti of Madurai district live in an isolate community close to the Sirumalais; the Valayar of Sendhi have their houses after the pattern that obtains in Ramnad district.

Now we many describe at some length the types of Valayar dwellings especially in Sendhi, Valayapatti, Chakkiliankodan and Rameswaram areas where the author had conducted field work, in this respect.

Sendhi Valayar

Sendhi in Sivaganga taluk, Ramnad district is in the interior. The Valayar in Sendhi live in a separate locality. Except a washerman's, all households (44) belong to the Valaya community. The pattern of houses, the design, the material used for house building, are all common among the Valayar, Pallar, Kallar, Pariaher, and some other caste-Hindus also. It is a paddy growing area. The houses are to be so constructed that they provide space for storing paddy (granary) space for the humans, cattle, sheep, goats, poultry and space for keeping agricultural implements and other miscellaneous household articles.

The area is abundant in palms (palmyra). The palmyra in the district is a multi-utility plant. Every part of it is used. It has economic, cultural and social significance. Its products are used in building construction, its fibre is used in farming and for domestic purposes, its tender fruits (nungu) are a cool delicious thing that are consumed by the young and the old, its fruits are consumed, its shoots, its toddy, its nuts, its baskets, etc. too are utilized. It pervades a vast segment of the life of the people there, and so the Valayar in their home district (said to be) live a 'Palmyra Culture' if one could call it so, similar to the Coconut culture of Kerala.

Sendhi Valaya locality is square in shape. It has one main street in the middle and four small lanes. The houses are constructed in rows. All are mud-walled, palmyra-leaf-roofed except one which is mangalore-tiled. They dig foundation, collect a variety of mud available locally at a distance of half a kilometer from the village. They remove small pieces of stone from the mud, prepare it properly at the house site, raise the mud wall, one and a half to two feet thick gradually. It may take several days for raising 10 feet of mud wall. It depends on the weather and season. When the mud wall is dry and well set, it is plastered with red mud and it can compete with brick and concrete wall in strength, beauty and durability. While the raising of the mud wall is in progress, other building material and palmyra leaves for roofing are got ready. The palm leaves (in the case of those who need purchase and those who do not own totally or adequate palmyra trees) are purchased at the rate of Rs.20.00 per thousand pieces. Sometimes the price ranges from Rs.15.00 to Rs.25.00 per thousand. The wage for cutting 1,000 leaves is Rs.3.00. One may have to climb 15 to 40 trees for collecting 1,000 leaves. These leaves are packed in bundles of 50 each. Twenty such bundles wherein the leaves are neatly placed one on the other make one thousand. The man who thatches (roofing one who attends to the thatching) is fed twice in the day and is paid a wage of Rs.3.00 per day. A house with 30 × 15 feet dimensions is thatched by two men in a day.

The beams, rafters, poles, supports for the roof are all of palmyra timber. The price of a palmyra tree, depending on its length and hardwood ranges from Rs.10.00 to 20.00. Palmyra is available locally and sometimes procured from the neighbouring villages.

The labour and material for building a house for a family comes to Rs.400.00 to Rs.500.00. There are expert mud-wall raisers and thatchers among the Valayar in the village.

Once in four to five years, new thatching or roofing is done. The old palmyra leaves used for roofing are not wasted. They are buried in the fields in small pits dug all over the field and covered with earth. This is one way of composting the leaves and within 3 months the material gets decomposed. The fields are ploughed after 3 months and the matter gets mixed up with the soil. The stems are collected, dried up and used as fuel for cooking food. The palmyra leaves are thus not wasted but used as organic manure in the fields in which paddy is cultivated.

The houses here are of two types square and rectangular. The front door is in the middle. On either side of the entrance are the pials over which is the extended slope roofing. The pials are two and a half feet to three feet in height, length depends on the length of the house but normally 12 to 15 feet and width 6 to 8 feet. The floors of the pials are either cement plastered or mud plastered. People sit on the pials, sleep, discuss matters, have their afternoon siesta, keep agricultural implements, cots, hay, hang in the roof above the pial, hunting and fishing devices, there are places for the guests to sit, wait, sleep and sometimes, at the dusk they eat on the pials, when it is already dark inside the house. While putting up the pials either on one or on both sides of the house, room is provided with a narrow entrance that could be closed and opened for the poultry. Sometimes there will be pial on one side of the entrance (frontal portion) and the other side with similar slope roofing is used as a cattle shed. Most of the cattle sheds are in the frontal portion of the house only. In case of those who have a large number of cattle, goats, sheep, they have separate sheds, that too on either side of the house; the criterion being that the cattle should be within the visible vicinity (for feeding, watering and protecting them from cattle lifters).

On either side of the frontal entrance, provision is made for placing earthen lamps or kerosene chimneys. Immediately after the entrance to the house, on the right side is provided the granary for storing paddy, beyond it, room, hall, living place and a store room in some houses. In a house of the above description, a square one, there is open place in the center of the house for ventilation. The open space in the center serves in side as a place for bath, wash etc. The rooms of the house on all sides are on a raised level, 9 to 12 inches to the central open place inside. The sullage water is let out to the backyard or to the lane or street through a narrow channel. The women during menstruation rest and sleep on the pials until they take the purificatory bath on the third day.

The foregoing description of a house is typical of some well-to-do families in Sendhi. In generality, the dwelling is a rectangular single-roomed hut with the same thick mud walls with palmyra leaf-thatch and either with pials adequate for sleeping or narrow ones for sitting and space enough for one man to sleep along the wall.

The Sendhi Valayar are comparatively better off than the Valayar of Valayapatti. The Sendhi people are rice growers and rice eaters and whereas in the case of Valayar of Valayapatti rice is a rare dish which they provide to themselves on festive or ceremonious or social occasions and so the housing of a people barring certain ecological or climatic influences is consistent with their levels of living. The Sendhi Valayar since they cultivate rice, they need storage facilities and so consequently they need houses with provision to store grain too. In view of the seasonal employment for the Sendhi Valayar, they have comparatively more leisure time and idle hours. This too seems to have something to do with the type of housing. The pials in front of the houses are in a way related to leisure and gossiping.

Valayar of Valayapatti

Valayapatti is an isolate consisting of 50 households, located about six kilometers to the west of Sirumalais in Madurai district. A settlement made over a century and half ago. The village has two streets running north to south; the main entrance to the village is from north. It has three rows of houses, the middle at certain points having houses facing east and west. Till ten years ago the houses were single-roomed narrow hovel-like things. During the past ten years in a phased programme, new houses, each measuring 15 x 10 feet have been put up by the Gandhigram Rural Institute with the monetary assistance received from a West German Voluntary Organization. Of the 50, 49 are mud-walled and tile roofed and one family lives in a small thatched hut. Except three houses which are double-roomed all the rest are single-roomed. Cooking, eating, sleeping, storing (far less) keeping clothing and household articles are all to be done and accommodated in a room measuring 15 × 10 feet. In one case a man and his wife and their ten children live and sleep in the same room; of these, there are two girls who have come of age. The parents are still in the reproductive age. There is no privacy, young parents and children, aged children and sexually active parents have to sleep in the same space. How it tells and acts upon the children, parents and adolescents is a matter for in-depth study.

No house in Valayapatti has any enclosure for bath, wash after nature call. Men and women have to bathe in the open.

The houses are whitewashed once a year. But the houses and the precincts of the houses are kept neat and clean. In Sendhi, there is no whitewashing of the walls since the walls are plastered with bright red mud. Both at Sendhi and Valayapatti, men and women during summer sleep in the open.

The dwellings at Valayapatti are simple. It is open drainage, and sullage water is let out to the street.

In brief, of the 94 houses in Sendhi and Valayapatti, mud-walled and thatched are 44, forty-three thatched in Sendhi alone and only one hut at Valayapatti. But the remaining 49 houses at Valayapatti are of a mixed type with mud walls and tiled-roof and all provided with cement windows. Windows and ventilation are conspicuously absent in Sendhi Valayar houses. In Valayapatti too they would not have gone for the windows, but for the agency that has provided the housing to them. In Sendhi, 5 houses (out of 44) are in a dilapidated condition and only one in such a state at Valayapatti.

Valayar of Chakkiliankodan

Chakkilankodan, in Shanarpatti block, Madurai district, is built on a bowl like depression on a huge rock on a hill top. The houses are built on rock, with no lanes, no streets. It is a cluster of mud-walled and lemon-grass thatched single-room huts. The entrances to these mud huts are too small. One has to bow too low to enter the house. You cannot just straightaway walk into the house. It is a house for the name sake. They resemble a mass of pig sties. Here, it is the extreme backwardness of the group and surrounding hills and forests that have patterned the dwellings of the Valayar of Chakkulankodan.

Rameswaram Islanders

It is the ecology and topography that determine the pattern of housing though, economic variable sometimes could overcome topographical difficulties. Sand is the omnipresent thing on Rameswaram Island of the Ramnad district. The building material locally available is some wild inferior saplings and *keeths* made of coconut leaves. The Valayar on the island, about eleven hundred households live in huts put up on sand. There is no flooring. It is sand inside, outside, and everywhere. The huts have neither mud nor brick walls. Thattis or coconut *keeths* are put up as walls. The *keeths* serve for walls, partitions, and roofing. The *keeths* are used as mattress for sleeping, sitting, for keeping fish, for sun-drying fish, for storing articles in the basket form. Palmyra leaf baskets are used as storing containers and carriers etc.

For instance, in the case of Karaiyur, a Valaya fishing community, close to the coast on the island, each household is assigned three cents of land by the government. There are about 250 Valaya households in Karaiyur, all engaged in fishing. The chief material for the huts is *keeths* of coconut which is available on the island and some wooden poles (small) beams and rafters are purchased. The huts are single-roomed and sometimes big in size with partitions. Defecation is in the open along the coast, or near water holes. Drinking water is not a problem. Fresh potable water is surface tapped within 3-4 feet. Almost each family has one tiny well improvised with moulded concrete rings (3 or 4 each about a height of one foot or one and a half feet with a radius of one and a half to two feet). These concrete moulds hold back the sand around. Water is taken straight from the wells, in vessels, containers or sometimes by means of rope and bucket.

These huts of coconut *keeths* stand the normal wind and rain. Since these houses have neither mud nor brick walls, sand is heaped up along the keeth wall. There is no problem of drainage since the houses are built on several feet of sand, and so there is no problem of sullage water. For washing, bathing, etc., they use concrete slabs, stone slabs (got from outside the island). Each hut may cost below Rs.300.00.

In summer they sleep in the open on the sand, and of course in the winter huddle themselves in the narrow huts. Storm and gales are a problem for the hut dwellers. They spend an uncertain, anxiety-ridden, unpleasant rainy season. And so the housing aspect for the Valaya fishermen of Rameswaram Island creates in them a sense of insecurity with their improvised impermanent dwellings.

The type obtaining in the criminally notorious village Rayarpalayam in Coimbatore district is, that of Chakkiliankodan. Back in Karaikudi, in Ramnad district, the Valayar live at two points in the town, their dwellings are thatched houses clustered in both the places. But in the case of Chembasi Valayar in Cittarevu in Madurai district, they live in a multicaste village, where they constitute a majority group. The Valayar in this village are socially (educationally) and economically better off and their houses symbolize this.

And so, while the generality of the Valayar are engaged in such pursuits in a survival-oriented economy, their housing also is consistent with their levels of living.

Ceremonies Associated with House Construction

Almost all Hindus in general, observe certain rules in terms of location of a house site, the direction the house would face when it is completed, number of doors and windows, auspicious time for digging the foundation and occupying the house, and consistent with their beliefs carry out certain ceremonies and rituals to ward off evil, propitiate deities so that the occupants would prosper in their new dwellings. The Valayar too observe certain ceremonies and rituals.

Before laying the foundation-stone (symbolic in mud-walled huts) for construction of a house, a ceremony is carried out at the site. A pit with one foot diameter and half a foot depth is dug up in the north-east corner of the site. In the center of the pit, a six inches high earth in conical shape is left intact. The top of the cone is flattened. A palai (a milk exuding tree) branch is planted at the center of the flattened cone. A quantity of cattle dung in conical shape is placed beside the flattened cone close to the palai branch that has been planted there already. A few pieces of aragam grass (cynodon doctylon) are tucked in on top of the cattle dung cone. This symbolizes the deity. Navadanyam (nine varieties of grain including pulses) are tied in a piece of cloth coloured with turmeric paste. This tiny cloth containing the grain with a knot at the neck, is tied to the palai branch. One pot full of water is poured into the trench. Arali (nerium odorum) and jasmine flowers are dropped into the pit filled with water. Since the water is poured swiftly into the pit there is swirling of it around the cone shaped earth that stands in the middle of the pit and the flowers too float around in the pit. The celebrants or any visitor to the ceremony may choose a flower of other species (Arali-jasmine) and follow it up when it floats around in the pit and if the particular flower stops finally at the north-east point, it is taken to be a good omen or a positive sign for act or work that the individual has in mind.

Puja is offered at the site, with burning of camphor, incense sticks and breaking of coconut and betel nut and betel leaves, puffed rice, boiled and fried bengalgram, banana are offered to the deity at the time of worship. Besides, the two species of flowers dropped into the pit filled with water or other available flowers are also used for puja.

The man who performs the puja gets half a slice of the coconut and three bananas. The visitors are given puffed rice, bengalgram and a little piece of copra each.

At Sendhi, we find a similar observance but with some minor variations. Instead of digging a pit, some earth is dug out in the north east corner of the site and the dug out spot is cleaned and daubed with a thick solution of cattle dung. A small lingam is made of turmeric paste and a few pieces of aragam grass are tucked on the lingam. Flowers are placed on the lingam. The articles of puja are the same as obtaining in the district of Madurai. The invitees to the ceremony are honoured with Chandanam (sandal paste). The whole ceremony is carried out by men, but women may be present and observe the ceremony.

A similar ceremony as obtaining in Madurai area is performed in digging irrigation well. In the case of engaging a mason, another ceremony is carried out at the time of laying the first stone for construction of revetment or steening wall. (First ceremony at the time of digging). On this occasion of having the first stone for construction, camphor is burnt after a coconut is broken, and betel nut and betel leaves are offered to the deity. The mason is paid Rs.1.25 as *kanikai.* This second ceremony is not performed when the Valayar themselves undertake the construction of the steening wall. It is necessitated in the case of a paid mason from outside the caste and the mason insists on the observance of this ceremony since it is remunerative to him. It is common practice in vogue in South India in the case of digging and construction of irrigation wells. Digging of a well sometimes is fraught with risk for the workers uncertainty for the farmer in tapping water and so puja is performed to gods to prevent any untoward thing and to seek good spring and good crops.

House-warming Ceremony

The House-warming ceremony (*Grihapravesam*) is common among all Hindus. The Valayar too in general observe such a ceremony. On the day the newly constructed house is occupied (even in the case of old house occupied by a family) milk is boiled on the new oven and this milk is given to the invitees. It is a sacred function, which is believed to bless the occupants with peace and prosperity. Sometimes puja is offered inside the house. Camphor is burnt, coconut is broken and betel nut and betel leaves are offered to the deity. Auspicious time is chosen to occupy the new house. Some consult the almanac and some seek guidance from knowledgeable persons in fixing the auspicious time. Usually, the 'House-warming ceremony' is performed in the morning hours before sunrise.

There is some variation in the performance of 'House-warming ceremony' in the Ramnad area. The ceremony usually takes place in the evening. Rice and some curry prepared in new earthen pots are offered to the deity. A plantain leaf (plate) is placed at the north-east corner in the house and rice and curry are placed on it. Incense is burnt at the time of puja. Usually the offerings are meant to the family deity. One of the elderly members in the households will eat the rice and curry offered to the deity. The invitees are served food. They dine in the premises of the new house. Women too are invited. The scale at which the ceremonies are performed depends on the level of living of the family concerned.

Appropriation and Use of the House

A large number of Valaya dwellings could be said to be single-roomed multi-purpose units. Big houses with rooms or halls appropriated for different purposes is negligible. The use of the house, and the time the members spend at the house, depend upon the occupation, profession and the leisure time the group enjoys. For the Valayar of Valayapatti, the house serves as a resting place during nights. Except a few days in rainy season and the days they declare to themselves as stay at home days, the Valayar spend the whole year from morning to evening on the hills, in the sea, in the fields, in the rivers or tanks. Small kids are either left in the care of elderly ones or old-people.

The Valayar who are chiefly engaged in collecting firewood, wild products, fishing, farm-labour and all other non-farm occupations, purchase their food commodities daily or in bi-weekly intervals. As such they have not much to store in the house. These people spend major part of the day outside their houses. In such cases, as mentioned earlier, their single-roomed dwellings (irrespective of the material used for the walls, for roofing) serve as all-purpose living places-cooking, eating, sleeping, etc. Seldom, they have privacy in the houses.

One of the reasons for the predominant number of nuclear families among the Valayar and economically backward groups is housing. The moment the son is married, he is obliged to establish his own residence. Two sets of couple (sexually active) cannot sleep in the same room. It is very rare that married brothers live with their spouses in a joint family. There is no such instance in Valayapatti and Sendhi taken for intensive study. When you go up in the economic ladder wherein you meet with increased income, adequate housing, you meet with extended families. This of course is in the case of farm-families and does not apply to the urbanized industrial society of the West.

Inadequate housing is felt in winter. The members in a family have to huddle themselves in their narrow dwellings. Summer though unbearable in certain districts, gives the Valayar (other groups too) a lot of relief. Accommodation for sleeping is not a problem. They sleep in the open, in front of their houses, in the streets, both adults and children.

In the Valayar houses in general, there is no provision for a special room for puja. A corner, a spot in the house is used for offering puja.

Sometimes, there will be no space or convenience for crèche inside the house. The cloth swings will be hung to tree branches outside the house.

Housing is one of the major problems for the Valayar. They are born, grow up, live and die in those narrow dwellings lacking ventilation and basic comforts.

A question was asked of all the 94 householders in Valayapatti and Sendhi as to their choice for living. Though all of them could not see any prospect of migrating to and living in town or city, the question was asked of them in order to know their attitude towards modernity. Cent percent of Sendhi and ninety percent of Valayapatti respondents prefer to live in villages. Eight percent of the respondents in Valayapatti expressed their preference to live in towns and one respondent's preference is city.

Household Belongings

Speaking of the material culture of the Valayar we may look into their household belongings. The household belongings chiefly comprise agricultural implements, weapons, traps and other contrivances for hunting game, utensils, kitchenware, furniture, dresses for ordinary and special occasions, ceremonial dress, boxes, toilet material and other personal effects. The kind of household belongings and the number of items in each category possessed by a Valaya family depends upon its occupation, location of habitat, economic level, size and adequacy of the dwelling, and social status of the family in respect to education and other offices held, barring the differences in the household

In the case of families that carry on agricultural activities, the implements possessed by them for various farm operations consist of ploughs, spades, crowbars, hoes, sickles, aruvals (Knives), winnowers, leather buckets used in lift irrigation and sometimes carts for transporting organic manure to the fields and farm produce to their homes from the threshold. The number of implements owned under each category depends upon the economic level and extent of farm activities carried on by the respective families.

In case of families engaged in fishing as a primary or subsidiary occupation, the chief accessories are fishing lines, nets, boats, and other contrivances such as *kachchal, kudam, dhuri*, and the latter are used in running water (streams, rivulets and rivers). The families that are engaged in collecting firewood invariably possess aruval and axe. A family may own a set of them depending on the number of persons engaged in the firewood collection in the family.

The hunting weapons and traps used by the Valayar chiefly comprise, musketeers, bows, with clay pellets used as missiles, *idikki, silukku* (for trapping rats, bandicoots), nets for trapping rabbits and birds, snares for catching birds, and spears and throws for hunting wild game. Majority of the families own the above hunting equipment, except musketeers which are used by a few individual families here and there.

In respect to utensils and kitchenware, as discussed earlier, the utensils for cooking and eating food, storing grain and water chiefly consist of mud vessels and ware made of aluminium, brass and sporadically of articles made of stainless steel. The kitchenware usually consists of one or two wooden churner, an earthen or iron pan for cooking meat and seasoning of curries, aluminium or glass containers for storing edible and non-edible oil, an iron tin or a glass bottle for fetching and storing kerosene for lighting purposes, and a stone mortar and one or two wooden pestles.

In respect to dress, it depends on the economic level of the family. The man or the woman owns a set or two of dress for daily wear and in some cases one or two shirts, dhotis and saris which compared to their ordinary dress are costly and they are worn on important social and ceremonial occasions. The samiyadis among the Valayar own a set of ceremonial dress which they don during the celebration of their deities. The ceremonial dress is kept in wooden boxes at the temple houses and never at the residential houses, since it should not get polluted. The rich and the middle class families in a relative sense possess a steel trunk or a wooden one. Most of the poor families either keep their clothes and other personal belongings and ornaments in earthen pots or vaults provided in the mud wall of their dwellings.

When it comes to furniture, a considerable number of families own string cots made of wooden or bamboo frame. We come across one or two wooden chairs in the families wherein we find educated members. Save this, furniture of any description is absent among the Valayar. In respect to dressing and toilet material, an ordinary family possesses one or two wooden or rubber combs, a mirror, a small wooden or metal container for vermilion and sacred ashes, a glass or aluminium container for oil, used in hair dressing.

Of late one or two families in some villages possess and use radio sets, cycles and wrist watches.

Thus most of the Valayar families own and use the core implements, weapons, contrivances, accessories in respect to their occupations like farming, fishing, hunting, collection of firewood and other wild products. But when it comes to clothes, domestic wear, furniture and toilet material, it is very minimal and of extremely utilitarian nature and there is negligible place for luxury goods among the Valayar.

Personal Care and Decorations

The habit of personal cleanliness and washing of bodies among the Valayar depends on variables such as the locality they live in, viz., hills, forests, sea coast, river banks, plains and drought stricken areas, the occupations they pursue, viz., collection of firewood, farming, farm-labour, fishing to mention the chief occupations, the sets of clothing they have for a change after wash, sometimes the level of living of other caste groups with whom the Valayar live and interact, further the washing habits of men, women, children and aged could be looked separately. The frequency of bathing varies in respect of region, occupation, sex and age.

The Valayar of Rameswaram island almost dip their bodies in the sea every day, or a couple of times a day. Strictly speaking, it is not a bath, but a dip in the sea water is necessitated by their occupation. Here there is no dearth of water and washing is so inconspicuous a thing in their daily routine. At homes almost each house has a small draw-well and for regular bath and the so-called oil-bath, they use this potable water.

In the same district in Sendhi most of the Valayar are farmers. Men folk after their farm operations (mostly rice cultivation) wash their bodies in the irrigation wells in the field, or in the irrigation tanks. It is a simple dip-and-dry bath, they do not use soap or any such material. The summer is so severe in Ramnad. The men-folk there, go for a dip either in the irrigation tank or irrigation wells even at midnight. Most of them know swimming. Hardly one can find a boy or a man among the Valayar of Rameswaram who does not swim. It is a must for the fishermen.

We have the other extreme at Chakkilankodan in Madurai district. There have been cases among them that the seed (pulses) that fell into the folds of their loin cloth around their waist while sowing, germinate after a couple of days. This is illustrative of the frequency of their bathing and bodily cleanliness. The type of house they live, the clothes they wear, the work they do, the bedding they use, the places they sleep in, the cleanliness of the places they sleep in, the facilities or civic amenities they command, all are consistent. It is in line with one another.

Back at Sendhi, youngsters in 10 families use toilet soaps for washing and soap nut powder for washing their heads. This is a change in their personal habits and it adds some modernity to their life in their view.

Men at Valayapatti do not use any material while they wash their bodies. Four women at Valayapatti (1) Santhamma, convener of the local Mather Sangham (women's club) (2) Wife of Madayanai who is from a town, and (3) Nagamma, though a native of Valayapatti is the wife of one Kulandaivelu, a peon in a High School who wants to be modern in his style of life, uses toilet soap for bath and face-wash. All women born at Valayapatti with the exception of Nagamma neither use soap nor soapnut powder for ordinary bath.

Men bathe at energized irrigation wells after their day's work in the noons and evenings. Women bathe usually after sunset since all houses lack any privacy or enclosure for bath. Darkness is the only privacy surrounding them. Women use both cold and hot water depending on seasons. The frequency of bathing among the Valayapatti folk ranges from once a day to once a week. The majority bathe once or twice a week. Some old women wash their bodies once or twice a month.

When they apply oil to their heads and bathe (the so-called oil bath) clay is used as shampoo. Nicely ground powder of uselam leaves (allizzia armora) is used exclusively and sometimes mixed with seekai (soapnut) powder for washing heads and also dried flowers of avaram (cassia auriculata) after applying oil. Flour of greengram, horsegram, cowpea is used for bathing children. This practice obtains among other caste groups too.

After the introduction of piped-water in Valayapatti, there is a slight increase in the frequency of bathing mostly in the case of children. The little fellows just go and sit or stand below the tap and turn it on. It is half play for them. Some children go without any wash for days together.

In case of some adults, the periodic bath is a small event. A day as well as the time is set apart. He may even casually mention it to others that he is going to have a bath or he had a bath that day, or others may inquire of him (on his appearance or change in clothes) whether he had a bath that day. Then the man goes on explaining how he had no time for a wash, how he had been postponing it for days on end, how his wife has persuaded him to have a wash and finally how he had a bath. Such inquiries and casual conversations are not uncommon among the Valayar.

Hair Dressing

Hair dressing and care of hair has some regional variation. Men who used to grow their hair and keep it in knots have taken to hair cutting as in the case of other menfolk. At Sendhi, Pasangarai, Rameswaram, Piranmalai in Ramnad district and at Valayapatti, Chittarevu, Anjikulipatti and A. Valayapatti in Madurai district, a couple of old men still go with the traditional type of hair style, no cropping. In majority of the cases, who go in for fishing, collection of firewood and farm labour, the hair is kept unkempt. Not much care is given to hair upkeep; occasionally they apply gingili oil and sometimes coconut oil. Neem oil is used for massaging the bodies and for head bath. In the case of women including the girls, the hair dressing takes after that of the lower class groups, viz., Kallar, Pallar and Pariaher. The Valayar in the districts of Ramnad and Madurai do not have the practice of plaits nor do they keep their hair in knots. They keep the hair loose and at the place where the knot is kept, they tuck in the hair upward drawing the ends inside, which could be learnt after a long practice. This may be called an art by itself. It does not require any combing; it could be while sitting, walking and talking. Some women do it with one hand, their left hand. It is not a permanent keep of the hair. It often goes off and the woman will be plying her hand (fingers) behind and tucking in the hair. In this style the hair appears bushy on the head.

Majority of the Valayar apply neem oil (melia indica) to their heads, but do not use it as a cosmetic; on the other hand use it when they have the so-called oil bath. They say the use of neem oil is good for the system, the system cools, acts as a detergent to lice and flies, though the odour is so strong and pungent for the by-standers. They apply neem oil to their heads profusely. Of late the young women in some Valaya villages have taken to gingili oil (sesame) and coconut oil. The working women, who are economically more active and who add to the income of their families have not much of leisure, to dress up their hair. The attention the Valaya men and women bestow and the time spent on their hair washing and dressing is far less.

Perfumes

The Valayar in general do not go in for any perfumes or scents. Some ten families both at Valayapatti and Sendhi use talcum powder for infants. But the Valayar use flowers on marriage and the festive occasions. They use jasmine, chamanthi (chrysanthemum) and (maragu) a sweet aromatic shrub. They either tuck the flowers on their heads or towards the frontal portion of the neck. The latter practice of using flowers is mostly prevalent among the Valayar and Kallar in the districts of Ramnad and Madurai. Especially when the Valayar celebrate their clan or village deities, one can see the jubilant womenfolk tucking jasmine to the frontal portion of their necks, not above the loosely tucked-in-hair knots.

Gopal's wife at Valayapatti has saradu (manglasuthram, string) only around her neck. It has no tali. She wears flowers just at the centre of the saradu that touches the central point between the breasts, the point at which tali should find place. It is on festive occasions. She wears short hair on her head (for she has offered her hair to a deity in recent months, a vow she has kept up) and she cannot adorn her head with flowers and so the flowers have come down to the chest. But as mentioned above, using flowers tucked to the front of the neck and keeping flowers fastened to the saradu is a unique style among the Valayar and also among the Kallar.

Tonsure

Before the advent of the western style of hair-cut, the menfolk kept their hair and once or twice a month they had their face-shave done by the barber, who comes under the Hindu jajmani system. Formerly, the barber received aya (remuneration) in the form of grain. His work then in terms of tonsure was less. Now, save a few old men who stick to their tufts, all go in for the hair-cut. The barber continues his service with an increased work load. Formerly, the adults had a face-shave mostly once in a month and some used to go in for a hair style in the forehead in an inverted 'U' shape or in the crescent shape.

Tonsure practices obtain among the Valayar irrespective of the styles and periodicity of hair cutting and face shaving.

Care of Teeth

Ash, earth, brick-powder, coal are used in brushing the teeth by women. Men use neem and karivelam sticks as brushes. Occasionally, a few families use Gopal tooth powder. We may say that over 99 percent do not spend any money toward brushing their teeth. Most of the Valayar chew betel-nut and betel-leaves. They use tobacco too. By constant chewing the teeth appear dark, light dark, a little brownish dark. The time they spend in brushing the teeth is considerably less; it may be at the work spot, farm, sea, river, tank, hill and so on. It is a quick brushing before they consume their morning meal. They do not seem to bother about the tint of their teeth.

Sanitary Condition

The question of environmental sanitation and upkeep of the houses again is a question which varies in terms of regions, occupation and economic status of the Valayar. For instance the Valayar in and around Aruppukottai community development block in Ramnad district live in spacious well-built, well-furnished and well-ventilated buildings. The streets are kept clean and the premises of the houses too. This population of course constitutes a negligible percentage of the Valayar population.

In Rameswaram there is no insanitary condition in the Valaya localities. It is sand for miles around. In Sendhi, the premises of the houses are well swept and well kept. The womenfolk take pretty care in keeping the precincts of the house clean. But the streets are dirty since they are nobody's concern. The environmental sanitation in Valayapatti is insanitary. There is no drainage. Each family has to wash, cleanse vessels outside the house. They rear poultry and that adds to the insanitation. They chew and spit indiscriminately. It is mud floors but of course daubed periodically with cattle dung paste. There is always collection of dirt from the ill-kept mud houses. Winter is a problem for most of the ill-housed Valayar. It is difficult to generalize the level of environmental sanitation in the case of Valaya settlements since majority of the settlements are constituents in multicaste village communities. There is always the regional, topographical, climatic, social and economic influence on sanitation of a people. There is some relationship between personal cleanliness and environmental sanitation. In the case of Valayar, both the aspects secure a low score.

As in the case of majority of the villagers, Valayar defecate in the open, in the fields. This is the one practice among the people which fouls and dirties the whole village environment. Men usually go outside the village, wash outside, at any water source. In times of emergencies and exigencies the menfolk cleanse the part with small stone pieces. Later they may have a wash.

The people are so accustomed to open defecation habits, that to wean them away from such a practice is difficult. Some fifteen years ago Gandhigram, located one kilometre south-west of Valayapatti, in its programmes of village work introduced a Wardha type of trench latrine (structure, enclosure made of bamboo thattis) in Valayapatti and need for such a latrine, with all seriousness was explained to the Valayar. The Wardha latrine is still there but it has not yet been accepted by the villagers.

Personal Ornaments

As all tribal and peasant women (not of course excluding the urbanized-sophisticated) like and wear jewels and ornaments, the Valayar women too crave for them. In the use of ornaments there are some regional differences as regards the type of ornaments and the points on the body they are worn. The description that follows mostly relates to the districts of Ramnad and Madurai, although the same pattern more or less holds good in other Valaya districts in the State with some variation in pattern.

Ornaments are used to adorn the nose, neck, ankles, waist, wrist, head, toes, fingers and ears, made of gold, silver, copper, brass, lead etc.

Nose

The Valaya women in their teens, youth and mostly upto their middle age wear nose screws on one side or on either side set with or without artificial stones. The girls in the age of 8-12 get their nostrils punctured. To begin with until the puncture is healed, they use a few millimeters length of grass stick (thodapakuchchi). Later they use sometimes brass screws. The vendors of these brass screws (Dasari by caste) puncture the nostrils as a free service to their clientele. These vendors visit villages and the Valayar visit the towns where these vendors reside and get their services. Even if a woman has no ornament on her person, she would like to have at least a nose screw. Certainly ornaments are on the decline, some old-fashioned ones. But the nose screw still stands firm, against changes in the world of ornaments and jewellery.

Ankles

Thandai made of silver are worn around the ankle by women. Girls and women in youth, before and after marriage wear *thandai*. It is a thick ring worn around both the ankles. It is becoming a little outmoded now and is on the decline among the Valayar. A few young women wear this silver ornament in some of the Valaya villages and by none at Valayapatti.

Waist

All male members wear (tie) around their waist a string, made of twisted cotton yarn, ark silk or some locally available fibre. In the case of children and some well-to-do families, the string is retained upto their second or third year. *Aramoodi* (tassel – pubic tassel) made of silver or alloy in spade shape is hung in front to shield the genital. It has an eye through which the waist string is run. *Aramoodi* was in use when female children were kept without any clothing upto 3rd or 4th year. This metallic genital shield is seldom used now since jattis and frocks are used considerably. It is an ornament and serves a purpose too.

Wrist

Glass, rubber, plastic bangles are worn by the female members. A married Hindu woman with a living husband is entitled to the wearing and use of five articles. They are (1) tali, (2) tilak, (3) turmeric, (4) flowers and (5) bangles. As a maiden, a Hindu girl is entitled as a custom to the last four and the addition of tali changes her marital status and she enjoys all the aforesaid articles and when she loses the tali (when widowed) she is deprived of the other four too, the ones she enjoyed as a maiden. Widowhood not only changes her marital status but cuts her social status and mode of life and habits also. As a widow the use of tilak (kumkum-vermilion), the use of turmeric paste as a disinfectant and as a cosmetic, use of flowers and wearing of glass bangles are a taboo. In lieu of *kumkum,* she can apply sacred ashes to her forehead, and in the place of glass bangles she can wear copper or gold ones, no flowers and no use of turmeric paste. Caste groups among whom widow remarriage is allowed, when a widow re-marries, she gains all the five. This custom of entitlement and deprivation of the five articles in respect of marital status of a woman is adhered to strictly among higher rungs in the ladder of caste hierarchy. We may say that the wearing or using of the five articles as the case may be can be said to have come under the Great Traditions pervading the divergent groups within the larger Hindu-fold.

Among the Valayar (Valayapatti) wearing of glass bangles is not considered important and symbolic of married state as in the case of middle aged and old women with their spouses living. Wearing of blouses has some relevance to age, but wearing of bangles, tali, at least a tali-less saradu is a must in the case of a married Hindu woman. The Valaya women (married) sometimes go without tali, saradu and bangles.

Wrist Watches

They are in use among a few educated and well-to-do Valayar. In Valayapatti, Ponnuchamy, Vice President of the village panchayat was the first man to buy and use a wrist watch. In a small socially and economically backward community, wearing a wrist watch or keeping a wireless set or a transistor radio is a status symbol and it enhances the user's status. Besides Ponnuchamy, Kulanadaivelu a peon, his brother-in-law (a little well-to-do) Nagarajan and Subbaiah, a goat-herd (getting ready for his marriage) have wrist watches. In some of the poor Valaya communities, the wrist watch and the radio still retain novelty.

Head and Forehead

They dress up their hair (women) using margosa oil. As mentioned earlier, the application of margosa oil to the head and body is believed to cool the system and relieve muscular, bodily pain due to hard work. The powerful-smelling oil is applied to the head and body either before they go to sleep or on the following day and wash their bodies.

Neck

Married women wear gold tali (badge) around their necks. There are cases of women who neither wear tali nor even the saradu. Married women in addition wear another ornament called sangili (chain). It is a necklace made of gold. A few wear sangili with pendant. Girls before puberty wear *karugumani,* a bead necklace of multi-colour. After reaching age, the girls cease wearing the karugumani.

The red-bead necklaces have been popular among the Chembasi Valayar. It is the custom of wearing of red-beads, by a group of Valayar which distinguished them as a sub-endogamous group among the Valayar. The red-beads have contributed to this social demarcation. Widows and old women go with bare necks.

Toes

Women at the time of marriage wear minji to both the second toes. The minji (rings) are made of silver and nickel. The ones that are worn at the time of marriage are made of silver. Even after wedding, most of the women continue to keep the minji in their toes for some years. The bridegroom also puts minji to his second toes at the time of marriage. The man removes them a few days after the marriage. These are used only in a full-fledged marriages that are celebrated in accordance with the caste regulations, not in the simplified emergent mandai marriages. The minji for the groom are presented by his mother or sister. She in turn receives a sari from the groom.

Fingers

Plain rings and rings set with stones made of gold, silver, nickel and copper are worn. None in the two villages taken for intensive study wears a gold ring. But Valayar in other areas (farmers) do wear gold rings. It is not a question of custom, but a question of economic status.

Ears

The ornaments or the jewellery are concentrated in the ear-zone. Different types and sizes are worn at different points of the ear. All women get their earlobes bored as infants. At one time or other they wear some type of ear-rings. The continuance of it and the make and name of it depends on the economic, marital and age status. Those who could afford use gold ear-rings. Thandatti and chavidi are worn as ear ornaments. In the case of thandatti one piece in each ear, sometimes one thandatti and two chavidis, on either side or three chavidis in each ear. Lac is used in stuffing the thandatti. It is gold plated, stuffed ear-ornament which is popular among socially backward caste groups. It is a regional ornament confined to the southern districts of Tamil Nadu. Besides lac, sacred ashes are stuffed in the thandatti to add sacredness to the ornaments. The wearing of thandatti by the Valayar has resulted in the establishment of Jajmani type of relationship between the Valayar and Koravar. Koravar were listed under criminal tribes until the repeal of law in 1948. Still they indulge in criminal activities. One of their caste occupations is weaving of baskets, mats, etc. It is the Koravar who bore the ear-lobes for the girls to wear thandatti and chavidi. The Koravar man makes a small incision in the lobes to begin with and a slender rolled-piece of soft old cloth is drawn through the hole in the lobe and left there, stuffing the hole. Eight days later, the size of rolled-cloth piece that is stuffed in the holes is increased in size in order to widen the hole in the ear-lobes. The Koravar applies some ointment for healing the wound. He visits his case once every five days after the second visit. On each visit, he removes the cloth stuffed in the ear-lobes and draws in new ones larger in size. The girth of the cloth piece is increased gradually in order to enlarge the size of the hole in the lobe to an inch vertically. In order to reach the desirable size of the hole, the Koravar cuts off some flesh around the hole on the fifteenth day of the first incision. By then, the edges of the hole become soft and so he prunes the flesh in a circular fashion to a needed size. When the bore (hole) is ready for distending the lobe, kunukus made of lead (thick heavy rings with nearly one inch in diameter) in the shape of chavidi are worn by the girls till they reach age. Even girls in the age of 8-12 wear kunukus. At this age, the hole in the ear lobes when distended would be an inch.

On attaining puberty, the *kunukus* are discarded and *thandatti* or *chavidi* made of gold are worn by the girls. This option and process last for one month. During this period, the Koravar comes in intimate contact with his client.

The Koravar is paid Rs. 30.00 per case for his entire services. This amount is paid to him on the day the girl wears the *kunukus* made of lead, somewhere after 30 or 35 days.

The ornaments of the ear, besides *thandatti* and *chavidi* comprise the following:

1.	Pudi	- A clove like ornament on either end, the middle being thinner.
2.	Alamurugu	- Worn on the upper portion of the ear.
3.	Onapathattu	- Worn in the central edge of the ear.
4.	Kunukuthattu	- Worn in the centre of the ear, worn 4 to 5 in a bunch made of gold and brass.
5.	Lolakku	- Worn in the lower end as an annexure to the earring.

During the last two decades, the distending of the ear-lobes, the long drawn surgical operation by the Koravar to enable the Valaya girls wear *kunukus*, *thandattis* is on the decline. Most of the Valaya young women, those who could afford, go in for ear-rings set with artificial stones. But the old fashion of *kunukus* and *thandattis* still rules high in certain parts especially the southern Valaya districts in Tamil Nadu.

Men are not an exception to wearing ear-rings. At Sendhi, four men (in their forties) wear ear-rings. They are a little better off in their community at Sendhi. They are proud and conscious of their ear-rings. Some of them in the village are referred to as ear-ring fellow (kadugukaran or kammalkaran in Tamil Nadu). Sometimes that may gain currency as a nickname and he will be popular in his nickname. Occasionally, we find young women using plastic flowers and hair-pins. Flowers are tucked in the loosely worked out knot at the back of the head. And flowers are used at the frontal portion of the neck. Some of the Valaya women use all sorts of flowers. Using of flowers is seasonal. Applying *thilakam-pottu* is not a regular thing among the Valaya women. It is only on festive and ceremonial occasions.

Tattoo

Tattooing has been in practice among the Valayar in the past. Women used to get different motifs tattooed on their bodies, shoulders, arms, foreheads, ankles. The motifs are parrot, fish, scorpion, eye of a peacock feather, *kolam* (a design) names, etc. In the two villages taken for the intensive study, there are 8 women and one man with tattoo marks. All the eight women are about 35, and the man about 50. Tattooing has been used as a treatment for rheumatism. Nagan abut 50, of Valayapatti had got his knee tattooed as a treatment for rheumatism similar to that of acupuncture, an ancient Chinese method of treatment of several diseases. After the tattooing, he was relieved of the complaint. It was a fashion among the older generation to get some motif tattooed on some part of the body. It is no more in vogue among the younger generation.

Clothing

The nature of work determines the type of dress though economic conditions do matter as determinants of style, adequacy and quality of dress. In conformity with the tradition, men everywhere wear white dhotis and put on also shorter cloth or towels over their shoulders. Middle aged and old men seldom wear shirts. Some of the youngsters do wear shirts, slacks. The boys wear a small under-cloth (*komanam-kowpeenam-tassel*) and a waist cloth or put on shirts and shorts. The adult men invariably use the *komanam*. When engaged in work they may stand with just the *komanam* and go about streets, fields and move freely in the houses etc. Formerly, longoat (a tassel like tight dress covering the genital and part of the nates and the waist) was largely in use by the Valayar. Even today, it is in use by the middle aged and the youth. The girls wear *pavadai* (skirt). The women usually wear coarse handloom cotton saris, six to nine yards in length. There are several ways of wearing the sari and each of these has a beauty of its own. Among the Valaya (among most of the non-Brahmin caste groups in the Valaya districts) the sari is passed around the waist and a knot is tied over one of the hips or on the back (among the young Valaya women it is shifting slowly to the front). The sari is then passed tightly around the waist and the end of it is brought up in front of the breasts, thrown over the left shoulder and tucked into the waist from behind or just left free flowing over the shoulders. The higher caste women show out a little of the ornamental fold, the rest being concealed beneath the sari, while the Valayar and the other lower caste women let it drop around the hip or at the back to a length of about a foot. The Valaya women (Kallar, Pallar, Pariaher too) wear the sari a little above the ankles. The Valaya women avoid wearing dark blue sari for fear of offending Karupuchamy to whom the colour is said to be sacred. The Valaya women since they toil in the fields, hills and forests go in for coarse deep red, brown colours. Girls in their teens those who could afford wear jackets and in some cases poverty keeps them bare bodied with skirt and a length of cloth covered in front of the body until they approach nubile age. Girls who have come of age, mostly wear blouses, this continues until they become mothers of one or two children. Wearing a blouse or going without it does not in any way impair the modesty of a woman in the group.

Vellayyanambalam of Valayapatti in his fifties has only two lungis, one to wrap around his waist and another to cover his body. He does not wear shirts or baniyans. These two pieces of cloth serve him as cover during nights. He had no change of lungis. He can't even put them for wash, since he has no change of clothes. By constant use, they are so soiled and have become thick and greasy. The only thing he could do is to buy soap and wash his two lungis at a pump house or a step well.

During winter when the nights are chill, men who go about with a loin-cloth and another piece half covering their bodies, make use of saries. A sari since it is the garment worn by women, gives a low status for a man if he uses it in public for want of proper clothes. This practice, however, obtains among certain Scheduled Castes and other socially and economically backward groups of people, viz., Pariaher, Pallar, Chakkiliar, Irula, Yanadi and the like. During winter nights, most of the Valayar who are poor just sleep on mats and gunny bags without any covering over their bodies.

At times of celebration of their clan deity, communal deities and during the celebration of Adi (July-August) and for Pongal (January 14), the Valayar go in for new clothes. In the case of garments for children, they go in for ready-made ones, no question of measurement. The tailor is given some idea of the person, age, and height. With this the tailor makes out the fittings.

On festive and ceremonial occasions, the whole group appears in its best. There is no specific dress for ceremonies or rituals except in the case of samiyadis who wear ritual dress during the celebration of deities. In Sendhi, tailors with hand sewing machines visit the village and attend to the needs of the people. Though the skinny mammae are flabby, the adult Valaya women (in a large number of cases) are not in the habit of wearing a brassiere and /or a blouse. Blouses are worn by teen-age girls and young women. We may safely say that the blouses are worn upto the 30th year. In the place of a skirt, a length of an old sari is tied around the waist by the adult women.

Washing of Clothes

It was reported that the Valayar of Valayapatti never used to wash their clothes themselves, but used the services of the washerman. It was especially so in the case of men's clothes. Two reasons are attributed to this practice, firstly, since it is the duty of the washerman to wash the clothes under the jajmani relationship he should do it; secondly, the same set of clothes are worn for a number of days, even for months together, and so removal of the accumulated soil and grease is rather out of question for the wearer. And so, he never used to wash it himself. When he buys a new set or a new piece, the old ones reach the washerman. In certain cases, a person may have a loin-cloth and a towel, and no clothes for a change, only on buying a new set could the old ones be laundered. Now, after the introduction of piped water in Valayapatti men, women and children have started washing their clothes occasionally.

"Food is first and foremost for a poor man, and clothing is secondary", an observation made by an old Valayan sums up the level and the importance of clothing among the Valayar.

Shoes and Sandals

Footwear has economic and social significance and these two factors determine the occasions the footwear is used and the sex that is privileged to use it. When west reigned supreme in India, till recent decades, members of Scheduled Castes, washermen and other so-called menial servicing castes were forbidden in using footwear and even if they used it, they were prohibited from wearing it in the streets where caste Hindus lived.

In the case of Valayar, there is significant divergence in their attitude towards the use of footwear. Use of sandals among men and women of Valayapatti is an occupational necessity. They go to the hills (Sirumalais) to collect firewood, honey, leaves of a variety of date (for making brooms) etc. Their job takes them to different parts of the hills and forests and they may have to tread on bushes, thorns and they are to be wary of reptiles on the hills. The terrain they have to walk daily form their village to the hills and back home and then to the neighbouring village or town for selling firewood, entails them the necessity of using footwear, not for fashion, nor for status, but to meet occupational requirements. Similar is the position in the case of men and women in Sendhi who go for collection of *gum* from *karivelam* (acacia) trees in the bed of Sendhi irrigation tank. But there is one difference in the women of Sendhi and Valayapatti wearing sandals. The women in Valayapatti wear them in the streets walk with sandals in the presence of and in the company of men. There is no bar in women using foot-wear at any point men use. The women in Sendhi avoid wearing sandals in the streets until they leave the outskirts of the village. This is as a mark of respect to the menfolk and not to pollute the area where the shrine of their deity is located. The women need sandals in the tank bed where they collect gum from the karivelam trees. It is full of thorns. They have to walk around and underneath the trees on bed of thorns. So the occupational imperativeness for footwear. The women carry footwear in their hands from the outskirts of the village. Except ten families (Sendhi 6 and Valayapatti 4) all the families in Sendhi and Valayapatti use sandals. One family in each community indicated that they could not afford to buy sandals on economic grounds.

In the case of these two nuclear villages in the study, footwear is an occupational necessity and both men and women use it, though there is a social difference among women not using sandals at Sendhi. This practice of Sendhi women not using sandals within the village precincts may be due to the presence of Brahmin families in Sendhi for several decades earlier (at present there is no Brahmin family at Sendhi), the location of a shrine and the temple-house in the village, as a mark of respect to the menfolk and finally Sendhi being a multicaste community with caste-Hindus such as Kallar and Konar who are a dominant group in the village. On the other hand, Valayapatti is an isolated community and to that extent Valayar are free from the negative sanctions of other caste-Hindu groups.

The situation in Piranmalai, which is said to be the ancestral home of the Valayar, is different. Here, using of footwear within the precincts of the Valaya locality is a taboo. The Saragu Valayar lives in two streets in a separate locality which is very close to the main village. Their shrine is located at the centre of one street. Decades earlier (the members do not know when) the community, in reverence to their local shrine, had decided that footwear should not be used within the Valaya locality. If any one were to wear sandals he has to leave them outside their residential locality. This self- imposed restriction has resulted in no member in the two hundred families using footwear.

On Rameswaram island, for two specific reasons-occupational (fishing) and topographical (the terrain is sandy) the Valayar seldom use footwear. The two factors do not necessitate the use of footwear.

Among the Valayar in general, the use of sandals by both the sexes is more of an occupational necessity, the social sanctions and status having less influence over the practice.

Diet Pattern of the Valayar

As said earlier, the Valayar are spread in eight districts in Tamil Naidu with variations in crops cultivated and dietary habits. Despite regional diversity, the basic diet of the Valayar consists of rice, millets, pulses, vegetable, meat and fish. The basic condiments that are used are salt, green and red chilies, tamarind, turmeric, and some spices. The better-off class uses more of spices and vegetables. The Valayar though meat-eaters are distinct from other meat-eating groups in India. The non-Brahmin meat-eaters in generality chiefly consume the meat of rams, sheep, goats, rabbits and birds including fowls. Some meat-eaters go in for pork and beef. But the Valayar, though not beef-eaters may be called omnivorous in a restricted sense. They eat a variety of animals, amphibians, birds, insects listed below and other available roots, tubers, wild edible fruits and of course the major and cheap cereals, millets, and pulses grown in the regions they live.

Non-Vegetarian Food

Animals

The animals they consume comprise rats, bandicoots, squirrels, monitor, sheep, wild sheep, goats, porcupine, wild and domesticated pigs, rabbits, water and ground turtle, langur, cats, mongoose, fowls, deer, armadillo (ant-eater) and fox.

Amphibians and Marines

The amphibians and marines they eat consist of frogs, crab, snail, fish, wild fowl, crane, kurugu (a species of crane), sengalunarai (red-footed water bird), pettakokku (a species of crane), sembothu (a species of bird), mandapura (pigeon), kadarai (patridge), serige (water fowl), mukkulippal (a water bird), neerukkakka (water crow), and ullan (a species of water bird which mostly forages on the banks and shores of water courses).

Insects

The insects they consume are winged-termites and eggs and nymph of musuru, a species of brown ant that habitate on trees, building homes with leaves.

And so the food of the Valayar may be broadly categorised as non-vegetarian and vegetarian food. Before, we discuss some of the non-vegetarian and vegetarian food, which are in a way conspicuous as food articles; we may look briefly into some of the recipes and food habits prevalent among a few Valaya communities.

In the case of Valaya fishermen of Rameswaram Island, food is prepared only once in the day that is in the evening. The left-over rice of the previous evening preserved with water and/or *kanji* (stained water) in mud vessels is consumed before twelve noon on their return from the sea. In the morning when they go afishing, they sip a cup of tea, no breakfast. The women take the *kanji*, the left over rice with water or mere *kanji* without rice. There is no lunch as such for men and women. They take only one full meal in the evening consisting of rice and fish. Fish is consumed by them almost every day. They seldom go for vegetables or greens. When raw fish is wanting, they prepare curry of dry fish exclusively and in combination with vegetables such as brinjal, drumstick and cluster beans. Rice is the only cereal they take.

They eat marines such as tortoise, turtle, crabs, besides, a variety of fish. Occasionally they net rabbits in the casurina plantations on the island.

The Valayar of Sendhi in Ramnad district prepare food only in the evening. Preparation of rice and other curries in the morning or afternoon is a rarity, but only on extraordinary, ceremonial and festive occasions. As in the case of Rameswaram Valaya islanders, the Valayar here eat rice. It is their staple food. Fresh or hot food is taken in the evenings only. The palasi, left-over rice of the previous evening preserved with water in earthen vessels is consumed in the morning as a breakfast at home or at the work spot. The same palasi if available will be taken in the noon in the place of lunch. Mud dishes are used in drinking *kanji*, or eating rice. Side dish *venjanam* if any is placed in a mud cup. Since, it is mere rice hot or cold, venjanam is a necessity. Most families in Sendhi prepare pickles of some lemon or other varieties. Green chilli and onions are used as *venjanam*. Meat is taken occasionally. They go for fishing during seasons and hunt rats too.

Idli, dosai (pan cake), paniyaram (an item prepared out of fermented rice flour with jaggery) are prepared on festive occasions. Flour of ulundu (blackgram), vendiyam (trigonella foenumgracium) and jaggery are mixed with rice flour for preparing *paniyaram*. This is a popular dish among the Valayar. They like it and often refer to it in their conservations. This is a big item for them, some sort of a finale (a feast) in treating a guest. *Attirasam* (a sweet preparation out of rice flour and jaggery cooked in the medium of groundnut oil) is a special for Deepavali (festival of lights). Rottis (cakes) and dosais are prepared from out of ragi flour. When a child is born, ragi (eleusive coracana gaerta), *kali* (semi-solid meal prepared out of ragi flour exclusively or cooked with broken grain of rice, cumbu, sorghum etc.) is distributed to each family in the local community at the time of announcing its birth. *Idli, dosai* and fresh hot food are served to a girl on her first menstruation

It is an unusual sight in the evenings, even after dusk in Valayapatti, that the women being busy at the mortars (stone mills) pounding, removing chaff of cholam (sorghum) for their evening meal. It is a daily affair in some cases. The pounding and cleansing of cholam cannot be done in advance for two reasons. The pounded, cleansed cholam (rice) cannot be kept too long, for it gets spoiled, since water is added at the time of pounding to remove the chaff. Another reason is poverty. They have to purchase grain almost every day with their day's earnings / wages. By the time they cook the cholam rice, it would be past eight in the evening and with some curry of pulses, they consume the only full meal for the day.

Cholam is the staple diet for the Valayar of Valayapatti. The left-over of the previous evening is taken in the mornings with water. Here too there is no lunch as such.

We may say that there are two major combinations in the diet of Valayar. Rice and fish are the combination in the districts of Tanjore, Tiruchirapalle, Tirunelveli and parts of

Madurai and Ramnad, and millets with negligible rice with meat and pulses and some vegetables in the districts of Coimbatore, North Arcot, The Nilgiris and parts of Madurai and Ramnad.

For instance, the Valayar in Coimbatore, North Arcot, parts of Madurai and Ramnad chiefly eat millets such as cholam (andropogon sorghum brot), cumbu (pennisetum typhoides), ragi (elusive coracana gaerta), thenai (seteria italica), samai (panicum miliaret), varagu (paspolum serobiculatum) and coarse variety of rice. In the case of Valayar of Valayapatti rice is a dish they could afford during marriage, festive and important social occasions.

The Valayar who live close to water sources and carry on fishing as an economic pursuit, collect some consumable marine products and eat them as main or substitute food as the case may be. In the case of those who live in dry areas, close to hills, forests, go about hunting, snaring game, catching rats, birds, insects, digging roots, collecting wild fruits, honey etc. for food. Procuring some of the game, birds and wild products are seasonal. We may discuss here a few non-vegetarian food items of the Valayar which are rather conspicuous.

Though the Valayar are omnivorous in their food habits, rodents (field rats, house rats and bandicoots) as food are very closely associated with their caste. Their catching and eating rats is a distinguishing factor and this singles them out as a rat-eating caste. Though many Valayar do not hide the fact of their eating rats and feel no qualms about it, it acts as a social stigma and the better-off and the educated among them despite this practice feel ashamed of their rat-eating community.

It is not a purposeless, wasteful killing, but it is used as food. It is the poor man's meat. The Valayar say (who are connoisseurs of meat of several species), that the rat meat is not inferior to others. But in the hierarchy of meats, it occupies a low position and so the consumer of it is looked down upon. Rat eating pulls down the Valaya community a great deal. Rat eating has been an ancient practice among them. Many of them do not make a secret of it. But some feel ashamed of it, but they are forced by custom and sanctions of tradition. There have been efforts made by some Valaya individuals to discourage their people in eating rats or to persuade them to give up eating rats.

Some of the Valayar do not stop with rats, but they go in for the bandicoots. They go on bandicoots expeditions. The Valayar of Ailur near Vadamadurai, Madurai district eats bandicoots. They go about with nets for catching rats. Bandicoots are caught especially during nights, since they are nocturnal in their habits. Sometimes the Valayar travel for miles, to different villages for collecting rats and bandicoots. But the bandicoots are eaten by a small minority of Valayar only. Once a Valayan, one of the village leaders of Valayapatti came across four men engaged in setting nets near a haystack on the way to Valayapatti. On enquiry the Valaya gentleman learnt that the laying of nets was for bandicoots and to his displeasure he came to know that they were his own caste people. The Valayapatti man asked them how they liked bandicoots. They told him that the meat of the bandicoot tasted fine.

As in the case of bandicoots, frogs are consumed by the Valayar in certain parts of Madurai district such as Alampatti, Katupatti, Manakatur, Checkuruchi, Pudupatti, Pandyanur, and Puttur of Vadamadurai block.

It is the same group of Karumbasi or Vannia Valayar who eat bandicoots in the Vadamadurai area. These bandicoot and frog eating Valayar are related to the Valayar of Valayapatti.

The frogs in the local dialect are called manakadai – 'mana' means manal – sand and kadai is a species of bird (sand bird). The frogs are collected from wet fields, wells, pools, tanks and other water sources. Baskets made of wild creepers/vines are used in collecting the frogs. Men, women and children go about collecting frogs.

The fresh frog meat is cooked as curry and eaten. The frogs are preserved like dry-fish. They are cut open at the abdomen, the vitals/intestines are removed, and then they are salted and exposed to sun until they are completely dry. Each family collects frogs in sufficient quantities during the season. The salted, dried frogs are stored, and they last for months. The Valayar use it for emergency purpose and during the off-seasons as a substitute for animal meat.

Oil is extracted when the frog meat is cooked with condiments and also extracted exclusively from frog fat. After collecting the oil, when it surfaces in the pot as a top layer in the water when the meat is boiled, it is heated again so that the water content in the oil is evaporated. The oil is taken out and preserved. It is added to food as a fat in the place of ghee (clarified butter). It is claimed that it has some medicinal value and it is applied externally for sprains and pain in the joints. It is also administered to animals mixing it with some feed for certain diseases. The oil is sold at high prices. People from distant places visit the Valaya villages to purchase the frog oil for medicinal purposes.

Eggs and Nymph of Musuru

The same groups of Valayar in Vadamadurai collect the eggs and nymph of musuru, a species of brown ants that are arboreal in their habits. Colonies of these ants build nests of leaves (usually they inhabit trees with broad leaves) sticking the leaves with a fine fibrous white substance produced from their bodies. These nets will be of a big coconut and pumpkin size. They lay eggs in these nests. The Valayar collect the eggs and nymph of these ants as a food article. The device for collecting is a long bamboo pole. A basket with a narrow neck is fastened to the upper end of the pole, leaving a ten inch to one foot pointed projection of the pole with which a hole is pricked in the leafy nest of the ants, and the basket is held up underneath the hole, and when the nest is shaken a little, the eggs and nymph fall into the basket tied to the pole. Once the basket is full, the contents are transferred to another basket kept on the ground. The eggs and nymph are consumed raw and fresh. They are also sun-dried on a flat stone and eaten. The Valayar keep it for a day or two. They consider it a delicacy. The Valayar in their leisure times go about collecting these eggs and nymph and eat them on the spot and bring home some for the children.

Eesal (Winged-Termites)

Another insect which is considered a delicacy by a large number of meat-eating groups in South India is the eesal - winged-termites. The Valayar relish them and avowedly look forward to the season. The winged-termites surface from their subterranean habitat following rain in the months of June, July, August, September and October. No Valayar group is an exception to the eating of winged-termites.

It is interesting to note that about 40 families (descendants of the first settler) at Valayapatti, own hills/mounds of winged-termites spread over a larger area on the Sirumalais (hills). These mounds/hills are all in the reserve forest on the hills. The ownership of these habitats of the termites is conventional (with no legal right) and their enjoyment rights over them are respected and seldom violated by the members of the community. Violation of this norm into the termite hills of another family is fraught with dire consequences – quarrels, clashes, and sometimes exchange of blows.

Usually, the winged-termites leave their underground homes after it rains, when the ground is wet or moist. They surface during nights and sometimes in the early mornings through a small opening (which they work out) on top of the mound in the form of a tunnel. The Valayar know (the other groups too) the time of their coming to the outer world and before the termites leave their dwellings on their own, the Valayar induce the termites to surface through the aperture they make on the hill.

The roots of *thalasurili* (aristolochina indica), kita, the leaves of kuttivelam (feroma elephantum), the seeds of kilachchi, the leaves of pancham, the roots of Ana and powdered minna are used as inducements for the winged-termites. Of the above roots and leaves of different species, the *kilachchi* seeds are a must. A combination of *kilachchi* seed with any one of the above would do the job. The seed alone or the seed plus other items are ground into a fine powder and this powder is blown into the hill through a small hole. The powder is held in the right palm and blown into, by the mouth. The powder is a sort of irritant, the termites start streaming out. There is another condition, though minor, the absence of wind for their coming out of their tunnels. A small pit is dug out near the hill, one and a half feet deep and one foot diameter. Two sticks are placed across the pit and a lighted hurricane lantern is placed on the sticks that are above the pit. The first to come out are the tiny wingless-termites. The winged termites when they surge forth from their subterranean home through the opening are instantly drawn by the light and in that act fall into the pit and struggle there only to be collected and put in a container or bundled in a cloth.

Back at home, the wings are winnowed away. Men prefer to attend to this winnowing business, though it is a woman's job, in order to prevent women munching handfuls or raw termites at the time of winnowing.

The termites are roasted in earthen vessels or iron pans. Salt and chilli powder and a pinch of turmeric powder are added for taste. Another recipe is to mix the roasted termites with roasted sorghum or rice. This is to increase the quantity. The grain is proportionally more. In order to make it more tasty cardamom, cloves, pepper, besides red chilli powder and salt are added. Another recipe is an equal quantity of palm jaggery (Palmyra sugar) and sorghum flour added to the roasted termites with all or some of the spices mentioned above. The roasted or the processed winged-termites are preserved for a month. It is used occasionally as a snack. Old people sans teeth who are fond of winged-termites get a few handfuls pounded in a poon (a tiny iron mortar measuring 7 to 9 inches in height, one to one and a half inches in diameter with a tapering bottom to which a small and sufficiently handy iron pistle is attached by a chain, and this is used for pounding betel-nut and betel-leaves by the toothless chewers) and consume it. When collected in sufficient quantities, the raw termites or the roasted ones (without any spices etc.) are sold. A measure of termites is sold at Rs.1.50 to Rs.2.00.

The first collection (the first haul) of the winged-termites is offered to the family deity. The place where the family deity is kept and offered puja at the house is cleaned, the vessel containing the termites is placed at the place and water is sprinkled around the vessel. They say a prayer in which they ask the deity to bless them with abundant winged-termites.

During the season, one can hear the Valayar recalling and reminiscing their experience in collecting these edible insects, the quantities their respective hills yielded, and so on and so forth.

Snails

Another article of food for the Valayar who inhabit areas along the water sources and paddies consists of snails. They eat a particular species, the size of which ranges from a gooseberry to a lemon. Women collect these snails, in tanks, paddy fields, irrigation channels, pools etc. They are collected in small earthen pots or palm leaf baskets. They are boiled first with shells, and then the shells are removed. The meat part remains as one piece. It is sliced and cooked and consumed as a side dish with rice or *kali* prepared out of ragi flour. They go in for minimum condiments or spices, chili powder, salt, a piece of garlic, seasoning or no seasoning.[3]

Vegetarian Food

Besides hunting and snaring game[4]now and then, there are a few seasonal food substitutes for certain Valaya groups: groundnut, wild edible fruits collected from hills and forests, jack, tender fruits of Palmyra etc.

Some of the Valayar are still in a semi-food gathering stage. For example, the Valaya women in some of the rice cultivating blocks (Narikodi, Melur, Madurai north etc.) in Ramnad and Madurai districts, visit the harvested paddy fields in the months of April-May (midsummer months). They dig out ant holes/hills for the granaries of paddy the insects had deposited in the tunnels. The black ants have the habit of collecting and depositing grain in their underground habitats. One such ant-hole may yield 100 to 300 grams of grain. The Valaya women can easily locate such ant-holes along the ridges, field-bunds in the paddy field. Despite simmering sun, one can see them engaged in digging the ant-holes with a length of iron or hard and pointed stick and collecting grain with all religious seriousness. They carry with them a basket made of palm leaf for bringing the grain home.

Speaking of certain seasonal food substitutes, we may say a word about jack, mushrooms, groundnut, wild fruits and greens.

Jack is cultivated and grown wild on the Sirumalais. Families who have plantations on the hills and others of Valayapatti make use of jack as food. The peak season for jack is June to August. The Valayar eat the fruit part and the seeds are fried and consumed. Further, the seeds are cooked with condiments or added to other curries. Children and adults will have cupfuls of cooked and spiced seeds.

Mushrooms

During April, May, June (after first showers) and November-December, mushrooms of various sizes grow. The Valayar are very fond of them and they consider it a delicious dish and a worthy substitute for meat (or a vegetable-meat if it may be called so). They know the places where they grow and they collect them during the seasons and prepare curry out of them.[5] Some of the strict vegetarian caste Hindus do not eat mushrooms considering them as tantamount to meat.

Groundnut

Whether the land owning Valayar cultivate groundnut or not,[6] they render labour for harvesting groundnut. During the groundnut harvest season it supplements their food.

Wild Fruits and Greens

Thorati (capparis grandiflora) and *kola* fruits are collected by the Valayar on the Sirumalais. These two are thorny plants, bearing fruits in the months of October and November. Besides their using these fruits as food substitutes, they sell their collections at 40 to 50 paise a measure (one and a half kg). Most of the families who have leisure during this season, go to the hills and collect wild fruits. During this season, a person engaged in the collection of fruits earns Rs.2.00 to Rs.3.00 per day.

The other wild fruits that grow on the hills are (1) narettam (Citrus aurantium) (September), (2) nave (July, August), (3) athai (ficus glomerata) (all through the year), (4) kollukoracha and (5) parangi, similar to thorati are also found in wild state. Besides, wild edible greens are collected and used. They are (1) thanda keerai, (2) kuppai keerai (amarantus viridis), (3) thakkali (a pygmy variety of tomato), (4) pulichi keerai (hibiscus cannacium), (5) molaya keerai, (6) minne keerai, (7) karum keerai and (8) chembu keerai. They do not go in for these greens exclusively. The greens are collected by both men and women in the course of their firewood collection and when they go for other wild products or for hunting.

Kottikalangu

Kottikalangu plant grows along river banks, tank bunds etc. The tubers of this plant are collected by the Valayar as a food article. It is the women who go about and collect k*ottikalangu*. The tubers are small in size usually measuring three-fourths to one inch in length and half an inch across. They have to dig the tubers with a dibble, spade or hoe. These tubers are either boiled adding some salt or roasted on coals and consumed. It is almost tasteless. The Valayar eat it forced by their poverty and collect it not for its taste but as an edible food article.

Since the Valayar are omnivorous and driven to certain food articles of fauna and flora, prescribed items of food are far less.[7] They do not eat meat during the mourning period.

Eating Habits

In regard to eating habits, seldom all the family members sit together and eat. It is the nature of their work that does not permit such a family eating. The only occasion that all the members get together is at the evening meal. In the case of children, right from the moment they are capable of helping themselves, some food (rice, cholam, or any food article) is put in the aluminium plate and placed before the child. It is a common sight among the Valaya (in the case of other caste groups too in the same or lower socio-economic conditions) villages to see toddlers with plates in their hands, placed in front of them, on pials, in the streets helping themselves in that childish awkward way. Some food is put in the plate and the child is to manage it by himself, no question of leisurely feeding of the child. In the morning and noon, sometimes it is the man and the children who have to serve themselves any left-over food, since the woman would be away collecting firewood or engaged in farm-labour. The woman serving food to the man is not universal among the Valayar. Either the woman is away on work or the food is so simple that it does not require somebody to serve it. In certain cases, as and when the members return home, each helps himself or herself.

Exceptional Foods

As mentioned earlier, the sweets that are popular are the sweetened paniyaram made of rice flour; idli and dosai are other items which are considered to be dishes prepared on special occasions, even though these two rice-flour items are in the daily menu of middle and a little well-to-do families. What is common at a particular level is a luxury at another level.

Any savoury or sweetmeats that the children could expect will be on festive occasions, and when the parents visit the towns or shandies (weekly markets) they bring atleast once a week something for the children – some savoury item – muruku, vadai, mixture, a length of sugarcane, puffed rice, roasted bengalgram.

Preparation of food and the food itself is a simple affair without much of complicated or cumbersome recipes or cookies. In general, it is food for existence and not food eagerly looking forward to.[8]

Some of the Valayar who are close to places where tea or coffee shops are located go in for a sip now and then. The Valayar of Valayapatti and Rameswaram Island are in the habit of taking tea in shops. They seldom prepare tea or coffee at their homes. It could be said that only a small fraction of Valayar are teetotalers.

Receptacles for Food and Drink

We find a culture-complex, in their levels of living. The receptacles they use for preparing, keeping and eating food and drinking are consistent or in harmony with their housing, clothing and dietary conditions. The vessels they use are simple, less costly and limited in number. Mud, brass, aluminium utensils are in use. Mud vessels are used in families, without exception. During the past couple of decades, there has been a slow change over to the metallic vessels for their unbreakable and long lasting characteristic.

Let us take a typical Valaya household and get an idea of the type of receptacles for food and drink it possesses. It owns a brass panai for fetching and storing drinking water. A chatti (vessel for cooking rice and curry) made of brass or aluminium, a brass chembu (a mug, a receptacle for keeping water by the side at the time of eating) one or two brass or aluminium tumblers (glasses). Normally, one aluminium eating plate for each adult and grown up child. These are all the brass or aluminium vessels that one may find in an ordinary Valaya household plus some earthenware for storing grain, pulses and some condiments and for cooking and eating and mugs were being used by the Valayar. Even now, in Sendhi and other Valaya households, earthen plates are used for eating. The use of aluminium vessels in a culture with a predominance of clay vessels is status-enhancing and not to speak of stainless steel utensils which are accorded a high position in the hierarchy of kitchenware. For instance, of the 94 households in Valayapatti and Sendhi, only 7 households (Valayapatti 5 and Sendhi 2) use receptacles made of stainless steel. Next to earthenware, it is aluminium followed by brass.

The food and the curries, the savouries they prepare are simple and the sweet dishes are rare. A household's kitchenware (excluding mud vessels) could be contained in a basket and carried by a woman on her head with all ease. Such are their material possessions. Some of the vessels/utensils available in a Valaya community are almost known to the entire community. These fewer utensils in a small community seldom get mixed up or lost. They can check up their whole utensils at a glance, in a moment. Such is the simplicity of receptacles for food and drinking among the Valayar in general.

SUMMARY

The material possessions and styles of life of the Valayar mark them off as a sub-culture within the Hindu population. They are very close to the lower castes in Tamil Nadu in respect to their dwellings, clothing, personal care and decoration. They live in diverse ecological and topographical conditions – hills, forests, sea coast and plains. Their houses are simple in most cases devoid of adequate space, privacy, ventilation and basic amenities. They keep their houses clean and tidy though the environmental sanitation is poor. The type of houses varies from region to region and most of the houses are mud-walled and thatched. Single room all-purpose dwelling predominates. They carry out ceremonies in the construction and occupation of the houses. They live in exclusively Valaya settlements as well as in multicaste communities.

The Valayar as other rural folk, are used to open defecation. Their dress, ornaments and personal upkeep are consistent with their housing. As an occupational necessity, Valayar in general use footwear. The women still keep on wearing traditional type of jewels and ornaments. They have their own style of hair-do.

The Valayar are omnivorous in a restricted sense. Their food chiefly consists of rice, sorghum, some millets, meat and fish. They eat a variety of wild and domesticated animals, birds, insects, roots, tubers, fruits and greens. They suffer from nutritional deficiency. Their food is simple. Most of them have one full meal a day. Their utensils for storing food grains, cooking and eating mostly consist of earthenware followed by aluminium. Their household belongings are limited to their occupational requirements and are minimal and simple. The Valayar are more anchored to tradition and closer to nature. They are a simple people with very basic survival, occupational oriented material possessions.

NOTES

1. In view of the price hike now the wages and rates should have reached a new high.
2. The author has come across reports that Valaya couples often have sexual intercourse on the hills when they go for collecting firewood. A place where every bush or rock gives you privacy. May be they feel it free there. Free from the constraint of lack of privacy at their houses.
3. In the course of field work at Sendhi, the author met an old woman (an acquaintance by then) in the street. She was carrying some thing in a small mud vessel astride her left side. On seeing the author, she covered it up with the loose end of her sari. Later it was learnt that the pot contained mollusk curry.
4. The hunting practices and the game hunted for food are described under occupations, in Chapter two.
5. It was a Deepavali day. Madayani of Valayapatti was in a fix as to what he should do for meat on that day. He had no money to buy meat. But that was a day meant for meat eating.

While pondering over the day's problem, he sighted a cluster of four beautiful large mushrooms near his lands close to the hills. With a sense of relief, he collected them, brought them home, and they served the family as substitute for meat. Deepavali passed off with a mushroom dish.

6. In Ramnad and Madurai districts, some of the Valaya landowners cultivate groundnut, but in the case of Valayapatti none cultivate groundnut and in Sendhi it is one of the crops cultivated by the Valayar.
7. Thammambalam is a native medical practitioner. He does not eat greens, vegetables cultivated in his fields until they are offered to the family deity on the Karthigai day (a festival that takes place in November). Since the man does not take greens etc. from his field until Karthigai the family members too eschew them until that day.
8. An informant from Valayapatti who works as peon in High School, who has some contact with the outside world complains of the monotony of the food. "Sir, it is cholam kanji in the morning, if available the same in the evening, though hot, and so it is cholam, and cholam. And not to speak of side dish. Sambar is a luxury. Food is not a pleasant part of life.

Economic Organization
II

The Valyar live and toil in different environmental settings. They come in close interaction with nature in the course of their economic pursuits. Barring other variables like education and intensity of interaction with other groups, the habitats and occupation to a great extent go to influence and determine the knowledge of their supernatural world and the intimate feel of the seasons and weather. The Valayar as a people are close to natural surroundings like sea, hills, forests, rivers, animals, birds and insects.

Keeping in view the Valaya fishermen, the firewood collector, the collector of wild products, and the hunter of game, his sense of change of season is linked with the fish and wild products that are seasonal. He believes in the creation of God. He believes that his destiny, availability of game, netting of abundant fish, and the phenomenon of rain depend on supernatural powers. And by his sacrifices, offerings and worshipping of his plethora of deities, he can secure things from them. This fact gets adequately reflected from a number of economic activities of the Valayar to be discussed in the following pages.

The Valayar are engaged in a variety of economic pursuits determined and influenced by the respective ecological and environmental conditions. There are more than thirty economic activities they are engaged in, the number of families, engaged in these occupations ranges from a very small to a large number.

OCCUPATIONS OF THE VALAYAR

In the following pages, an attempt has been made to describe and discuss the economic organization of the two nuclear communities of the present study – Valayapatti and Sendhi – and a general picture of the distribution of the Valaya population in Tamil Nadu in terms of different occupations followed by a brief discussion of each occupation. The Valayar are engaged in single as well as in a combination of two or three occupations as the sources of their livelihood. These economic activities broadly relate to farming, fishing, collection of firewood and other forest or wild products of economic value, farm and industrial labour, petty services, house-building and manufacture of house-building material and in petty business. Discussion in this section relates to single occupation and important combination of occupations broadly in terms of the percentage of the Valaya population engaged in pursuits. The general discussion of economic activities of the total Valaya population is followed by the economic activities of Valayar of Valayapatti and Sendhi under the respective categories. The occupations of the people in Valayapatti and Sendhi are categorised as primary, secondary and miscellaneous depending on the quantum of income through each such occupation. There are 50 households in Valayapatti and 44 in Sendhi and most of these households in these two Valaya communities have more than one occupation which is characteristic of the lower strata in the rural communities in India.

As shown in Table 1, farming is the primary occupation for the majority in both the communities though a large number is engaged in it in Sendhi. We could see that ecology has a bearing on the economic pursuits of people, while collection and selling of firewood is totally absent as a primary occupation in Sendhi; seventeen households (34%) in Valayapatti primarily depend on it as a chief source of their livelihood. Valayapatti is located at the foot of the Sirumalais (hills) and hence this occupation. Farm labour as a primary occupation is in some five households in each community, compared to farming, the collection and selling of firewood. It is interesting to note that one family in Sendhi, the head of which is a 'Kodangi' (conjurer-cum astrologer) lives on his earnings primarily on sooth-saying while rearing of goats is the primary occupation for one family in Valayapatti.

TABLE 1: Distribution of Households in Terms of Primary Occupation

Category	Valayapatti No.	Sendhi No.	Total
Farming	27	38	65
Fire wood	17	—	17
Farm Labour	5	5	10
Rearing Goats	1	—	1
Soothe-saying	—	1	1
Total	50	44	94

TABLE 2: Distribution of Households in Terms of Secondary Occupation

Category	Valayapatti No.	Sendhi No.	Total
Farming	—	1	1
Farm Labour	19	36	55
Fire wood	28	—	28
Gum Collection	—	1	1
Basket Making	—	1	1
Attached Labour	—	1	1
Total	47	40	87

In Valayapatti out of 50 households, 47 have secondary occupations, besides primary occupation, while 40 out of 44 in Sendhi have secondary occupations in addition to their primary ones (see Table 2). In respect to secondary occupations too, we find the same influence of land and geographical features. Sendhi with considerable paddy cultivation provides work to the farm-labour and so out of 44 households, 36 depend on farm-labour as a secondary source of their living while farming is the primary occupation for 38 households and so in the case of Sendhi it is farming and farm-labour which constitute the chief occupations of the Valaya community. But the position in the case of Valayapatti is different. Here it is the collection and selling of firewood, chief secondary occupations for 56% of the households while 34% pursue it as a primary occupation. At Valayapatti, farm-labour is a secondary occupation to 38% of the households.

Besides the primary and secondary occupations, a few subsidiary occupations are carried on by the two communities. Seventy-four (80%) out of 94 households (Valayapatti 38 and

Sendhi 36) carry on some subsidiary or miscellaneous occupations. These occupations as shown in Table 3 supplement their income.

The forest (Sirumalais) helps the Valayar rear goats and that is why while 19 (38%) households rear goats at Valayapatti, it is just two households in Sendhi. On the other hand perhaps in view of paddy cultivation and the availability and adequacy of fodder (hay) dairying as a subsidiary occupation is carried on by 19 out of 44 households in Sendhi, while it is totally absent in Valayapatti though the cattle population in Valayapatti is 168 as against 63 head of cattle in Sendhi. Poultry is commonly reared by all the Valayar. Eating of birds is occasional, mostly on festival and ceremonial occasions. One family in Sendhi runs a small grocery shop and one man in Valayapatti works as an office-boy in a High School.

TABLE 3: Distribution of Households in Terms of Subsidiary Occupations

Category	Valayapatti No.	Sendhi No.	Total
Dairying	—	22	22
Rearing of Goats	19	2	21
Poultry	37	33	70
Rearing of Sheep	—	3	3
Vending Articles	1	1	1
Employed (Job)	1	—	1

The occupations mentioned above are the primary, secondary and subsidiary occupations of the two Valaya communities at Valayapatti and Sendhi taking family as a unit of study. But within the family, members have division of work and a member in a family may work within the family occupation, or outside of it, or may attend to one item of work or more than one item of work, or one may be economically active and productive in terms of services and goods or one may be a dependent and a non-earning member. And so an attempt has been made to find out how the members of these two communities are occupied.

The total population of these two groups is 475, Valayapatti 272 and Sendhi 203. This population comprises 226 males and 249 females. Table 4 shows the population under different categories, i.e. earning and non-earning population.

While male members of the community are engaged in field work such as farming, farm-labour, collection of firewood, etc., some female members, attend to both field and domestic work, cooking, tidying up the house, attending on children and most of the chores concerning the home. We find that one-third (159) of the total population, predominantly male members engaged in their main family occupation such as farming, farm-labour, and collection of firewood as the case may be, while a small number of men (13) are working outside their families' chief occupation.[1] It may be noted here that the Valaya woman works at two fronts – the field front and the home-front. Usually it is a small number of women who attend to domestic work exclusively. We find here that only 24 women out of 249 (inclusive of children) just attending to their households only. But on the other hand, a little less than one half (114) of women work in their family occupation and also keep the home. The Valaya women outnumber men in certain economic activities. This has been brought out in the census of 1921. The ratio between male and female workers engaged in economic activities is shown in Table 5.

TABLE 4: Distribution of the Population in Terms of Economic Activities or Otherwise

Category	Valayapatti No.	Sendhi No.	Total
(a) Working within the Family occupation	83	76	159
(b) Working outside the family occupation	6	7	13
(c) Domestic work	13	11	24
(d) Attending school	62	9	71
(e) Not working	46	46	92
(a) + (c)	62	52	114
(a) + (b)	—	1	1
(b) + (c)	—	1	1
Total	272	203	475

It is clear from Table 5 that in the case of 'land owners and tenants', 'agricultural labourers' and 'miscellaneous labourers' it is women who outnumber men. In the case of land-owners and tenants per 1000 men workers, there are 1635 women workers, 63.5% larger than the men workers. The highest ratio (97.4%) almost double of female workers to male workers is under miscellaneous labour. So it is female Valaya who bears the major burden and works harder for the sustenance of the family.

TABLE 5: Ratio of Female Workers per 1000 Male Workers and Occupational Distribution of the Valayar per 1000 Population[2]

Occupation	No. per 1000 Workers Engaged in Each Occupation	No. of Female Workers per 1000 Male
Cultivation, Owners and Tenants	463	510
Land Owners and Tenants	139	1635
Agricultural Labourers	152	1034
Fishing and Selling Fish	58	387
Miscellaneous Labourers	91	1974
Others	97	334

In respect to the distribution of the population in the two communities in terms of how each person is occupied, 22.42% of the population in Valayapatti attends school and 4.4% at Sendhi. This difference could be attributed to two factors. In case of Valayapatti it has been under the service area of the Gandhigram Rural Institute and secondly, the primary school is located in the hamlet itself which serves exclusively the Valaya children (a situational factor) and further Valayapatti has been exposed to a lot of outside influence through the educational institutions at Gandhigram. But in the case of Sendhi, though the primary school is located in the village, only 9 children out of 44 children in the age group of 5-14 attend school. It is due to the social environment and the values of the group.

The population categorized as non-working comprises children below five years, children of the school-going age that do not attend school, and old and infirm people who are non-workers in the economic sense. Of the total population of 475 of the two valaya communities a little over one third (34.3%) of the population is unproductive and dependent-population. That is, in the population under study, for every two workers (earning members) there is one non-worker. This position varies considerably in the individual (children attending school and the not-working category) in unproductive and dependent while only 27% comes under this category in Sendhi.

Division of Labour

All this point, we may briefly discuss the division of labour based on sex and age as it obtains among the Valayar. The division of labour among them we may broadly categorise into activities confined to the house and home and outside the home. Activities outside the home again comprise both economic and domestic and the economic activities that men, women, aged people and children carry on further depend on the nature and kind of occupations the family pursues. For example, in agricultural operations, men right from the age of sixteen attend to preparing the soil, ploughing, leveling, hedging, broadcasting seed, bailing out water for irrigating the fields, while women attend to transplanting and weeding. Harvesting of crops is mostly carried on by women, but men also attend to harvesting and weeding sometimes. In an agricultural family, old people of both sexes who are not strong enough to carry on operations which require strength, keep watch over the crops or guide youngsters in the operations by giving directions and sometimes play a supportive role.

In a family which depends upon farm-labour both men and women right from their fifteenth-sixteenth year hire themselves as labourers-men in ploughing, sowing, harvesting, winnowing and cleaning the grain. Similarly, in the case of families that live on collection of firewood and other wild products as a primary or a supplementary source of income both men and women until their early fifties, engage themselves in such activities. On the other hand, in the fishing community, fishing is solely the men's job. It is the man as discussed under fishing who weaves the net or lines, and mends it and keeps it in good repair. The women's role in fishing family involves her helping the man when the catch is brought to the shore or home as the case may be, in grading the fish by size or variety, in selling, sun-drying, salting, storing and sometimes selling the dry fish at home or at the local market.

It may be pointed out that barring minor differences in the economic burden borne by the women in certain occupations, they are equal participants with men in all means of livelihood that the Valayar pursue. This is necessitated by their level of living.

The old people (beyond sixty) who have ceased to be economically active as mentioned earlier look after minor chores, watering and feeding animals, sometimes tending cattle, keeping watch over crops, taking care of small children left at home while their parents are engaged in work. Laziness is a rarity among the old and the young in the Valaya community.

When we come to the domestic or home front, jobs connected with cleaning, daubing the floor and tidying the house, and cleaning, pounding, husking and milling the grain and cooking are carried on by the woman. Sometimes, the man also helps her in these chores. But household work predominantly is the domain of the woman. In respect to purchase of grain, condiments and other day-to-day consumer articles both men and women attend to this. But it is the women who take initiative in these and remind the man the need for an article. In regard to monetary transactions, though women are consulted and taken into confidence, it is mostly men who carry on such activities. Thus, we find natural division of labour based on sex and age, which is almost universal among the caste-groups similar to the Valayar in the region in economic pursuits and levels of living.

Juvenile Labour at Valayapatti and Sendhi

Children among the Valayar in the age group of five and sixteen are a source of economic asset and support to the families, despite their young age, they are engaged in several economic activities. The juvenile labour as it obtains in Valayapatti and Sendhi may briefly be discussed here (see Table 6)

As mentioned earlier, there is considerable prevalence of juvenile labour among the Valayar. In respect to the two villages with a population of 475 (Sendhi 203, Valayapatti 272) there are 79 children ranging from five to sixteen of age. Of these 79 children, 36 are males and 43 females. Thirty children (male 18 female 12) are engaged in farming and farm-labour, 20 in tending cattle (males 13 females 7), fourteen girls are engaged in farming, farm-labour, 20 in farming, and another eight girls in exclusive domestic works, helping mothers and managing and carrying out household chores. Three boys and two girls in Valayapatti supplement their family's income through collection of firewood. Two boys in Sendhi who are ten and twelve of age are attached labourers.

Of these 79 juvenile workers, 42 (male 18, female 24) are from Valayapatti and 37 (male 18, female 19) are from Sendhi. Female juvenile workers outnumber (more in Valayapatti) male workers.

In respect to the juvenile workers in terms of age categories in the two villages, the highest number 29 (male 13, female 16) is in the age group of 5-10 followed by 25 (male 12, female 13) in 11-12, and 25 (male 11, female 14) in 13-16.

For instance, one girl in Sendhi who is in her fifth year tends cattle, and another in Valayapatti in her seventh year does the same job. Further, in Valayapatti, two girls in their eighth year, one in ninth, two in tenth and three in their 12th year are put to grazing of cattle.

Occupational Distribution of the Valayar of Tamil Nadu in General

We may briefly look into the occupational distribution of the Valayar in Tamil Nadu and discuss each occupation separately. The Valaya population is engaged in several types of occupation, some in one and others in a combination of occupations where each such occupation supplements the other for others.[3]

Twenty-four occupations, single as well as a combination of occupations are shown besides a few other occupations pursued by a small number of families discussed separately. The major occupations are farming, farm labour, fishing, collection of firewood and a combination of these followed by occupations such as masonry, digging of wells, match works, fire works, mat weaving, keethu making, brick work, bangle selling, coir work, weaving, village menial service, etc.

We may recall that Valayar live in eight districts in Tamil Nadu and there are 98255 Valaya households in these eight Valaya districts. Of this total, 33.58% are engaged in farming followed by 26.72% in farm-labour and next to it fishing as a single occupation is pursued by 12.4% of the households. But in terms of percentage or size of population, farm-labour is followed by farming and farm-labour as a combination is carried on by 20.44% of the households and the rest of the single and combination of occupations are pursued by two and less than one percent of the population.

Table 5 gives the distribution of Valayar as per 1921 census in terms of their occupation. It is seen that 46.3% and 13.9% of the population is engaged in farming as owner cultivators and tenant cultivators followed by 15.21% as farm-labourers and 5.8% in fishing, 9.1% in miscellaneous labour and 9.7% in other occupations. Compared to the occupational distribution in 1921, the position as of today varies considerably in respect to farming and farm-labour. It is significant to note that nearly 60% of the Valaya population in 1921 is shown as pursuing farming but as per the returns received by the author, about 34% is engaged in farming. But the percentage of the population engaged in farming becomes equal to the position obtaining in 1921, when the percentage of population today (20.44%) engaged in farming and collection of firewood is combined. Based on the Census data (1921) and the data related to the present study, relatively, the largest population is engaged in farming and the percentage to population taper down to 0.01 percent when it comes to weaving and bangles selling as full-time family occupations.

We may briefly discuss the spread of the Valaya population in the eight Valaya districts in terms of each occupation.

Farming

Of the total household population (98.255) 33.58 percent (32,998) is engaged in exclusive farming. Of this farm-population, the highest percentage (37.40) is found in Madurai district followed by Tiruchirapalle with 30.40%, Tanjore with 17.67%, Ramnad with 13.34% and Coimbatore with 1.19% (392 households). Farming as an exclusive occupation of the Valayar has not been reported from the districts of Tirunelveli, The Nilgiris, and North Arcot and farming as a secondary occupation too is not found among the Valayar in the above three districts. In the case of the Nilgiris district the major factor for absence of farming appears to be ecology and the terrain. Though the largest Valaya population (28.7%) obtains in the district of Tanjore and despite it being a rice-rich area, only 17.67% of the farm-population is found in the district and similar is the case in respect to Ramnad district which is next to Tanjore in terms of Valaya population (27.5%). When we come down to the district level, we find that 16.27 percent of the Valaya population in the district of Ramnad is engaged in farming, but in Madurai it is 62.29 percent, 9.19 percent in Coimbatore, 64.01 percent in Tiruchirapalle and 20.69% percent in Tanjore district. If district is taken as a unit, the highest population engaged in farming is found in Tiruchirapalle followed by Madurai, Tanjore, Ramnad and Coimbatore in the declining order.

Farm practices and crops grown in Tamil Nadu vary from district to district. For instance, the districts of Ramnad, Coimbatore, parts of Madurai and Tirunelveli are dry areas, chiefly dependent on monsoonic rains and well and tank irrigation. In the case of Tanjore, Tirunelveli, parts of Madurai, Ramnad and Tirunelveli they enjoy irrigation facilities and wet crops like paddy are grown in these parts.

In general cereals, millets, pulses, oil seeds and cotton are grown in these districts by the Valayar as others do.

Valayapatti and Sendhi

Let us look into the nature of farming in the two nuclear villages of the study. In Valayapatti, 54% (27) of the 50 households and in Sendhi, 88.37% (38) of 44 households carry on farming as their chief occupation. Of the 50 households in Valayapatti, 64 percent (32) and of 44 households in Sendhi, 88.64% (39) own land. The percentage of land owners in both the communities is 75.5% percent. The size of the individual holding too varies. The extent of land owned by the respondent families varies from below one acre to above five acres. Of the 71 land-owning households, the highest number (39) own from 1-3 acres followed by 16 from 3-5 acres; 11 above 5 acres, and 5 below one acre. The majority is marginal farmers and the rest are small and medium farmers.

The 71 land-owning families in the two communities own an extent of 210.39 acres. The group at Valayapatti owns 87.51 acres and the Sendhi Valayar an extent of 122.88% acres. The land owned by the Valayar of Valayapatti is technically classified as dry, though it is locally categorised as dry, garden and forest land, and the extent under the above local classification is dry 55.63 acres, garden 14.77 acres and forest land 17.11 acres. Garden land is dry land which enjoys irrigation facilities. The land categorised as forest land is situated on the Sirumalais (hills). But in the case of Sendhi, nearly one-half of (59.26 acres) land is wet land and paddy is cultivated in this land. The Valayar at Sendhi own 61.55 acres of dry land and 2.07 acres of garden land. This garden land mostly consists of vacant house sites and backyards.

There is an interesting contrast between the two valaya communities of Valayapatti and Sendhi in respect to land. The first three to four generations of Valayar at Valayapatti reclaimed and purchased nearly 300 acres of land around their habitat but during the last and the present generation, most of the land was sold out for very small sums of money to the neighbouring villagers especially to the Gounder of Chettiapatti and the weaver community of Chinnalapatti. The manner in which they lost their lands shows two things, mainly their poverty and their less dependence on, and low value for lands. There has been a case of one Valayan who has disposed of fifty cents of his land for a few vadais (a savory prepared out of ground bengalgram or black-gram with or without spicing in the medium of groundnut oil) during those days each piece cost a pie and now from 20 to30 paise.[4]

But the story in the case of Sendhi is different. The land in Sendhi enjoys tank irrigation. Paddy is the main crop grown, the value of land is higher and farming has been the chief occupation of the majority of the Valayar at Sendhi. The story goes as briefly referred to in the Introduction that the Zamindar of Sakkondi in Sivaganga taluk invited the first Valaya settlers at Sendhi and offered them lands. Subsequently, the same Zamindar invited a few Brahmin families to Sendhi and over a period of time the Brahmin became dominant and they grabbed the lands from the Valayar and purchased some form the Zamindar and ultimately most of the Valayar were reduced to the position of tenant cultivators and share croppers. This continued for several decades. But with abolition of Zamindari and Inamdari (land tenure systems) and with the enactment of tenancy laws, the Valayar of Sendhi after a prolonged civil dispute secured their rights over the lands they were cultivating as tenants and share croppers. The lead and support for the Valayar at Sendhi was given by a Marxist communist leader of a neighbouring village.[5] This major help in securing the individual rights over the lands brought them under the communist fold and the whole Sendhi Valaya community swears by Communism irrespective of their knowledge, understanding and implications of Communism.

While land is the chief source of sustenance for the Valayar of Sendhi it is not so in the case of Valayapatti. The pattern or type of land owned also varies. Of the 39 land owners in Sendhi, 56.41 percent own 'wet, dry and garden' land and none come under this category in Valayapatti, while 18.75 percent of the 32 land owners in Valayapatti own dry-forest-garden-land such a combination of land ownership is not found in Sendhi, and while 59.38 percent of land owners in Valayapatti own dry land only, there is no farmer in Sendhi who owns dry land only and at the same time 36.46 percent (out of 39) of the Sendhi Valayar own wet and dry land. Obviously the type of land and irrigation facilities determines the type of crops cultivated.

Paddy is the main crop cultivated in Sendhi; and in the case of Valayapatti it is dry crops and mainly millets. The following crops are cultivated in both the villages. They are kuthiraivali (Echinochola Colona var), ragi (Elensine coracama goertu), tenai (Setaria italica) varagu (Phaseolous mungo var), cowpea/(Vigna catjang walp), green grams (Phaseolous aurous Roxb), Pigeon Pea (Cajanus Cajan milsp), sesame (indicum tit; mochecia-dolichos lab var lignousus). Of the above crops, millets extent in Sendhi. Six farmers of Valayapatti own land on the Sirumalais. These are plantations on the slopes of hills. A hill-variety of banana, jack, fruit, lemon, coffee, pineapple, and guinea sized tomato are cultivated on the hills. Besides the above crops and fruits cultivated, the Valayar collect a variety of edible wild fruits, roots, tubers, and wild greens on the hills. They collect these wild edible fruits locally called thorati, kela, Nava, narettam, athai, kollu koruchcha, parangi, rakkota and wild edible greens such as thaandakeerai, kuppaikeerai, pulichi keerai, molaya keerai, minne keerai, karum keerai, chembu keerai etc, and consume them as food substitutes. They consume these fruits on the spot, at the point of collecting or at home. If the quantity collected is larger it goes in for the market. For instance, thorati and kela fruits (thorny plants) are collected by the Valayar (Valayapatti) in the month of November and a measure (1-1/2 kg) of these tiny fruits is sold at 40 to 50 paise. Most of the families in Valayapatti along with the collection of firewood exclusively collect these fruits on the hills and sell them. During the season, a full time collector of these fruits earns from Rs.2.00 to 3.00 a day. Both men and women, young and old collect these fruits.

In respect of the plantations on the hills, banana and lemon are planted largely and these fruits are sold in the Dindigul market usually once a week.

A Test to Ascertain the Prospect of Rain

Agricultural operations depend upon seasonal rains and the Valayar have their own way of finding out whether it would rain in a particular season or not. It may be relevant here to discuss such a practice among the Valayar and their association with fauna and flora.

When rains fail in the Tamil months of Adi (July-August) and Puratasi (September-October) malaikuri which is a test to find out whether it would rain or not is observed. This test indicates whether it would rain at all during the year, and if so, when? such an observance is discussed by the entire Valaya community in a given locality and all the households are informed of the observance and a date is fixed for the ritual.

A new earthen vessel is brought from the potter. It is filled with ash to the brim collected from the ovens of five to six houses. A square, 4 feet by 4 feet is marked with ash on the ground. A pistle is used in the marking. The ash-filled pot is placed at the centre of the square. Across each corner of the square (outside the square) four persons lie keeping their heads towards each other. The person who lies at the south-east corner keeps his head toward north-east, he who lies at the north-east keeps his head south-east, the north-east corner man toward south-west and the south –west corner man toward north-west. They lie face down with their hands stretched on the ground. A fifth person sits on the pot, keeping his feet on the ash, that is, he keeps his weight on his heels. He does not touch the ground. He has to sit on the pot in the same posture until the pot, rotates on its own axis. (*Chatti Suthinathan arul yarangum* – the God's grace will come only when the pot spins). When the pot spins fast, the man sitting on it balances himself on it by keeping his hands on the ground. It may rotate in that fashion for several minutes and the finale comes when the pot breaks into pieces. Until then the same person or another person has to sit on it. While the pot spins fast, it breaks into pieces and the man balancing on it gets the *arul*. He gets 'possessed' of the divine and falls to the ground, and kicks the four persons lying at four corners, and each falls a few yards from the point where he was lying and usually (as they say) the one lying at the south-west corner does not roll.

Immediately after the kicking by the 'possessed' is over, the pot shreds (broken pieces) are counted. Supposing the pot was broken into seven pieces, it will rain in 7 days, the man who sits on the pot and gets possessed announce the days within which it would rain.

If the pot spins slowly, there would be moderate rain in the month during which they seek knowledge of it. Supposing it spins fast, it means heavy rain in the month. The four persons who lie at the four corners symbolize the four directions. The *malaikuri* is carried out at the *mandai* (village common—an open ground).

We have said earlier that the Valayar are one of the peoples who are close to a natural environment and come in intimate contact with the elements: wind, rain and sun. For example, the Valayar of Valayapatti since their childhood, have intimate knowledge of the topography of the hills, the fauna and flora on the hills. They collect wild products, set snares, and hunt game on the hills. They are familiar with the lairs and the behaviour of game animals and birds. On occasions, they discuss and share their experiences of animal behaviour. Children will be curious listeners of such discussions. These are lessons for them in setting snares and in catching/hunting game. The Valayar are familiar with the food habits of animals, habitats, their behaviour after they are wounded, how to follow the trail of a wounded bear, deer, mountain sheep, etc.

In the evenings during the game seasons, the menfolk discuss the hunting strategy, snaring and trapping devices, recall how they encountered certain game, how miraculously they escaped, or how the game escaped being shot at and so on. These discussions on hunting are so lively; they revolve around guns, rifles, and types of rifles. They recall how so-and-so secured a trophy— a giant wild boar. Some of these over a period of time become legendary. These stories enthuse the youngsters and strengthen their kin bond. The youth are trained in setting snares, improvising snares, traps and hunting game. The young men accompany the adults as helpmates in hunting game. Similar is the knowledge on the part of the Valaya fishermen (coastal) in respect of sea, marine life and weather. For instance, the Rameswaram islanders know all the species of edible and non-edible fish and other marine life that are found in that part of the sea. They lay nets in accordance with the behaviour of a particular species of fish. They understand nature and coordinate with her. They live more in harmony with nature.

The Valayar of Valayapatti during the last two generations have done this malaikuri six times. Every time within the number of days as indicated by the number of pieces the pot has broken into, it had rained. It reinforces their faith in the supernatural and their belief in the ritual and the *Arul* (grace) of God. It is seeking divine guidance, not praying for rain, but to find out the date within which it would rain. This is their meteorology and the Valaya ways of weather forecasting.

Implements

The farm implements used in both the villages are traditional except iron ploughs used in Sendhi. The possession and number of farm implements owned by a family is an index of a family's economic level. The farm implements and allied ones in the villages comprise wooden plough, iron ploughs, spades, hoes, crowbars, levelers, sickles, aruval, axe, gum cheepi (a tool used for collecting gum producing trees), *seethuki (*used for collecting green grass), cart, *chedi vetti* (wood and tree cutter), *silukku* (used in catching rats).[6]

Except a few items of money crops such as pulses, banana, lemon and oil seed, the rest of the produce is consumed by the community. In view of the marginality of their farming, the entire produce of millets in Valayapatti (save a family) is consumed by the producers and there is no marketable surplus. But in the case of Sendhi Valayar, some of the families do sell a quantity of paddy to meet farm and domestic expenses. Such expenses in most cases in Valayapatti are met through their collection and sale of firewood. Theirs is subsistence economy.

It is paradoxical that though the community development programme has been in operation in the Athoor (Madurai) and Sivaganaga (Ramnad) blocks for the last fifty years, the Valayar of Valayapatti and Sendhi have not been touched by any CD programme. Not even the field level worker has visited these two villages all these years. If at all there are new farm practices in these two villages, it was only a radiational effect. No respondent in the two villages has received any help from the block agency.

As part of this study, an attempt was made to know the attitude of the Valayar in respect to certain improved farm practices.

To a question as to what extent the traditional practice of cultivation with a wooden plough is outdated or otherwise, of the 94 respondents in Valayapatti and Sendhi, 61.70 percent think that the wooden plough is not at all outdated, 34.05% opine that it is partly outdated while a small percentage (4.25) feel that it is absolutely outdated. It may be noted here that Sendhi is advanced in farm practices compared to Valayapatti. This is evident in the attitudes of the respondents, while only 36.36 percent of the Sendhi respondents say that the wooden plough is not at all outdated, in the case of Valayapatti it is 84 percent who hold that attitude. But in the case of necessity of green manure and fertilizers, there is a shift in the attitude. Nearly one half of the respondents consider them absolutely necessary (Valayapatti 48%, Sendhi 43.18%) and over one-third consider them partly necessary (Valayapatti 36%, Sendhi 36.36%) and a little over one-fifth of the respondents say that green manure and fertilisers are not at all necessary.

In the case of improved seeds, a little over one half of the respondents (Valayapatti 74%; Sendhi 13.64%) indicate that improved seeds are absolutely necessary and a little over one-fourth hold that improved seeds are partly necessary and almost the same percentage feel that improved seeds are not at all necessary.

Farm-Labour

Next to farming it is farm-labour in which 26.72 percent (26.258 families) of the total Valaya households are engaged as their chief and sometimes their only occupation. Of the 26.258 farm-labour families, 54.37 percent, (the highest percentage) is found in the district of Ramnad followed by Tanjore with 21.46 percent; the Nilgiris with 0.28 percent with 0. 25 percent in Tiruchirapalle. It is significant to note that while 30.40 percent of the total Valaya households pursue farming as their exclusive occupation in Tiruchirapalle, only 0.25 percent of the total population lives on farm-labour in the district. Sometimes the occupation also reflects and secures to the practitioners the social position *vis-à-vis* other castes and occupational groups. Thus, we find over 85 percent of Valaya farmers are found in the districts of Madurai, Tiruchirapalle and Tanjore and at the same time over 90 percent of Valaya farm-labourers are distributed in the districts of Ramnad, Tanjore, Madurai and Coimbatore in the declining order. The land-owning and the landless within a caste emerge as not too-well demarcated classes. Labourers are mostly from the lower castes especially the Scheduled Castes. Even though one belongs to a middle ranking caste, he is landless-labourer in rural community. It sometimes assigns him a position different from the one enjoyed by his land-owning kinsfolk or casteman. We find over one-fourth of Valaya population in Tamil Nadu being farm-labourers; Ramnad district which tops the list in the Valaya farm-labour population has its highest Valaya labour concentration in the Singampunari C.D. block. As per the returns, all the 10.196 families in the block are farm-labourers. It is not to be taken literally so, but the chief source of livelihood for the Valaya population there, is farm-labour. But the position becomes different when we move on to Madurai district. Here it is only 19.97 percent of the Valaya population that is engaged in farm-labour as against 52.59 percent in Ramnad district. In The Nilgiris district, 85.06 percent of the Valayar work on plantations as labourers and in Coimbatore, it is 57.47 percent, and in Tiruchirapalle, it is just 0.41 percent and in Tanjore, it is 20 percent, engaged in farm-labour. We find that the Valaya labour population has a wider geographic spread in the districts of Coimbatore 18 C.D. blocks, Ramnad (11), Madurai (19), Tanjore (9) and in The Nilgiris it is limited to two blocks and in Tiruchirapalle it is only in one block (Jayankondan).

In the case of Valayapatti and Sendhi, 87 out of 94 families (Valayapatti 88% and Sendhi 97.73%) are engaged in farm-labour. In terms of male and female and children hiring themselves as farm labourers, a total population of 218 male, female and children are engaged in farm-labour in both the villages. That is, a little less than one-half of the total population of these two Valaya communities partly sustain themselves on farm-labour. In the case of Valayapatti it is 40.86% (38) men, 41.94 %(39) women and 17.20% (16) children out of a total labour force of 93 and in the case of Sendhi with 125 persons engaged in farm-labour, the split-up is 30.40% (38) men, 38.40% (48) women and 31.20% (39) children. It is seen that between these two communities a higher percentage of men and women is engaged in farm-labour in Valayapatti but at the same time, the juvenile labour is nearly double in the case of Sendhi Valayar, since over Ninety percent of the school-going age children do not attend school.

Farm-labour is seasonal and so they do not find work all through the year. The number of days a family is engaged in farm-labour depends on factors such as availability of work, the other occupation of the family, the health and the ability of the worker to work. Importantly the seasonal nature of farming limits the number of days of employment in the case of labour. In respect of Valayapatti and Sendhi, of 87 (out of 94) families engaged in farm-labour, 34 families secure work for days ranging from 51-100 and another, 34 for 101-150 in a year. Only 16 families find labour for over 150 days and only 3 families in Valayapatti engage themselves in farm-labour for below 50 days a year. Thirty families hire themselves as farm-labourers for51-100 days in a year in Valayapatti, only 4 families come under this category in Sendhi, and on the other hand, 24 and 15 families work for days ranging from 101-150 and above 150 respectively in Sendhi. In the case of Valayatti it is only ten and one in these two categories. In terms of population and number of days in a year, it is Valayar of Sendhi who are larger in the size of the population and number of days engaged in farm labour in a year. One main reason for this greater absorption of the labour force for a longer period is paddy and garden cultivation in Sendhi.

Nature of Farm-Labour

The Valayar in general are engaged in various types of farm-labour and this is determined by the regional and local practices and the crops cultivated. In the case of Valayapatti and Sendhi, the labour force there, is engaged in reclamation of land, ploughing, bund-forming and transplanting, ridge trimming, interculture and weeding, fencing work, harvesting, digging wells, wood cutting and collection of coffee beans. Table 7 shows the distribution of the farm-labour families in the two villages activity-wise. It is seen that harvesting has a high frequency followed by ploughing and 'bund-forming' and 'ridge trimming'. Next in frequency are 'interculture and weeding' and 'transplantation' and 'reclamation of land'. But harvesting naturally has the highest frequency; one reason for this frequency seems to be the wages which usually in the case of harvesting are paid in the shape of grain that is harvested.

Employee-employer Relationship in Farm-Labour

We discern a pattern of relationship between the Valaya labour and the farmer–employers. We find that the Valaya labourers (for that matter most labour-force in the village) serve particular families belonging to their own and other castes. Usually the farmer-employer contacts the particular families and the labour families on the other hand feel obliged to answer and respond to the call of such farm-families. This relationship over a period of time in the local area, in the limited territory, gets established and results in a sort of diluted form of jajmani relationship. There develops a patron-client reciprocal relationship between the farmer and the labourer. The caste-groups the Valayar serve also indicate the inter-caste relationship, its closeness and intensity.

TABLE 7: Distribution of Farm-Labour Families in terms of Activities

Farm Activity	Number of Families engaged in it
Reclamation of land	11
Ploughing	25
Bund-forming and Ridge-trimming	24
Transplantation	12
Interculture and weeding	16
Harvesting	35
Collection of Coffee Beans	4
Digging wells	8
Wood-cutting	11
Fencing-work	1

Since Valaya labourers in generality are poor, they hire themselves as farm-labourers to caste-Hindus who mostly own land and carry on farming. The Valaya labourers work as farm-labourers for their own caste and other caste-Hindus equal to them, superior to them and seldom they serve the Scheduled Castes, since the latter themselves mostly are landless-labourers and on one hand, they may not go in for outside labour and on the other, the castes higher to them are reluctant to hire themselves as farm labourer to them. Eighty-seven out of 94 Valaya families in Valayapatti and Sendhi are engaged in farm-labour. These 87 families serve a total of 583 farm families in the respective villages and in the neighborhood. The largest number of Valayar work for the largest number of families of their own community. Seventy-six families serve 208 Valaya families in both the villages. That is, the highest Valaya labour-force in the two villages is employed internally. The period of service of Valayar to Valayar ranges from below five years to above 20 years. Some of the families out of the 76, have been serving 81 Valaya farmers for over 20 years, 69 families during the past five years, 32 and 23 for the past 6-10 and 11-15 years respectively. Next to the Valayar, it is the Kallar (at Sendhi) who are the largest in number served.

Fifty families have been serving 175 Kallar families and the largest numbers (91) of Kallar families have been receiving service from the Valayar over twenty years. It shows a long economic and social interdependency between the Valayar and the Kallar. Next in frequency in the number serving and the number of families served is the Valayar-Konar: 22 families serve 42 families of Konar caste. In Sendhi, Konar enjoy a considerable economic and social status and 22 Valaya families in Sendhi have been working for 24 Konar families over 20 years. This period may extend over decades. It is significant to note here that 20 Valaya families (at Valayapatti) have been hiring themselves as labourers to cobblers on the plantations on the Sirumalais. Normally Valayar do not work for Scheduled Castes as farm-labourers, but the case of the cobblers in Pudur and Pazhavur in the Sirumalais is different. Though they are leather-workers, they have settled on the hills, started planting banana, lemon and other fruits. Their labour and nature helped them, and a few cobbler planters have grown relatively prosperous. These planters live now in big and well furnished houses, their styles of life and levels of living have changed and consequently despite their low social status, they have become people to be reckoned with and so in view of their newly acquired status, their previous social position is ignored and the Valayar work for them on the plantations. While one cobbler planter family has been receiving Valaya farm-labour for over 20 years, the other 28 cobbler families have been employing Valaya labour during the past ten years only and 20 cobbler planters have been employing them during the past five years. In the case of Gounder farmers (at Valayapatti) though the Valaya men are rather critical of their working for the Gounder, the Valaya women go in for harvesting of sorghum and groundnut and thus we find even though it is to their distaste, fifteen Valaya families work for 28 Gounder families. Besides, the Valayar work for Muslims, Naicker, Naidu, Nadar, Vellala, Chettiar, Brahmin, Pandaram, Nair and Barber, Excluding their own caste, the Valaya labour families serve fourteen castes higher, equal and lower to them in the traditional social hierarchy.

Of 583 farm families for whom the Valayar work as labourers, 197 families (Kallar 91, Valayar 81, Konar 24 and Cobbler 1) have been using Valaya-labour for over 20 years, 187 families comprising all the fifteen castes for below five years, 113 families mostly of Kallar, Valayar, Konar castes for a period of 16-20 years, 76 families from 6-10 years and 10 families from 11-15 years.

The Valaya labour have economic and the resultant social contact with several caste groups through their labour. Besides their local labour, they migrate yearly to Tanjore district for paddy harvesting.

Migrant Labour

The question of prestige and social status matters much in a local community. Here there is face-to-face relationship and the people are sensitive and conscious of their caste-rankings. It is unusual to find a high caste man hiring him as a farm-labourer to a low caste man in a rural situation. But the services rendered and supplied in what is called the Hindu *Jajmani* system are different. Theoretically they are considered to be mutual, reciprocal and based on the principle of equality. But the service of a priest is not labour in the strict sense of the world. The priest serves his caste people and castes inferior to his. His services are such in the hierarchy of values of the group served, that they always secure him and keep him in a higher status. A carpenter in the *Jajmani* system may serve a member of a Scheduled Caste in making a plough and receive his aya (remuneration) from his Scheduled Caste ayadakula (clientele), but at the same time the carpenter may not work as a labourer on the farm of a Scheduled casteman.

The Valayar of Valayapatti refuse or resent hiring themselves as farm labourers to the Gounder of Chettiapatti (their closest village in terms of physical distance and social contact) as a matter of prestige. The Valayar assume that they are superior to the Gounder in caste rank and at the best they concede that the Gounder are their equals. This consciousness of prestige-rank operates at a high degree in the local community and tapers off considerably when the individual moves to newer areas and farther places. The Valayar of Valayapatti besides their reluctance to hire themselves as farm labourers to the Gounder though the Valaya women work as harvesters to the Gounder, do not like to work also in the company of or along with the Gounder. According to the Valayar, the Gounder are not efficient and skilled in ploughing and the Valayar avoid hiring themselves as ploughmen on the farms of Chinnalapatti (the nearby town) people, when they learn that the Gounder too will work on the same farm. The Valayar are afraid that the inefficiency of the Gounder will reflect upon them (Valayar) and the reputation they have earned as hard and sincere workers would be tarnished. But the same people behave in a different way in a new setting. This is finely illustrated by the Valayar. Some menfolk (sometimes women too) migrate to Tanjore district as paddy harvesters. They take refuge in their anonymity and hire themselves as labourers to whatever caste that offers them the job. In one case, a group of Valayar and Kallar (a denotified tribe), 16 in all, worked for about 20 days at Ammapatti in Tanjore district. During this period, they worked for a Pariah (Scheduled caste man) for ten days and all of them stayed there at the employer's house. Five days later they discovered (as they put it) to their discomfiture that their employer-host was a Pariah-Christian. Immediately they started cooking their food separately (they should have excused themselves for this change on some gounds or on some pretext). Though they made their own arrangement for food, they did not leave their employer and the harvesting job continued for another five days. There at a distant place, there was no question of any hesitation and reluctance on the part of the Valayar to engage themselves as farmhands to castes inferior to them. They take refuge in their anonymity.

There are situations in life, in the context of social stratification in India, wherein one feels free and proud of disclosing one's caste and ashamed of making a mention of it. This behaviour is patterned after the rewards, recognition, privileges, status, and treatment traditionally accorded to that particular caste. On the other hand (where it cannot be known apparently) when the social identity or disclosure meant suffering from some disadvantages, disabilities and lower estimation in the eyes of the people, the individual tries to conceal the caste or tries to evade the question or simply lies; mentions a high caste as his.

There was such an instance. During a recent paddy harvest season, a group of Valayar from Valayapatti and their kinsfolk from other villages went to Tanjore district as paddy harvesters; introduced themselves as Kallar. The reason was (as explained by the group) that Kallar enjoy a respectable status in Tanjore district and other caste groups (in certain parts of the district) are a little afraid of and apprehensive of the Kallar community. The Kallar in the district are a dominant group and enjoy comparatively a higher social position. At the sane time, the Valayar in Tanjore district because of their economic and educational backwardness enjoy a low status. The Valayar at home, assign to themselves a rank higher to Kallar, but once in Tanjore they could not reveal their social identity for fear of suffering a low social estimation at the hands of the farmer-employers there. Another aspect of the question is observance or adherence to rules governing commensal relations. The concept of pollution loses its effectiveness and seriousness when a person leaves his local area and comes in contact with members of other castes elsewhere. There he conveniently takes shelter (there is no generalization here) in his anonymity; there is no botheration about commensal rules and his getting polluted.

To digress a little here, it is not always that a low caste in the old order of Hindu society suffers from all the disabilities and disadvantages. The system secures and sanctions the members certain freedom of action, economic or otherwise. He can eat such and such food, dress in a particular way, may appear in dirty clothes, could approach you for alms, for food, for patronage, can marry and divorce with all ease, can live in a hut, could go abegging, can indulge in filthy language, etc., all justified and rationalized by virtue of his low status in the caste hierarchy.

One may frown upon able bodied professional beggars but they take refuge in the tradition, in the value system, in the *Kula dharma* (caste duty or function). One may say that the economic or social functions of his caste are to be perpetuated. Begging has been one such profession. Their fathers, forefathers did it and so they are bound to carry on the tradition of caste and so live on mendicancy.[7]

Groups of Valayar from Madurai district migrate to villages in Tanjore district in the months of January-February. They stay there for three to four weeks. They bring back their wages in the shape of rice, since they are paid in grain. They par-boil the paddy, dry it, mill it in the villages where they work, and bring back the rice to their houses in small gunny bags. They work and are paid on contract basis— a fixed quantity of grain for harvesting an acre of paddy field. The work comprises harvesting, bundling, carrying and stalk bundles to the threshing floor, threshing, winnowing and reaching the grain to the residence of the farmer. Normally for a man-day it works out upproximately to 7-1/2 kg. of paddy. When the Valayar take women with them to Tanjore district for paddy harvest, the women attend to cooking and they too get an equal share in the wages. Wages for various kinds of farm operations are paid both in kind and cash. Usually grain is paid as wage in the case of harvests and in respect to sowing, transplanting, hoeing which take place when an ordinary farmer is at a low ebb in regard to his grain stock and so usually money is paid for on the extent covered. The unit of field is *panam.* A *panam* is equal to ten cents (one-tenth of an acre). The wages for transplanting a panam of field is 4 kg. Harvesting also is done on unit basis and so is contractual. For harvesting one acre of paddy 12 to 14 marakkas (I marakka is equal to 7 kg) are paid. The labourers organize themselves into groups and work on contractual basis. The groups may be small or big. Usually it is close kin and in-laws that work in groups.

In the case of Valayar of Valayapatti, thirty to forty years ago, most men from the village used to work on the plantations on the Sirumalais. They were chiefly hired by other planters on the hills. The work was both on contract and daily wages. The daily wages for a man was twelve annas (75 paise). They used to stay on the hills for a fortnight to a month at a stretch. During those days, when there was no good market for oranges and jack fruit, the Valayar used to live on these fruits and drink the spring water there. Some two decades ago, some men on their return to the village from the hills, fell ill with swollen stomachs and high temperature. This peculiar disease took away a few lives of men. This has discouraged them to hire themselves as plantation workers on the hills.

The planters on the Sirumalais are Cobblers, Muslims, Naicker, Servai, Nadar and Valayar. The planters used to advance money to the Valaya labourers. Now the number of Valayar working on the plantations on the Sirumalais is reduced.[8] But the families (6) who have plantations on the hills work on their own plantations.

Fishing

The Valayar are known through two distinct occupations — fishing and collection and selling of firewood besides other economic pursuits. One of the stories explaining the birth or the origin of the Valayar runs that once Lord Siva during a traverse on the earth lost his ring in the ocean. In order to retrieve it he created this group and they were provided with a fishing net and with the help of it they restored the ring to Lord Siva. Since then they have taken to fishing and since they use 'Valai' (net) for fishing and netting game they are called Valayar. Though one of the chief occupational attributes to the Valayar is fishermen, only 12.14% (11,924 families) of the total Valaya population in Tamil Nadu is engaged in fishing.

The sources of fishing are inland, tanks, rivers, ponds, wells and sea. Of the 11.924 Valaya fishermen families in the State, 67.18% are in Tanjore district. It is here we find the heaviest concentration of Valayar engaged in fishing. They are mostly fresh water fishermen. The Valayar in the district known as Muthuraja, Servai, Pillai, Ambalakaran and Pujari are mostly inland fresh water fishermen and they claim that they are different from the off-shore fishermen. Next to Tanjore it is in Tirunelveli district with, 22.87 percent of Valayar are engaged in fishing followed by 21, 64 percent in Tiruchirapalle district, 6.78% in Ramnad district and 0.81 percent in North Arcot district.

In the district of Tanjore, of the 28, 176 Valaya families, 28.43 percent (8,010) families carry on fishing as their only occupation and only source of livelihood. Within the district the Community Development block of Sambanarkoil with a total of 6,700 households, is returned as entirely engaged in fishing and the next largest concentration of valaya fishermen in the district is in the Community Development block of Sethubavasamudrum (1,0200) and one hundred families in Vedaranyam block and the remaining scattered over the district. It does not mean that other Valaya families do not go a-fishing. They do, but in their case, fishing is not their main stay and source of livelihood.

It is interesting to note that of the 3,078 Valaya families in the district of Tirunelveli; all the 2,703 families in the Sri Vaikuntam block are engaged in fishing as their chief livelihood. The total number of families engaged in fishing in the district is 2,727. Of the remaining fishermen families, 16 are distributed in the Manu block and 8 in Kallavodu block. Though Tiruchirapalle district stands third in the total Valaya fishermen population, fishermen (fulltime occupation) constitute only 1.65 percent of the total valaya population in the district. The total fishermen population of 258 families in the district is spread in four C.D. blocks - Vembur 129, Karum 65, Aravakuruchi 34 and Thirumanur 30.

In the case of Ramnad district where the Valaya fishermen carry on their fishing operations off-shore, they constitute only 2.99 percent (808) of the total district Valaya population. The largest concentration (542 families) is in the Mandapam block which includes

Rameswaram Island and 180 families are spread in Sakkotai block followed by 66 in Kalayarkuruchi and 20 in Tiruppulani.

As pointed out earlier, the preceding figures of Valaya fishermen population relate to those Valaya families whose only economic activity is fishing.

But there are other Valaya families in the State who pursue fishing as an occupation along with farming, farm-labour, and collection of firewood as a secondary or subsidiary occupation. This is discussed under the respective sub-headings.

In the district of Coimbatore where farm-labcur is the predominant occupation for the group, only 25 families (0.59%) of the total district population in the Kodumudi block carry on inland-fishing as a full time job. In the North Arcot district, out of 111 Valaya families, 86.49 percent (96) are engaged in fishing. Of the 96 families, 75 are distributed in Vandavasi block and another 21 families in the Annakavoor block.

We may briefly describe some aspects of off-shore fishing especially among the Valayar of Rameswaram Island and inland-fishing among some groups in Madurai and Ramnad districts.

Fishing among Rameswaram Islanders

Fishing is the only occupation for the majority and a secondary occupation for about 800 Valayar on the Rameswaram Island. It is offshore fishing along the coastline. The fishing equipment and the appliances are made by themselves. They continue to carry on their fishing with their traditional craft and techniques, though mechanized boats are in use on the island by other fishing communities.

Fishing equipment consists of country craft (boats) *Karivelam* (net used in off-shore fishing with closely knit cotton net at the tail end) and nylon nets. They use fishing lines and hooks. Fishing is done in groups. It is collective work. The fishing groups are viable and consist mostly of kin-groups. Each group is headed by a leader who directs and guides the operation while in the sea. He is called *semmati* or *mandadi*.

There are families who own boats and fishing nets of their own. They hire the equipment sometimes. In case of lending the equipment, the owner (who does not join the group in fishing) gets 30 percent of the sale proceeds of the catch on the day. The balance of amount will be shared by the group engaged in that boat and the *semmati* will have an extra share. Irrespective of number of men engaged in a group, the semmati will have two shares. Sometimes, there will be two *semmatis* for a boat, and each of them will have two shares in the catch and occasionally the *semmatis* will be the owners of the fishing craft. It is the owner-lender of the boat, which bears any damage to the craft and fishing nets.

In case of fishing, employing country craft and cotton nets, by the Valayar, the value of an average catch is about Rs. 100.00. If luck favors, they will be rewarded with a catch worth Rs.4000.00 to Rs. 5000.00. There are days when they return home almost empty and with a catch hardly enough for them for the curry for the day[9]

This sort of fluctuation in their catch forces them to borrow money for their food from the master-fishermen (those who own and rent craft). The Valaya fishermen once they get indebted to a master-fisherman, they are obliged to sell their subsequent catches too him until they repay the loan. This selling is always at lower rate and fishermen of this dependent category find themselves in the vicious circle incapable of extricating themselves from such fishermen money-lenders. Their economic dependency deprives them of good prices for their catch of fish. Their buyer is fixed and so they are placed in a disadvantageous position. These Valaya fishermen the poorer sections (among other fishing groups too) centre around an owner – rentier of fishing craft and trader in fish.

Fishing Zone

TheValayar fish off-shore in shallow waters, going upto 4 to 6 km. The Paravar (a fishing community) do deep-sea fishing. They use power craft and go upto 15· to 25 km. deep in the sea. The Valayar limit themselves to off-shore fishing. Normally, there are no clashes between off-shore and deep-sea fishing groups, but sometimes, the mechanized craft cut across the lines laid by the Valayar (karivelam) causing damages to the nets and the pulling-ropes.

The number of men engaged in each *Karaivalai* fishing group ranges from 15 to 100. This group comprises young and old. Strength is required in pulling the lines. When they fail to get any catch on a day, some of them have to starve. Their economy in a way is based on chance factor. They do sòme piloting and reconnaissance work; go about the coast and watch for the fish. The moment they sight a school of fish near the shore, they rush to their houses, fetch the nets and launch their boats into the sea and drop the lines. The reward for each group may range from Rs. 300 to 1000.00 on such occasions.

Six kilometers to the south of Rameswaram town there is a shallow coast, free of rock and rocky reefs. At a time, ten to twelve karaivalais could be set along the length of the coast (at that particular part). There is no fixed place for any fishing group to lay its lines, but whosoever that goes early to the coast, will have the first place (from a point along the coast), the second place for the group that reached the spot second and so on.

Daily Routine

The Valaya fishermen leave their homes at four O' clock in the morning with their nets (the boats lie on the coast) and launch the boats into the sea. By the time they get into the sea with the craft and lines, it would be around six. One end of the line (net) remains and is held on the coast and the other end is dragged into the sea with the help of the craft rowed by the men. They go about 4 to 6 kilometers off-coast and then in an upside down 'U' shape and other end of the *Karaivalai* is laid upto the coast. It would be 7.30 or 8 in the morning when the laying of the lines is over and from then onwards pulling or dragging the lines (net) at both the ends begins. If they sense that they would secure a good catch, the lines would be dragged to coast around twelve noon. If they think that a second round is promising they launch boats into the sea again and it would be dusk when they collect their second catch.

Ten to fifteen men on either side of the Karaivalai pull the lines (a cluster of small ropes to which the net is tied). They tie ropes around their waists for hold and convenience and also hold the ropes with both hands and leaning side ways and backward, pull the ropes at a time with a chorus. When the karaivalais near the coast, small nets on either wing are pulled to close up the fish into the main net and prevent them escape side ways at the approach to the coast.

There are certain species of fish which are to be netted on sighting a school of such on its movement. Some species of fish could be netted any time without sighting it. It tells of the nature of some species of fish. The peak season for off-shore fishing is from January to June.

Marketing of Fish

Fish are sold fresh, salted and preserved in ice. Some exportable varieties and some varieties that are transported to distant points in the country are preserved in ice boxes at proximity of the coast. Some varieties are salted. The salting is done at the coast itself. The fish are cut open in the lower portion and stuffed with salt and put in the sand pit. The bottom of the sand pit is covered with palm mats (Palmyra) and after the pit is filled with salted fish, the pit is covered with palm mat with a thick layer of sand on top of it. The fish in the pit will not get spoiled even if it rains. After a couple of days, the fish are exhumed and they would be ready for market. Some varieties of small fish are sun-dried and sold.

In many cases, the individual fishermen are obliged to sell their share of catch to the master-fishermen and they in turn sell to the traders from whom they (master-fishermen) borrow money in advance. So, one is linked with the other. In a figurative sense, it is a question of a big whale swallowing a small whale and the big being swallowed by the bigger and the bigger by the biggest. It was reported by the Karaiyur Valayar on the island that if they sell 10 kg. of fish to the money lender-trader, they get Rs. 16.00 and if the same quantity is sold on the market directly it fetches them Rs. 25.00. Sometimes, the womenfolk sell the fish at the market place in Rameswaram and go about vending in the streets. This selling of fish by the fisher women is on the permission of the master-fishermen and usually the fish that are marketed in this fashion are the ones that the master-fishermen have rejected. This type of marketing of fish is mostly in the case of offshore fishing but in the case of inland and fresh water fishing by the Valayar the marketing of fish is individual and there are no intermediaries there.

The Valaya Children collect pebbles and shells of different marine species that are washed ashore on the Rameswaram Island. These pebbles and shells of varying sizes, shapes and hues are sold to the traders in the town. Necklaces and ornaments made of beautiful multi-coloured pebbles and pieces of shells and conches have a flourishing sale at Rameswaram. The pilgrims are the buyers and these shells of marine species find a market in different places.

Fishermen Cooperative Societies

There are 9 Fishermen Cooperative Societies in and around Rameswaram Island. They are the FCS of (1) Rameswaram, (2) Olaikuda, (3) Sudukattanpatti, (4) Thangachchimadam, (5) Anthonipuram, (6) Souriyamagar, (7) Soosaiyapparpatnam, (8) Pamban and (9) Dhanushkodi. The FCS of Dhanushkodi which was organized in 1950 was the first fishermen cooperative organized in the area. The total membership in these 9 cooperatives is 1837.[11]

The fishermen community in this area comprising the nine fishermen cooperatives consist of Paravar (Christians), Valayar, Karaiyalar (Hindus) and Muslims. Valayar are members in some of these cooperatives. The membership in the cooperatives ranges from 105 to 542. The highest number of members is in Rameswaram Fishermen Cooperative organized in

1952 About one-third of its members are Valayar belonging to Karaiyur, a hamlet of Rameswaram situated close to the coast, one kilometer to the south-east of Rameswaram town. In terms of caste, the Valayar constitute the majority in the cooperative on the island. The first president of the cooperative was a Valayan and now (November 1972) two of the directors of the society are the Valayar from Karaiyur.

The fishermen cooperative grants loans to the members for purchase of Karaivalai, nylon nets, boats, buoys and life jackets and loan toward working capital and construction of godowns. Subsidy is also given by the government through the cooperatives in respect of all the above items. The loans are long term and short term. The Rameswaram cooperative has one mechanized boat and it is used for fishing and the catch is disposed of locally. In the Rameswaram-Dhanushkodi area, there are approximately 200 mechanized boats and 3000country craft. The Valayar as a group have not so far taken to nylon nets. Usually, nylon nets are used by those who operate mechanized boats. After the 1964 cyclone, the master-fishermen [12] were advanced each from Rs. 4,00,000 to 5,00,000 towards country craft and nets, and in the case of ordinary members of the cooperative, without boat and nets of their own, the amount advanced was Rs. 100.00 to 500.00. The Valayar of Karaiyur are making efforts to organize themselves into an Association of Fishermen (besides the existing cooperative) in order to reduce and gradually eliminate the exploitation by the master-fishermen and traders.

Inland Fishing

Valayar as a rule go a-fishing wherever it is possible and fish are available. Only those groups who live close to hills, forests and in dry areas lack opportunities for fishing. In their case, it is hunting and netting of game. Fishing as a means of livelihood and fishing for food among the Valayar is to be distinguished. And so fishing and fish are so dear to them. [13] Fishing for food among the Valayar is universal, wherever facilities for fishing are available.

The Valayar around Madurai are engaged in inland-fishing in the irrigation tanks. The devices used (in the case of all inland-fishermen) are nets that are drawn held at either end of its mouth, thrownets (visurvalai), long nets (kandaivalai) that are dropped across stagnant waters, the upper end of it is kept afloat with the help of corks and the lower end touching the floor or distended vertically with iron or burnt clay balls, and *kuchchal, kodam, dhuri, panaichari,* etc. (all devices for catching fish in running waters along small streams, canals, supply channels). Fishing in the tanks is usually in the summer months. It depends on the depth of water in the tanks. Though, the Valayar start fishing right from January, the peak period is from March to May. Some of the Valayar are employed by contractors enjoying usufruct rights over fish in the tanks. The Valayar go about fishing in the tanks at six in the morning and stay in the tanks till 10 A.M. They are paid wages at the rate of Rs. 5.00 per day (for 4 hours work). Besides fishing on wages, they fish in the ponds and tanks which are free and open to all. Sometimes they go about fishing in the tanks during nights without the knowledge of the contractor.[14]

The Valayar in Sivaganga, Ramnad district, fish in the tanks on contractual basis and on their own. Either they purchase as a group, the usufruct rights over the fish in the tanks in the year, fish and the share the sale proceeds or if somebody is the contractor they fish for wages. They form into small groups, fish and sell the catch themselves in

Sivaganga and Madurai city. The average per capita earning per day in the case of men is Rs. 5.00. Inland fishing is seasonal. The Valayar knit and mend their own nets. In 1968, a fishermen cooperative society was organized for the Valayar at Sivaganga. Only 28 families have enrolled themselves as members in the cooperative. Each member was supplied with yarn for the nets. Sometimes they sell fishing nets. The price of a net (pulling type used in tanks) ranges from Rs. 50.00 to Rs. 80.00. When they are rewarded with a heavy catch and some quantity of raw fish is left out without selling, it is sun-dried, preserved and sold later. Besides fishing, they go about collecting frogs, snails, and turtle for food besides their catching rats for food and snakes for their skins.

In sum, fishing is a way of life for some of the Valayar and fish are a food they cherish and relish highly.[15]

Collection of Firewood

Next to fishing, it is collection and sale of firewood which is associated with the Valaya community as their traditional occupation. Again as in the case of fishing as an occupation, collection of firewood as a means of livelihood is determined by the sort of area the Valayar habitate. The Valayar living in the proximity (within range of 6 to 10 kilometers) of hills, forests, hilly-forests, places with dense vegetation, places where they could manage dry or fresh wood go about collecting and selling firewood as a full-time job and as secondary or as subsidiary occupation. The other populations though not for sale, collect firewood for their home consumption.

Though it is one of the characteristic caste occupations of the Valayar, 0.39 percent (386) of the total Valaya population only, is engaged in the collection and sale of firewood as the only means of their livelihood. Of the 386 families under this category, 87.05 percent (336) are distributed in the district of Tirunelveli, 11.66 percent (45) in Madurai and 1.30 percent (5) in Tanjore district. The Valayar who live by this occupation constitute 10.92 percent of the total valaya district population in Tirunelveli. Within the district, 251 families are distributed in the blocks of Kodiyanallur and 85 in Vasudevanllur. The 45 families in Madurai district are spread in Sanarpatti block close to the Sirumalais and the five families in Tanjore district are found in the Papanasam block.

Collection and selling of firewood is primary occupation for 34 percent (16) of families and secondary for 59.57 percent (28) families in Valayapatti. That is, 44 out of fifty families are engaged in the collection and selling of firewood as primary and secondary occupation. In the case of Valayapatti, 43 male, 38 female and 9 children belonging to the 44 families pursue collection of firewood as a means of livelihood.

Since collection and selling of firewood is self-employment and under nobody's command, authority or mercy save periodic encounters with the forest personnet (in reserve forest areas), they feel at home with this occupation. They earn through this, more than what they could earn through farm-labour. In farm-labour they contend, they are under somebody's obligation and in the firewood business, they are their own bosses. Once a while, they are caught by the forest personnel (since their cutting is illegal) and are fined. These fines are despite the forest officials being supplied with firewood by each Valaya member collecting firewood in the forest area.[16] Sometimes the Valayar make friends and satisfy the forest officials with supply of honey. It is an usual practice everywhere with all those persons or groups engaged in the collection of firewood in the reserve forest.

The Valayar collect both dry and fresh (raw) wood. The head loads of firewood they carry from the hills/forests are unbundled at the village and bigger ones are rebundled into two, so that the bundles appear larger and impress the potential buyer. Arranging the lengths of firewood and making them into a long bundle is an art by itself. They spend considerable time in arranging the pieces into bundles. They give a facelift to the bundle. Sometimes two persons attend to this arrangement of firewood into headload.

In some cases, it is the man who collects firewood on the hills and carry the bundle home, and rebundle the pieces into one or two, looking bigger and attractive to the buyer and it is the women who sell them.

During the winter season (October to January) the price of firewood goes high. A man's headload of dry wood is sold at Rs. 5.00 to Rs. 7.00 and wet wood at Rs. 4.00 to Rs. 6.00 and a woman's headload dry at Rs. 3.00 to Rs. 5.00 and wet at Rs. 2.00 to Rs. 4.00. In the other seasons too, the price of a woman's and a man's headload ranges from Rs. 3.00 to Rs. 6.00. A man is able to earn Rs. 6.00 per headload of firewood per day in winter equivalent to what he would earn in two days in summer months. The increase in the price per headload of firewood tends to make the Valayar work for a fewer days in a week. Say that an average man works for four days in a week in the rainy and winter seasons and five to six days in the summer. The frequency of the Valayar engaging themselves in the collection of firewood in summer is high due to low prices, conduciveness of the weather and more supply of the material in the market and, on the other hand, in the rainy-winter season, weather is not conducive and so the frequency of their going for firewood is less, and this results in low supply and high prices. In the winter-rainy season, the leisure in their case is forced leisure, and further the tendency is to work for fewer days in view of higher prices.

The families, who live on their day-to-day earnings, have to buy food grain after disposing of the firewood they have collected during the day. The market for the firewood is Chinnalapatti and Chettiapatti. After selling their day's collection of firewood, they buy sorghum and other condiments and back at home, the woman pounds the grain, cleanses it of the chaff and cooks it. The meal that is taken in the evening is the full meal for the day.

Sometimes, women are found busy at the mortars, which are usually stationed in front of their houses, pounding sorghum at eight and nine in the evening. This is the routine of the day around the year. In this, it is the woman who toils more. She shares the larger part of the burden and responsibility. She has either collected the firewood singly or along with her husband or children. She carries the firewood back home by the evening and at the village it may be rebundled. After a short respite, she leaves the home for selling the firewood. She carries the bundle of firewood on her head, goes about street to street until it is disposed of. After selling the product of her day's labour, she goes in for food grains, etc., and hurries back home and attends to cleansing of the grain and cooking the evening meal.[17]

Hunting, Collection of Firewood, and other Wild Products

Though hunting, snaring of game, collection of wild/forest products, besides collection of firewood, have been the basic and ancient occupations of the Valayar, today only 0.63 percent (616) of the total Valaya population is engaged in the above as a full time occupation.

The population with hunting, collection of wild products and firewood as a combination of occupations is spread in the districts of Ramnad, Madurai, Coimbatore and The Nilgiris. The highest number of this occupational category (54.87%) is found in Coimbatore district followed by The Nilgiris with 2.11%. Thirteen out of thirty –seven families in the Kotagiri block in the district of Nilgiris are engaged in hunting and collection of forest products as their chief source of life. Here it is the terrain and the tradition that determine the occupation of the group.

The hunting or snaring of game varies in frequency and intensity from group to group and it is mostly seasonal. It depends on the environment they live in. The Valayar use different types of nets, snares, devices, contrivances for catching wild game and birds. Animals such as wild pigs, porcupine, rabbit, wild sheep, monitor, spotted deer, turtles, mountain squirrels, rats, armadillo (ant eater), langur, tree dog, and birds of different species which are edible are hunted or snared.

Hunting in the case of Valayar is both an individual and a group activity. It depends upon the game hunted and the device used. Besides snares, nets, baits, (poisoned), of late some of the Valayar have started using rifles and muzzle loading guns. Sometimes, when the cartridges are expensive and not easily procurable, the hunters improvise cartridges using the cases of fired cartridges. But the use of firearms for hunting by the Valayar is very much limited. Hunting or catching game and birds is carried on employing age-old devices. Of several such devices the following two traps deserve a brief description.

Idikki

It is a device used for catching rats. It looks like a bow with a string. It is made of a stick, about a metre in length. It is bent in bow fashion and strung with string made of fibre. At the lower end of the device, a lever is attached made of a small length of string with a two inch slender stick fastened at the end. The idikki is set in the fields along the tracks the rats use, and when a rat passes through the lever end of the idikki, it automatically snaps and the victim is nailed to the device.[18]

The idikki is employed to a considerable extent as a mechanical rodent control. In some paddy rich pockets in Madurai and Ramnad districts, farmers engage the Valayar in setting the idikkis for trapping rats along rat tracks (familiar to the Valayar) before sunset and collect the victims on the following morning. For each set of 30 idikkis laid in the paddy field, the farmer pays Rs. 3.00 irrespective of the number of rats trapped. The fee varies from place to place. The rats trapped are the property of the Valayan who has set the idikkis. Either he uses them all or shares them with his kinsfolk. While speaking of catching rats, another appliance may be mentioned here. Locally it is called *silukku*. It is a wooden or bamboo stick measuring one and one-fourth metres or one and a half metres, to the lower end of which a length of iron piece forked at the end is fastened. On sighting a rat, the *silukku* is used in nabbing the rat to the ground with the forked appliance. It is used chiefly for catching rats though the same is used for catching snakes for their skins.

We may have a brief account of their practices in going about catching rats for meat and as an economic activity or as a means of livelihood.

The Valayar search rats in the dark nights and during days. Usually they begin the operation after nine in the night. They carry with them either hurricane lamps or torches and a tool called *silukku*, referred to above. The rats when they go about foraging along the ridges, fences, field-bunds and fields, are located with the aid of light. When the light is focused on the victims, they get blinded and immobilized, then is the time for the Valayar to hold them or pin them down to the ground with *silukku*. Later, the victim is picked up and pulled apart holding the head in one hand and hind limbs in the other. With this pull, the ligaments snatch and the joints sever and after some time the creature dies. This small game after it is collected is put in a bag or basket they carry about or tucked in the loin cloth around the waist. It was told that one Valayan managed to catch forty rats and tucked them all around his waist. He did not require any bag or basket to carry home his catch-his food. It serves them as meat and supplementary food.

When the Valayar are free in the months from March to October they go about catching field rats during the days succeeding rainy evenings or nights. In the newly worked out earth, the rat tracks are the tell-tale things which help the Valayar dig out for the rats.

Catching rats is a group affair and it involves some division of work. It requires atleast two persons. They go in groups. Women seldom go about catching rats. It is a man's job. The rats trapped are consumed by the trappers and also given to families in their community free or for a nominal price. When a Valayan traps a large number of rats, he takes them to his kinsfolk who live in the neighbouring villages. As destroyers of rodents which compete with human beings for food and survival, the Valayar are the friends of the farmers and they do a service to the nation. We may cite here an incident of interest.

Some fifteen years ago, a Sub-Inspector of Police of Nilakottai Police Station (Madurai district) was on a routine round near the village of chittarevu with a few constables with him. The time was between 9 to 10 P.M. They were walking across some fields. Presumably they were on a prohibition raid. At a distance in the fields, the police saw several figures moving about with hurricane lanterns and sticks in their hands. The inspector became curious about the persons and what they did at that nightly hour in the fields with lanterns and sticks. The men with him (perhaps inadvertently) told him in a slighting and a lighter tone "Sir, they are the Valaya fellows going about in search of rats". This pricked the Inspector since he was a Valayan (may be that the Police Constables did not know the caste of the Inspector or even if they had known, made the observation on the Valayar inadvertently). Further, as if to add disgrace and much to the chagrin of the Police Officer, some of the constables with him were Pariaher and Pallar (members of Scheduled Castes). The Valayar who were on a rat hunt were from Chittarevu, where there are 450 households of Chembasi and Vannia Valayar.

The Police Officer, it is reported felt that catching rats for food was shameful and degrading and it brought down their caste rank in the eyes of other caste groups.

On the following day, the story goes; the Inspector went to Chittarevu without any of his men, met some of the Valayar and warned them that they should refrain from that base avocation of catching rats, failing which they would meet with severe punishment. He collected all *idikkis* and *silukkus* and made a bonfire of them in the presence of the confused and helpless members of the Valaya community.

As a result of the warning and threat left by the Inspector, there was a lull in rat hunting for a couple of years (may be so long the Inspector was in the particular police station) at chittarevu.[19]

That custom persists and habits die hard is illustrated through another episode, wherein in a Valaya conference, moments after a strong advocacy that Valayar should refrain from the degrading habit of eating rats, a Valaya member sights a squirrel and shouts "squirrel-squirrel" and runs after it in the conference hall in order to catch it.

Yadal

It is a trap or a contrivance set on the ground along the usual tracks used by animals. It is set for trapping wild boar, wild sheep, spotted deer, langur, porcupine and other game. The trap is worked out on a small pit (dug out for the purpose) with sticks and heavy boulders (stone) with a lever which works with a slight touch or pressure by the victim. Once the Yadal is set, it could be used for a long time, with the change of broken sticks whenever needed. The setting of the trap requires great skill. A Valayan who sets this trap on the hills visits it in the morning or day time. All the families in Valayapatti have their exclusive places on the Sirumalais (hills) for setting these traps. As in the case of winged-termite hills, these Yadal spots are the property of the families concerned. Each family has the right over the spot (usual animal track) and this right is seldom impinged by others. When a Valayan finds a game trapped in the Yadal of another man, either he informs the owner of the Yadal or retrieves the animal (dead or alive) and reaches it to the owner.

Formerly the knowledge and skills of setting these traps were highly-guarded secrets and seldom shared with the members of non-Valaya communities.

Group Hunting

Hunting or snaring of game is carried on by individuals, families and groups of men belonging to several families. Before they start for hunting, they look for certain signs or omens and when they think it is favourable, they go for hunting. Sometimes, prior to proceeding for hunting, their deities are consulted for directions and blessings.

It is the belief of the Valayar that if any member of the hunting group violates any caste rule, the gods of the Valayar will not help them with any game. On their hunting expeditions, when they do find any game or miss any game in shooting or snaring, they make a fire at a spot (on the hills-forests) and say invocative prayers to their gods to help them discover the culprit in the team who has violated some community tenet as a result of which they were not successful in hunting any game.

Any one of their deities will speak to them through the medium of one of them who gets the *arul* (getting possessed of the spirit and becoming the medium of the deity) and reveals the identity of the culprit in the group.[20] Such a person is excluded from the group for the then hunting expedition. During such group hunting, on securing a game before the Valayar start for home, they flay the game or cut it open as the case may be and the lungs are removed from the animal. The lungs are cut into small pieces and these pieces are driven into five small sticks (measuring about 16 inches of one tree) and a fire is made and these sticks are held in hand and the meat ends are held in the flames and after thus roasting the meat pieces, the sticks are stuck to the ground in a slanting position. The hunters stand in front of the meat sticks and offer prayers to their gods for helping them with game.

Of the five sticks with roasted meat-pieces, one goes in full to the man who killed the game and the rest of the four are shared by the remaining men who participated in the hunting. The meat of the kill is shared equally by all. Sometimes, depending on the number of game and quantity of meat, it is given to the kindred of the same village and neighbouring villages.

In the case of the Valayar of Valayapatti when they kill any game on the hills (Sirumalais), the meat is worked on the hills or the game is brought to the village and the meat is distributed to the kinsfolk free of cost and sometimes sold to them.

In the case of four families in Valayapatti who use muskets as well as traps, baits and nets, hunting is a source of income for them. The meat of wild boar, sheep, deer, and porcupine are readily purchased by the people on the hills and on the plains. The Valayan who kills a game has some obligations towards his kinsfolk. He keeps a portion for his family's consumption and distributes some to his close kindred. Some times, this distribution of meat will show one's range of kinship relationship. Occasionally, one comes across mild complaints and discontent expressed by some individual families who have been ignored by their people in obliging them with meat.

Hunting has the commercial end also. A wild boar, ewe or ram may fetch the hunter from Rs. 30.00 to Rs. 60.00. The price of this meat is lower to that of the meat of the domesticated animals.

One such commercial and medicinal game on the Sirumalais (Valayapatti) is langur. The langurs are sensitive and cautious animals. Despite their wariness they are shot by the Valayar.[21] The animal is flayed. The head (perhaps due to its ugly, frightening appearance and at the same time resembling human face) the palms and the feet with fingers and toes (cut at the wrist and ankle point) are discarded. Every bit of the remaining meat including the skin is consumed as food or as medicine. Salt and turmeric paste are applied to the skin and meat, before they are sun-dried, in case they are to be preserved. It is believed that the meat of langur possesses high medicinal value. The dried meat or skin of langur is cooked in the medium of sesame oil and it is given to children suffering from whooping cough. A small piece of langur meat (20 grams) is sold for a rupee. People visit the Valaya village from different places traveling 20 to 30 kilometers for buying the dried meat pieces of langur for medical use.

The langur meat is preserved for a couple of years without it losing the medicinal properties. The intestines and other vitals which could not be preserved are cooked and shared by all those who helped in flaying and working the meat. This has been the practice in Valayapatti in the case of killing a langur.

Both adults and boys in Valayapatti go about trapping and snaring birds, wild fowls and migratory birds, and the latter visit the Sirumalais in large numbers in the months of July and August. The Valayar set nets and a single catch may yield about one hundred birds. Down the hills the Valayar study the course of their flight and set the nets and keep waiting. Boys and adults while tending cattle on the hills employ themselves in setting traps and snares for catching birds and also collect eggs of some birds for consumption.

It may be mentioned here that some of the hunting families train and employ dogs in hunting. When a game is shot at and when the victim escapes with lingering life, the dogs are sent to fetch them or to intercept them and immobilize them. Sometimes, when an animal on being killed falls into or gets lodged at an inaccessible point, the help of the dogs is sought to retrieve the game. The Valayar especially the regular hunters take sufficient care of the dogs and train them for hunting purposes.

Mention may be made here of the manner in which the triumph of a sizeable kill is announced by the people who went on a group hunting to their folk at the village. They blow the horn from the hill top or forest as the case may be and on their back home at the approach of the village precincts. On receiving the message, the folk at the village go forward, receive the hunters with all joy and give them a hero's welcome.

Similar is the practice when they go on ritual hunting during the celebration of their deities. This ritual hunting is part of their religious ceremonies[22]

Catching Snakes

Catching snakes for their skins, as an economic activity is associated with most of the Valayar, but this activity as means of livelihood among the Valayar is negligible. It is causal, occasional, fortuitous and seldom a distinct economic pursuit.[23] But when they meet with any chance, they catch the snakes for skins. The price of a skin depends on its length and width, ranging from Rs.10.00 to Rs. 100.00.

Catching snakes as an economic activity is naturally found among the Valayar who live close to hills, forests where economically useful snakes abound. In the case of the Valayar of Valayapatti, the Sirumalais (hill) are a source for this. Snakes of several species and sizes are found on the Sirumalais. In the course of their collection of firewood and other wild products, the Valayar of Valayapatti when they sight snakes which have a skin value, they catch them. The skin of the snake is to be peeled off when the victim is alive. No damage should be caused to the skin, for the damaged skin will fetch a very low price. The peeling of the skin requires a lot of skill, care and dexterity. It is an art and the Valayar are adept at it. A snake when caught is held tight at both ends, the skin is cut just below the head and slit open in the middle if the lower part from head to the tail end, and holding the head tight with one hand and keeping the tail under the foot, the skin is peeled off from head downward the tail. The actual skinning takes a few seconds. Immediately, after the skin is rolled to a small length of stick a little lengthier to the width of the skin.

A Few men in groups (in threes and fours) from Valayapatti and Karaikudi (Ramnad district) go to Kerala during winter and stay there for two to three months for catching snakes in the Kerala forests. Sometimes the traders (primary buyers) advance money to such Valaya groups who stay in Kerala and buy the skins from them. The Valayar return home after earning some money. On their return home the men share their adventures, their catches and their experiences in another part of the country with their fellowmen. People enjoy listening to such accounts.

Collection of Wild Products

The Valayar, depending upon their habitat (nearness to hills, and forests) engage themselves in the collecting or gathering economy. They collect mangoes, edible, commercial wild fruits, roots, tubers, honey, medicinal herbs, date leaves, etc.

The Mangoes

In the case of Valayar of Valayapatti the month of April is the season for collecting tender and unriped mangoes from giant trees on the Sirumalais. Some of these mango trees are in the reserve forest on the hills and some in privately owned plantations. There is a large number of mango trees on the hills. The mango crop is both leased out to private traders and collected by individual owners.

The Valayar go about in groups for collecting mangoes, climb the towering trees, pluck the tender mangoes and stuff the sacks they carry about them. The collection is transported to Madurai and sold there, in the market in measures (not by weight or number). The mangoes are sold locally also. The sale proceeds are shared by the members in the group. These mangoes are used for making pickles and sundried chips. The Valayar of Valayapatti sometimes collect mangoes in private plantations amounting to stealing.[24]

Date Leaves

A species of date grows abundantly on the Sirumalais. The leaves are long, soft and the tips of the leaves are not thorny. The leaves are used for weaving mats, and the leaves with stems are used for making brooms for domestic use. The leaves with stem (the end part) could be collected for about six months in a year (June to September and January to March). A day's collection of these leaves fetches an individual Rs. 4.00 to 5.00. About twenty families in Valayapatti and 32 families in Erasakkanaickanur, chinnamanur block, Madurai district (men, women and children) engage themselves in collecting the date leaves. The traders in the date leaves collect bundles of leaves in Lorries once a week or ten days. The traders sometimes advance money to the Valayar.

During this season, there is considerable shift from collection of firewood to the collection of date leaves. Comparatively, it is easier in collection and it is remunerative in terms of time spent over it. In the case of Valayapatti, the Sirumalais regulate the economic life of the Valayar considerably.

Honey

Collection of honey though not economically an important activity among the Valayar, it is a traditional occupation associated with the Valaya community. The Valayar who live in the proximity of hills and forests in the course of their collecting firewood, wild products and grazing cattle, collect honey. Either they sell the honey in the neighbouring villages and towns, or to the traders. Most of their collection is sold.

About ten families in Valayapatti go about collecting honey for commercial purposes though on a small scale. In the case of Valayar of Valayapatti, the peak period for collection of honey is June, July and August. They are experts in collecting honey (in scaling peaks, precipices, climbing down peaks with help of ropes made of wild creepers) though not as skilled and dexterous as the Paliar of Sirumalais.

Herbs

The Valayar who practice herbal medicine for human and animal ailments and diseases collect herbs. Sometimes on requests from others they collect the requisite herb or root and receive payments from such employers. The Valayar believe that the herbs and roots for medicinal use are to be collected during auspicious moments otherwise they will be ineffective.

The Valayar whose economic activities are associated with hills and forests, collect several wild products such as edible fruits, barks, timber for making agricultural implements and furniture, leaves of some plants for domestic and commercial uses and lemon grass used as thatch for houses. A variety of wild products are collected by the Valayar for their own consumption and for commercial purposes.

Farming and Farm-labour

It may be recalled that of the total Valaya population, 33.58 percent and 26.72 percent are engaged in exclusive farming and farm-labour respectively. But in the case of marginal and small farmers, they supplement their farm income by engaging themselves in farm-labour. And so, in the case of 20.44 percent of Valaya population, farming and farm-labour as twin occupations go together. A little over one-fifth of the population is engaged in farming and farm-labour, that is, 20,092. Valaya families depend on these twin occupations. Of this population, the distribution is in the following descending order: Tanjore 35.34% (7100), Ramnad 31.38% (63,04), Tiruchirapalle 19.23% (3864), Madurai 10.72% (2154) and Coimbatore 3.83% (670). This combination of farming and farm-labour obtains only in the districts (the above-mentioned) where farming is practiced by the Valayar.

We may briefly look into the nature of distribution of this population in the districts. In Tanjore district, 25.20 percent of the population is engaged in farming and farm-labour. The highest concentration is in Orathanadu block (3,634) followed by Thirumarukal block (1,021), Tanjore (847) and in six other blocks ranging from 42 to 677 families. In the case of Ramnad district, the distribution of this occupational group is similar as that of Tanjore district. Of the total Valaya families in the district (27,055), 23.30 percent (6.304) carry on farming and farm-labour as their chief occupations. The highest concentration of this population in the district is in Aruppukottai (2,655), Karayapatti (1,513), Tiruchuli (1,057), and Sivaganga (585) blocks and in the case of four other blocks; it ranges from 10% to 20%. This category of occupational group is distributed in eight blocks in Ramnad district out of twenty-three for which data are available.

Tiruchirapalle, a rice-rich area, has a little less than one-third of the total farming population. While 64.01 percent of the district Valaya population is engaged in farming, 24.65 percent of the population is engaged in farming and farm-labour. Interestingly, this category is distributed in two blocks only: Amaravathi — 2,491 families, Thiruvaramgudam — 1,373.

Madurai district presents a slightly different picture. Only a little over ten percent of the district Valaya population depend on farming and farm-labour. As in the case of Tanjore and Ramnad, this category of population is distributed in eight C.D. blocks.[25]

In Coimbatore district nearly sixty percent of the Valaya population is engaged in farm-labour and in the case of farming and farm-labour, the percentage is 15.21. Farming-cum-farm-labour population (670 families) is distributed in seven blocks in the district, the number of families ranging from 50 to 310. It may be mentioned here that about one-tenth of the Valaya population in the district is chiefly engaged in farming while one and a half of that population carries on farming and farm-labour.

Farming, Farm-labour and collection of Fire-wood

The above three occupations as a combination is carried on by 1.19 percent (1166) of the total Valaya population in Tamil Nadu. This category of population is distributed in three districts: Tiruchirapalle 1066 (91.42%), Coimbatore and Madurai with 50 families each

(4.29%). It is interesting to note that this occupational group in Tiruchirapalle district is found in Annavasal block only. Similar is the case in respect to Coimbatore and Madurai districts.

Farming and Fishing

Fishing among the Valayar is carried on both for their own consumption and on commercial lines. Fishing here as a combination with farming is taken as a means of livelihood for the Valayar. Of the total Valaya population, 1.79 percent depends on farming and fishing. In terms of distribution of this occupational group, Madurai district tops the list with 63.11 percent (1107) followed by Tanjore 17.05 percent; Ramnad 11.40 percent, Tiruchirapalle 7.58 percent and Tirunelveli with 0.86 percent (15).

Farming and fishing are seasonal and the Valayar who fall under this combination of occupations spend most of the summer months in fishing. It is off-season for farming and it is season for inland fishing (tanks, pools, etc.) in the interior as well as coastal districts in Tamil Nadu. The entire farming-cum-fishing Valaya population in the Madurai district is concentrated in the Madurai west block. In the case of Tiruchirapalle the one hundred and thirty-three families are located in Lalgudi block, but this category of population in Tanjore district is distributed in six blocks with the majority located in Seerkali and Ammapet blocks and a small number (34) in Papanasam, and ten and below ten families in the other three remaining blocks.

Farm-labour and Fishing

The landless labour among the Valayar either go in for collection of firewood, other forest products or supplement their income through fishing. Same is the case of the Valayar who chiefly live on fishing. While the men are engaged in fishing, the womenfolk hire themselves as farm-labourers. Men also hire themselves as farm-labourers during farm season when it is slack period for fishing. But the percentage of population with farm labour and fishing is very small (0.21%), 210 families: 100 in Tanjore, 25 in Tiruchirapalle and five families in Coimbatore districts.

It may be pointed out here that no Valaya family combines fishing and collection of firewood as sources of its living. Naturally, in dry-hilly and forest areas, there is more of collection of firewood and in such areas fishing is negligible and in view of the terrain differences, fishing and collection of firewood do not go together.

Farming, Farm-labour and Fishing

We find 0.37 percent (359) of the total population engaged in three occupations — farming, farm-labour and fishing. Of the 359 families under this category, 91.64 percent (329) are from Ramnad district and the remaining percentage of 8.36 (36) is in the district of Tanjore.

There are a few occupations and professions which are not traditional in the case of Valayar but pursued by small number here and there and such economic pursuits of life which have in some cases a mingling of religious and social background are briefly discussed in the following pages.

Services Associated with Shrines and Palaces

The Valayar of Algarkoil Valayapatti are the bearers of the ornament-boxes of the deity, carried along with the Alagar deity, that is taken in a procession-fashion to Madurai from Alagar temple during the festival of Chithirai (April-May). They carry the boxes containing costly gold ornaments used in decorating the deity to and fro Madurai. The Valayar feel proud of this service, for, they are entrusted with Valuable ornaments.[26] It takes six days for to and fro journey. For this particular service they are remunerated as follows:

1. Rs. 12.50 in cash
2. Ten sadams, - each sadam rice-broth may be sufficient for an adult.
3. Ten measures (15 kg.) of raw rice.
4. One temple dosai (pancake)

The money that is paid them by the temple authorities is so inadequate in terms of the expenses they incur during the six-day journey and so they raise among themselves about Rs.300.00 for augmenting their expenses.

As a preliminary to their attending to the sacred duty of carrying the ornaments of the deity, the local Valaya community council is convened, and it settles all outstanding issues and disputes. The whole community is involved in this. This community picks out men from such households in which the women in the six days of the celebration are free from menstruation. During the six days of to and fro journey carrying the ornament boxes, the men do not eat anything outside. They prepare their food on their way at places where the deity and the entire procession stop for brief periods for rest and food.

The entire Valaya community of A. Valayapatti is associated with this service of Alagar temple.[27]

The Saragu Valayar at Piranmalai serve the Siva temple there as watch and ward. During the annual festival, the Valayar carry the vahanas (wooden platforms over which an animal or bird figure is fixed over which the idol representing the deity is seated and taken in procession along the streets) and drag the chariots (theru) along the streets. For the service they render as watch and ward, they are paid a nominal monthly salary. On festive occasions they are paid 30 measures (45 kg.) of rice and Rs. 6.00 for their exclusive service as the bearers of the vahanas and the draggers of the chariots. The grain and the money are shared by all the two hundred Valaya families at Piranmalai. The temple has leased to 85 families, each forty cents of temple land. Valaya families are leased out forty cents of the temple land each. They cultivate the land and share the produce (fifty-fifty) with the temple.

Some twenty young Valaya men on the Rameswaram Island have been for some years now engaged in transporting giant granite blocks to the precincts of the Ranganatha temple from the Rameswaram railway station. At the temple site, the stone is sculptured into idols, columns, and used for various items for the new building and renovation of the temple. These giant blocks of stone weighing several metric tones are transported from a quarry in Ambasamudram in Tirunelveli district by railway to Rameswaram station. The distance between the temple and the station is about one and a half kilometers. No Lorries are used on the island. The blocks of stone are to be transported from the station by manpower. The blocks, one at a time, are lifted over a long-sized rectangular four-wheeled cart to which ropes are tied in the front side. Some men drag their cart in the front and some push the cart from behind. The men engaged in this job are in the age group of twenty and thirty years. The wage is based on the volume of the block. It is calculated at the rate of Rs. 1.25 per cubic foot. The wages are divided equally among the workers.

In order to ease the strain while the cart is being dragged, one leads in the rhythmic song followed by others in a chorus. The pulling and pushing of the loaded cart (the movements) are in tune with the song. In a day, they transport four to five blocks.[28]

There is another association of the Valayar with the temple. Cooked rice is used as offering to the deity. Hand-pounded rice is used for such offerings. It is the Valaya women who pound the paddy in the corridors of the temple. The wages are paid in kind. This hand-pounding of paddy goes on all round the year. This jajmani type of relationship between the Valayar and the Ranganatha temple has been in vogue for a number of decades.

A few Valaya families in Sivaganga (Ramnad district) have been in the employ of the Raja of Sivaganga since the princely state had come into being. They were employed as the bearers of the palanquin used by the royal household. Even though the princely states have lost their entities as independent administrative units, the former rulers of Sivaganga state, still continue some of their old practices. In the place of palanquins they use automobiles now. And so, the Valayar who have been in the service of the former Rajas, still carry on another job for them. They have been and are the pall-bearers in the case of members of the Raja family. It is the Valayar who attend to the washing, dressing of the dead, and building the bier and carrying the dead to the cremation ground. This service has been hereditary. Besides being fed on that day, the Valaya men who carry the bier are paid Rs. 60.00 to Rs. 100.00 (no fixed amount). This amount is shared equally by the members of the group. The Valaya families who are in the Raja's service are provided with a length of silk cloth which the men don on their heads or wrap around their waists when they carry the dead of the Raja family. They used to don the silk cloth to their head, etc., when they worked as palanquin-bearers and on important occasions. This silk scarf on the person of the Valayar was a symbol of the Raja's patronage and a status symbol irrespective of their job in the Raja's family.

Quarry and Masonry Work

As pointed out earlier, some of the Valayar as groups and village communities are engaged in professions and jobs traditionally not associated with Valaya community. May be the local conditions and the skills developed by the Valayar made them to take to such avocations. One such profession is quarry and masonry work. One hundred and eighty-four families are engaged in this work. In Thiruparamkundrum a suburb of Madurai city, 162 families are engaged in quarry work, blasting and stone cutting, and twenty households in quarry work in the Manickyapuram village in Palladam block, Coimbatore district and two families in Virudhunagar, Ramnad district are stone masons by profession.

Well Digging

A total of 189 households are engaged in digging irrigation wells. Of these, 118 families are distributed in P. Naickenpalayam block and the remaining 71 in a cluster of six Valaya communities in Sulur block, both in Coimbatore district. The digging of new wells and deepening and silting of old wells are done mostly during the summer seasons. Lift-irrigation through wells is the chief irrigation in Coimbatore. Traditionally, it is the Vodda caste that engages itself in this profession. Perhaps owing to the local demand and a regular supply of such a job some of the Valayar have taken to the profession of sinking and deepening of wells. They do the work on unit basis. Both men and women engage themselves in this work. Men dig and blast stone in the well and the women attend to the lifting of the excavated earth, kankar and stones as the case may be. These Valayar attend to the masonry part of the work also.

Brick Making

Brick-making is another rural industry some of the Valayar are engaged in. A total of 473 Valaya families in the villages of Thirunagari, Neppathur, Managaimadam, Vanagiri in Sirkali block, Tanjore district carry on the profession of brick-making. As in the case of digging and silting of irrigation wells, brick-making is seasonal and carried on all through the year except during the rainy season. It is also unit work and contractual, wages paid per thousand pieces. Both men and women are engaged in this work. They dig the earth, lift it, heap it, prepare the clay and cut or mould the bricks. In some cases, they help the employer or the contractor as the case may be, in firing the bricks for which they receive extra wages. Brick cutting is the chief occupation for 473 families; some of them carry on with a little farming and go about fishing on commercial lines.

Match and Fire Works

Sometimes it is the location of an industry in a particular locality that attracts labour from non-traditional sectors. Sivakasi in Ramnad district is an example in this case. It is the main centre in South India for match and fire works industries. A total of 382 Valaya families, 150 in Sivakasi, 230 in Venpanatham block, Tiruchirapalle district and two families in the Udumalpet block, Coimbatore district, work in these fields. The 150 families in Sivakasi work both in match and fire works industries, but the families in Tiruchirapalle and Coimbatore districts are engaged in match works only.

Mat Weaving

Mats are woven from a type of reed grown in marshy places, in some pools, stagnant, waters, along canals and river beds. The reed is cut; each reed is sliced into two, vertically, and sun-dried. The fibre used as twisted yarn in weaving is collected locally. The Valayar themselves set the looms. A total of 496 Valaya families, 462 in Thirupulani, Ramnad district, 31 in Moppiripalam and 3 in Padvarampalle in Sulur block, Coimbatore district are engaged in mat-weaving. The mats woven are of different sizes and vary in fabric and quality. In the case of these families, mat-weaving is the chief occupation and farm-labour is reported as a subsidiary one. The thirty-four families of Coimbatore district engaged in mat-weaving also manufacture ropes from palm fibre.

Another specialization of one hundred Valaya families in Thillayyambore in Kumbakonam block, Tanjore district is making of 'keethu' (coconut palm leaf thattis) from coconut palm leaf. These keethu are used for roofing the houses, pandals and also used as mattress during summer.

Weaving and Bangle-selling

Seventy-five families in Sedarpalayam in Uthukuli block, Coimbatore district are weavers by profession. These Valayar go about hunting too during leisure time.

Some fifteen Valaya families in the North Arcot district have taken to and carry on bangle selling, a profession no way related to the Valaya caste by tradition. These fifteen families are from four villages of Pernamallur block in North Arcot district.

In the Podakkudi group of villages in the Mayuram block of Tanjore district, 36 households are engaged in house building especially in thatching work (roofing). One or two members in each family carry on this profession.

Seventy-five families in the Uthukuli block, Coimbatore district are full time handloom weavers. We find that fifty Valaya families in the Dindigul town who have settled there from the Tiruchirapalle district and 378 families in Tanjore district are petty shop-keepers and small enterprises. In the case of Dindigul town, the Valaya families mostly deal in vegetables and fruits at the market place. Another one hundred families in Tanjore district chiefly live on coconut trade.

In respect to professions based on educational qualifications, three of the Valaya[29] are lawyers; four are graduate civil engineers; one an M.B.B.S. medical practitioner; one; a Circle Inspector and a few Police Constables; One, a Sub-Inspector; one District Survey Officer and here and there especially in Madurai, Ramnad and Tiruchirapalle district, one could meet matriculate and graduate Valayar working in white collar jobs. It may be pointed out here that the number of educated employed is insignificant in terms of Valaya population. In some villages in Coimbatore district, the Valayar are the hereditary talayaris (village menial servants).

The Criminal Habits of Valayar

Indulgence in criminal offences may be termed as a social malady in respect to the offenders and a social problem in the case of the affected. Criminal behaviour cannot be attributed to economic factors alone. The Valayar in a relative sense are poor and backward, but poverty alone does not contribute to criminal behaviour. The Valayar in the Coimbatore, Tiruchirapalle and Madurai districts were listed as 'notified tribe' during pre-independence India. The Chettinad Valayar of the Ramnad district were also notified tribe. Besides Valayar, Ambalakaran in Tanjore and Tiruchirapalle, Servai in Tiruchirapalle and Padayachi in the district were included in the list of notified tribes.[30]

A large section of the Valaya community of Coimbatore district possesses criminal propensities. They commit crimes such as dacoity, robbery, burglaries and thefts and a good bulk of organized crime is traced to the Valayar.[31] This phenomenon may be attributed to a combination of factors, viz. (1) physical and mental characteristics of the group; (2) hereditary characteristics; (3) economic factors; and (4) social factors. It appears to be more a regional phenomenon in Coimbatore district. It is dry district. Of the total Valaya population in the State, 1.19 percent only is engaged in farming in Coimbatore district. It may be said that non-economic factors with the nucleus of economic conditions of the Valayar in the district of Coimbatore account for the high incidence of crime among them. In the districts of Madurai, Ramnad, Tiruchirapalle, Tanjore, Tirunelveli, North Arcot and the Nilgiris districts the percentage of Valaya crime is infinitesimally small. Since there is, relatively speaking, high incidence of crime among the Valayar of Coimbatore and comprehensive data are available on Coimbatore Valayar only, the discussion on Valaya criminal habits begins with Coimbatore district and at the end, a brief account is given of Madurai Valayar.

Crime is not a socially sanctioned means of livelihood, but some of the Valayar in Coimbatore district have taken to crime as a profession and as a way of life and hence its relevance and inclusion in the economic organization of the Valayar.

The following account of the criminological survey of Valaya crimes is confined to the period 1959 to 1963 in Coimbatore district. Though up-to-date figures are not included here, the details are illustrative of the criminal behaviour of the Valayar community in Coimbatore district and Palani Taluk, Keeranur and Chatrapatti areas in Madurai district.

The total Valayar population in Coimbatore district as per 1921 census is 13,975 constituting about 0.38 percent of the total population of the district. Valayar live in 329 different centers in the district as against a total of 34 towns and 897 villages.[32] Valayar reside in large number in Karamadai, Cheyyur, Karumathampatti, Annur, Nambiyur, Mettupalayam, Tiruppur, Avanashi, Sulur and Pullyampatti Police Station limits than in other areas. Out of a total population of 13,975 as many as 1,804 Valayar were convicted under prohibition offences and 669 for property offences during the years 1958-63, that is nearly five percent and 13 percent of the total Valayar were involved in property and prohibition offences respectively.[33]

It is seen that the Valayar in the district commit crimes coming under all heads of classification and that they have been operating fairly uniformly during the years 1959-63. Although there have been no offences of murder for gain committed by the Valayar during the years 1959-63, they were responsible for cases under this head also during 1954 and certain other years. The incidence of Valaya crime shows an upward trend during 1962 and 1963.

The Valayar indulge in dacoity, robbery, house-breakings, major and minor thefts and cattle thefts. They contribute heavily to grave crimes especially dacoity and robbery and have a fair share in cattle theft also. House-breakings and thefts come next in the order of percentage.

In respect to dacoity cases convicted in the year 1962, the Valayar of the district constitute 74 percent and 71.4 percent in 1960. Similarly in respect to robbery cases, the Valayar account for 60 percent in 1963, 45 percent in 1962, 40 percent in 1961, 33.3 percent in 1959 and 28.6 percent in 1960. Their share in house-breaking for the period (1959-63) ranges from seven to about seventeen percent and the range and percentage are more or less similar in regard to thefts.[34]

There were 384 property offences during the years 1959-63 in Coimbatore district specifically known to have been committed by the members of the local Valaya community. In a few cases, the Valayar of Palani taluk are also known to have operated. Except in one case where a Valayan of Srirangam (Tiruchirapalle district) came to notice, the Valayar of Tiruchirapalle, Ramnad and Madurai do not appear to have operated in the district. The local resident Valayar did not extend their sphere of operation beyond the district except in a limited number of cases where they came to notice in Palani taluk and Kezhirjambarai in Kerala. Even these few cases were promoted by geographical contiguity and presence of relatives there.

The Valayar of Coimbatore district was under the obligations of the Criminal Tribes Act until it was repealed. By 1963 only eleven Valayar were under the provision of the restrictions of the Habitual Offenders Act.[35]

Criminal Organisations

Some of the Valayar in Coimbatore district have been indulging in criminal activities in organized groups. A criminal organization headed by Govindan alias Ranga Valayan engaged in committing a series of burglaries and house-thefts came to the notice of the Police in 1963. The gang consisted of eighteen Valayar drawn from the villages of Periakumarpalayam (the village of Govindan alias Ranga Valayan) and Karadibavi. This gang of 18, besides individuals consisted of three sets of brothers, one set consisted of four and the other two, two each. There were two other subsidiary gangs one led by Rama Valayan son of Amasai Valayan of the same village. The whole formation was responsible for a series of burglaries and thefts in Coimbatore district and in Kerala during the year 1960, 1961, 1962 and 1963. Forty one cases were detected. The gang operated in Sulur, Perur, Perianaickenpalam, Madukurai, Karumathampatti, Koilpalayam, Mettupalayam, Thruppur Rural, Kinathukadavu (Coimbatore district) and Palghat.

The *modus operandi* used consisted of masks and stones to be flung at the victims whenever circumstances necessitated.

The three Valaya gangs were inter-related and inter-connected who operated in batches for a prolonged period. This came to light in 1962. Of the 41 cases committed by these gangs, five of them were grave burglaries.

Another criminal organization of earlier origin which came to the notice of the Nambiyur Police in 1956, consisted of eight Valayar of Rangarapalayam headed by Vagaram alias Karuppu Valayan son of Algavalayan.

Besides organized crime through gangs, individual Valayar have been responsible for a series of offences such as stealing of gold, jewel, wrist watches, vessels and house-breakings.

Types of Crimes and Their Distribution

The crime records of the police stations of Coimbatore district show that during the year 1959-63 as many as 381 property offences were Valaya crimes.[36] The figure includes offences under various sections of IPC (Indian Penal Code).

Tiruppur Taluk Police Station tops the list with 26 cases followed by Nambiyur Karamadai with 24 each. Next in the order are Kumdadam having a figure 21, Annur and Perianaickenpalayam with 20 each and Kottar 19. Pullyampatti Police station follows with 17 offences. Mettupalayam and Avanasni with 13 each, and Sulur, Madathukulam, Pollachi town and Cheyyur with 12 each, and Thomdamathur and Dharapuram have 10 each. The rest of the stations have crime in single digit. The circle-wise figures of Valaya crimes are given in Table 8.

Mettupalayam circle first with 82 cases, followed by Pollachi with 46, Coimbatore Rural with 41, Tiruppur with 35, Udumalpet and Dharapuram with 33 each, Gobichettipalayam with 27, Sathyamangalam with 26, Podanur with 25, Palladam with 21, Coimbatore town East and west with 5 each and Perundurai and Erode taluk with one each.

In regard to the incidence of Valaya crimes, the months of June to September have heavy crime figures under thefts, house breakings, dacoities and robberies. April, May, and December are lean months under all heads of Valaya crimes; January, February, March, October and November are moderate in the incidence. Crimes by Valayar show a tendency to increase as the month advances and also the incidence of crimes was great on the days of shandies (weekly markets) in the respective police station limits.

We may have a brief account of the Valaya crimes crime-wise for the period 1959-1963 for which details are available.

TABLE 8: Distribution of Valaya crimes circle-wise between 1959-63

Name of the Circle	Total Valaya Crimes
1. Mettupalayam	82
2. Pollachi	46
3. Coimbatore Rural	41
4. Tiruppur	35
5. Dharapuram	33
6. Udumalpet	33
7. Gobichettipalayam	27
8. Sathyamangalam	26
9. Podanur	25
10. Palladam	21
11. Coimbatore Town East	5
12. Coimbatore Town West	5
13. Perundurai	1
14. Erode Taluk	1
Total	381

Dacoities

In the year 1959, there were two dacoities, one on the highway and the other on the field, in which Valaya complicity was strongly suspected. During the year 1960, there were eight dacoities of which seven were detected. Five of the seven detected cases were the work of Valayar. In all the five occurrences, inmates of houses were either assaulted or threatened with sticks, aruvals or spears. Twenty –nine Valayar, one Gounder and four Chetty were prosecuted. Some of the Valaya accused wore white banyans and white shirts and had painted their faces black.

The year 1961 recorded seven dacoities of which one was the work of Valayar. The dacoities during the year 1962, numbered four, of which three were detected and found to be the work of Valayar. All three were field dacoities. In one case, seven Valayar of Rayarpalayam were involved.

Robberies

Nineteen out of the 49 cases detected during the period were traced to be the work of Valayar.

In 1959, two of the three valaya crimes occurred on the highway and one on a field. The two highway robberies were at Annur, on Wednesdays, the Avanashi shandy days, one from a shandy cart and another from a lorry driver. K.D. Mosuvan alias Karuppan, his brother Sadayan Madan alias Karuppan son of Royapaalathan alias Rasivalayan and Surai alias Raman of 'Thotiapalayam, Annur police Station, armed with 'bitchuva' (dagger) threatened the complainants in both the cases and removed bengalgram from the cart and cash from the lorry driver. In the second case, when the lorry was proceeding slowly on an ascent, the accused cut some of the groundnut bags. The complainant stopped the vehicle on suspicion, saw that the bags had been cut and followed the trail of groundnut to a distance of about quarter kilometer when he was surprised by K.D. Mosuvan and three others and relieved of his purse containing cash at the point of 'bitchuva'. In the third case, a gold 'tali' was snatched away from the complainant when she was grazing cattle, and cash was removed from four passers-by on the Pollachi Valparai road at point just beyond Angalakurchi village. The four passers-by were made to sit and cash was removed.

Valayar were found to be responsible for four out of the 14 cases of robbery detected during the year 1960. Local K.Ds were responsible for two of these cases and casuals for the other two. The properties involved in these cases were gold, jewels, cash, wrist watch and vessels valued at Rs. 5,010. About forty percent of the robberies in 1961 were traced to the work of Valayar of Rayarpalayam, Jangamanaicken-palayam, Kurubapalayam and Thudiyur. Two of the Valaya occurrences were in field cattle-pens in Nambiyur police station limits. The articles involved in these cases were goats, sheep, vessels and gold chain. In the year 1962, five of the sixteen cases were committed by the Valayar. Two of these five cases were field robberies, two house-robberies and one was a highway robbery. In 1962, three of the robberies of the year which occurred in the limits of the Cheyyur, Kangayam and Kottur police station limits were found to be the work of Valayar.

Dacoities and robberies committed by Valayar have been far too many at Gudimangalam, Tiruppur taluk, Nambiyur, Perianaickenpalayam, Annur, Cheyyur, Avanashi, Avanashi-palayam and Pullyampatti. More occurrences took place in Annur and Cheyyur than in any other place.

House-breakings

A general study of the house-breaking cases in Coimbatore district discloses that Coimbatore city has had a very high contribution to make in all the five years under report, followed by Pollachi, Udumalpet, Mettupalayam and Erode town. During the period, 148 house-breaking are known to be the work of Valayar.

Thefts

During the period 1959-63, out of a total of 379 property cases, there were 208 cases of thefts attributable to Valayar of which 210 were ordinary thefts, 31 house thefts, two servant thefts, and 65 cattle thefts.

Only nine police stations out of 39 were free from ordinary thefts for which Valayar were responsible. These thefts include garden produce, grain, pocket picking, clothes, lanterns and vessels.

History-sheeted Bad Characters

Three hundred history sheets are maintained in Coimbatore district under the classifications of dossier criminal, habitual offenders, known depredators and suspects. Six of them are D.Cs, eleven are habitual offenders, 201 are K.Ds and 82 are suspects. These history sheets are distributed among 38 police stations wherein Valayar have taken up residences. There are 29 sheets in Nambiyur (Rayarpalayam having the lion's share), 18 in Cheyyur, 17 in Kottur, 13 in Tiruppur taluk, 11 in Avanashi and 10 in Kamanaicke-npalayam. The other stations have fewer numbers of sheets.

Thirty percent of the total villages having resident history-sheeted Valayar lie in Mettupalayam circle. It has a Valaya population of 4,113 out of a total 13,975 Valayar for the whole district. As regards Valaya ex-convicts, Mettupalayam circle accounts for 203 out of a total of 669. Twenty-two percent of the total Valaya property crime is contributed by Mettupalayam circle, the actual figures being 82 cases, for a total of 38%. One D.C., one H.O., 43 K.D., and 24 suspects among Valaya criminals are in Mettupalayam circle. This amounts to 23 per cent of the history sheets maintained in the district.

Other Offences by the Valayar

Valayar came to notice in respect of a few cases of cycle thefts, temple thefts. Electric starter and switch thefts also. One Ranga Valayan son of Sokka Valayan of Karamadai was concerned in the case of temple theft in the year 1944. He removed cash from a box kept for the devotees to offer their donations, and he was convicted.

Rayarpalayam Valayar (Coimbatore district) is a terror in the area. It is reported that the whole community is engaged in criminal activities as a profession and as a way of life. They have earned such notoriety, [37t]that people dreaded going alone within a radius of 5 km, of Rayarpalayam. It is said to be the nucleus/origin of the Valaya population in the district. It is situated in Nambiyur police station limits in Gobichettipalayam circle, attached to Mettupalayam sub-division in Coimbatore district, Rayarpalayam is a hamlet of Emmampoodi 10 km. south-east of Nambiyur. Emmampoodi village is on the bus route between Nambiyur and Kunnathur (via) Malapalayam. The village consists of 96 households, with single room tenements put up with mud walls and thatched roof.[38] There is only one tiled house belonging to a K.D. The economic condition of the Valayar is deplorably bad. The clothing of the men and women is as poor as it is sparse. The household articles will hardly be a bag load. The village is not electrified. It has a drinking water well. The lands west and south of the village belong to Rayarpalayam village and are very underdeveloped and are not economic agricultural holdings. The result is most of the land remains fallow. Crime has thus become a means of livelihood for them. The population of the Valayar in the village is on the decrease, for the more enterprising moved to place of greater prosperity either for employment or for purposes of crime. Some of them are engaged in farm-labour. During the period under report, the Valayar of Rayarpalayam were involved in large numbers in the detected cases than those from any other village. In a case of 1963, Rayarpalayam Valayar K.D. Muthan alias Muthuswamy son of Mulyan Karuppan, H.O. 252, Maran alias Velveti Maran, Rangan alias Rangaswamy with the assistance of Rangaswamy, son of Karuppan alias Karuppuswamy settled at Thottonnatham in Kolakambai Police Station limits (The Nilgiris district) entered the house of one Thavathula Rowther of Manalada estate on the night of 11th April 1963, in police uniform posing as police officers on prohibition duty and committed theft. A recent report said (a private communication) that law enforcement authorities finding it difficult to cut down the incidence of criminal activities indulged in by the Rayarpalayam Valayar, set fire to their dwellings, so that when their huts are gutted and destroyed they may scatter and migrate to other places. Though (as the report goes) the huts were reduced to ashes, they came up again in a short period. They defy authority, persist in their criminal behaviour.

Steps for Rehabilitation

As a measure of reformation in the late 1950s, a scheme of single teacher elementary school was evolved by the Superintendent of Police, Coimbatore, in consultation with the District Collector. A school at Rayarpalayam and the road leading to the village were constructed under the local development scheme, the police force meeting its half cost by contributing labour. The road and school were opened in 1957. A constable was posted as the first teacher. Classes for children were conducted from 8.30 A.M. to 10.30 A.M. and for adults from 7 P.M. to 9 P.M. daily. On July 11, 1958, the Sub-Inspector of Police of Nambiyur conducted a prohibition raid with the Armed Reserve and detected 31 cases in the village. Neither child nor adult would attend the school from that date and the school was eventually closed at the end of the year. All subsequent efforts to reclaim or reform them proved futile. And so it continues to be a problem.

As a contrast to Rayarpalayam, the Valayar of Valayarpalayam and Molakalipalayam in Karumathampatti Police Station limits are fairly above want. The former village has a Valaya population of about 160, of which about 30 are men and 30 women while the remaining are children. Men, women, and children wear decent dress; women have jewellery of modern taste and many of the children are school going. The houses are built better and the lives of the inhabitants indicate healthy and progressive trends.

The Valayar of Thandukarampalayam in Cheyyur Police Station limits are mostly converts to Christianity. The church at Lourdupuram about 2 km. from Thandukarampalayam is giving the necessary help and guidance to these people. There are about 30 adults and 45 children in the village. Five of them are ex-convicts under property offences. Thirty – two have been convicted under the Prohibition Act. The Valayar of Managarasu Valayapuram is also converts to Christianity. Adults are about 30 and children 35 in this village. Only two are exconvicts under property offences and more than 25 have had convictions for prohibition offences.

Though Madurai district is one of the five main Valaya districts in the State, the incidence of criminal activities is mostly confined to the police station limits of Palani taluk, Keeranur and Chatrapatti. The Valayar in these parts are identical with the Valayar of the criminal tribe before the repeal of the Act. In these police station limits of Palani circle, about 750 Valayar live in 24 villages, some isolates and the other constituents in the multicaste communities. The Valayar in the Palani taluk constitute only 0.25 percent. Out of 221 adult male population, 41 are ex-convicts for property offences. The largest number (26) is found in Keeranur Police Station followed by Chatrapati and Palani taluk 2; 18.5% of the Valaya population are ex-convicts. During the years 1959-63 fifty-seven Valayar were convicted under the Prohibition Act, and 14.8 percent of the adult Valaya population in Palani taluk happened to be convicted for offences under the Prohibition Act.

Palani circle-crime history shows that there were 642 offences under dacoity, robbery, house-breakings and thefts during the years 1959-63, 470 of these cases were detected and only 16 were traced to the Valayar. Valaya crimes are 3.4% of the total volume of crime.

About 4 percent of the Palani taluk Valayar, 16.5% of Keeranur Valayar and 18% percent of the Chatrapati Valayar (24 in number) are history-sheeted.

The foregoing account of the Valaya crimes is what has surfaced and come to the notice of the authorities. There should have been several cases uncomplained and sometimes undetected. Besides the Valayar engaging themselves in criminal acts exclusively, there have been, in parts of Madurai and Ramnad districts accomplices or assistant to the Kallar criminal tribe until the Act was repealed. The Valayar, wherever the Kallar have been dominant, have played a subordinate role in the organised and individual criminal acts of the Kallar.

Two to three decades ago, the Valayar of Valayapatti used to steal banana, coffee, jack, lemons from the plantations on the Sirumalais on a high scale.[39] But now, there is so much of decline in this activity since some 6 families have their own plantations on the hills and they are afraid of reciprocal behaviour on the part of other people, if they steal from other plantation. But even now, during summer, some of the young men in Valayapatti go in small groups and collect tender mangoes from trees on the Sirumalais belonging to other caste-groups. There is no question of their feeling it a shame. They take pride in such things when they succeed uncaught.

There is another factor associated with their occupation which is likely to develop a tendency among the Valayar to do things surreptitiously with the knowledge of the authorities. Collection and sale of firewood is one of the chief occupations of the group. Usually they collect fire wood from reserve forests. They do not simply go in for dry wood, but cut raw wood, fell saplings for construction and agricultural uses. These are all unauthorized and unlawful cuttings. But they have to live on that. They make friends with the forest personnel, grease their palms periodically, supply them firewood, honey or any other wild product and occasionally lend themselves to be booked and fined for unlawful cutting of trees and firewood. This is a problem wherever the Valayar collect firewood in the reserve forests and their interaction with the forest personnel and the periodical prosecutions under forest regulations are an ever continuing phenomenon. So, their occupation of collecting and selling of firewood, honey and other forest products breeds in them a tendency to do things secretly, hide facts, always trying to please (satisfy) or hoodwink the authority. Sometimes, they argue and satisfy themselves that they "cut and collect wood from the government's property. It is no individual property. It is not tantamount to stealing. We have a right to live. Collecting firewood has been our way of life. There is no alternative avocation for us. Let the Government provide us some alternative. The forest personnel are a menace to us and somehow we may have to live on this and so depend on the forest". And so go their arguments.

Thus, we find the criminal activities of the Valayar in the State is confined mainly to Coimbatore district and its fringe areas and it does not reflect the ethos of the group as such.[40]

There are other groups such as Kepmaris, Thotti, Naickers in Tamil Nadu who as ethnic groups wherever they are, engaged in criminal acts. With them, till now it is a group characteristic, the whole-caste is involved. But in the case of Valayar, thousands of whom are below poverty line do not indulge in criminal behaviour. And so it is not mere poverty, it has not been their social heredity but a phenomenon as a result of a combination of factors in the case of Coimbatore Valayar which needs a depth-study.

Livestock

The Valayar as farmers, farm labourers, as collectors of firewood and sometimes as fishermen are associated with livestock and they rear cattle, sheep, goats, pigs and poultry. Livestock supplements their income to a small extent. They rear cattle for draft and for organic manure purposes. The Valayar who live close to the forests and hills own larger number of cattle. In such cases, the use of cattle is in terms of draft work and dung as manure and sometimes they sell bull calves, but there is no significant dairying activity. Most of them do not milk their cows and buffaloes. A larger number of Valaya families in Madurai and Ramnad districts engage cows for draft purposes-for ploughing, drawing water, carting manure, etc., and so dairying activity among them is so low. This is evident from the sample study made in the villages of Valayapatti and Sendhi. Here we may briefly look into the livestock position in these two communities.

Of the total ninety-four households, seventy-four households own some livestock. In Valayapatti 82% and in Sendhi 72.73% of the households own livestock. In Valayapatti 41 families own 94 cows, 35 bullocks, 11 he-buffaloes, 28 calves, 140 goats and 123 birds. In the case of Sendhi, the cattle wealth of Valayar is poor. The thirty-two livestock-owning families in Sendhi rear 24 cows, 39 bullocks, 12 calves, 75 sheep and 56 birds. It must be noted that in Valayapatti and Sendhi, livestock has not been taken up seriously since pedigree animals or birds have not so far entered these two villages. For instance, even though 86 percent of the respondents of Valayapatti and 22.73 percent of Sendhi have heard of artificial insemination, fifty percent of the Valayapatti and a small percentage (4.55) of Sendhi respondents are not in favour of artificial insemination. Further, though a key village sub-centre is located at a distance of $2^{1/2}$ kilometers of Valayapatti, no livestock-owning family at the village has availed itself of this opportunity. The Valayar who are not in favour of artificial insemination, state that it is against nature the method is not always successful and that the offspring of such insemination are not useful for draft purposes in the area. In short, livestock is neither a chief source of livelihood nor a substantial subsidiary occupation for the Valayar.

Income and Expenditure

The Valayar as a community is included in the list of backward and most backward groups in the State. Their levels of life vary in terms of occupation and regionally too. The affluent section in the community in a relative sense could be said to be negligible. At a micro-level, the sources of income, monthly income, lending and borrowing, monthly expenditure and family budgets of Valayapatti and Sendhi give us an insight into the economic life of the generality of the Valayar in Tamil Nadu.

As noted earlier, the chief occupations of the Valayar of Valayapatti and Sendhi (samples from the two districts) are farming, farm labour, collection of firewood and to a small extent collection of gum in case of Sendhi. We may briefly look into the economy of these two villages.

Table 9 shows the source-wise income and percentage distribution of fifty households in Valayapatti and forty-four in Sendhi. The 94 households have an annual income of Rs. 112.982, Valayapatti: Rs. 64,116 Sendhi: Rs. 48,866. While the largest percentage of income (32. 48) for Valayapatti is firewood, Sendhi derives its highest income of 68.68 percent from food crops. Looked at village-wise, Valayapatti next to firewood, derives its 24.56 percent income from money crops, 19.96 percent from farm-labour followed by 14.69 percent product from food crops and 8.31 percent mostly from forest products. In the case of Sendhi as mentioned above, 68.68 percent of its income is through food crops (mainly paddy), 21.28 percent from farm-labour, 4.67 percent from money crops followed by 3.26 percent from gum and 2.11 percent from other miscellaneous economic activities. It may be noted that in between Valayapatti and Sendhi, while the highest percentage of income in the case of the former is firewood, this occupation as an economic activity is totally absent in the latter though in its place there is collection and sale of gum to a tune of 2.11 percent. While food crops as a source of income constitutes 68.68 percent in case of Sendhi it is only 14.69 percent in case of Valayapatti and while nearly one-fourth of Valayapatti's income is through money crops it is less than one-twentieth in case of Sendhi, Percentage of income through farm-labour is a little higher in Sendhi compared to Valayapatti.

The percentage distribution of the combined income for the two villages takes a different turn. Food crops constitute 38.04 percent followed by farm-labour 20.53 percent; firewood 18.43 percent, money crops 15.26 percent, others 5.63 percent and gum 1.41 percent.

Based on this annual income the per capita income in the case of Valayapatti (population 272) is Rs. 235.72 and Rs. 240.72 in case of Sendhi and the average per capita income for the two communities is Rs. 237.86. The national average per capita income in India as of 1971-72 was Rs. 645 at current prices, and the difference between national average and the per capita income of the Valayar in the sample is sharp. At the same time, per capita income in Tamil Nadu (1971-72) was Rs. 774 at current prices. Compared with the all-India and Tamil Nadu per capita income, the per capita income of the Valayar in the sample is less than one-half.[41]When we take the family as a unit, the average per family annual income works out to Rs. 1202 and the monthly average of per family Rs. 100 and so based on this all the Valaya families in Valayapatti and Sendhi are below poverty line.[42] We may safely observe that the same economic level applies to the majority of the Valayar in Tamil Nadu. When we stretch it further and look at the per capita per day income of earnings, in the case of 475 persons in Valayapatti and Sendhi it works out to 65 paise. In a statistical sense individual has to live, eat, clothe and shelter himself within this income. This statistic of 65 paise per day (average) speaks of the Valayar's food, in terms of quantity and quality, and in a word their levels of living.

Within this low level of per capita income, there is diversity within a community.

Of the 94 families of Valayapatti and Sendhi, 63.82 percent of them enjoy annual income ranging from Rs. 1001.00 to above Rs. 1500.00 and between the two villages, while 72.74 percent of the families in Sendhi come under over Rs. 100.00 slab, the percentage of this category of population in Valayapatti is 56. The Valayar in Sendhi are comparatively better off than the people in Valayapatti. On the other hand, 4.55 percent of the population in Sendhi has an annual income less than Rs. 300.00 The intra-community class structure based on income in Valayapatti is graded more or less with equal number of families under each category while over one-half of the families in Sendhi are concentrated at a higher

TABLE 9: Sources and Income

Village	Food Crops Rs.	Money Crops Rs.	Farm Labour Rs.	Fire Wood Collection Rs.	Gum Collection Rs. Rs.	Labour miscellaneous Rs.	Total Rs.
Valayapatti	9420*	15745	12800	20826	—	5425	64116
	(14.69)	(24.56)	(19.96)	(32.48)		(8.31)	(100)
Sendhi	33562	2282	10399	—	1593	1030	48866
	(68.68)	(4.67)	(21.28)		(3.26)	(2.11)	(100)
Total	42982	18027	23199	20826	1593	6355	112982
	(38.04)	(15.96)	(20.53)	(18.43)	(1.41)	(5.63)	(100)

* Figures in parenthesis are percentages.

TABLE 10: Percentage Distribution of Valaya Families in Valayapatti and Sendhi in Terms if Annual income

Village	Below 300	301-500	501-750	751-1000	1001-1250	1251-1500	AboveRs.	Total1500
Valayapatti	-	1*	10	11	11	3	14	50
		(2)	(20)	(22)	(22)	(6)	(28)	(100)
Sendhi	2	5	12	3	5	8	19	44
	(4.55)	(11.36)	(4.55)	(6.82)	(11.36)	(18.20)	(43.18)	(100)
	2	6	12	3	5	8	19	44
	(2.13)	(6.38)	(4.55)	(6.82)	(11.36)	(18.20)	(43.18)	(100)

*The figures in parentheses are percentages.

income level (Rs. 1251.00 and Above) while families coming under lower income slabs are smaller in number. In short, it may be observed that the Valayar in general, are at subsistence (economic) level (see Table 10).

While income is an index of level of living, it is more so in the case of expenditure. While incomes were worked our for the families in Valayapatti and Sendhi per annum, month was taken as a unit for expenditure. Expenditure as such mainly comprises food, clothing, social and religious ceremonies and functions. But in order to understand the pattern of expenditure in the two Valaya communities, a sample of twenty households, ten in each village was chosen randomly and family budgets were worked out. These budgets help us understand the consumption pattern among the Valayar in the two villages (see Table 11) of the two Valaya communities, 50 percent of the families spend monthly, amount ranging from Rs. 51 to Rs. 100. Community-wise 52 percent of the families in Valayapatti and 47.73 percent of Sendhi Valayar come under this category. There is much similarity in the number of families in both the villages in different expenditure ranges. Over 80 percent of the families under study have a monthly expenditure of less than Rs. 150. In the case of the general study of monthly expenditure of 94 households, food items, fuel and items such as chewing and smoking were taken into account. But in the case of the twenty families, a number of other items have been included and hence the difference between the average of the total numbers of households (94) and the average of the twenty households, taken up for a detailed budgetary study.

TABLE 11: Distribution of Valaya Families in Valayapatti and Sendhi in Terms of Monthly Expenditure

Village	Below Rs. 50	51-100	101-150	151-200	201-250	Total
Valayapatti	4	26	16	2	2	50
	(8.00)	(52.00)	(32.00)	(4.00)	(4.00)	(100)
Sendhi	6	21	12	3	2	44
	(13.64)	(47.83)	(27.27)	(6.82)	(4.55)	(100)
Total	10	47	28	5	6	194
	(10.62)	(50.00)	(22.82)	(5.31)	(4.25)	(100)

Pattern of Consumer Expenditure

A general study of total income and expenditure of a community does not very much help us to have a feel of their life. In the case of the Valayar, it would be worth while examining, even if briefly, the standard and quality of living at their level. A simple index to judge the standard of living is the distribution of the total consumer expenditure between major items such as food, fuel, clothing, etc. A detailed study of consumer expenditure was made of twenty families. The items in the household budgetary analysis comprise cereals, pulses, leafy and other vegetable, milk and milk products, fruits, meat, poultry products, edible and non-edible oils, sugar, nuts, spices, medical treatment, clothing, housing, education, transport, recreation, festivals, light and fuel and intoxicants and smoking items.

The twenty households have a population of 127: adults 62, children below 18 years 65 and the consumption units are 95 (actually 94 ½) rounded off to 95 at the rate of one unit for an adult and half a unit for a child below 18 years), the consumer expenditure is worked out for a month. Some of the items of expenditure which are occasional and annual are worked out to monthly average. The monthly consumer expenditure for the twenty households is Rs. 4396.45 and the average per household expenditure is Rs. 219.82. This works out to Rs. 36.19 per capita and Rs. 48.38 per consumption unit of the population in the sample[43] The expenditure toward cost of cultivation including cattle feed had been excluded from the monthly consumer expenditure, since it involves farm and occupational expenses and the income thereof. The expenditure coverage is restricted to the items noted above.

The per capita or per consumption unit expenditure includes food and non-food items, and so for as expenditure on food is concerned it gives an idea of their food consumption and the nutritional level of their food. As per the percentage distribution of the consumer expenditure, the Valayar in the sample spend 76.10 percent exclusively for food items such as cereals, pulses, oils, vegetables, sugar, spices, nuts, fruits, meat, poultry products, milk and milk products. The remaining 23.90 percent of the expenditure is distributed over clothing, travel, intoxicants, medicine, recreation etc.

Of the food items, cereals constitute the largest percentage. A household in the sample spends 51.00 percent towards cereals. The cereals in the case of Valayapatti consist chiefly of sorghum, millets, and an occasional luxury of rice, and in the case of Sendhi it is mainly rice followed by ragi. The monthly per household expenditure ranges from Rs. 65 to Rs. 200 with an averages of Rs. 112.10. Spices constitute the next highest percentage with 4.98. The spices in the case of Valayar are chiefly chillies, salt, tamarind, coriander, turmeric, mustard, pepper etc., but the essential condiments to their curries are chillies, salt and tamarind. They may go for other spices on special occasions and for preparing meat. Some spices like cardamom, cloves are luxury items for them. In the sample of twenty households, the expenditures in a month toward spices range from Rs. 2 in one household to Rs. 25 in another. Fifty percent of the households' spend from Rs. 8 to Rs. 12 and another twenty-five percent between Rs. 15 to Rs. 25 towards spices and the average per family is Rs. 20.92.

The third item in the order of descendency of percentage is the vegetables that the constitute 3.82 percent of the total expenditure and Rs. 8.38 as average per household expenditure per month. It may be said that majority of the Valaya farmers are small and marginal farmers and the majority of them do not grow vegetables. For instance, no family in Valayapatti cultivates vegetables except a few households cultivating snake gourd. The Valayar neither cultivate vegetables on commercial scale nor to any considerable extent for their own consumption.

In the 20 households under study, the per household per month expenditure on vegetables ranges from Rs. 2 to 15. If we work out the per household monthly average (Rs. 8.38) it comes to about 28 paise per day. Consumption of vegetables among the Valayar is insignificant though vegetables constitute 3. 82 percent of the total expenditure.

Related to vegetables are the leafy vegetables which constitute only 0.21 percent of the expenditure and in terms of money, the household per month amount is 46 paise only. The

Valayar of Valayapatti mostly collects greens from fields and hills and rarely buy them, but in Sendhi the position is a little different. They buy greens in the weekly markets. Leafy vegetables or greens are only occasional items in the diet of the Valayar.

Next in percentage of expenditure in the descending order under food are edible oils. In this the major consumption is groundnut oil. Oil is used in the seasoning of curries and occasionally as a medium for cooking meat, preparing pancakes and paniyaram. The edible oils constitute 3.13 per cent in the total expenditure and the average expenditure per family towards this item is Rs.6.48. Every household uses edible oils. In the sample household, expenditure toward edible oils ranges from forty paise to Rs. 21.60. The edible oils they consume are the main sources of fat for them. It may be mentioned here that some very backward groups of Valayar in Singampunari block area, Ramnad district, use frog oil as a medium for seasoning and cooking in a few cases, coconut oil in small quantities is used mostly for hair dressing.

Meat is the next item with 3.07 percent of the total monthly consumer expenditure. Meat as an item includes meat purchased locally and the value of the meat they secure through game. Though they are traditional hunters and look for the game, now and then once or twice a month, they go in for meat in the village market or consume a fowl. Meat as an item consists of pork, chicken, meat of sheep, goats and wild game and birds. Of these, in some cases, rat meat constitutes a major chunk, chicken, is an usual course when important kin visit the family. Meat on festive occasions and religious celebrations,[44] is a must besides it being consumed occasionally. The family per average expenditure toward meat in a month is Rs.6.76. This amount in terms of quantity of goat or ram meat means a little over half a kilogram per family per month. At this rate, members in a family may have a taste of it once or twice in a month. When it is a game hunted, the question is different, but when it comes to buying, it turns to be a luxury. The amount spent towards meat in a month ranges from Rs. 2.00 to Rs. 20.00 in the case of the twenty households. Especially in respect to consumption of meat by the Valayar in general, in terms of frequency and quantity of meat, it varies from area to area in Tamil Nadu.

Pulses are next in frequency to meat, which constitute 3.05 percent of the total expenditure. The average per household expenditure towards pulses is Rs. 6.70 and the amount spent by the individual households in the sample ranges from Rs. 2.00 to Rs. 15.00. The pulses consumed by the Valayar consist mainly of redgram, blackgram, green gram, field gram, horsegram, and cowpea. All households consume some pulses or other. After meat, pulses are the major protein giving items in the case of the Valayar.

Rearing of poultry is common among the Valayar. The pattern of consumption of eggs and birds varies from group to group among them. In some cases both eggs and birds are consumed domestically and in some, eggs are sold, birds consumed and sold too. But in most of the cases, rearing of poultry is not an income adding activity. It is mostly for domestic consumption and for ritual requirements. The Valayar rear cocks to be sacrificed to their deities. Usually sacrificial cocks are reared by the individual family and seldom purchased.

In the sample of households under study, the percentage distribution of expenditure toward poultry products is 2. 38 and per household average expenditure on this item is Rs. 5.21. The amount spent by individual households ranges from twenty paise to Rs. 25.00

in a month. The twenty paise case may be an egg consumed by the household in a month and in the case of family with Rs. 25.00 under this head, they may be rearing a large number of birds and consume one or two in a month besides eggs. It is a practice among the Valayar to treat a guest with chicken and so birds are so associated with the life of Valayar.

Though milk and milk products constitute 2.35 percent of the total monthly consumer expenditure, only 35 percent (11) of the sample households consume these products. In the case of the 45 percent of the households, milk and milk products are absent in their diet. The average household expenditure toward milk and milk products is Rs. 5.16 and the range of expenditure on these items among the sample households is from twenty paise to Rs. 30.00. In most cases, milk products in the shape of buttermilk and curds are consumed and seldom they use butter or clarified butter.[45] Further, even though teatotalling and coffee sipping habit obtains among urban influenced Valayar they usually (men only) enjoy coffee or tea at eating-places and seldom make use of milk for preparing tea or coffee at their homes. It is interesting to note that the per capita consumption of milk per day among the Valayar is very low.

If we take the pattern of consumption of milk by the population in the sample as an indicator, based on the average amount spent by individual household, the consumption of milk per month is about 2500 milliliters and in the case of average family (five members) its works out to about 17 milliliters per day per capita. At this level the consumption of milk or milk products in the case of the Valayar is quite insignificant.

Fruits constitute 1.65 percent of the total expenditure. The month per household average expenditure under this item is Rs. 3.62. Fruits are consumed by all the households in the sample. Eating of fruits is seasonal, but the consumption in Valayapatti is more. It may be recalled that some Valaya families have their plantations on the Sirumalais. A hill variety of banana, pomegranate, orange, jack are cultivated on the hills and so in the case of Valayar of Valayapatti there is more(comparatively) consumption of fruits especially banana, jack and other wild fruits. The facility is absent in Sendhi and the consumption of fruits there is limited. The chief consumers of fruits are children. When the parents visit a weekly market or the neighbouring town, depending on the season, they buy fruits for their children. The common fruits are banana and mangoes. The other varieties of fruits are costly and beyond the reach of the majority of Valayar.

Sugar constituents a negligible percentage (0.24) in the total consumer expenditure population. The average per month per household expenditures on sugar is 54 paise and it ranges from 10 paise to Rs.2.50. Sugar is consumed as a sweetmeat, occasionally as an ingredient of a dish. It is taken in the form of jaggery and sugar (white).[46] It is a fringe item in their diet.

Another fringe or minor item is nuts constituting just 0.22 percent of the expenditure. Groundnut is the only item under nuts. Normally, the Valayar do not buy groundnut, they earn groundnut as wages and as a friendly consideration from other cultivators of groundnut. It is an item which wets the mouths of both adults and children. During the harvest season of groundnut one can see every one munching groundnut. Sometimes, groundnut is used by the Valayar for chutney.

The food items discussed above are both produced and purchased locally and from the neighbouring towns, on cash and on credit basis. In some cases, cereals are produced and consumed and the marketable surplus is sold. In some cases, the home-produced cereals will suffice the household for a few months and during the remaining period, they buy cereals from other farmers, or in the local grocery shops. In regard to pulses, most of the pulses are produced by some Valaya households and some buy in the local shops. Spices and edible oils are all purchased locally and in the neighbouring towns both on payment of cash and on credit. Usually, the frequency of buying the condiments is weekly, especially in the shandies or in the town. In some cases, the purchase may be a daily affair, quantities enough for a day or two. This practice speaks of their abject conditions.

We may discuss the non-food items that go into the consumer expenditure.

Medicine or medical treatment for men and animals constitutes 1.00 percent of the total expenditure and per household average per month is Rs.2.19. That is, a household in the sample spends Rs.2.19 on average in a month both for men and animals. This expenditure in the case of twenty households in the sample, ranges form 10 paise to Rs.10.00. The medicine may be a tablet, a herb, decoction of leaves of medicinal value, or the fee paid to the native practitioner or a modern physician.

Though clothing is a major item next to food, only less than one tenth of the expenditure on food is spent over clothes. The percentage distribution over all items of food is 76.10, but in the case of clothing it is 7.74 percent. The per month per household expenditure on clothing is Rs.17.02. In the case of the twenty households, it ranges from rs.6.00 to Rs.30.00. Though expenditure is not incurred every month on clothing, it is the monthly average of the amount spent in a year on clothing. The Valayar go in for clothing on festive and ceremonial occasions and when absolutely forced for another piece or set of clothing.

Housing as a head of expenditure is neither an annual feature nor is it a monthly one. A householder, once he constructs a house (mostly thatched) goes in for a new thatched roof once in four or five years. Once a year, he whitewashes and gives a new look to his dwelling. It is mostly done by the members of the family and such items of housework are not expressed in terms of expenditure. And so, only five out of twenty respondents have reported some expenditure on housing. This expenditure per month ranges from Rs.5.00 to Rs.42.00.

In respect to the expenditure on education (0.19 percent) as in the case of housing, only five out of twenty respondents in sample have reported. The monthly expenditure on education ranges from one rupee to two rupees. Children in all the twenty households either are only at the primary school level or not attending school. There is no fee at the primary level. In the case of children in Valayapatti, text books and note books are supplied to them by Gandhigram aided by German voluntary Organization. Educational expenses are insignificant and it does not bother them much. Perhaps in households wherein children are in high schools and colleges, there may be considerable expenditure under this head.

When we come to travel and transport, the picture is different. All the twenty households in the sample and for that matter the majority of households spend some amount over travel. They visit their kin in the neighbouring villages, blocks and districts. Sometimes they have to travel on bus. It may be a friendly visit, or attending a puberty ceremony, marriage, celebration of a deity or a funeral. The Valayar keep in close touch with their kin and meet social obligations. The percentage distribution of expenditure on transport is 3.39 and on average a household in the sample spends Rs. 5.65 in a month. This expenditure ranges from Rs. 1.50 to Rs. 10.00 for a month. This is an expenditure which the Valayar do not grudge and try to evade.

The Valayar are a toiling and hardworking class. The most popular recreation for them is the cinema. The percentage expenditure on recreation is 1.25. People who live within about ten kilometers to a cinema hall see films. They may visit a cinema whenever there is a film that attracts the rural people. In the case of Valayapatti and Sendhi, cinema – going is a regular feature. Men, women and children enjoy the films. The boys especially do not miss a single Tamil film. Films are a source of knowledge and information for them. Usually, they go to the late show (9.30 p.m.). By evening they would finish their work, have their meal and go for the late show. The frequency of their going to films in Valayapatti is rather high, because the boys and the girls (who have a high frequency of visit) earn their money for their ticket and the parents also allow this.

Though there are some traditional recreations among adults and children such as story-telling, gossiping, reading (in a few cases) listening to radio, playing some rural game (mostly in the case of children), there are no items costing any money. The cinema is the major area where they spend money.

Expenditure on Festivals

The percentage distribution of expenditure on festivals is 1.84. The household per month expenditure over festivals ranges from Re.1.00 to Rs.10.00. The religious and community festivals, the celebration of clan and community deities are excluded from this head, since these religious celebrations are not carried out every year. Usually, these clan and community deity celebrations are held every alternate year. Preparations for these celebrations are elaborate involving considerable amount and time. The expenditure under the festivals in the present context relates to the year-round common festivals such as, Deepavali (festival of lights) Pongal, Varsha Porappu (new year day) and so on. Besides the Valayar observing some common Hindu festivals, they do attend festivals of other communities in the neighbouring villages and towns. Visits are mainly to enjoy the fun there.

Savings

Savings as a habit, as a feature with the Valayar in the sample is almost nil. Of the twenty households only one household saves a rupee per month. This does not mean that the Valayar do not save, but these savings are not regular and atleast in the case of the sample households, it is not a habit.

Non-edible Oils

The non-edible oils in the case of Valayar consist of neem oil (though other groups make use of mohuva, kusum, pungum). The neem oil is used as hair oil and before taking what is called oil-bath, they apply this oil to the head profusely and smear the body then take bath. The neem oil they say, acts like a detergent and as a pesticide on the lice and that it has also medicinal value and so they use it. Though the neem oil is so strong and pungent smelling, the Valayar like it and use it. They claim that the neem oil when applied to the body before one goes to bed after a day of hard toil, relieves bodily pains. Though in terms of cost it is not much, the percentage distribution of expenditure over the non-edible oil is 0.59. All the Valaya families in Sendhi make use of neem oil, but its use in the case of Valayapatti is negligible.[47] Only one household in Valayapatti makes use of this oil. It may be mentioned here that it is mostly Valaya women who use neem oil as hair oil.

Light and Fuel

Though 100 percent of the villages in Tamil Nadu are electrified, it may be safely said that over ninety percent of the Valayar could not afford electricity for their dwellings.[48] Most Valaya villages and localities in bigger villages enjoy street lights. This is only to emphasize that the Valayar chiefly depend upon kerosene and other oil lamps. They are small iron chimneys, hurricane lanterns, and earthen oil lamps and oil used in the latter types are pungum and groundnut. They make use of these lamps very economically. Usually, they buy kerosene in small quantities (quarter to one litre). This is only for the lamps. This expenditure is a must for every household. One may not see more than two chimneys burning at a time at any Valaya residence. In most cases the households manage with one lamp.

When we come to fuel for cooking, all the Valayar use firewood except perhaps some Valayar on Rameswaram Island. No Valaya household spends any money on firewood. Even in the case of those Valayar who are not engaged in the collection of firewood as an economic activity, they collect and manage enough of fuel for their own domestic consumption. And so, the expenditure under this head is only on kerosene and other oils used for lamps. The monthly expenditure spent for light and fuel constitutes 1.00 percent. The amount spent over this in the case of the sample ranges from Rs.1.20 to Rs.4.60.

Intoxicants, Smoking and Chewing

Chewing betel-nut and betel-leaves and without tobacco is universal habit among the Valayar. The habit of chewing is more among women than among men. Close to the chewing habit is the smoking habit among adult men and the youth. They smoke bedies (an indigenous variety of smoke) and cigarettes. Here and there, a little well to do young men smoke cigarettes. These two are very steadfast habits, and expenditure on such items everyday is a must. Some strongly addicted persons may even forego their food than their chewing and smoking..[49]

Further, Valayar in a considerable number of villages in Tamil Nadu indulge in intoxicating drinks such as toddy and arrack (alcohol). For instance, men in nearly one half of the households in Sendhi and four in Valayapatti are addicted to drinking toddy and arrack.[50] Under the non-food items, the highest percentage of expenditure is on intoxicants, chewing and smoking; 5.14 percent of expenditure is on intoxicants, chewing and smoking. Of course, chewing and smoking are open, but drinking is a little concealed. The expenditure under the above items ranges from Rs.2.00 to Rs.36.00 per month in the case of the families in the sample. A Valaya family may have either chewing or smoking or both plus drinking strong beverages. In other words, no Valaya family is free from atleast one of the three habits.

In the case of Valayapatti, smoking is common among the youth and the adult men, and almost all adult men and women chew. In chewing betel-nut and betel-leaves, they add tobacco but in the case of Sendhi the number of men that smoke is far less, but chewing is almost common among men and women. Except two or three men in Valayapatti who occasionally smoke cigarettes, beedis are smoked in both the villages and it is common among all the Valayar. It may be relevant at this point to compare the percentage distribution of consumption expenditure object-wise of the Valayar with that of the population in Tamil Nadu.

As Table 12 indicates, the Valayar compared with all classes of people in Tamil Nadu spend more on food than the general population. The Valayar spend more on cereals and meat. Their spending on clothing and housing is also high, but when it comes to fuel and lighting and beverages and intoxicants the percentage of expenditure is considerably low. In respect to non-food items, the expenditure is low by over six percent to that of the general Tamil population. It may be pointed out here that it cannot be generalized in respect to the Valaya population in Tamil Nadu.

TABLE 12: Percentage Distribution of Consumption Expenditure Object-wise of the Valayar and the General Population in Tamil Nadu

Object	Valayar	Tamil Population
1. Cereals	50.94	45.20
2. Pulses	3.03	3.20
3. Vegetables	4.00	3.20
4. Milk	2.34	2.73
5. Fruits	1.85	1.40
6. Meat	5.42	3.76
7. Edible Oils	3.12	3.23
8. Sugar	0.24	1.90
9. Spices	4.94	5.06
10. Sub-total food	75.88	69.79
11. Clothing	7.69	3.96
12. Housing	1.74	0.43
13. Fuel & light	1.01	7.23
14. Beverages & intoxicants	5.12	8.43
15. Others	8.56	10.16
Sub-total non-food	24.12	30.21
Total	100.00	100.00

Source: National Sample Survey: 23rd Round (July 1968 – June 1969)

Nutritional Quality of the Food

The foregoing description of the food consumed by the Valayar indicates in general, quantitative and qualitative deficiencies in their food. This has been brought out in a study of 'Nutritional Status' of pre-school children in Valayapatti. The major findings of the study are that vegetables, fruits, pulses, nuts and oil seeds, fats and oils and jaggery are consumed in very little quantity when compared to the recommended allowance, that the main bulk of the diet consists of cholam (sorghum) and rice occasionally, that eighty percent of their income is spent on cereals and only twenty percent on body building and protective foods and as a whole, the diet is found to be an ill-balanced one. And the report adds, the diet of the children is deficient in protein, protein calories, calcium, iron, Vitamin A, and Vitamin C. This is the nutritional level of the children who are provided lunch in the Balwadi (kindergarten) and we can very well surmise the nutritional level of the generality of the Valaya community.

Modes of Reckoning, Measures and Weights

Though the Valayar too as part of the general populace in the country are subject to changes in weighing, measuring, still they cling on to the old order in measurement of grain, weighing articles, measuring distance, surface, expressing distance, etc. Though metric system has been in use over fifteen years (with reference to the time of this study), even today they still reckon and make use of the old measures such as:

1. Marakkal = 5 Madras measures = 7(1/2) kg.
2. 12 Marakka = 1 Kalam (one bag)
3. Arapadi = 1/2 measure = ¾ kg
4. Kalpadi = ¼ measure
5. Arikalpadi = 1/8 measure
6. Veessam = 1/16 measure
7. Araveesam = 1/32 measure
8. Kalveesam = 1/64 measure

Though the weighment is in terms of kilograms 'vis' (1400 grams) as a weighing measure is in local use in some of the Valaya communities. Kilometre as a measure of distance is a long way to reach the Valayar. Kallu or mile is the unit used in respect to distance. Similarly, seldom do they use metres to measure lengths of cloth, etc. It is the old jaanu (about 9 inches), molam (one and a half feet) and gajam (yard) that are understood. Though hectare is the official unit of land, almost everybody speaks of his land, keeps account of his land, thinks of his land in terms of kuzhi. A kuzhi in southern districts of Tamil Nadu is 60 cents but in Chingleput and North Arcot, it is 6 ½ cents, called "gunta" in Telugu.

The use of old measures in measuring volume, surface and distance are found among many caste groups. The changeover to modern metric system or the common units used all over the country, depends on education of the community, their interaction and commerce with urban population, the nature of the community's occupation and profession. The change will be slow in the case of people who have far less to buy, sell (measurable things) and who are predominantly illiterate and far from urban social intercourse.

On Rameswaram Island, where the Valayar eke out their livelihood by fishing, kilogram is in common use among them. Fish are weighed and also sold as single pieces. At the same time, the Valayar in Valayapatti when they sell honey they speak in terms of and use 'padis', arapadis, ozhakku, all old measures, and not in terms of litres or milliliters. They are at home when they use the old local measures. Naturally, the adherence to the old system is found mostly among women and the old among both the sexes.

TABLE 13 : Range of Indebtedness of Families in Valayapatti and Sendhi

Name of the Village	Below Rs. 100	101-300	301-500	501-750	751-1000	1001-1500	1501-2000	2001-2500	Above Rs.2500	Total
No. 50 Valayapatti	12 (30.77)	9 (23.08)	7 (17.95)	1 (2.56)	3 (7.68)	2 (5.12)	1 (2.56)	- -	4 (10.24)	39 (100)
N44 Sendhi	4 (11.76)	9 (26.47)	7 (20.59)	1 (2.99)	2 (5.88)	4 (11.76)	5 (12.70)	1 (2.94)	1 (2.94)	34 (100)
Total	16 (21.91)	18 (24.65)	14 (19.19)	2 (2.74)	5 (6.85)	6 (8.22)	6 (8.22)	1 (1.37)	5 (6.85)	73 (100)

* The figures in parenthesis are percentages to the total number of debtor families.

TABLE 14: Sources of Borrowing

Village	Government	Coop	Money-lenders	Traders	Farmers	Relatives	Others
Valayapatti	1	12	6	4	3	18	25
Sendhi	-	1	1	1	32	11	2
Total	1	13	7	5	35	29	27

Problem of Indebtedness

Under the foregoing conditions of income and expenditure with all simplicity in their food, dress and shelter, the majority of the Valayar are forced to go in for loans around the year. The indebtedness, the range of indebtedness, sources of borrowing and purposes for which money was borrowed are discussed in respect to Valayapatti and Sendhi

Of the 94 families in Valayapatti and Sendhi, 77.66 percent (73) of the families are indebted; in the case of Valayapatti, it is 78 percent and in Sendhi it is 77.27 percent. In respect to the total population of the two villages the highest percentage (24.65) are indebted in the range of Rs. 101-300, followed by 21.91 percent below Rs. 100 and 19.19 percent from Rs. 301-500 and others come in the range of Rs. 501 and above Rs. 2500. Looking at both villages individually more or less the same percentage distribution of families in terms of range of indebtedness is seen. As pointed out earlier, the Valayar of Valayapatti are economically a little backward compared to Sendhi and this phenomenon is seen in the number of indebted families in the lower range. While 30.77 percent of the families in Valayapatti are indebted below Rs. 100, the percentage under this category for Sendhi is 11.96 percent only.

Sources of Borrowing

The main sources of borrowing for the two communities are government, village credit co-operative societies, professional money-leders, traders, farmers, relatives, and others. Farmers who are non-Valayar (outsiders in the case of Valayapatti and insiders and outsiders in the case of Sendhi), relatives and others constitute the chief sources of borrowing for both the communities.

As shown in Tables 13 and 14 the highest number (25) of Valaya families out of 39 in Valayapatti had borrowed from 'others'. The item called 'others' in the case of Valayapatti is the Gandhigram Rural Institute, which had carried on some extension and service programmes in the village. The Institute had advanced interest-free loans for food, farm expenses and social functions. But in the case of Sendhi, out of 34 indebted families, 32 had borrowed from 'farmers'. This is owing to the economic relationship between the Sendhi Valayar and non-Valaya farmers from Sendhi and neighbouring villages. Since farming and cultivation of paddy is the chief occupation of the Valayar of Sendhi, the need created by their farm expenses and credit worthiness and security it affords to the non-valaya farmers, bring them and the farmers into this economic interaction. Next in frequency in the case of both the villages is 'relatives': Valayapatti-18, Sendhi, followed by Cooperatives-12 in the case of Valayapatti. Though there is a co-operative society in Sendhi, and farming being the chief occupation for the Valayar, it is interesting to note that only one family has obtained credit from the village co-operative society. Money-lenders constitute a considerable source for Valayapatti and it is negligible in case of Sendhi. Traders matter a little, as source of credit for Valayapatti. This is as a result of their contact with their forest products and crops of the plantations on the Sirumalais. But a trader as a source of credit is negligible in the case of Sendhi. It is significant to note that government as a source of credit is nil in the case of Sendhi and with a sole case in Valayapatti. Still the Valayar are shy of approaching government sources. It is not fear, but a vast gulf persists between the governmental bureaucracy and the villagers especially backward groups like Valayar.

The Valayar (true in most other cases) depend on multiple sources for their credit needs. An individual family may borrow from more than one source, but usually such multiple-sources cases are few. In the case of the two villages, 24 households from each village have borrowed from a single source, 9 again from each village from two sources, one family in Sendhi from three sources, four in Valayapatti from four sources, and two of Valayapatti have borrowed from more than four sources.

In respect to interest charged on loans it is fixed in the case of government and co-operatives. Farmers, depending on the amount and time taken for repayment charge interest at the prevailing rate. The question of charging interest depends on the intimacy between the lender and the borrower. Usually, short terms hand-loans are interest free. The question of charging interest by relatives depends on the degree of relationship. Traders normally advance money to the Valayar toward some farm produce or forest products. It is the professional money-lender (a well-known fact) who charges a high rate of interest. Further, pawnbrokers are another source of credit for the Valayar. In times of emergency and acute conditions the Valayar pawn brass utensils, silver and gold ornaments. Brass utensils are pawned more frequently. This practice obtains in Valayapatti and Sendhi in the case of considerable number of families.

Purposes of borrowing

The majority of the Valayar are at subsistence level and their credit needs are related to their food, clothing, medicine, socio-religious ceremonies and occupational requirements. The major purpose for which money is borrowed comprises food followed by clothing and medicine. During the off-season or part of the year as the case may be to sustain themselves, the Valayar go in for short loans for purchasing foodgrains. They buy clothes on certain festive and ceremonial occasions. When it is obligatory to wear new clothes, and when they could not afford buying by themselves they go in for credit. In the present study, 25 families of Valayapatti and 23 families of Sendhi have borrowed money for the purpose of food, clothing and medicine. Socioreligious functions such as puberty ceremony, marriage, celebration of a deity, etc., as purpose, have a frequency of 16 and 10 families respectively of Valayapatti and Sendhi. Besides, they go in for loans to meet the cultivation expenses. Nineteen families in Sendhi and twelve in Valayapatti have obtained loans for meeting occupational expenses. The Sendhi Valayar cultivate paddy and they apply chemical fertilisers to paddy. The cost of cultivation in the case of Sendhi is higher than it is in Valayapatti and this makes the Sendhi Valayar go in for more of occupational loans. Only one family in Sendhi has incurred debt for the purpose of house construction.[52]

Jajmani Relations

The Valayar as Hindus come under the socio-economic relationship with other caste-groups. They receive services and goods from Washerman, Barber, chakkiliar, Thoti, Kottukaran, Urimikaran, Valluvan, Carpenter, Blacksmith, Koravan and Potter and in return, these servicing and occupational caste-groups are paid remuneration in kind in the shape of grain or any farm produce. The jajmani relationship as a complex institution prevails all over rural India. But this institution in respect to certain servicing and caste-groups is fast changing and this change is a universal phenomenon and the Valayar too experience these changes. We may briefly discuss here the jajmani relations and the changes thereof in respect to the Valayar. Though data on the institution were restricted to Valayapatti and Sendhi, what is discussed here holds good in the case of all other Valayar in Tamil Nadu.

Washerman

The washerman collects the soiled clothes of his Valaya jajmans twice or thrice a week and washes them.[53] Washing of clothes is a regular and major service. Besides this, the washerman or the washerwoman figures at certain events in the life cycle of an individual. It is the washerwoman who cleans the room where the confinement has taken place and she washes the blood-stained clothes of the mother. When a girl has her first menses, it is the washerwoman who conducts the girl to a well or a stream and helps her in her bathing and supplies her a set of washed clothes after every bath and washes the soiled ones. On the occasion of the marriage, the washerman supplies white cloth and puts up the canopy underneath the green pandals and he supplies the groom a change of clothes (a dhoti and a towel) after the groom's ritual bath before he changes over to the marriage clothes. The washerman figures in the funeral processions and funeral rites. The Valayar of Valayapatti and Sendhi receive these services. In case of Sendhi, one washerman family has been serving them for the past several generations. The washer man's residence is located in the Valaya Street in Sendhi. The washerman is paid grain after harvest of paddy in the case of Sendhi Valayar and the quantity of remuneration depends upon the size of the family. The remuneration per annuam ranges from 20 to 50 kg. Besides the annual payment of grain, the washerman collects food in the morning and evening from his clientele households. The washerman is paid both in kind and cash for his specific services on the occasions mentioned above. There is every likelihood of the washerman family at Sendhi serving the Valayar there for years to come for there is no thinking on their part to change the washerman.

But in the case of Valayapatti the position is different. Earlier, two washerman families, residents of Chettiapatti were serving the Valayapatti people. Now there is no such jajmani relationship with any washerman family. But the services of some washerman and women are solicited. In the case of Sendhi there is sustained income for the Valayar from farming and further Sendhi is a multicaste community and the washerman there serves other caste-groups also. In the case of Valayapatti, since the majority live on collection and sale of firewood, it is a question of their earning in terms of money and once they started introducing money in the place of grain, the jajmani sort of relationship could not be sustained and so there is no fixed washerman family having jajmani relationship with the Valayar of Valayapatti. It may be observed that of all the caste-occupational groups that come under jajmani relationship, the washerman appears to be viable and not so much affected by the changes taking place in the jajmani institution. This applies to the Valayar also.

Barber

The ritual or ceremonial importance of the barber in the life of the Valayar has not changed but his jajmani relationship with Valayar in terms of his services—face shaving, head shaving, hair cutting have been undergoing changes. The barber in the case of Sendhi is a native of the village and resides in the same village serves the Valayar and receives remuneration in the shape of grain. As in the case of washerman, the remuneration depends on the size of the family. Here it is the male members that are reckoned with.

In the case of Valayapatti also, it is a particular barber family (residing at Chettiapatti) no servicing or occupational caste-family resides at Valayapatti) that serves the Valayar there. Usually, for tonsure services, the barber in the case of Valayapatti visits the village on Thursdays (self-declared holiday for Valayapatti market day at Chinnalapatti) and stays throughout the day (of course depending on the number of clients) in the village attending to tonsure services. Though still the hereditary jajmani relationship is maintained in the case of Sendhi Valayar, it has changed in the case of Valayapatti. While the Sendhi people continue to pay the remuneration to the barber in kind (20 to 30 kilograms) annually or after harvest of paddy crops, in the case of Valayapatti, for some ten to fifteen years now, they pay money to the barber (shaving – twenty paise, hair- cutting –fifty to seventy-five paise). But the fee paid (kanikai) for the service rendered by the barberman of woman has not undergone any change.

Besides the tonsure services, the barber woman in Sendhi (in many Valaya villages) attends to midwifery cases. She attends to the delivery of the child, cuts the umbilical cord, washes the child, and acts as a medicine man for the mother and the child. She is fed on the days she is employed on such work, and she is paid for in cash (Rs. 2.00 in Sendhi). In the case of tonsure ceremony, (in the case of first shaving of the children both at Valayapatti and Sendhi –for that matter among all Valayar) the barber is invited and he attends to tonsure. He is given food and a fixed fee (in Sendhi and Valayapatti it is fifty paise). Any extra payment depends on the ability of the client-family.

The barber figures on the funeral day also.[54] In some villages where the Valayar too are his clientele, the barber functions as a native physician and surgeon. Further, in some villages the barbers are the drum-beaters 'nadaswaram'. They are engaged on marriage occasions and for such services they are paid a fee agreed prior to their engagement.

The barber, with changes in some cases in the pattern of remuneration paid and the kind of services rendered by him, continues to play his role in the jajmani system.

Chakkiliar

The Chakkiliar are the leather workers. In Tamil Nadu, they are known as chakkilians and Madharis. They are migrants from Andhra Pradesh and Karnataka and speak Telugu and Kananada. They make and mend leather buckets used in lift-irrigation. Wherever lift-irrigation through mohte (device for drawing water) is prevalent, the Chakkiliar (cobblers) attend to the making and mending of the leather buckets. In the case of Valayapatti and Sendhi, a few Valaya households still continue to receive this service from the Chakkiliar. The remuneration depends on the number of leather buckets maintained by the farmer at the rate of 40 kg. per leather bucket. Most Valaya farmers who still continue lift-irrigation through mhote will maintain (use) only one leather bucket. The Chakkiliar for Valayapatti are from Chettiapatti and for Sendhi from a neighbouring village. Formally, the cobblers used to (even now to a considerable extent) make sandals for the Valayar.

In some cases (for example Valayapatti) the chakkiliar attend to the disposal of dead cattle, flaying of the dead animal and processing of the hide which is given back to the jajman. For flaying one head of cattle, they are paid Rs. 3.00 to Rs. 5.00. The Chakkiliar in the case of some Valaya communities, are engaged as drum-beaters during marriages. These functions (in the case of Sendhi) in some valaya and non-Valaya villages are traditionally carried on by the Pariaher. They are paid on each such occasion an amount ranging from Rs. 10.00 to Rs. 15.00 and also fed on that day.

In the case of Valayar of Valayapatti, the Chakkiliar of Chettiapatti are the hereditary drum-beaters when the Valayar celebrate their deities. The drum-beaters are paid their fee in cash besides perquisites like food on the festive occasions.

But by large, the jajmani relationship between the Valayar and the Chakkiliar borne out of farming is on the decline. One chief reason for this decline is the installation of electric motor pumpsets by farmers for irrigation. Here it is a technological innovation on the part of the jajmans that brought in the change in the jajmani relationship.

Pariaher

The Pariaher are the Tamil-speaking Scheduled Caste. As in the case of Chakkiliar, the Pariaher serve the Valayar (as they do innumerable caste-Hindus and artisans) as disposers of and flayers of dead cattle, as drum-beaters, menial village servants and messengers (Thoti). In Sendhi, till recently, the Pariaher in the village were serving the Valayar. They were paid money and fed and supplied with toddy or other intoxicants – whenever they were engaged for drum beating. The Kottukarans (drum-beaters) and Thotis (village menial servants-cum-messengers) are from Pariaher. It may be noted that Kottukarans are from chakkiliar too.

The 'thotiship' is a hereditary right held by a Pariah community. Within the Pariah community, year after year, it may go in rotation among men in a clan or several clans in the same village or it may be retained by one family, the incumbency passing on from father to son and so on.

In the case of Valayapatti, the Thoti is from Chinnalapatti (3 km. from Valayapatti). The Valayar call him 'Pillaikutti Thoti'. He is considered to be a son of the Valaya community. In the case of death of a destitute Valaya (theoretically), the Pillaikutti Thoti plays the role of a son to the deceased. He is paid remuneration by every Valayar household at the time of harvest of crops or in lieu cash. The quantity of grain given to him ranges from 3 kg. to 6 kg. depending upon the status of the jajman family. Usually, he goes to the threshold and collects his grain from his jajmans. If he wants, he can collect food from his clientele both in the morning and in the evening. The Thoti functioning as the son of Valaya community in a given village is prevalent in Madurai and Ramnad districts.

As mentioned earlier, the jajmani relationship between the Kottukarans and the Valayar continues, since it is related to their celebration of their deities. It is a religious and ritual necessity.[55]

Urimikarans

Urimikarans are a Scheduled Caste. They speak Telugu. They are a sub-caste among cobblers though they claim themselves superior to the cobblers. They style themselves as 'Naidu', middle ranking caste-Hindus. They play a drum originally called 'Devadhundhubhi'.[56] The instrument is played by both hands, and on the left side, it is played with a curved stick and on the right, with hand. The curved stick when passed over the skin with pressure produces a 'rrum' sound and so it is called 'Urumi' and the group that plays it is called' Urimikarans;. These drums are mainly used in rural areas and that too in the celebration of village deities. The Valayar invariably engage the Urimikarans when they celebrate their deities. It is a jajmani relationship. The Urimikaran collects his remuneration in the shape of grain from each Valaya household once a year during the harvest of the main crop in the area. Besides this annual collection of grain, the Urimikaran is fed during the days he is engaged in playing the drum and he is also paid cash (about Rs. 5.00). He also collects money (small changes) from the individual Valayar during the festival.

As in case of several servicing and occupational caste-groups, the Urimikarans serve some villages and they have jurisdictional right over those villages. The profession is hereditary and the sons in a family divide among themselves the number of villages in the family's jurisdiction.

The Valayar of Valayapatti and Sendhi engage Urimikaran when they celebrate their caste deities and the jajmani relation between the Valayar and the Urimikarans continues as of old days.

Valluvan

Valluvan are a Scheduled Caste, but by virtue of their profession as astrologers and medicine men, socially they are far above the Pariaher and Chakkiliar. The Valluvan is an astrologer for the Valayar. In case of Valayar of Valayapatti, the Valluvan (who resides in a village near Kodai Road 12 km from Valayapatti) visits them during the harvest time and collects his remuneration from his Valaya clientele is interesting. The Valluvan keeps his palm upside down and drives the palms into the grain heap and draws the grain. He repeats drawing grain in this fashion five times. He could collect only a limited quantity of grain in this way. This method of his collecting remuneration shows that no importance is given to the quantity of remuneration. The manner in which the Valluvan collects the grain and quantity thereof shows that the remuneration collected is nominal and symbolic of his jajmani relationship with the Valayar. The Valluvan (the term 'Valluvan' is used both in singular and plural form) are placed low in the caste-hierarchy.

As in the case of other groups, the Valluvan has certain villages under his jurisdiction. But his jajmani relationship with the Valayar (for example in the case of Valayapatti) is on the decline.

Carpenter

The Valayar who are farmers have jajmani relations with carpenter. He makes the plough and other wooden agriculture implements for the Valaya farmers. Besides this, he helps the local Valayar with the making of doors, windows and other sundry household equipment. The carpenter receives remuneration from the Valayar for the ploughs he makes and cash payment in respect to other items of work.

In the case of Sendhi, the carpenter (the same man does the smithy black also) resides in Sendhi itself, and for generations, the same carpenter family has been having jajmani relationship with the Valayar. Since farming and that too paddy cultivation is the chief occupation of the Valayar of Sendhi, the jajmani relation of payment of the remuneration is in the shape of grain. The remuneration per annum per farm-family depends on the number of ploughs the individual family maintains, and it ranges from 15 to 30 kg. of paddy.

On the other hand, the position in the case of the Valayar of Valayapatti is different. At the moment, they have no carpenter with whom they have jajmani relation. It was reported that about two decades ago, a carpenter family resident at Chettiapatti served the Valayar under the jajmani system, but since then the jajmani relationship slowly declined. One of the reasons in the case of Valayapatti may be that theirs is dry farming and the crops are rainfed. There is always uncertainty of the crops and further, farming is not the occupation for the majority of the Valayar of Valayapatti.

Since there is no regular carpenter for them in the jajmani sense, they get their ploughs and other wooden implements made by the carpenters in Chinnalapatti and Chettiapatti on payment of cash. Of all the Valaya farm-families in Tamil Nadu the above two are the possible patterns. But on the whole, in view of the new type of ploughs and new farm practices, the jajmani type of relations between the carpenter and the Valaya jajmains is on the decline.

Blacksmith

In the case of blacksmith also, the jajmani relations are mostly in the case of Valaya farm-families. The blacksmith makes and sets the share to the plough, makes spades, crowbars, hoes, aruval and iron implements for the Valayar. The above items of work fall under jajmani system. Besides these, the blacksmith attends to work connected with construction of houses for which he is paid cash either on contract or piece-work basis. As in the case of carpenter, the blacksmith also collects his remuneration during the harvest time from each of his jajmans and the quantity of grain ranges from 10 to 20 kg.

In the case of Sendhi, the jajmani relations between the blacksmith and the Valayar continue in full measure, but in the case of Valayapatti, the meeting of black smithy needs of the Valayar are not institutionalised. The Valayar of Valayapatti get their implements (aruval, pickaxe, silukku, plough shares, hoes etc.) made by the blacksmith resident at Chettiapatti and Chinnalapatti, the two neighbouring centres. Sometimes, they buy these implements from the Dindigul town. In respect to other Valayar population in the State, it may be said that both the jajmani system and cash purchase of implements and other domestic appliances prevail.

Potter

In view of the level of living of the Valayar in general, and the domestic utensils they use and could afford to use, the jajmani relationship between them and the potter is enduring and strong. As discussed earlier under material culture, the majority of the Valayar use chiefly earthenware for cooking and storing grain.

The potter supplies his Valaya clientele, usually in the month of January on the eve of Pongal, a set of earthenware varying in size, type and utility. The clientele visit the potter and collect the set of ware. In addition to the domestic earthenware, the potter supplies small saucer like earthen lamps, for the festival of 'Kaarthigai' which is celebrated in the month of November. Further, the potter supplies two earthen pots on the funeral day. One is used for cooking rice and the other is used for carrying burning faggots, both of which are carried to the burial ground. The above supplies come under the jajmani arrangement. Besides, the potter supplies the bridegroom family, a set of painted and decorated pottery in different sizes which are placed near the marriage dais. Though this service and supply are customary, the potter is paid money for this exclusive service. The potter is one of the important non-Valayar that figures in the Valayar marriages.

The potter does not dine at a Valayar house (for that matter the smiths also do not). He collects his remuneration in the shape of grain during the harvest of the main crops in the area. The Valayar of Valayapatti and Sendhi have jajmani relations with their respective potters. In case of both the communities, the potters are from the neighbouring villages.

While mostly men deal with the Carpenter, Blacksmith, Kottukaran, Urimikaran, Chakkilians in respect to securing their services and supplies, it is predominantly women who deal and intensely interact with the potter. It is the women who choose, who are to be satisfied in respect to the earthenware supplied to them. It is interesting to observe the dialogue, arguments, quarrels between the potters and the Valaya women when the latter visit the former to pick up their wares.

Koravar

The Koravar in Tamil Nadu are a denotified tribe. Their occupation is mat and basket weaving and they bore ear-lobes of Valaya girls facilitating the wearing of *'thandati'* and *chavidi.* The Koravar though spread in the South India, they appear to have jajmani relations with a few castes in the districts of Madurai, Ramnad and Tirunelveli. They have jajmani relations with the Valayar and they supply their clientele with mats and Palmyra baskets once a year, the number ranging from 2 to 4. They also mend old baskets at the residence of their clientele or at a common place in the jajman's village. The Koravar are paid paddy or any other grain once a year during the harvest of crops, the quantity ranging from 8 to 12 kg. They camp in the villages of their clientele in the months of January and February for weaving and repairing baskets. During their stay in the villages, they collect food from the houses of their clientele (who include non-Valayar also). As in the case of other servicing caste-groups, Koravar have hereditary rights of their profession over certain villages. The jajmani relations between Koravar and the Valayar continue even today. There has been no change in the pattern of their relationship. Both men and women among the Koravar weave and repair baskets. In the case of the Koravar too, it is the Valaya women who interact more and carry on business with them. Baskets and ear-boring relate to Valaya women. It may be noted here that the jajmani type of relation between the Valayar and Koravar is localised in the districts of Madurai, Ramnad and Tirunelveli.[57]

SUMMARY

The Valayar are a poly-occupational group. They are engaged in a variety of economic pursuits determined and influenced by the ecological and environmental conditions. They are engaged in more than thirty economic activities. The number of households engaged in these occupations and professions ranges from a very small to a large number. At one end of the continuum the Valayar are engaged in hunting and collection of wild products and at the other end in farming farm-labour, fishing, collection of firewood and a combination of these. Farming, farm-labour and collection of firewood are the chief occupations of the Valayar of Valayapatti and Sendhi and the majority of the populations in the two villages are engaged within their family occupations. In the case of land-owners, tenants and farm-labourers, women workers outnumber men-workers. The women have equal share in the economic burden of the family.

In respect of the Valaya population in Tamil Nadu, a little over one-third is engaged in farming, one-fourth in farm-labour and about one-sixth in fishing and the rest of the population pursue miscellaneous occupations and professions, (brick works, match and fire works, piggery, well digging, bangle selling, etc.) and a combination of farming-farm-labour and fishing. Most of the farm implements used by the Valayar are traditional. As farm-labourers they work in their own and neighbouring villages and serve both Valaya and non-Valaya farmers. There is a little seasonal migration of labour within and outside the districts. There is considerable juvenile labour among the Valayar. There is a considerable incidence of crime such as dacoity, robberies, and thefts among the Valayar of Coimbatore district and to a less degree in Palani taluk and sporadically in other places.

The Valayar own livestock like cattle, sheep, goats, and poultry and the cattle serve them for draft purposes in farming and sheep, goats and poultry supplement their income. In respect to the sources and income in the case of Valayapatti and Sendhi, the major income for Valayapatti is through sale of firewood and in Sendhi it is through farming. One-half of the households in Valayapatti and Sendhi have an annual income ranging from below Rs.300.00 to Rs.1,000.00 and the other half in the range of Rs.1001.00 to above 1500.00 and nearly two-thirds of the households incur a monthly expenditure below Rs.100.00 and in the case of the remaining households the monthly expenditure does not exceed Rs.250.00. About four-fifths of their income is spent over food. The Valayar in general are habituated to chewing and smoking and some to drinking toddy and alcohol. The nutritional quality of the food consumed by the Valayar is poor.

A majority of the Valayar in Valayapatti and Sendhi are indebted and they borrow money mostly from farmers and relatives. They incur debt chiefly for their food and social and religious ceremonies.

The Valayar have jajmani relations with castes such as Washerman, Barber, Koravar, Carpenter, Blacksmith, Valluvan, Potter, Chikkiliar and Pariaher. In some cases these relations are on the decline and in some enduring as of old days.

The Valayar as a group are economically backward, traditional in the styles of their occupations with their moorings in the past.

REFERENCES

1. For example, when the chief occupation of the family is farming, a member in the family may mostly work in collecting firewood or as farm-labourer besides his/her attending to family occupation (partly).
2. Census of India, 1921, Volume XIII, Madras, Part-I, P. 220.
3. We have a considerable preponderance of combinations of occupations among the Valayar.
4. A few cases of those who have lost their lands in the above manner may be given below:

(i) Chinnakannu, w/o Muthukala had sold one acre of land on the Sirumlais to a Muslim of Dindigul for a paltry sum of Rs, 100 for buying foodstuffs and the present value is above Rs. 3000. She sold a sixty cent piece to a Gounder for Rs. 25. These two sale deeds took place twenty-five years ago.

(ii) Ilunganambalam s/o Vellayanambalam disposed of one acre of plantation land on the hills to a Muslim for buying grain for food and his son ten years ago, sold half an acre of garden land for Rs. 500.00 which is worth now Rs. 5000.00 Most of the lands were thus lost and now the extent of their land is reduced to one-fourth of what it was fifty years ago.

5. A.R. Ayyadorai of Kumarapatti, three kilometers from Sendhi village.
6. See Table 2 in Appendix I.
7. The author in the course of his field work chanced to meet a group of mendicants who were professionals. They were from a village called 'Andipatti' in Madurai district. The village gets its name after the personal noun 'andi' in Tamil and it means 'mendicant'. When translated it means 'mendicants' or 'beggars' village'. When questioned as to why they were going for alms they answered we are professional beggars. This is our 'Kula Vrithi' (caste occupation). We do own houses and some lands too. But we spend six months in a year going about villages for alms. If we do not go for alms we shall be failing in our duty and thus get ourselves ruined'. This is how one justifies or rationalizes one's behaviour.
8. It was reported that a Valaya youth some twenty years ago working on the hills as an attached labourer to a Konar planter while plucking a jack fruit, lost his hold, fell down from the tree and lost his life. This tragic end of a Valaya youth has discouraged them to hire themselves as plantation labourers on the hills for a couple of years.
9. A catch which the author noted at the coast on the Rameswaram Island in the month of November 1972, was auctioned just on the spot immediately after coasting the net, for Rs.7.50. Twenty-one men were engaged in this group that was their earning for the day.
10. Some of the Valayar on the island who are not engaged in fishing are employed as domestic servants by Brahmin. The Brahmin section have no liking for the fishing section of the Valayar..
11. Figures as on 11-11-1972 obtained from the office of the Asst. Director of Fisheries, Rameswaram.
12. There are 20 master fishermen among the Valayar at Karaiyur and in the neighbouring hamlets on the island.
13. In the Aruppukottai area of Ramnad district, the Valayar go about fishing in the summer months – right from January to April in ponds and tanks. Even if paddy harvests are going on, and when work is available for them, and a male paddy harvester is paid 3 measures of paddy (4 ½ kg) per day as wage, they prefer going afishing, even if the monetary value of their catch per day is far less than what they would earn as farm labourers. A simple question of values, taste, food and independence.
14. The Valayar living close the irrigation tanks cultivate cucumber and melons in the tank bed during summer. They pay a nominal rent of Rs. 1.25 per acre to the local village Panchayat.
15. See Appendix I Table 13 for a list of off-shore and inland fish the Valayar catch.
16. Forests have considerable importance in the life of the Valayar, not only do they draw part of their sustenance from forests but living close to the forests, they are spiritually, economically and emotionally attached to them. Some of their deities reside in the forests (Asalai, the seven virgin deities in the case of Valayapatti). They go to the forests for game, work in the forests as forest labourers and plantation workers, collect firewood, get their medicinal herbs from the forests, and also collect minor forest produce.
17. At Valayapatti for instance during the slack-season, ninety percent of the families buy their provisions every evening required for the day. It may be sorghum, rice, (very rarely), chillies, salt, tamarind, kerosene (for lamp) and spices. During the harvest of sorghum and other millets (November-January) for want of time to sundry the sorghum, the grain is roasted in mud pots, then pounded and chaff removed and then cooked.

18. A specimen of idikki is found in the Madras government Museum. It appears to be an ancient device and mostly used by the Valayar in Tamil Nadu.

19. The author, during his field work in Chittarevu in the beginning of 1973, was informed by the Valayar there, that they do go about catching rats as usual nowadays for food.

20. The following incident was reported to the author—Thirty years ago, a group of men from Valayapatti went to Sirumalais on hunting expedition. They sighted a male deer and they fired ten shots at it with the two muzzle loading guns they were carrying about them, but the guns did not fire. They felt it strange and Alagunambalam, a member in the group asked the gunmen to fire into the sky and all the five shots were successful. The group was convinced that some one in the group has played some thing foul incurring the displeasure of the gods and so the guns failed when aimed at the game. On the suggestion of the ambalakarar, a fire was made and the gods were invoked to help them know the culprit in the group and the reasons for the strange behaviour of the muskets when aimed at the game. While the gods were being invoked, Andiabalam, one of the men in the group got possessed and he gave a blow to watcher Chedayanambalam (a then important man in the village) and admonished him that though he was not to be blamed, the deity was drawing his attention as man that mattered in the village, and so saying the medium caught hold of one Ganapathi, whose brother, the medium declared, had committed an act amounting to incest. Thought it was Ganapathi's brother who was alleged to have committed incest, Ganapathi was dropped from the hunting group. The deity through the medium, directed the group to proceed in a particular direction and assured them that they would be rewarded with game. The group did as directed by the deity and killed the very same deer they encountered earlier in the day Naganambalam, brother of Ganapathi was alleged to have had a sexual union with wife of one of his paternal uncles which according to the norms of the community amounts to incest. The media of gods work as control on the deviants and potential deviants in the community. May be the persons who become the media of deities have knowledge of some violations on the part of some individuals in the community. Celebration or propitiation of deities is the occasion on which such persons are exposed (through the media) and ridiculed at. The revelations and observations made by the deities through the media play

21. The author had an opportunity of witnessing a male langur being flayed and worked into meat. The man who shot it down carried his precious game all the way from the hills to the village. The shooting of the langur locally called mandai was an important event in the village community. It was nine o'clock in the night. Almost the entire community gathered at the residence of the man (Chembagam) who killed the game. The ambalakarar (the caste council chief) himself attended to the flaying of the animal with all ceremonious seriousness. There were others who busied themselves cutting the meat into size. This operation was carried late into the night.

22. The Saragu Valayar of Algarkoil Valayapatti go on hunting expedition on the third day after the celebration of Karuppuchamy. If they succeed hunting any game, they arrange drum-beating on their return home. They celebrate their triumph with fire works and they spend Rs. 500.00 to Rs. 1000.00 over such celebration.

23. The Irula, a Scheduled tribe in South India, more especially in Tamil Nadu and Andhra Pradesh are professionals in catching snakes for skins. The Irula too go about catching rats, squirrels, birds for food and engage also in fishing, collection of firewood, honey and wild products.

24. On one occasion six men from Valayapatti had collected tender mangoes in a plantation belonging to a Naicker planter of Pudur on the Sirumalais. When the group entered the plantation and were preparing themselves to climb the trees for plucking mangoes, the watchman there, objected to their plucking mangoes. On this objection one of the men (Kalimuthu) questioned

the ownership of the plantation and asked the watchman to produce the patta (revenue record showing the ownership of the land) as evidence of ownership. The watchman took it as an insult and ridicule, and while the Valayar were engaged in the illicit plucking of mangoes ignoring the watchman, the latter went to the planter and reported the incident to him. Then one of the sons of the planter came to the Valayar and summoned them to his residence. All the six men were beaten severely and let off with the mangoes they have plucked.

It was reported that until a decade ago some of the Valayar of Valayapatti used to steal coffee beans, banana, lemon, mangoes, etc. They used to go to the hills during the night and steal things form private plantations. A few years ago a Valaya boy of Valayapatti was caught while stealing lemons and he was beaten so severely by the planter, the boy died the same night. The planter made it that the boy fell from a tree and died. During the past ten years the incidence of this type of stealing is on the decline.

25. See the occupational distribution of the population Tables 5-10 in Appendix I for details of distribution occupation-wise.

26. This temple employ has been there for the Valayar of a Valayapatti from remote times. The Valayar of this village claim that one of their ancestors discovered the (buried) idol of Alagar on the hills there while digging for wild roots. The first priest of this temple according to them was a Valayan but latter on, in view of the Valayan pre-occupation with hunting, etc., he or the community entrusted the priestly functions to Brahmin and retained to themselves the job of bearing of armament boxes of algar deity. They lament in a plaintive tone that they are economically and socially backward and so they have been relegated to a very minor status vis-à-vis the temple functions. Formerly, as bearers of the ornament boxes, they were enjoying 40 acres of the temple land. This manyam (gifted land-land with tenancy rights) has been since discontinued. In the words of the Valayar "The temple authorities know that we are god-fearing and that we consider material remuneration secondary and so they exploit us. Despite insignificant reward, we continue to discharge our sacred duty to our God by carrying His ornaments".

27. Besides the community's customary service to the temple, ten Valaya men are in the regular employ of the Alagar temple. One is a graduate clerk, another a matriculate accountant, three as weepers, three Para (watchmen) and two gardeners are paid a monthly salary of Rs. 75.00 and one Prasadam (two types of rice preparation—pepper rice and tamarind rice broth locally called milagusadam and pulisadam).

28. Renovation and extension of the Ranganatha temple is being carried on for some years now.

29. A census survey could be carried out on the number of Valaya educated-employed. The data that are furnished here were collected through personal contacts during the field work.

30. Government of Tamil Nadu, Notification Governing the Grant of Scholarships by the Department of Backward Classes—General Rules, 1971-72

31. Most of the material in this section is based on 'Criminological Survey of Valaya Crimes' Publication by Research Centre, CID, Madras, government of Tamil Nadu, 1965.

32. Figure according to the Criminological Survey of Valaya Crimes.

33. See Table 14 in Appendix I for the number of Valayar convinced (1959-63) for property and prohibition offences police station-wise in the district.

34. See Tables 15 and 16 in Appendix I for the numerical and percentage distribution of the Valaya convicts in the district for the period 1959-63.

35. See Appendix I for a brief account of the Habitual Offenders.

36. See Table 17 in Appendix I for the distribution of Valaya crimes, station-wise in Coimbatore district.

37. One educated non-Valaya acquaintance of the author who hails from a village near Rayarpalam warned him that he should not visit Rayarpalayam for his field work with watch, cash, any valuable article including the pen, lest they will rob of the visitor of such things.
38. In 1963, it was 115 households.
39. One of the nuclear villages for the present only.
40. The reasons or causes for the high incidence of crimes among the Valayar, suggest a separate depth-study which would throw light on their indulgence in criminal behaviour, when their caste people elsewhere are free from it.
41. Statistical Outline of India 1975 – Tata Services Limited, Department of Economics and Statistics, Bombay House, Bombay, p.7.
42. A family defined as a unit consisting of five members with a monthly income less than Rs.160 is considered to be falling under below poverty-line.
43. See Table 18, for details on the per capita consumer expenditure in Appendix I.
44. In the case of professional Valaya fishermen, fish is consumed almost every day.
45. The author has not come across a single Valaya family consuming ghee (clarified butter) as a constituent of their diet.
46. In the case of Valayar of Valayapatti who had provisions to draw sugar (one kilogram per month) through their ration cards from the Cooperative every month, no card-holder in the knowledge of the author drew his sugar quota. Instead, they allowed petty shopkeepers and others to draw the sugar every month against a payment of 75 paise to one rupee every month.
47. A Valaya informant informed the author that the use of neem oil as hair oil indicates the backwardness among them do not use neem oil.
48. The author in the course of his visits to Valaya villages in the districts of Madurai and Ramnad has not come across a single Valaya house electrified.
49. In the course of a group interview after nightfall, when the author requested the group to furnish details on Muniyandi deity, one Valaya gentleman by name of pricked chinnayya 46, a leader of the local community (Sendhi) said "If you could provide us with Vethalaipakku (betel-leaves), we would comply with your request". This has pricked the ego of Odayar a member in the group and he observed "You see sir, it is unfortunate that the Valaya community has gone down in the esteem of other caste-groups because of this practice of asking others for betel-nut, betel-leaves and tobacco".
50. The Kambli of Sendhi (Mayan) lamented that he was ashamed of his drinking. As the chief of the Sendhi Valaya community, he very much tried (as he said) to give up drinking in respect to his office but the habit had an upper hand and grip over him.
51. Nutritional Status of pre-school Children in a Rural Community (Valayapatti) (C.S. Gita Nalinakshi and R. Subramanian), Bulletin of the Gandhigram Institute of Rural Health & Family Planning, Vol. VI, No. 1, July 1971.
52. Unthoughtful and indiscriminate borrowing on the part of a few families in Valayapatti from the neighbouring Gounder resulted in the Valayar losing their lands in part on their failure to repay the money and further the creditors so manipulated in order to grab the lands of the Valayar.
53. Jajman is the one who receives services and supplies and the one who serves or supplies is called the Kam Karne Wallah in Hindi. Some other terms also are in use in respect to the above. 'Aya' is the remuneration paid for service rendered or the goods supplied, 'Aryadakula' is the service and goods receiver and 'Ayagara' is the one who serves and supplies goods.

54. The Pariaher in Sendhi as a measure of Sanskritizing themselves have stopped disposing of the dead cattle and beating of drums for the caste-Hindus including the Valayar.
55. The rate of change and discontinuance is more in occupational Jajmani relationship and less in social and religious areas.
56. It is claimed by the Urimikarans that this instrument was played in the court of Indra, the chief of Devas. They say they are the descendants of the players this skin instrument in the Indraloka.
57. As far as the author could gather.

CHAPTER 19

Model Schemes for Self-employment: Individuals, Families and Groups

One dependable and substantive and long term means of wriggling out of poverty is to go in for some micro or mini enterprise development either by the individual, family or a collectivity of a few individuals or families or sometimes a segment of the poor community taking up the enterprises listed below which have been designed and recommended by the Khadi and Village Industries Commission of India. The KVIC will provide and guide the initiatives of these projects. There are other agencies/banks which would help and support the sponsors. In the following pages, a list of small-scale mini or micro enterprises is listed with brief details in respect to the background of the enterprise and the prospects thereof. In respect to the prospects, the whole input and output details will be supplied by the Khadi and Village and Industries Commission and the entrepreneurs could approach the extension personnel working in the District Industries Centres (DIC's) in India. The list of enterprises or entrepreneurial prospects is the traditional and potential areas for any new venture that would gradually elevate the poor from the trap of poverty.

PROCESSING OF CEREALS AND PULSES INDUSTRY

Paddy Processing Unit

Product - Rice

I. Background

Processing of Cereals and Pulses Industry is an age old traditional industry which serves three purposes: (a) conserving foodgrains especially rice, (b) giving more nutritive and whole-some food and (c) providing employment to rural people especially women folk. It is accepted by one and all that hand pounded rice (less polished) has higher nutritional value than that of the milled rice. Rice being the staple diet for nearly 75 percent of Indian population, particularly in the poorer sections, it is all the more necessary that they are supplied with rice having more nutrition, and all possible efforts should be made to retain that nutritive content during the processing. When paddy is polished in the hullers and rice mills, many of these important elements contained in the grain are lost which can be retained and protected by hand pounding the paddy. Higher percentage of recovery is yet another feature of the activity.

II. Prospects

The decentralized processing of Cereals and Pulses Industry under the purview of KVIC has capacity of generation of large employment opportunities in the rural areas, especially for women folk. Introduction of handy, simple and efficient power driven equipment like paddy dehusker and rice polisher will increase the earnings of artisans and also the quality of the rice processed.

Dal Processing Family Unit

I. Background

Pulses and its various products are in common use in Indian food and diet. For almost all the families in India, both in urban and rural areas, pulses and its number of preparations are more or less indispensable part of their food. Among the different varieties of pulses grown in the country Tur dal, Moong dal and Grams are prominent. Pulses processed on hand operated chakkis are more nutritious and tasty than the mill processed pulses. It is one of the oldest traditional activities of India and it has large scope for generation of employment opportunities among women folk in rural areas, especially during off season. The marketing of pulses and its products is not at all a problem. It is easily sold at the nearby areas of production. By introducing improved tools and implements, it can increase the earnings of the artisans without any loss of nutritional value of the pulses.

Papad Making Family Unit

I. Background

Papad making is fairly common activity in all the states. With the changing pattern of living and urbanization, the practice of purchasing Papad from the market is growing fast. The family unit envisaged in the scheme can provide quality Papad to consumers and employment to 5 women in their own houses and thereby provide net annual earning of Rs. 1,200 to each of the working women.

I. Assumptions

As papad making is a traditional work in our families, the ladies do not require any training for a long period. But as the commodity is for commercial sales, the uniformity, quality control and systematic packaging etc. will no doubt be necessary.

It is presumed that with the growing demand for the commodity the family would not be facing any problem as far as the marketing is concerned.

Poha and Murmura Family Unit

I. Background

Poha (beaten rice) and Murmura (Puffed rice) are in common use in India. Varieties of Preparations are made out of poha and murmura which are quite tasty. Moreover they possess high nutritive value. With commercialisation of the activity, the sale of these eatables is on the increase both in villages as well as in urban areas. The traditional artisans require financial assistance to carry on these occupations in the self-employed sector. It provides employment at the place of residence of the artisan and such individual artisan processes and sells the products in the nearby areas. Consequently they do not require any help for marketing their products.

II. Assumptions

With a view to assisting the traditional artisans in the self-employed sector who are finding it difficult to get necessary finance for the activity, this family unit has been proposed. Two to five members of the family will be employed on full time basis and their earnings would be increased due to continuous work. The productivity of the artisans will also be increased by providing improved tools and equipment. The family members of the artisan will also be assisting in the activity.

Bakery Products Family Unit

I. Background

Bakery is one of the schemes of Processing of Cereals and Pulses Industry which has been included under the purview of the KVIC with a view to generate employment opportunities in small towns and in villages. With a small investment, enriched food products like breads, buns, nankhatais and biscuits etc. can be produced and made available to the common man. It can provide full time employment to one baker and two helpers or a baker and two members of his family. There are two types of bakery units under the purview of KVIC. "A:" type bakery is for small towns with a population of about 10.000 each and "B" type unit is for villages with a population of about 5,000 each.

Bhar Bhuja, Roasting Channa, Dalia and Murmura - Family Unit

I. Background

Parched channa (checkpeas), murmura (puffed rice), dalia etc, are the nutritious eatables. The sale of these eatables is common in the villages as well as in urban areas. The traditional artisans require some financial assistance to carry on this occupation in the self employed sector. Since, it provides employment at the place of residence of the artisan and he can market his product in the nearby areas, he does not need any assistance for marketing.

II. Assumptions

This family unit is proposed with a view to assisting the self-employed artisans who find it difficult to procure necessary finance for the activity. Two persons will be employed on full time basis.

GHANI OIL INDUSTRY

Ghani Processing of Edible Oil Seeds

I. Introduction

The edible oil production activities on ghanis are carried out by village artisans known Telis, ghanichi, chettiar, vaniyan etc. Due to the importance of edible oil in human diet, the activities of oilseed pressing found an important place in socio-economic life of the rural India since ages. With the advent of industrialization and in-roads of mechanized expellers of different sizes in urban and semi-urban areas, the artisans were affected adversely in their traditional occupation and large number of them was compelled to search new avocation for their livelihood. It was at this stage the KVIC embarked upon this programme and extended financial, technical and organizational assistance. The application of power to ghani improved considerably the remunerative capacity of ghani. According to nutritional experts the desirable level of edible oil and fat consumption per capita has been 57 grams per day as against 9 Grams available today.

II. Prospectus

The introduction of power ghani in place of the traditional bullock ghani will certainly help both artisan and consumer i.e. the former by way of increased income/earnings and the latter in getting pure, fresh and nutritious product at a reasonable rate at their door step. There is a definite consumer preference for the product and it does not face any marketing problem. However, they may face financial difficulty in stocking raw materials which are usually seasonally available and finished products in beginning for about two or three months. This problem can be solved either by providing adequate financial assistance to the artisans or by setting up of service institutions in centrally located areas from where they can avail of the facility of purchasing raw-material as and when they need.

III. Assumption

(i) Khadi and V. I. Commission may arrange to supply standardized tools and equipment to the artisans through the approved manufacturers. It may also help the artisans in the procurement of raw materials.

(ii) Khadi and V. I. Commission may also arrange for adequate training facilities, if required.

(iii) The scheme is intended for self-employed, educated unemployed, agricultural landless labourers and the traditional ghani artisans who want to switch over to improved methods.

(iv) It is therefore assumed that the family members of artisans would also assist him in the activities.

(v) Bank Finance has been recommended only to the extent of 80 percent of the total financial requirement for setting up of the ghani unit including working capital. It is expected that the individual would invest his own funds to the tune of balance 20 percent as seed capital.

VILLAGE LEATHER INDUSTRY

I. Manufacture of Footwears

I. Background

Footwear manufacture is one of the ancient household village crafts of the country. By and large the cobblers in rural area are doing the work as a traditional and hereditary occupation. The artisans of this industry come from the socially and economically backward strata of the community and are working in their houses with the members of their families. Because of their illiteracy and financial difficulty the rural cobblers are finding it difficult to change their work habit and adopt improved methods of production. However, they are hardworking and prefer to work on individual basis along with the members of their families. Therefore, it is proposed that they may be encouraged by giving the required improved tools and implements. Due to the continuous persuation by the various agencies especially the KVIC, the cobblers are now gradually changing their habits and adopting modern techniques in their work. However, this process is slow.

II. Prospects

The footwears manufactured by the cobblers who are residing in the tehsil towns or in district places have good retail demand locally. Sometimes they sell their footwears to wholesale merchants. They are quite conversant with their crafts and some of them are ready to accept changes in designs and patterns. With the overall improvement in the standard of living of the people, the demand of footwears is bound to increase.

III. Objectives

The main objectives of the scheme are to enable the cobblers to provide fuller work and higher earnings. For this, it is intended to (i) supply improved tools and implements, (ii) encourage cobblers to upgrade their skill and improve the quality of the products and (iii) to improve their social and economic conditions.

II. Manufacture of Tanned Leather

I. Background

Tanning and footwear manufacture are ancient household crafts of the country. The tanners and cobblers are doing the work as traditional and hereditary occupations. The artisans of the industry are socially and economically backward and are traditionally working in the small pits in their houses with the members of their families. Because of their illiteracy and financial difficultly they are not readily willing to change their work habit and adopt modern technology. However, they are hard working and prefer to work on individual basis along with the members of their families. Therefore, it is proposed that they may be encouraged by giving required tools and implements. Due to continuous persuasion by various agencies especially the KVIC, the tanners are gradually changing their work-habits and adopting the modern techniques in the work. However, this process is slow.

II. Prospects

The village tanning is mostly done by adopting bag tanning process and the leather thus produced is mostly used for *charas* (water lifters) and country type footwears. This leather has demand for the most part of the year. Therefore, the tanner and shoemakers are mostly engaged in the work for 9 to 10 months and for the rest of the period they work as agricultural labourer.

III. Objectives

The main objectives of the scheme are to enable the tanners to have fuller work and higher earnings. It is intended to

(i) supply improved tools and implements.

(ii) Improved pits with shed,

(iii) encourage tanners to upgrade their skill and improve the quality of the products and

(iv) improve their social and economic conditions.

MANUFACTURE OF CANE GUR AND KHANDSARI INDUSTRY

I. Background

India is one of the major producers of sugarcane in the world and consequently sugar, khandsari and gur. Sugarcane is an important cash crop of the country playing an important role in the village economy. According to 1966 Census of Agricultural implements and machinery in use, 6.50 lakh bullock driven crushers were working in the country. In the 1971 population census. (Occupational classification 20 percent sample by the main activities) the number engaged in the activity of khandsari and gur manufacture in the country was shown as nearly 1.08 lakhs. Although about 225 large scale sugar factories and over 25,000 power driven sugar crushers are working in the country, about 54 percent of the total production is still by the self employed artisans/cultivators.

II. Prospects

It is estimated that about Rs. 8 to 10 crores are annually lost because of wasteful processing techniques. The majority of artisans/cultivators do not use efficient tools and implements by which the above loss can be avoided. The use of improved techniques and implements cannot only add to their income but also improve the lot of small cane growers who are generally poor if financial and technical help is not extended to them. Thereby it may make a substantial recurring contribution to the national economy. This will also help in more fruitful marketing of the product at opportune time, protection against malpractices of intermediaries etc. envisages equipping the artisans/small cultivators with a small oil engine and power driven attachment to convert the bullock driven crushers into a power driven machine. The availability of a small oil engine will equip the artisan to utilize power for various useful purposes also, such as pumping water for irrigation and household use, running a chaffcutter for feeding the cattle etc.

PALMGUR INDUSTRY

I. Manufacture of Date Palmgur

I. Introduction

The sweet sap of the palm viz., neera after processing can be converted into date palmgur. Manufacture of date palmgur has been known in this country since time immemorial much before the introduction of cane sugar manufacture. The country used to export huge quantities of date palm sugar to the various countries. Even in those days the manufacturing activity was concentrated in the then State of Bengal. This is the traditional area for the industry. The date palmgur is superior in nutrition compared to cane gur. In these areas, large numbers of date palm trees are available for this production activity. It provides employment opportunities to the poorer strata of the society. It is essentially a seasonal activity wherein all the family members of the artisans can participate.

II. Prospects

Date palmgur is facing competition from canegur. However, the date palmgur is more nutritious, and it helps the country to release large fertile area now under sugarcane for production of foodgrains. It also provides employment opportunities to rural people by utilizing neglected natural wealth for productive purposes.

II. Manufacture of Palmyrah Gur

I. Introduction

The sweet sap of the palm viz., neera after processing can be converted into palmgur. Manufacture of palmgur has been known in this country since time immemorial much before the introduction of cane sugar manufacture in the organized sector. The country used to export huge quantities of palm sugar to the various countries. Even in those days the manufacturing activity was concentrated in the States of Tamil Nadu, Andhra Pradesh, Kerala and West Bengal. These are traditional areas for the industry. The palmgur is superior in nutrition compared to cane gur, In these, areas, large number of palm trees are available for the production activity. It provides employment opportunities to the poorer strata of the society. It is essentially a seasonal activity wherein all the family members of artisan can participate.

II. Prospects

Palmgur is facing competition from cane gur. However, the fact is that palmgur is more nutritious and it helps the country to release large fertile area now under sugarcane for production of food grains. It also provides employment opportunities to rural people by utilizing neglected natural wealth for productive purposes.

III. Manufacture of Palmyrah Palm Candy

I. Introduction

In addition to the manufacture of palmgur and palm sugar, by processing sweet (palm juice) i.e., neera, palm candy or crystalised sugar is also obtained. Candy is a concentrated form of sucrose. In the commercial world candy means fairly large crystal of sucrose. Like plamgur, candy manufacture is one of the traditional village industries of this country. Its origin is hidden in the annals of history. However, the ancient treatise on Hindu medicine, 'Susrut' narrates a number of uses for which candy was put to and could be used for. However, with the advent of cane candy in the market the production of palm candy considerably declined. In certain parts of the country, especially in Southern India, it is still manufactured on a sufficiently large scale. Its demand is, however restricted compared to palm gur since it has very limited uses. It is mainly used as one of the ingredients in medicinal preparations and for distribution on religious occasions. Today, the manufacturing activities are concentrated in certain parts of Tamil Nadu especially in the districts of Ramnad, Tirunelveli and Kanyakumari. For centuries, palm candy is manufactured for commercial purposes in Tiruchendur, Udangudi, Thisayan-villai, Kottandadu, Sirunadau, Kundiruppu, Sathankolam, Adaikaipuram areas and certain parts of Kanyakumari district. These areas almost exclusively account for the entire production of palm candy within the country. The candy manufactured in these areas is pooled at Virudhanagar in Ramnad district and it is sent to different consuming areas in the country. Few years back, palm candy used to earn some foreign exchange when it was exported from the Tuticorin port. Its export market was Sri Lanka.

Palm candy is graded on the basis of colour, brightness and size of crystal. It was estimated that the respective shares of big, medium and small varieties of palm candy were in the neighbourhood of 5.45 and 50 percent of the total output. Since a very small quantity is retained by the manufacturer himself for self consumption, most of the production is available for the commercial sale. However, due to low keeping quality, there are some wastages arising out of melting.

II. Method of processing

KVIC has recently introduced improved methods of manufacture of palm candy. However bulk of the production is still in the traditional sector. Traditional method of manufacture is time consuming and it also affects the quality of product. The present scheme visualizes introduction of improved methods of manufacture of palm candy. Under the new methods, rectangular shape iron pan is used and palm juice is boiled on the furnace, crystallization is done in U shaped GI crystaliser. It is experienced that this new candy crystaliser gives better recovery of palm candy compared to traditional earthen crystaliser. Moreover, it is possible to obtain first candy crop in a shorter period of ten days as against the protracted period of 40 days in the traditional method. Palm candy obtained in the improved crystaliser gives attractive appearance, hence it fetches relatively higher price.

II. Prospects

It is true that palm candy faces competition from sugar candy on various counts. However, in view of the paramount need for conserving sugar cane for other uses it is worth considering the use of palm candy in place of sugarcane candy. Palm candy is more nutritious than sugarcane candy.

IV. Manufacture of Palmyrah Palm Fibre

I. Introduction

Apart from tapping for obtaining sweet juice viz., neera, or its conversion into various edible products such as palmgur, palm sugar and palm candy, different parts of palmyrah palm are also exploited for manufacturing variety of non edible products. Palmyrah fibre is obtained from the sheath or the portion at the base of leaves stalk of the palmyrah palm. It is an important raw material for brush manufacturing industry. It is either exclusively used or mixed with other fibres. Normally, from the 10th year, the palmyrah tree starts yielding fibre and continues to yield till about 25th year. On an average, 10 to 15 sheaths are obtained annually from a tree. Each sheath yields about ¼ to ½ kg, of fibre. Pakmyrah fibre has an export market and about 10.000 tonnes of palmyrah fibre is annually exported to different countries. It earns about Rs. 4 to 5 crores worth of foreign exchange. Palm fibre activity is concentrated in two States viz., Tamil Nadu and Andhra Pradesh and it is exported from Kakinada and Tuticorin ports. In Tamil Nadu the areas of concentration are, Thisayanvillai, Udangudi, Kolachal, Ramnad, Erode, Chermalai, Morakka. In Kerala the production is concentrated in Palghat and Malabar districts. In Andhra Pradesh it is heavily concentrated in East and West Godavari, Visakhapatnam, Krishna and Karimnagar districts.

II. Prospects

The Palmyra fibre after processing is graded according to the quality and used appropriately. Since India is in the tropical belt it has abundant raw material for the manufacture of palmyrah fibre. It should be possible to extensively develop the manufacturing activity in the country. It would generate employment opportunities to a large number of people in the country. It is possible to develop manufacture of finished articles and export them to various consuming countries. Internal market for the product also can be developed considerably. There is further scope for improvement in processing of fibre as well as manufacture of finished articles. The present scheme visualizes the manufacture of finished products for internal consumption.

Manufacture of Mats (Weaving)

I. Introduction

The manufacture of mats from palmyrah leaves is in vogue in certain parts of the country. A large number of palmgur artisans are also engaged in this manufacturing activity. It is difficult to precisely estimate the quantity and value of production of mats available for commercial use. According to an estimate, there are about 600 lakh palmyrah palms in the country; out of which nearly 50 percent are available for obtaining palm leaves. In spite of the fact that palmyrah leaves are available in many parts of the country, the manufacturing activity is by and large concentrated in southern parts of the country. The State of Tamil Nadu has got the largest share i.e. about 80 percent followed by Andhra Pradesh and Kerala.

II. Prospects

The principal demand for palmyrah mats comes from textile and sugar mills and is essentially required as a packaging material. Preparation of mats of out of palm leaves is a simple process. Fresh leaves are dried under the Sun for a couple of days and cut according to the requirements with the help of small knife. The leave strips are made flexible by sprinkling little water and then are woven into different sizes. In view of the fact that the country is facing acute problem of raw material for packaging, it is appropriate that activity should be given attention it deserves. By encouraging this activity, it would be possible not only to utilize the wealth which at present is neglected but also generate employment opportunities to the rural people. The activity is labour intensive in character and requires a small capital investment. The family members of palmgur artisan can also attend to this activity in their leisure hours. The palmgur manufacturing activity is seasonal in character and if support is provided by this activity it should be possible to provide work throughout the year.

NON-EDIBLE OILS AND SOAP INDUSTRY

Manufacture of Laundry Soap

I. Introduction

There being no appreciable improvement in the overall output of the major edible oilseeds, the shortage of edible oils in the country continues, consequently raising the price of oils very high. This has caused considerable concern to the edible oil based industries and has posed great problem before the nation.

The use of non-edible oils in soap making has been introduced so as to release the edible oils used in it exclusively for edible purposes. The collection of non-edible oilseeds of free origin such as Neem, Mahwah, Karanja, Castor, Undi, Pise, Punna, Pilu, Khakhan, Dhupa,

Thumba etc. available in the forests of the country in numerous quantities and otherwise going waste, would add to national economy and oil bank of the country, if tapped and utilized fully, thereby giving employment opportunity to millions of rural and tribal people, supplementing the earnings of seasonal workers and sizeable wages to full time workers in oil pressing and soap making.

The potentiality of various non-edible oilseeds has been assessed at 66.71 lakh tonnes of which about 10 lakh tonnes of oils could be available. These oils would not only be additional resources to the country towards self-reliance in oils and save the foreign exchange being spent on imports of oils and fats but enable the country to earn foreign exchange with the export of various fats and oil cakes.

II. Prospects

The laundry soap manufactured by small scale sector with non-edible oils particularly could be of consumer's preference due to its economical rates and better quality and in view of lower investments and limited over-head charges to producers.

Though the availability of non-edible oils could be a problem for such units in certain areas, it has become a regular market commodity in most parts of the country.

The model scheme for individuals has been formulated with definite formula for soap composition and has been based on the present rates of machines and materials. The economics is likely to differ with change in the composition and rate variation and as such is subject to appropriate modifications and alterations.

The individual owning land and shed may be able to run this unit more economically, provided he manages the work with the assistance of his own family members.

The choice of the local market in rate and quality is required to be balanced with composition of the soap.

Manufacture of Toilet Soap

I. Introduction

India produces about 10.21 lakh tonnes of soap annually out of which 1.60 lakh tonnes of toilet soap is produced exclusively by the organized sector. A sizeable quantity of toilet soap is exported after meeting the country's needs. Even though the bulk of the laundry soap requirement is made by the small scale and V.I. sectors, the production of toilet soap has not yet been undertaken because of heavy investments on machinery/ equipment and requirement of moderate sophistication, training, wider publicity and campaigning.

The Khadi and V.I. Commission has been able to scale down the heavy machinery and fabricate suitable machines and equipment which can undertake toilet soap making in the cottage and V.I. Sector.

II. Prospects

The Country's need of toilet soap is growing by about 7 percent every year. In the context of new industrial policy which emphasises the rapid expansion of Cottage and V.I. Sector about 500 units of this type have to be established every year to meet the requirements.

BEEKEEPING INDUSTRY

I. Background

Honey is the most nutritious and bounteous gift of the nature. It is the best source of heat and instant energy not only for infants but also for sick, invalid and manual workers who are in need of immediate replenishment. One kg. honey releases 3,500 calories of energy. Therefore, it is called "Nature's Energy Bank'. Flowers of a variety of plants secrete sweet juice which is called "nectar". This nectar is collected by bees and converted into honey. Bees collect this nectar as their own food and after digesting or partial digesting convert it into honey. The bee compensates the flowers by helping cross pollination which enhances the yield. Though it has been the natural phenomenon, the KVIC has revolutionized the process by proper bee management and scientific production of honey, which has also increased the production of honey. These modern bee farms are called 'Apiaries'. This process fundamentally involves transference of natural or wild bee colonies into man made wooden hives, a site, where colonies are housed extractors. This gives very pure honey which is called Apiary honey. There is another type of honey which is called 'squeezed' dorsata (rock bee), and is found freely in the natural environs of forests in the mountaineous and sub mountaineous regions. Rock bee is a good gatherer of honey and a single honey comb may produce upto 20 kgs. of honey and ½ kg. of the wax. But the honey thus produced has a very poor keeping quality as it is usually unclean. Besides, its collection entails mass destruction of the bees along with their eggs and the young ones which are squeezed out while obtaining honey. Forest departments usually give contracts for the collection of rock bee and wax to private parties.

Bee wax is a by-product which is an important element in comb foundation of artificial hives. It is used for furniture, manufacture of floor polishes, dressing and water proofing of leather goods etc. It is all essential ingredient in shoe polishes, cosmetics, face creams and lipsticks. The crude bee wax is purified by indirect heat and melting it with water. The wax melts and floats on the surface. On cooling, the pure wax is solidified at the top and it can be removed as a slate. By repeating the same process, it gets further purified.

By conservative estimates, the total annual production of bee wax is placed at 1,00,000 kgs. Out of which about 30,000 kgs. of bee wax is from Apis indica bee colonies and about 70,.000 kgs. from wild bee colonies.

Another important by-product is bee venom which is used in the pharmaceutical industry.

II. Prospects

In India about 20-25 lakhs of colonies can easily be supported due to inexhaustible reserves of flora and diverse environment. Himachal Pradesh, Jammu and Kashmir and Uttar Pradesh having rich fruit belts are yet to join the front rank in honey products. If it is properly managed and fully exploited on modern lines, the annual honey production may increase to the tune of Rs.20-25 crores. It will also help in increase in the income in agriculture and horticulture, thereby provide gainful employment to over 15-20 lakh persons on household basis in the country. There is a great demand for tropical honey in Europe due to its purity.

VILLAGE POTTERY INDUSTRY

I. Introduction

Almost all the villages in the country have potters. By and large, it is a traditional and hereditary occupation. It is estimated that about 13 lakh persons are engaged in the manufacture of various types of utility and fancy articles including conventional pots, pans, building materials such as bricks, roofing and firing tiles. Of them, about 12 lakh persons are engaged in the manufacture of earthen wares and earthen pottery as well as structural clay products, out of which about 10 lakh persons are estimated to be in the rural sector. The KVIC's development programmes have so far covered about only a lakh of persons. However, the fact remains that there is a vast scope for expansion of the activities in this field. It is likely that some of the potters might have been assisted through banks and other development agencies.

II. Prospects

Demand for improved pottery articles is on the increase. The other factors which would influence the future expansion of the industry are the changing industrial scene in the rural areas and increase in construction activities involving the use of bricks and roofing and flooring tiles. Supply of improved pottery wares is unstable and low. This is mainly on account of slow change in the habits of the potters, production not demand oriented etc. Public taste in designs and quality of wares is fast changing and the artisans have to be provided the needed help and guidance. Providing facilities like raw materials, fuel and improved equipment and training in better methods of production of quality pottery products and marketing to traditional artisans would not only increase the productivity of potter but also would ensure higher earnings and quality and quantity of the products to suit the changing need of the people.

FIBRE INDUSTRY

Rope Making

I. Introduction

In India, almost all the States have large quantities of vegetable fibres. Among the wide range of fibres, sun-hemp, sisal banana and jute are the most important fibres, which are generally used for rope making for various agricultural, industrial and trade purposes. The manufacturing activity of fibre and fibre products is one of the age-old traditional activities which is carried out in rural areas especially by Harijans, adivasis and backward classes i.e. the weaker sections of the community. The extraction of fibre of any origin is done by these methods, viz. a) Chemical (b) Mechanical, (c) Retting system. Among them the retting method is the best suited method for extraction of fibre in large quantities and is generally used in process of sisal fibre, besides decorticators and raspadors which can be done either by hand or by machine. It is suitable only when large quantities of raw materials are available for processing on commercial scale.

II. Prospects

Due to the abundant availability of vegetable fibres in India (which are both naturally grown and cultivated) there is immense scope for generation of gainful seasonal employment opportunities in rural areas especially amongst Harijans, adivasis and backward class of people. It can also serve as a means to revive the age-old traditional handicraft activities in the country based on vegetable fibre.

III. Objectives

Maximum coverage of larger number of existing artisans by development and make them self-reliant by introducing improved tools and equipment to enable the artisans improve the quality and quantity of production and ensure higher earnings are the main objectives of the scheme.

Ban Making

I. Introduction

The production of two ply yarn, popularly known as 'Ban' made mostly out of grass fibres like "Moonj" and "Bhabar" is an important activity under the fibre industry in northern parts of India. Ban is used for Charpai (cot) weaving and for general tying purposes. It is the coir of the north.

II. Prospects

The traditional method of preparing ban (yarn) is to twist the grass fibre on palm and charkha. The ban making machine introduced by KVIC has become popular in Himachal Pradesh, Punjab, Uttar Pradesh, Rajasthan, Bihar and Orissa. The machine helps the artisan to earn double of what they normally earn by using traditional method and this scheme is suited for self-employment. The raw material grows in abundance and it is one of the established traditional industries of north. The use of ban is extensive and is likely to remain so for years to come. It has thus a secure market. There are substitutes such as "niwar", cotton sutlies or plastic rope but they do not pose any serious threat. The activity provides employment especially to women-folk and it is a subsidiary source of income for many agricultural labourers. In other words, both from the supply and demand sides, the activity appears to be stable. According to the existing pattern of trade, the intermediaries collect the finished ban from the artisans and send it to the main distribution centres. A small portion finds its way in the local markets through weekly bazars. This is done directly by the producers themselves.

III. Objectives

There is immense scope for generation of gainful seasonal employment in rural areas, especially amongst weaker sections of the community by making productive use of the abundantly available grass fibres which grow naturally or are cultivated to meet the requirements of growing population in the country-side.

CARPENTRY AND BLACKSMITHY INDUSTRY

Manufacture of agricultural implements, bullock' carts, building materials and other utility furniture

I. Introduction

Almost every village in India has a carpenter/blacksmith. The same artisan often performs both the functions. Both are essential service industries and can be construed as trades.

The artisans in smaller villages are generally bound by contractual arrangement for work with the farmers for which they are paid in kind. Their activities include manufacture, maintenance and repair services. The village carpenter/blacksmith is required to undertake servicing of ploughs, agricultural implements and residential quarters of the farmers. Both the activities are capable of generating work opportunities to the artisans throughout the year.

According to 1971 census, occupational classification (20 percent sample) by main activity the number engaged in these two activities in the country was as follows:

Activity		Total (Nos.)	In Household Sector (Nos.)
A.	Carpentry		
1.	Carpenters	9,83,200	4,79,800
2.	Cabinet makers	1,08,400	41,500
3.	Wood working machine operators	15,000	2,200
4.	Cart builders and Wheel wrights	24,100	15,000
5.	Other related carpentry workers	70,200	23,800
6.	Supervisors and foremen (Carpentry Cabinet making and related wood working processes)	6500	1,400
Total		12,07400	5,63,700

There are 8.80 lakh carpentry and blacksmithy artisans in the household industrial sector, but number of the artisans in rural areas is not available. Generally, the tools of the village artisans are antiquated and limited in range of production. Average investment in improved tools is estimated at Rs.2,750/- to Rs.3,000/-. The antiquated tools would cost Rs.750 to Rs.1,000. At present, the village carpenters/blacksmiths have virtually no access in markets outside the village as they are not equipped with skills and tools to manufacture the articles required in urban areas. In certain areas, where agriculture has become prosperous, there has been a spurt in construction and other activities which have provided boost to these activities. The demand for their services is on the increase. These artisans sometimes undertake even repairs, maintenance and servicing of complex tools. In such cases, they purchase iron sheets, iron rods, girders etc. from the iron merchants in the nearby towns whereas the village carpenters/blacksmiths are deprived of great deal of business due to lack of adequate range of sophisticated tools and the requisite skills to handle them. The basic objective of the programme, therefore is to enable them to get fuller work and consequently higher earnings.

II. Prospects

The demand for carpentry and blacksmithy articles is bound to increase with the pace of the improvement in general standard of living both in rural and urban areas. With the expansion of rural electrification there would be expansion of improved technology. Besides, the educated unemployed especially among carpenters and blacksmiths would easily be able to take up these activities with a view to earn their livelihood.

LIME MANUFACTURING INDUSTRY

(I) Manufacture of Quick-lime

I. Introduction

There is no other material in commerce that has diverse uses and varied functions as lime. Its uses are too numerous to list. With the increasing tempo of rural and urban housing programme, the demand for lime is on the increase. As such to keep pace with the increasing demand, it is felt necessary to help the individual artisans to take up the task of producing lime with the help of his own family members. This will not only help the artisans to retain the self-employed character but also help in increasing employment opportunities in the rural areas. Hence, a scheme for quick lime production is designed for the individuals.

(II) Chalk Making

I. Introduction

Chalks are generally prepared by admixture of plaster of paris (95 percent) with China clay (5 percent). Because of the heavy demand for plaster of paris in other industries, it has become absolutely necessary to substitute it to the extent possible by lime. The cost of manufacture of chalks has increased due to rise in the price of plaster of paris in some measure. The experiments conducted by using different compositions of plaster of paris and slaked lime have shown that chalks made out of 70 percent plaster of paris and 30 percent slaked lime are good in quality for writing purposes.

II. Process of manufacture

In accordance with the norms of production, a particular quality of plaster of paris (70 percent by weight) and slaked lime (30 percent by weight) have to be mixed in dry state thoroughly in a tray. The mixture so formed should be put in a bucket and water added to it with constant and vigorous stirring till it becomes slurry (then liquid paste). Soon after formation of slurry it should be taken in a beaker and poured into moulds which are already applied with cleaned oil (one part of coconut oil and 3 parts of kerosene oil). The moulds containing the mixture should be allowed for 10 minutes for drying. The drying of the mixture can be confirmed by the finger touch. Care should be taken while taking out the chalks in semi-dry condition from the moulds without causing much breakage. The semi-dry chalks should be dried in the direct Sun-light. When it is completely dried, it is ready for sale.

(III) Manufacture of Conch-Shell Products

I. Introduction

It is a general practice in the eastern parts of the country to use articles manufactured from conch shells as art pieces. Especially women folk in those areas have a special liking for them. It is reported that nearly 75,000 persons are engaged in the manufacture of conch shell products such as ladies bangles, finger and ear-rings, buttons etc. These conch shells are collected in Tamil Nadu coast and Andaman Nicobar Islands in the Bay of Bengal. These raw materials are then sent to West Bengal, Assam and Orissa for manufacture of decorative articles. The artisans use simple hand tools and work in their cottages.

II. Prospects

With the increasing demand of conch shell products, there is every possibility of widening the opportunity for accommodating more unemployed people in the activity. At present majority of the artisans are using hand tools such as hand drill, hacksaw, hammer etc. If power operated tools and implements such as cutting machine with 2 HP. motor and drilling machine are provided with adequate financial assistance, the average earnings of the artisan will certainly increase.

(IV) Manufacture of Agarbatti-stand, Table Lamps, Candle Holder, Paper Weight etc.

I. Introduction

All along the coastal areas, sea-shells are abundantly available. The sea shells being purer quality of $CaCo_3$, is a good raw material for lime industry. Sea shells are of various types. Fancy artwares can be made out of them. Many of them have different colours, shades and natural luster. Fancy articles such as agarbatti stands, table lamps, candle holders, paper weights etc. are manufactured. In addition to this, the lime can be used as poultry feed. It is observed that, large number of people are engaged in this activity in Kerala, Tamil Nadu and Orissa. But due to poor financial resources, most of the artisans work as labourers.

II. Prospects

The artisans in general lack financial resources, marketing facilities and capacity to stock the products. As a result, either they have to work as labourers or they have to sell their products at low prices. This results in depressing their earnings. If adequate financial assistance is given on reasonable terms and necessary facilities are provided, it would be possible to improve their lot. Even the educated members of their family will be able to work and manufacture many more utility ware articles with varied designs and increase their earnings.

(V) Manufacture of Edible Scented Lime

I. Introduction

The lime shells are abundantly available in the coastal regions, backwaters and lakes. These lime shells are the purest source of fat lime which is used as edible lime also. Besides, calcify stones are also the purer form of calcium carbonate, commercially termed as chemical or pharmaceutical grade. In rural areas, the requirements of edible lime for consumption with betel leaves are generally met by small artisans family who supply shell lime by burning shells in their bhattis. The consumers generally purchase the burnt lime and convert it into a pasty edible substance.

II. The process

The tank admeasuring 4'×2'21/2' is constructed out of brick masonry. The gunny bags are spread at the bottom of the tank for absorbing the moisture. Thereafter a weighed quantity of fresh lime is taken for tank slaking. The water is poured over the lime in the tank for slaking. When the slaking operation is completed, the milk of lime is kept for a overnight to settle. The contents are then decanted and the white lime paste is taken out and pressed under hydraulic press, so that the extra moisture is removed and the mass becomes a soft paste. Thereafter the perfume (rose scent), raodamine, Vaseline and glycerin in suitable proportions is added to the paste and processed in a power operated mortar mill (2 h.p. motor). The functions of the above ingredients are to impart perfume and colour to reduce the caustic in the paste. The paste is then passed to the mould where the scented lime is packed in bottles of 100 grams capacity.

III. The prospects

At present limeshell collection for utilization in the manufacture of scented edible lime on individual basis is limited and scattered activity, therefore the exploitation of this natural wealth, abundantly available in the coastal areas on commercial lines is not made to the fullest extent. Besides, this traditional activity does not give substantial earnings to the family members since the quality of product is not upto the standards. If it is organized scientifically, with the supply of improved tools and techniques, the available resources can be utilized to the maximum extent. The expansion of this activity, on scientific and economical basis will generate continuous employment to families of poor and backward class directly and indirectly engaged in this activity and their earnings will also increase substantially. Hence there is a general scope for expansion of this activity.

(VI) Manufacture of Sigol Plaster

I. Introduction

Different types of mortars are used for plastering walls internally and externally because of its inherent qualities like adequate water retentivity, prevention of cracks after drying, adequate strength and workable, to adhere well to masonry or other surface and to prevent moisture going into the walls. In any building construction, internal and external plaster is essential due to the reason well known to all. Because of the shortage of cement considerable attention is paid to use of other indigenous materials in building construction activities. Lime is the most important building material in addition to some other puzzolanic building materials.

II. The process

The success of plaster depends upon the techniques of preparing the surface to which the plaster is to be applied and of applying the plaster. It is very essential that all joints of the brick work whether in clay or lime should be raked out to a depth of ½" and surface of wall thoroughly washed and all lime mortar and other loose matters removed. The face of the wall should then be kept wet for two days before plaster. The plaster is applied in two coats and has an average thickness of two inches when applied on brick work and ¾" over stone masonry. A product consisting on well fired bricks, fine sand and dry slaked hydrated lime is pulverished in very fine state and is extensively used as a plaster on the masonry without following the usual practice of applying cement plaster.

III. Prospects

There is an acute shortage of cement. In that case, this plaster can serve as a alternative indigenous material for building construction activity. It can fulfill all the qualities of cement plaster. This plaster is also cheaper nearly about 40 to 50 percent as compared to that of cement plaster having good weather resistance, workability and building strength. It also develops shining properties and any colour can be added to the plaster as desired. There is no need of applying extra colour. It has more cooling effect than cement. Neru is also an identical product in the days of scarcity of cement. This type of ready prepared coloured plaster is 50% cheaper in cost and it is well received by the public. Because of increase in demand of housing, the building construction activities are day by day are on increase. Therefore, there is a great scope for manufacture of sigol plaster which can generate additional, employment directly or indirectly both in construction of building activity and manufacture of sigol plaster in the rural areas.

(VII) Manufacture of Sand Lime Tiles, Hollow Blocks and Jallies etc.

I. Introduction

In manufacturing of pre-fabricated materials like sand lime tiles, hollow blocks and jallies nearly 87 percent of local sand is used. The red clay being the prime raw material for manufacture of above items is not available in all the parts of the country. As estimated about 30% of the total land of the country is of alluvial soil. Clay of quite a large area is not suitable for red bricks or tiles, hence sand lime tiles and hollow blocks can be substituted in such places. There is a practice in our country to prepare hollow blocks and roof tiles by using sand and lime in a bigger proportion, especially in the states of Andhra Pradesh, Karnataka and West Bengal. Some of the units of KVIC in Andhra Pradesh and Karnataka are producing these materials on commercial scale without hampering the constructional requirements laid down in I.S.I. specifications.

II. The Process

Sand and lime along with cement is made to mortar and same is cast over one hand press and wooden moulds are used. The cost of machine is very less and it can be fabricated in local work shops. Thereafter the green staged tiles are kept in open air for 24 hours. The materials are taken out from wooden moulds and kept under water for 21 days for curing. Then the tiles are directly marketed.

III. The Prospects

As stated above that the red clay needed for tiles making is not available in all parts of the country. Besides, the clay deposits in some places required some additional alteration in composition which is costlier affair for rural people. The timely availability of fuel both in quantity and quality is another difficulty for the centres producing red bricks and tiles. The clay products can serve the purpose when it is properly vetrified (fired). Therefore, fire is a must. Because of the short supply of fuel, the production of bricks and tiles was affected which ultimately resulted very slow pace of development of building industry in the country. In this context, manufacture of sand lime tiles and hollow blocks has immense scope for development as an alternative answer of building industry. The Government is also keen in suggesting some alternative building materials in rural areas. Besides, it would create additional employment opportunities for professional artisans as well as educated unemployed youths in the rural areas on regular full time basis.

FRUIT PROCESSING AND FRUIT PRESERVATION INDUSTRY

(I) Home Scale Unit

I. Introduction

It is estimated that only 0.5% percent of the fruits and vegetables are processed for preservation and about 25 percent of fruits and vegetables are lost either in orchards and fields or in transit indicating that there is a considerable scope for activities indicating related to the local processing and preservation activities.

II. Objectives

It has twin objectives of providing employment opportunities to skilled and educated persons and also reducing the cost of processing so as to ensure continuous supply of a variety of fruits and vegetable products within the means of common man.

(II) Individual Unit

I. Introduction

The high potential for the development and expansion of the fruit processing and preservation industry would be obvious from the fact that out of the estimated total production of fruits and vegetables of about 20 million tonnes in the country, only 0.5% is processed and about 25 to 30 percent is wasted in handling, transport and storage which can be utilized to ensure continuous supply of variety of fruit products within the reach of the common man.

II. Objectives

1. To provide employment opportunities to skilled and educated persons.
2. To ensure continuous supply of variety of fruit products within the reach of the common man.
3. To improve the quality and quantity of production through improved techniques.

III. Assumptions

The model scheme for individual has the following assumptions:

(i) The Khadi and V.I. Commission may arrange to supply improved tools, equipment and machines to the skilled and educated persons.

(ii) It may assist in procuring the raw materials for processing of fruits and vegetables.

(iii) It may arrange for marketing of the products, if so required.

(iv) It would extend adequate training facilities, if so required.

(v) The family members of the workers would also assist in the activities.

BAMBOO AND CANE WORK INDUSTRY

I. Introduction

Bamboos are amongst the most versatile of plant materials and have been put to variety of uses since the beginning of human civilization. Articles of daily use such as baskets, mats, teapoys and chairs etc. are made of cane and bamboos. Similarly, cane and bamboos are also used for scaffoldings, rafters, roofs, walls and interior decoration and myriad of toys and fancy articles. The kangri made of willow wickers in Jammu & Kashmir is one of the world famous products of cane work. This is an ancient craft which needs revival and preservation. If encouragement is given, it would be possible to manufacture variety of value added items. Besides, bamboo is the single most commonly used material for construction of human dwelling throughout the world.

II. Prospects

The industry provides vast scope for generating employment opportunities in rural areas especially for weaker sections of the community. Their earnings can also be increased by improving the production techniques and diversification in production. The KVIC aims to assist as large a number of artisans as possible who are mostly scattered through its developmental activities.

III. Assumptions

The basic objective of the model scheme is to enable the artisans to have fuller work and higher earnings, improve the quality and quantity of the products and achieve diversification in production. The model scheme has the following assumptions.

(i) The KVIC may arrange to supply improved tools and equipment to the artisans through the approved manufacturers.

(ii) The KVIC may arrange for training of the artisans in improved techniques and also assist in improving the traditional techniques, if required.

(iii) The family members of the artisans may assist in the activity.

(iv) The KVIC may help in timely procurement of raw materials at reasonable prices, if required.

Source: Model Schemes of Village Industries for Individuals, Khadi and Village Industries Commission, Gramodaya; Mumbai, 5th Edition, 1983.

Grateful thanks are expressed to KVIC.

CHAPTER 20

Measures to Alleviate Poverty

In contrast to many other developing countries, a comparatively sophisticated redistribution system for the poorer sections of the population was established during the sixties and seventies in India. There are benefit programmes for marginal farmers, rural development programmes, crash schemes for rural employment, intensive rural employment programmes, food for work programmes, programmes for ecologically disadvantaged areas and minimum needs programmes.

If poverty went down during recent years it was probably much more the effect of these deliberate efforts than of economic growth as such. Nevertheless, it is much easier to finance these programmes in a situation of growth. The Indian government has spent Rs.37 billion on anti-poverty programmes during the sixth plan period (1980-85). This is an impressive amount in absolute terms but it represents little more than 0.5% of the national product during this period. This relative figure is indeed very small if one compares it with unemployment and social security schemes in western industrialized countries. Dandekar has recently calculated that it would cost 98.600 Million Rs. per year to bring all the poor, including the urban poor in the unorganized sector, above the poverty line.

This would constitute one third of the government revenues. Such a programme would drastically change the structure of government outlays but one cannot argue that an antipoverty programme which would wipe out absolute poverty completely in India is inconceivable. A substantial increase in expenditures on antipoverty programmes should be vigorously supported by development assistance. India is now one of those countries which receive very limited amounts of development assistance in per capita terms.

DEGRADATION OF URBAN ENVIRONMENT IS CAUSED BY RURAL POVERTY

As far as sanitation and the provision of clean drinking water are concerned, these tasks are being undertaken through time-bound programmes by State Public Health and Water supply Organizations. However, it is necessary to look beyond the statistics of targets and achievements complied by these authorities and recognize the fact that sanitary conditions are deteriorating rapidly in almost all towns and cities, primarily because of the continued influx of the rural poor who set up slum colonies and even start living on pavements in search of livelihood. Municipal bodies are finding it increasingly difficult to cater even to the minimum sanitary needs of such immigrants. Open defecation and urination have become familiar sights in and around slums, and constitute a grave threat to public health.

The caste-Hindus have a stake in adding fuel to the fire. They sow the seeds of discord amongst the poor to prevent their uniting, and exploit the underprivileged as landowners, employers, traders and money-lenders. They not only try to nip resistance in the bud, wherever and whenever it occurs, but misuse those programmes designed to improve the lot of the poor for their own benefit. And one of the main reasons for this is that they want to prevent the poor from becoming economically independent of them.

ANIMATION AND FACILITATION THROUGH VOLUNTARY AGENCIES

The poor and underprivileged are hardly in a position to improve their lot on their own, but need impulses provided by well-meaning outsiders. These are people who do not belong to the poor but, for different reasons, want to help them by establishing non-profit organizations. In the past century, in Europe, too, industrial workers, craftsmen pressed hard by industrial enterprises and petty farmers, needed such persons to found cooperatives, trade-unions and labour parties.

The Voluntary agencies (VAs) fulfil usually several tasks, which fall into two categories: animation and facilitation. In reality, one cannot clearly distinguish one from the other. Animation means, first of all, conscientization of the poor. Animators help the poor to regain their self-confidence and self-assertiveness. Only when the poor regard themselves as equal human beings and citizens do they question the reasons behind their poverty, realize their rights, request changes, discover the abilities and capacities at their disposal, have the confidence to change established patterns of behaviour and dare to use their assets to promote their own interests.

Once the poor have been motivated and activated by conscientization, the animator changes into the role of the facilitator. He assists the poor in forming groups, in deciding which measures should be taken and in executing the same.

He acts as their intermediary to get access to governmental or commercial services. He, for example, manages to establish first contacts between the poor and the official banking sector by helping to provide the securities banks require (seed, money, incentive deposit, group guarantees), and by helping the banks to change their procedures in such a way that they meet the requirements and abilities of the poor.

VAs provide legal aid to the poor and their groups in their disputes with the rich and the government authorities, they encourage them to unite in federations or to take part in support net-works in order to promote their common interests collectively, and establish themselves as institutions at the service of those of the poor who have no access whatsoever to any services.

Those VAs which are serious about grassroot development are aware that they themselves do not know the direction in which the poor will move. They present themselves, therefore, not as teachers and know-alls, but as equal partners and, by skilful questioning, make them conscious of their problems, prompt them to identify the causes and to propose solutions. VAs should not be hierarchically structured, but need a code of conduct and an organizational form conducive to participation.

Even though there are tens of thousands of VAs in India, many of them are only of local importance, and others do not work as altruistically and efficiently as would be required in the best interest of the poor. And this is the reason why, so far, they could not contribute to a large extent and with a lasting effect towards the eradication of poverty by strengthening the demand system.*

But anti-poverty programmes are probably far more difficult to implement, vastly more expensive and also likely to take time. The land reforms programme, with all its many limitations, belongs to this category. But the effects of the land reforms vary from State to State, depending on the nature of the reforms and the earnestness with which they were implemented. But, by and large, the reforms have removed from the scene holders of concessional tenures such as zamindars, jagirdars amd inamdars and have made it extremely difficult for absentee landowners to keep their land except where they belonged to the dominant castes. The reforms have also benefited tenants and cultivators in some States. Further, special programmes have been devised for two categories of poor peasants, called "small" and "marginal" farmers, which have proved to be helpful, though here again there are differences between States in the seriousness with which the programmes were implemented.

The food-for-work programmes, in areas where they exist, enable landless labourers, the weakest section of the rural population, to find work during the lean agricultural seasons. Some States have modest housing schemes for the weaker sections: The importance of such schemes is often not so much in the quantum of relief provided but in making known to the people that a new order is round the corner. The same may be said of some other programmes such as attempts to provide free lunches for school children, low-interest bank loans to the poor to enable them to be self-employed and very modest pensions to poor widows and old men. In this connection, the abolition of the institution of "bonded labour" is important, in as much as this category of agricultural servants have worked very hard and paid very low wages. Informed observers of the rural scene in India think that the institution still survives in the more backward areas and besides, not all emancipated labourers have been rehabilitated. Some State Governments are also actively trying to provide electricity and pure drinking water to villages in backward areas. The total effect of all these innovations has been to instill hope in people who had long suffered neglect. The quality of life in India's villages is beginning – only beginning – to change. And that is a big thing.

But the removal of poverty, stupendous as the task is, is only part of the struggle to control population growth. Further, the initial effects of the removal of poverty may only be to exacerbate the problem. It is time that disincentives were also thought of for promoting family planning, instead of relying entirely on incentives, as is being done so far.

Rural society is hierarchical in more than one sense, though it is usual to refer only to caste while considering hierarchy. But there is also a hierarchy based on the ownership of land and everyone who owns a sizable quantity of land has to become a patron in order to have an assured supply of labour and services. Patrons generally come from the high or dominant castes. When the members of a dominant caste own the bulk of the arable land in the village or local area, then the caste as a whole wields substantial power over the artisan, servicing and labouring castes which supply the clients. Here the point needs

---

***Source**: Adopted from the material – Problems of International Cooperation – "*viertel jahres berichte*" December 1987.

to be made that traditionally, that is, in pre-British times, it was not land that was scarce but labour, and a landowner had to look after his labourers reasonably well in order to retain them. But with the enormous rise that has taken place in India's population during the last 150 years, the quantum of arable land has shrunk drastically, and concomitantly, competition has sharpened greatly among clients in order to have access to land. Naturally, this has drastically reduced the ability of the clients to hold their own against exploitative patrons.

The patron-client relationship was traditionally a multi-stranded one, the patron being employer, creditor, arbitrator, and generally, friend, and protector, while the client was bonded labourer, tenant, sharecropper, debtor and general factotum. The client was expected to serve his master loyally, and have his interests at heart and promote them. In rural India, several groups of patrons and clients came together to form a faction, and a village is usually split into two or more factions. While the personnel of factions changes over time, and bits of one faction hive off occasionally to join another, an outside threat frequently leads to the closing up of the factions except when factionalism runs very deep. Factionalism is a part of the rural social structure, like caste.

A patron's clients included the members of the artisan and servicing castes who worked for him, and their families. The clients were paid fixed amounts of grain at harvest. They also had roles in the patron's house at life cycle rituals, and they were paid for this separately.

But a radical transformation is beginning to take place in the relations between patron and client. Clients are now increasingly paid cash, and this is particularly true of the agriculturally prosperous areas. Now infrequently, outside labourers are employed in preference to traditional clients, as they are more hard-working, and cheaper. The rules of noblesse oblige are giving way to the exclusive consideration of profit, to the disadvantage of clients.

This leads us to rural migrations. During the last four decades, agriculturally prosperous regions are attracting labourers from far and near. Labourers from dry or unirrigated areas gravitate to prosperous areas in search of work. In a sense, immigrant labour acts as a depressor of wages, but it is also a source of income to some of the poorest people. In a society without the benefit of state-supported social security schemes, poor immigrants would have gone to the wall but for the new work opportunities available in the rich agricultural regions.

Nowadays, mass migrations occur of seasonal workers from Orissa and Eastern U.P. to Haryana and Punjab. Similarly Marathi speakers in the north-western region of Maharashtra migrate to neighbouring Gujarat for seasonal work. Besides inter-state seasonal migration, there is much intra-state seasonal migration all over India. Such migration is welcomed by landowners who would not be able to transplant, weed or harvest their crops otherwise. But while landowners may welcome immigrant labourers, indigenous labourers do not. Immigrants not only bring down wages but they are also used to "discipline" indigenous labour. Since a good proportion of the latter will be members of the Scheduled Castes, they will be antagonistic both to their high caste employers and to the immigrants. This may lead to conflict between the affected Scheduled Castes and their high caste patrons, or assume the form of a conflict between indigenes and outsiders.

A most depressing scenario for the future is that concerning the relations between dominant, landowning castes and the Scheduled Castes. The conflict between the two is likely to become more and more bitter, and violent. It will be a primary arena for the struggle for equality in India.

Traditionally, as is widely known, the Scheduled Castes performed certain essential tasks in the villages, some of which like sweeping and scavenging, removal of dead animals, and doing leather work, were considered polluting as well as degrading. They were also important as agricultural labourers. They suffered from a number of collective disabilities, and were also obliged to show deference to the higher castes in speech and gesture, failure to do so being punished by the latter.

But the position of the Scheduled Castes is changing, and the pace of change likely to be faster in the near future. Thanks to the policy of protective discrimination, many members of the Scheduled Castes have been to school and college, and are holding white-collar and professional jobs. Some members of the Scheduled Castes have a higher standard of living than many members of the high castes. Again, thanks to reservation, some members of the Scheduled Castes are elected legislators at various levels while a much smaller number have become ministers. Not only do high caste candidates, seeking election to a legislative body, have to approach members of the Scheduled Castes for votes, but many members of the high castes have to approach Scheduled Caste ministers for a variety of favours. And it is well to remember that these events are happening for the first time in the history of India.

But in spite of the changes which are occurring in the relations between the high castes and Scheduled Castes, large numbers of the latter are acutely dissatisfied at what they consider to be the slow pace of change. The young and educated members of the Scheduled Castes are particularly dissatisfied, and angry. Open defiance of the authority of the high castes is encountered increasingly, especially among some groups such as the Mahars in urban Maharashtra. During the early seventies, the Mahar had an organization called the Dalit Panthers, deriving inspiration from the Black Panthers, which was committed to the promotion of the cause of the Scheduled Castes through recourse to violent revolutions The Panthers were responsible for producing a body of protest literature called "dalit sahitya", rejecting caste, inequality and exploitation. Now "dalit sahitya" exists in other Indian languages also, contributing to the militancy of the Scheduled Castes and the "weaker sections" generally.

While the Scheduled Castes have made some substantial gains, and as already mentioned, pollution ideas have weakened somewhat, large numbers of people, particularly those in the rural areas, do not accept the idea that the Scheduled Castes are their equals. The progress achieved by some Scheduled Caste members, has only roused the anger and envy of many members of the high castes who attribute the formers' success to the special treatment accorded to them. The refusal of some Scheduled Castes to perform one or other of the many traditional duties imposed on them, is seen by the dominant castes, as an affront to their dignity. They think that the government is pampering the Scheduled Castes, and encouraging them to defy the authority of the higher castes. No wonder then that violent clashes occur frequently between bands of the dominants and the Scheduled Castes: the latter are beaten up, their huts set fire to, and their women raped. Such clashes are not confined to rural areas though they are far more common there. They seem to be more frequent in the Hindi-speaking regions than elsewhere, but the latter areas are not free from such clashes.

It is likely that such clashes will increase in the coming years. As more and more members of the Scheduled Castes get educated and assert themselves, resentment against them is likely to increase. The fact that even in 2006 A.D. about 70 percent of the population is likely to be rural, will mean that India's villages will each become a mini-battlefield for inter-caste conflict. Since resentment at the progress of the Scheduled Castes, the conflict might bring together all the caste Hindus, including those which are just above the untouchability line, against the Scheduled Castes. Under the circumstances, the latter might look to conversion to another religion as a way out of their problems, and also, as a way of scoring off caste Hindus for their cussed hostility. But such a step might only worsen the situation, inviting even greater wrath from the Hindus of the entire region.

The benefits and concessions which the Scheduled Castes (and Tribes) are enjoying may be renewed for some more years. Political parties, anxious to secure the votes of the Scheduled Castes (and Tribes), will only be too eager to extend them for another decade. But in the process they may antagonize the other sections of the population, especially the castes just above the untouchability line who feel that they are lagging behind the Scheduled Castes in the gains they have made.

There is a positive aspect to the conflict between the dominant (and high) castes on the one hand, and the Scheduled Castes on the other, which is important, and needs to be mentioned. The bloodshed, death, rape and incendiarism have all to be viewed in the long run, as an integral part of the process of translating into reality the rights which the constitution of India grants to the Scheduled Castes and Tribes. To say this is not to condone the savage attacks on the Scheduled Castes, but only to recognize the important fact that the conflict has a positive dimension castes, it attracts a good deal of media attention. As a result, questions are asked in Parliament and the State legislatures, voluntary bodies visit the scene of conflict, and the police, who are generally reluctant to take action against the powerful village leaders, are forced to act. More importantly, there is a general raising of consciousness about the rights of the Scheduled Castes, and the latter become aware of the fact that they have supporters and friends in the world outside their village. If social conflict is indispensable to the improving of the living conditions of the Scheduled Castes, then its presence is a healthier sign than its absence.*

1. Before any measures and strategies could be adopted there is need to know the types and causes of poverty. This could be done by sponsoring village level survey by competent groups. Governments while arranging for such surveys should take care that information on all factors such as income, availability and access to social amenities, housing, dietary levels etc. location of the areas inhabited by the poor are taken into account;
2. Availability of infrastructural facilities, agricultural production levels, housing needs etc, are some of the factors that should also be considered to demarcate areas with

---

***Source:** Adopted from the Chapter "On Living in a Revolution" by M.N. Srinivas, *Problems of International Co-operation*, – "*viertel jahres berichte*", December 1987.

large incidence of poverty. Governments especially of Afro Asian countries should locate such areas on the basis of above mentioned factors;

3. For quantifying poverty, it is essential to know the nature of poverty and also to have a comprehensive and updated data base. Necessary steps need therefore to be taken to strengthen the data base regarding all aspects of poverty viz. income, consumption expenditure, basket of goods in the normal diet;
4. Alleviation of poverty can be successful if the indirect causes such as literacy levels, bonded labour, exploitation by land owners etc, are also dealt with. Governments of the developing countries may like to take necessary steps in that direction;
5. The poverty line expressed in terms of consumption expenditure is by far the most common determinant of poverty. As the consumption expenditure for availing the basic necessities of food, clothing and shelter may vary depending on dietary habits, availability of natural resources and attitude to subsistence, the economic system of the country in question has to be studied in detail for quantifying poverty. Governments of the Afro-Asian Rural Reconstruction Organizations (AARRO) member countries may take necessary steps towards that direction.
6. Parity of income is a factor that should be kept in mind while determining poverty through the poverty line. The poverty line, which is expressed in terms of consumption expenditure, may vary from region to region depending on the parity of income of the population. A basket of goods may not cost the same in two countries and, therefore, it will be wrong to use the same expenditure levels for determining the poverty line. Although the World Bank specifies the range of $ 275-$370 per capita per annum, it is necessary that each country should determine its own poverty line depending on the cost of living prevalent in that country. This may also vary for different regions in the same country.
7. According to the World Development Report, poverty has been defined as "the inability to attain a minimum standard of living." The concept of a minimum standard of living" has two elements; one that can be measured in real terms like cost of basic necessities, and the other which is subjective including the cost of participating in every day life of society, such as education levels, entertainment facilities etc. An index, therefore, needs to be framed considering the factors such as health, education, and other social amenities apart from consumption expenditure for determining the poverty line;
8. It has been observed that poverty is widespread in the rural areas of the developing countries which are largely dependent on agriculture. Agricultural production is thus closely related to the incidence of poverty in years of scarce rainfall, agricultural production is low and a majority of the population is deprived of their only source of income. Governments of the AARRO member countries should, therefore, ensure that alternative sources of income are made available to them and poverty alleviation programmes are taken up particularly in water deficient areas;
9. Countries which suffer from the problems of poverty have devised various measures for its alleviation. Some countries have been more successful in dealing with this problem than others. Programmes for alleviation of poverty in the AARRO member countries should therefore be studied and evaluated for their levels of success in

a common forum. The successful strategies should be mutually studied and exchanged so that poverty could be fought on a global level. Once the effective strategies have been identified; they need to be suitably modified before the transfer of technology to other countries. Various factors affecting poverty, unique to a country need careful consideration while modifying these strategies. There is thus a need for a closer cooperation among AARRO member countries in this direction;

10. In many less developed countries poverty is not only a rural characteristic but also often times is parallel with agriculture (under-development and under-employment). Although improvements in labour and land productivities can be a source of income improvements through multiple cropping, planting of high value crops and undertaking of similar activities, etc. and therefore should be further promoted. The stimulus for integration and linkages with other sectors in particular manufacturing offer further opportunities for marketing agricultural surplus and utilization of farm labour in higher value-added off-farm and/or non-agriculture employment. Agro-based industrialization in rural areas is very effective in generating additional employment and income in these areas. Agro-based industries should therefore be developed so as to use locally available raw materials, expertise and labour;*

11. A majority of the rural poor under poverty consists of landless laborers. Their income is restricted to the seasonal demand of labour for on –farm activities. Agro-based industrialization is one way of providing them with alternative sources of income during the off- seasons. Cooperative is another way of organising the landless labourers for productive use. Allied sectors such as dairy, poultry, fisheries, handicrafts etc. need to be developed for providing income to the rural poor. Specific alleviation programmes should be devised keeping the landless labourers in mind. Besides providing them with alternative sources of income and their social condition has also to be improved through these programmes by making available education, health and recreation facilities to them;

12. Long–term poverty alleviation measures can be effective only if they take into account developments in the entire economy. Factors such as macro-economic policies, development of agriculture, infrastructure, rural industries, health, nutrition, sanitation, water supply, education etc. have all to be considered while formulating the long-term measures, close cooperation of all the agencies involved in these areas is imperative and necessary steps need to be taken for coordinating the attitude towards the achievement of these objectives;

13. Specific programmes of poverty alleviation should have specific objectives and approaches. Different regions suffering from poverty will need different programmes as the causes of poverty will vary depending on the socio-economic conditions of the people. The immediate concern should be to provide the basic amenities for subsistence to the poor;

14. The Integrated Rural Development Programme (IRDP) is an important instrument of the strategy to alleviate poverty. The objective of such a programme, which has been successful in some member countries, is to assist the families below poverty

---

* A chapter detailing mini and micro enterprises is included in the book.

line in rural areas by taking up self-employed agro-based ventures. The other developing countries should take up this programme modified according to their local conditions and provide income generating assets including working capital through a package of assistance comprising subsidy and institutional credit;

15. The broader area-based IRDP approach to rural development whilst useful in many cases has limitation in the sense that being a general and non-focused approach, leakages have taken place and the poor have not fully benefited from such projects. A specially and directly targeted approach bearing upon the identified poor could be more effective either independently and/or in combination with IRDP approach. Such an approach should not be precluded in the package of measures to tackle poverty;

16. Another programme which could usefully be taken up by the member countries of AARRO is Minimum Needs Programme. In India, this was designed to secure to the rural areas within a reasonable time frame, certain basic amenities in the field of education, health, drinking water, electrification, roads and home sites and it has been a great success;

17. The Malaysian experience shows that industrialization is the fastest means to alleviate rural poverty. Governments of the member countries may, therefore, consider the possibility of locating the industries/factories in rural areas which will alleviate rural poverty. To attract the industrialists to come to rural areas for setting up industries, suitable incentives may be provided. This will also serve the purpose of bringing down migration from rural to urban areas and will reduce pollution problem in large cities/towns. In this context, it would be worthwhile to mention that most of the developing countries are shifting the already established factories from urban to rural areas at a very high cost to combat problems created by pollution;

18. Studies in Malaysia have brought out that the development and adoption of improved technology was instrumental for increased productivity, output and income to farmers. The availability of credit facilities and use of improved farm production technology have resulted in enhanced productivity and income. The Governments of the AARRO member countries are, therefore, well advised to make available to the farmers credit on easy terms, for at least for the increased net cost whenever a new improved technology is introduced this will facilitate taking up the new technology by the farmers;

19. Governments may provide adequate facilities for small scale and cottage industries to be set up in rural areas on cooperative basis. Credit facilities at concessional rates may also have to be provided at least in the beginning for the success of the project. Governments may also arrange for marketing of the products so that those engaged in small scale and cottage industries could get remunerative prices for their products;

20. For the efficient management of any rural development programmes initiated either by the Government or voluntary organization, people's participation is necessary.* The Government should take necessary steps to decentralize the decision making

---

* In view of its vital importance for success of any programme meant for the development of especially rural people a separate chapter is included on people's participation.

process within the framework of national policy, promote local government institutions and increase the delegation of responsibility to other rural masses for rural development activities. The peoples' participation approach should also encompass self-help and self-initiated schemes and projects;

21. Cooperatives play a leading role to bring about effective social change and improvement in the rural economy which will result in alleviation of poverty. As such, the Government should encourage multi-purpose rural cooperative activities, such as, production, marketing, credit and human resource development. The cooperative members should be encouraged and motivated to take initiative in developmental activities thereby creating more avenues for rural employment.
22. The contribution of Non-Government Organizations (NGOs) is very effective in activities related to rural development programmes which are aimed at helping the rural poor. Governments should encourage, promote and support voluntary agencies as these grass-root organizations could play a significant role to supplement and complement the role of Government in the management of rural development programmes. A case in point is the credit programme ala' the Grameen Bank of Bangladesh and implemented by an NGO in Malaysia as "Project Amanah Ikhtiar." NGOs can also act as a liaison between masses in the rural areas and the Government in ensuring smooth flow of funds and optimal utilization of resources;
23. International organizations should contribute liberally in the form of financial aid and human resource for rural development work for alleviation of poverty. The assistance from international organizations is vital for the developing countries which are starved of resources and trained manpower;
24. The women organizations should be associated with poverty alleviation programmes from the very beginning;
25. Concurrent monitoring to assess the stages of implementation and its evaluation at periodic interval is necessary to critically analyse achievement and results of projects, programmes and policies vis-à-vis intended objectives. The Government should create the facilities for monitoring and evaluation of anti-poverty schemes. This will help in the adjustments of strategies in response to performance gaps and other problems of implementation;
26. It is desirable to create and build up a data base as this information, if suitably utilized, will enrich the management capability for successful implementation of projects. The Government should take necessary steps in that direction considering the importance of data and information to the policy makers, scholars and researchers which will assist in the formulation of policies and preparation of projects for poverty alleviation;
27. A number of poverty alleviation programmes have been introduced by the various member countries at different points of time. These programmes vary with conditions in various countries and the causes of poverty. There is a need to train the staff responsible for the eradication of poverty, particularly when a new programme is introduced. There is also a need for training whenever an improved technology, successful in some of the countries is to be transferred to and adopted by developing countries. To train both trainers and farmers in particular. In alleviation programmer

and projects including self-help projects and to exchange knowledge and expertise to other countries with experts from other countries, a need has been felt to have an institute having requisite facilities for training as well as for research.*

Lessons learned

Unless the poor take interest and recognize their own capability, external support may not help to bring about change in their condition. Even if inputs were externally injected without considering the value system and needs of the beneficiaries, programmes might not be sustainable once the external support is withdrawn. Thus a feeling of self- reliance has to be generated. Programme intervention should only follow when there is real will among the intended beneficiaries to change their condition. This requires attitudinal change on their part. Likewise the external agency should not unnecessarily raise their expectations. What was most important was to raise awareness and help the beneficiaries to develop a feeling of self-reliance. For that, awareness generating measures in the form of functional literacy programmes etc. could be initiated.

It was also desirable for any external agency to have a change agent on the spot. The change agent, first of all, should observe the value system of the intended beneficiaries and their ways of life, and make them aware of their potentials and limitations as a way of gaining their confidence. Once the confidence was gained and the change agent felt assured that the external input would not be detrimental to the feeling of self-reliance, he/she should try to obtain the support for the income-generating activities that the beneficiaries themselves had decided on. It was advisable to explore activities which were traditional and family-based and which had market value, and accordingly to assist beneficiaries to design the programmes for their benefit.

Poverty reduction was a time-consuming process, in which one faced ups and downs. Often times, it was a frustrating exercise. Hence, the programme period had to be reasonably long so that sufficient time could be devoted to establishing rapport with beneficiaries.

The beneficiaries of a programme have to take interest and recognize their own capabilities in order for external support to be effective. Sensitizing programme management of the needs and priorities in setting programme goals is essential to the success of a programme. It is therefore desirable for any external agency to have some body in the form of a change agent at the programme site that should observe the value system of the intended beneficiaries, their way of life, and make them aware of their potentials and limitations as a way of gaining their confidence. Once, the confidence is gained and the change agent feels assured that the external input would not to detrimental to the feeling of self reliance, he/she should try to get the support for the income generating activities that are decided by the beneficiaries themselves. It is advisable to explore the activities which have been traditionally family based and have a market value, and assist the beneficiaries to design programmes based on these activities.

---

* **Source**: Adopted from the *Report of International Workshop on "Rural Poverty and Ways & Means to Alleviate It"*, Malecca, Malaysia, January, 1992.

The question of poverty alleviation is a stupendous task. In the name of humanity the entire administrative system and all sections of people need recognize the deplorable conditions of living by the poor. Though, efforts have been there in the past, they were not strong and fully action oriented atleast now in the twenty first century in the name of humanity respecting the precious life of people suffering in the mire of poverty everyone should strive to work **Unto To The Last.***

***Source:** Adopted from the material "Employment Strategies for the Rural Poor", United Nations, New York, 1994.

Index